Indian Land Tenure

The Library of American Indian Affairs

From the Indian Claims Commission Series

Microfiche Publications
Decisions of the Indian Claims Commission
Expert Testimony before the Indian Claims Commission
Transcripts of Oral Expert Testimony before the Indian Claims Commission
Legal Briefs before the Indian Claims Commission
General Accounting Office Reports on Offsets
Legislative History of the Indian Claims Commission Act

Books
Index to the Decisions of the Indian Claims Commission
Index to the Expert Testimony before the Indian Claims Commission
Index to the Oral Expert Testimony, Briefs and GAO Reports
    (in preparation)

Other Publications

The Office of Indian Affairs, 1824-1880: Historical Sketches
    by Edward E. Hill
Indian Land Tenure: Bibliographical Essays and a Guide to the Literature
    by Imre Sutton
Guide to the Annual Reports of the Lake Mohonk Conference of Friends
    of the Indian; Introductions by Dr. Larry E. Burgess and Dr. Laurence
    Hauptman and Foreword by A. Keith Smiley
Index to American Indian Documents in the Congressional Serial Sets,
    1817-1899, by Steven L. Johnson
Annual Reports of the Lake Mohonk Conference of Friends of the Indian
    (microfiche)
Indian Committee of the Society of Friends: 1696-1974 (microfilm)
The American Indian Oral History Collection (audio tape),
    Dr. Joseph H. Cash, General Editor

Editorial Advisory Board

Vine Deloria, Jr., author, attorney and member Standing Rock Sioux
Dr. William Sturtevant, Curator, Department of Anthropology, National
    Museum of Natural History, Smithsonian Institution

Indian Land Tenure

Bibliographical Essays and a Guide to the Literature

by

Imre Sutton

Professor of Geography
California State University, Fullerton

Clearwater Publishing Company, Inc.

New York and Paris

Library of Congress Cataloging in Publication Data

Sutton, Imre, 1928-
  Indian land tenure.

  (The Library of American Indian Affairs)
  Bibliography: p.
  Includes indexes.
  1. Indians of North America—Land tenure—Bib-
liography. 2. Indians of North America—Land
transfers—Bibliography. I. Title.
Z1209.U5S95   [E98.L3]   016.333'2   74-30668
ISBN 0-88354-104-1
ISBN 0-88354-106-8 pbk.

CLEARWATER PUBLISHING COMPANY, INC.
50 Rockefeller Plaza, New York, New York 10020

Manufactured in the United States of America

To
J. E. Spencer,
Professor, mentor,
and friend

Foreword

Imre Sutton's study of Indian land tenure in the United States is significant not only for its subject but for its organization. Professor Sutton has isolated what is perhaps the critical issue in Indian-white relations and the basis of the physical and cultural existence of many tribes. He has brought to light in a comprehensive fashion the vast but scattered literature on the subject. No historian or student who wishes to examine the relationship of the Indian and the land in the past or present can ignore the pathways and directions that Professor Sutton has so carefully laid out.

The essays into which Professor Sutton's work is organized provide all readers—novice, general, and specialized—with informed critical discussions of the relevant literature. The specialist can approach the material through categories of tribe, region, or subject. The novice and the general reader, on the other hand, have a sure guide in Sutton's essays through the thicket of conflicting interpretations, high- and low-quality articles and books, and obscure sources. Only a scholar thoroughly familiar with this complex literature and dedicated over many years to its collection and analysis could write such illuminating essays on Indian land tenure.

Bibliographical work, while vital and laborious, is less glamorous than other types of research and is often ill-acknowledged and ill-rewarded. I hope not only that Professor Sutton's work will be acknowledged by those scholars who use it, but also that it will be imitated by others who have the capacity similarly to combine encyclopedic knowledge of the literature in several fields (in Sutton's case, anthropology, history, and geography) to illuminate a particularly vital topic. Sutton has accomplished this purpose for Indian land tenure. To the extent that lawyers, anthropologists, historians, geographers, librarians, and government officials wish to understand the special role of the American Indian (the only truly "territorial" minority in American life, as Sutton points out) in our multi-ethnic society, they will owe Sutton a lasting debt of gratitude.

Wilcomb E. Washburn

Smithsonian Institution

Preface

Recent events at Wounded Knee, South Dakota, on the Onondaga Reservation in Upstate New York, in Palm Springs, California, and on other Indian lands have reminded us anew of the Indians' presence in this nation. These events have involved confrontations with white society of a kind that all too often goes unnoticed; it is only when major events like those at Wounded Knee gain national or regional attention that America rediscovers its Indian population.

In recent years the Indians' reaffirmation of their desire for self-determination has been spirited, in part, by parallel movements for recognition by blacks and Chicanos (cf. de la Garza et al. 1973). But only the Indians represent a truly "territorial" minority, and their constant quest for equity in American society stands alone in being founded on a recognized body of treaties and laws.

Whether on the reservation or in the city, whether among Indians at tribal council meetings or at pan-Indian pow-wows, it is apparent that the tribes and individual Indians are taking an active part in a movement to change the policies that have abridged their rights in the soil and their rights to autonomy as self-governing or jural communities. If the tribes must continue to deal with the frustration of adverse changes in the institutions affecting their land rights in a society that has openly promised to preserve historical guarantees, then Indians will continue to confront the government, form alliances, and go to court.

The literature of recent years reflects the rise and maturation of Indian leadership. It also reflects the vigorous efforts of Indians and their non-

Indian allies to redress grievances in the courts. New organizations have been formed, for example the Institute for the Development of Indian Law, the Native American Rights Fund, and the American Indian Movement (AIM). Several Indian scholars have ably articulated the Indians' position in the vital affairs of their land. Kickingbird and Ducheneaux (1973), associated with the Institute for the Development of Indian Law, have demanded that the government now permanently disclaim the intention to take any more of the acreage now remaining in trust. The right to, and the hope for, tribal autonomy within reservations, so frequently under attack in several states, has been voiced by other Indian leaders, such as Russell Means, Dennis Banks, and Vine Deloria, Jr., the last perhaps being the best-known spokesman for Indian self-determination. However, the new literature on the Indian and his land is still too predominantly non-Indian, despite the fact that more and more Indians are writing on issues that concern them. Many of the interpretations, mine included, are by non-Indians seeking to comprehend the Indian viewpoint.

Currently, there is a great urge to commit to print almost everything readable about the Indian. He makes good copy in all forms, fiction and non-fiction alike. He is newsworthy and demands the attention of scholars in a dozen disciplines. While there is no dearth of literature, the mass of printed material on the Indian awaits the willing compiler, bibliographer, or classifier who would sort, classify, and evaluate what is in print on any number of subjects useful to students of Indian affairs. Past and present writings in the Indian field underscore an acknowledged fact: land continues to be the crux of the conflict between Indian and white in this country.

Some years ago I became convinced that the literature on Indian land tenure needed a synthesizer, that it needed to be brought together in one place, subjected to critical review, and made accessible to students of Indian affairs. In my estimation, a simple bibliography would not do; several already existed and had been found to be incomplete, unstructured, or lacking in critical evaluation. A decade ago I discovered that even the trained scholar had difficulty finding applicable studies on this subject in print or in manuscript. Not only was there no critical bibliography on Indian land tenure, but a guide to research themes, major land issues, maps, and the like was also lacking. Current anthologies and related works fill only part of the demand.

It is my view that a working bibliography in any field should be accompanied by its compiler's views on what are the major issues and themes and what is the best way to perceive the structure of the subject matter. My purpose in this book goes beyond classification of the literature by relevant topic, tribe, or place: it is to provide a structure to the literature that may facilitate research in Indian land tenure. This structure, which derives from empirical observation, is expressed in a typology (see Figure 1).

The entire organization of this book revolves around the typology. By means of the typology I have tried to demonstrate to the relatively uninitiated that Indian land does not stand isolated from the entire national environment, nor do our institutions governing Indian land form a microcosm insulated from the rest of our society: to be sure, to best understand the field of Indian land tenure one must take into fullest account our national land history and our relevant laws. I have sought to put the Indian and his land in the context of time and place within the changing American scene. Historians have helped establish this perspective. I have also sought to draw attention to the relevance of ethnographic literature and research methodology in the courtroom and in administrative practice. Scholarly fields have been enriched by the invention of ethnohistory, much of which got under way as part of the research on Indian land claims. Of necessity, I have dipped, though sparingly, into Canadian and Mexican literature, and because I can see the direction of future research toward a comparative view of the administration of indigenous land rights, I close the volume with a brief heuristic essay that places the Indian in the context of all post-colonial indigenous populations.

The publishers and I have developed several indexes to facilitate the use of this study. Researchers who would prefer to approach questions and topics through the tribal and geographic indexes can locate useful titles without referring to the essays. The subject index, on the other hand, leads to pages in the essays. Using the indexes in conjunction with the table of contents opens additional avenues to the literature. However, if one starts with the essays, a much wider range of studies becomes available. In addition, in the bibliography we have cited page references to textual treatment of authors. In general, we have retained the spelling of tribal names as they appeared in the works being discussed; in the indexes, however, we have resorted to the most commonly utilized spelling (e.g., Navajo).

The development of this study has a long history, beginning with my first encounter with Zuni Indians when I worked for the U.S. Forest Service. It was then (1947-48) that I had more than a passing concern to ask why able-bodied male Indians had to leave their reservation all summer, during the height of the agricultural season, to work fighting forest fires. When I first attended college a year or so later I continued this interest in Indian resource problems; at that time an enthusiastic young scholar, Professor Valene Smith Golay (now at California State University,

Chico) expressed deep conviction over the plight of the Indians and generated in me a lasting interest in the study of their land problems. The interest, however, was postponed for another decade until I undertook doctoral studies at UCLA and embarked on a dissertation dealing with Indian land tenure in Southern California (completed in 1964). Meanwhile, I had prepared a very preliminary review essay on the geographical literature of the American Indian. In 1963 one of my referees, Professor Homer Aschmann (Department of Geography, University of California, Riverside), advised me well by suggesting that I focus my attention mainly on the land tenure theme. Although neither he nor I knew where this would ultimately lead me, I thank him for his counsel and his more recent critical examination of this book in manuscript.

Others along the way have also contributed to my thinking, or given me encouragement, or have added countless references that I had overlooked, and I would like to acknowledge a debt of thanks to each of them: as editor of the series, *Indian Affairs* (Brigham Young University), Dr. Arturo deHoyos saw in my study, even before it was set down on paper, a worthwhile contribution to the literature and committed himself to publishing it; he later graciously released me to seek an eastern publisher when the opportunity came along. Dr. Wilcomb E. Washburn, Director of American Studies, and Dr. William Sturtevant, Curator of Anthropology, both of the Smithsonian Institution; Professor Omer C. Stewart of the University of Colorado, Department of Anthropology; Dr. Monroe E. Price, of the law school at UCLA; Professor Raymond Fogelson at the University of Chicago, Department of Anthropology; Professors Jackson Putnam (history) and Otto Sadovszky (anthropology) of my home university each critically read the manuscript at one stage or another. Dr. Nancy O. Lurie, Curator, Milwaukee Public Museum, added candid remarks. I must especially single out Dr. Washburn, who encouraged me to submit the manuscript to the Newberry Library's Center for the History of the American Indian in Chicago. Through his efforts and those of Dr. Robert Bieder, Associate Director of the Center, the Newberry has generously underwritten the financing of the critical evaluation of this work. The Newberry has also provided the publisher with a modest but appreciated publishing subsidy. The association with the Newberry Library in this venture has been personally rewarding and I am deeply grateful for their gesture of confidence in my research efforts.

It would be a serious failing on my part if I were to overlook the numerous scholars who gave ready assistance through advice, encouragement, reprints of their works, or commentaries on work in progress. To economize on space, I cite them without reference to their affiliations and thank all of them heartily: David Aberle, Alvar Carlson, Elizabeth Colson,

Louis De Vorsey, Marshall Harris, Leslie Hewes, Francis Jennings, Joseph Jorgensen, Kenneth Narvey, John Stafford, Wayne Suttles, Douglas Wilms, and Paul Wilson. Glen Wilkinson of the law firm Wilkinson, Cragun, and Barker graciously provided me with copies of expert witness testimony in land claims cases. My colleague, Prof. Glenn George, helped clarify the use of set theory and Venn diagrams, which figure in the typology. And although the epilogue is merely a fragment of a more thorough study, I would like to thank my colleagues Wayne Untereiner (Anthropology) and Ronald Helin (Geography) for advice on the pitfalls of comparative interpretations. Thanks must also go to Janet Skinner for research; to Nancy Hunter for interlibrary loan assistance; to Martha Beecher for typing the original manuscript; and to Sue Lirette Hannes, Floyd Hickok, Beth Tufft Huning, Don Severson, and Mike Stannard for cartography. Many of the early ideas for this book and related Indian studies were shared with colleagues and Indian students when I was chairman of the Native American Studies program at California State University, Fullerton; I have especially appreciated the candor and counsel of Beth Voien. I would also like to acknowledge the assistance of my own university in providing two small grants to further my research and a sabbatical leave in fall, 1972 that freed me sufficiently from campus duties so I could embark upon the writing of this book. Finally, I must compliment my editor, Martin Lubin, on his able craftsmanship and patience. I warmly thank everyone involved.

My closing comment is reserved for a brief testimonial to a scholar who has, in my estimation, no peer in the study of land systems. Joseph E. Spencer, Professor of Geography, University of California, Los Angeles, more than any other scholar has stimulated my thinking in this entire field; my years at UCLA and since have benefitted immeasurably from his stimulating insights, his systems view of agrarian life, and his eclectic approach to the craft of the geographer. I only hope this small volume measures up to the expectations he has quietly held for me in the decade since the completion of my doctorate.

Imre Sutton

California State University, Fullerton
January, 1975

Table of Contents

Table of Illustrations

Indian Land Tenure: The Structure and Content of the Literature

INDIAN LAND TENURE AS A STUDY

The Indian and His Land

Earth and nature are inseparable from the Indian himself. Even the urban Indian must continue to feel some orientation to the land, all the more so to a given place, cherished and sustained in the mind as a homeland or, at least since contact times, to the locus of Indianness called a reservation. As a non-Indian student of Indian land tenure, I, and many like myself, can only approximate in words what Indians must perceive about earth, nature, and the land upon which they stand (cf. Collier 1949; Dukelow and Zakheim 1972; Whalen 1971). But the historical circumstances of Indian-white relations over land can be understood and fully explicated, as can the legal and political constructs under which the tribes and individual Indians must function in our society. While much has been written about Indians and about their lands past or present, only a few studies encompass the full complexities of Indian land rights or comprehend the multidisciplinary nature of the Indians' problem vis-à-vis the role of land in the expression of tribal self-determination. Perhaps only an Indian can put into words what so keenly disturbs his brethren today:

> Among the more surprising elements of Indian land tenure is the aspect of continual experimentation with property rights which has been visited upon the individual tribes by Congressional fiat. Rather than advocating a profound, logical and rigorous relationship of

ward-guardian, or trustee-ward, the United States policy has fluc-
tuated between the strictest enforcement of trust duties and the
most lax and benign neglect worthy of a Moynihan tome. (Vine
Deloria, Jr., in the introduction to Kickingbird and Ducheneaux
1973, p. x.)

Land sustains the lifestyle of countless tribes, even when little acreage
is in production or has productive value. Land sustains far more than
subsistence, and indeed many Indians recognized decades ago the folly of
attempting to sustain their daily needs on acreage that is marginal, both in
resources and in per capita size. But land has emotional meaning, a
psychological significance for the Indian that is far more intense than our
nostalgic longing for the family farm and a rural way of life.

Readers of these bibliographical essays and those who seek only a
specific reference via the indexes should accept the fact of the continuing
importance of land to most Indians. They should not infer, from the fact
that nearly half of today's 800,000 Indians have migrated to cities or have
been born away from rural circumstances, that land has declining meaning
to tribal Americans. It is difficult enough to ascertain how many of the
Indian families now in cities or in rural non-Indian places really prefer
living and working distant from their brethren; in addition, it is even
harder to explain all the factors contributing to the almost involuntary
urban relocation. Moreover, the statistics on returning Indian families can
only approximate the number who cannot adjust to white society or who
feel the irresistible pull of ethnicity, the locus of which is the reservation.
Even if the aspiration to return to the land is only momentary for many
Indians, there always remains the historical tie established by and en-
trusted to the federal government. Recent activist protests by "eastern"
Indians, advocating a return of tribal lands taken even earlier than those in
the West, testify to the strength and endurance of the Indians' feeling
toward the land.[1] More than one scholar has observed that the reservation
not only has sustained tribal culture, but also has formed the base from
which to generate new native nationalism.

So much pivots around the land as a locus of tribalism that in many
ways land tenure constitutes *the* fundamental access, the one through
which, as if it were a window, observers must look in order to discover the
Indian. No matter how hard one tries to look elsewhere, land comes into
view. For example, factors such as religion, diffusion of cultural traits and
material culture, the impact of commercialization and industrialization,
urban relocation, and education all contribute to the ways land may be
used, acquired, or disposed of, and to the ways Indian peoples aggregate in
social, political, or other terms.

The church, to expand on one of these examples, has played a direct role in several aspects of Indian affairs since colonial days. Religious motivations formed the basis for much territorial conquest (cf. Deloria's introductory remarks in Wise 1971). Moreover, ministerial personnel became Indian agents for a time and administered (often quite inadequately) many land matters during the Grant Administration, and missionaries were among the vanguard in advocating the allotment policy and private property in land throughout the eighteenth and nineteenth centuries. Native religious revival has been suggested as a factor in the resurgence of tribal claims to former territory. Certainly native religion inspired the restoration of Blue Lake to the Taos Pueblo. To cite another example, the introduction of the horse into North America permitted many Plains people to attain greater mobility, and in turn necessitated their entry into alien territories in quest of food. The changing territorial demands and the conflicts among tribes and bands over counterclaims to land are only part of the story that the entry of the horse set in motion. And, of course, the introduction of agriculture among former hunting and gathering peoples directly influenced the establishment of new configurations on the land: farm units of small acreage as compared to the vast territory that hunting demanded. With land allotment, agriculture came to mean living in dispersed homesteads, with parallel declines in village community life and a general movement to agency towns. The advent of trade and commerce among the woodland tribes of the northeast, triggered by the Europeans' desire for furs, is cited by some ethnologists as a key factor in the shift from tribal or band hunting practices to the family hunting territory.

More recently, the establishment of factories on some reservations cannot be fully understood without reference to the nature of tribal corporate authority over land resources as revitalized by the Indian Reorganization Act (IRA), 1934, which granted tribes considerable powers over the internal management of lands held in common. Land tenure must partially account for urban relocation, although its role is understated or neglected in some recent studies (cf. Neils 1971). The tendency of conflicts within tribes over the assignment of land to families or individuals to lead to out-migration has been noted among many Indians born since the allotment of land, and especially since the IRA, which discouraged allotment and curtailed further programs to effect private ownership of Indian resources.

Finally, the education of Indians all too often relates to factors of land tenure. For example, in order to receive financial assistance for education, tribal Indians must route their request through the tribe, despite the fact that they may live in distant cities or even in other states. Further, many tribes have protested the unnecessary and emotionally wasteful need to transport children beyond the reservation's borders to schools dominated by whites or to domicile Indian children for long months far from the family hearth simply because reservation communities cannot afford to support their own schools. And many returning Indian college graduates have made their new competence felt in tribal land management.

Some apologists for the seeming neglect of major Indian land issues have asserted that preoccupation with the land theme has overshadowed efforts to rehabilitate and help Indians to participate in a society in which, perhaps, the ownership of land has declining meaning for the general populace. Such an assertion seems misplaced in the light of the disastrous effects of the urban relocation program upon the vitality of Indian initiative and aspirations. Even if almost all Indians were to abandon their reservations for reasons of livelihood, the land would represent a sanctuary and a jural place in which tribal autonomy could flourish (cf. Castile 1974). Thus perhaps its political meaning to Indians persists even if economic opportunity declines and Indian families move away. And surely the Indian's historical land relation to the federal government predicates the perpetuation of a preoccupation with land themes.

On the Nature of Land Tenure and Its Application to Indians

Since this study deals with the intrusion of Euro-American culture upon the lifestyles of a group of indigenous peoples culturally differentiated one from another, interpretations of property and law become important to any understanding of the nature and kind of land tenure that we identify with the tribes. If we accept the idea that modern society expresses its rights in land through polity and, in turn, that polity governs law and justice, we find that the body of federal Indian law—which embraces the whole of Indian real property as well as tribal and personal property rights—may be characterized as a species of colonial law (cf. Bohannan 1965; Thomas 1966 a/b). In a construct of unicentric power involving two or more cultures, such as the United States, the minority culture (in this case, the tribes) are a dependent people, and although they may exercise considerable self-rule, the laws and institutions of western culture determine the range and parameters of indigenous expression. In this regard land is no exception.

Tenure of land, like land utilization, is markedly variable in time and place. Tenurial institutions are place-oriented: i.e., they attach to specific parts of the earth's surface and lie within the law of the jurisdiction in which they are located. In origin, land tenure grows out of the basic property institution and its relationship thereto has been hypothesized by Herskovits (1952), whose study is highly relevant to a consideration of

Indian land tenure (see Section A). Property, as the basic institution which gives rise to most of the customary (traditional) or more codified practices of land tenure, is a universal of culture—a "basic cultural category" in Wissler's terms (1938a). Hallowell's (1943, 1957) now-classic statement underscored the importance of distinguishing "property in its *purely* economic or legal aspects and property considered as a *social institution*" (1955, p. 238; his italics). But one cannot always distinguish the political and social meanings of land from the more purely economic. In the Indian field, such distinctions may blur; one finds that economic disuse of land by an Indian allottee cannot be fully separated from that same Indian's participation in the sociopolitical activities of the tribe based upon his membership and his right to share in tribal resources. Hallowell evaluated the close relationship of property and law in western culture, and concluded that although they stem from separate origins, they seem never to have been separate in their functioning.[2]

A specific time, place, and people must be considered in any understanding of the role of land tenure in land-use expressions. Like land use, tenure changes through time, owing to innovation within a society, cultural interaction, and the kind of intrusion that leads to the superimposition of new institutions upon those of another culture. When two quite different cultures interact, as Fried asserted (1952) when comparing European conquest over Indians to Chinese subjugation of tribal people in southeast Asia, "it is in the struggle over systems of tenure or ownership that the contest between social systems for the control of an area is to be understood" (p. 392). The laws of the conquering society come to extinguish or diminish the effectiveness of the customs and laws of the vanquished people. Indian land tenure may be understood only in this context. Thus it is germane and instructive to relate Indian land tenure to the ways Euro-American institutions have evolved and flourished on this continent.

Native land tenure, from what we have learned in three or more centuries, differs fundamentally from European land institutions and those developed uniquely on this continent by Euro-Americans. Tenures may be defined in terms of how the land is held—e.g., tribal, communal, freehold, tenancy, public, or national—and in terms of the "bundle of rights" concept. One may distinguish three subsets of the bundle: rights to the use of land (and to nonuse in certain instances), rights to lease or permit others to utilize land held by one person or group, and rights to alienate, sell, or encumber the land. Not all societies sanction unlimited rights to the use of land resources, nor do they all allow for the temporary transfer of such use rights to others. In many traditional societies functioning at the tribal or communal level, alienation does not exist as a right of the individual, since the land belongs to the tribe or the group (village, community, or band). Also it is often necessary to recognize clearly a difference between rights to use and rights to convey those rights to use, for such differences are important in distinguishing traditional views of land rights among many peoples, including certain American Indian tribes, from those of Euro-American societies.

This bundle not only expresses rights, but also enumerates restrictions, which generally emanate from the people who exercise the tenure system, but which may also originate as regulatory measures invoked by the intruding people who constitute the dominant society. Nonetheless, society in general, through its law-making institutions, exercises constraints over both the use and the allocation of land resources. The taxing power is one such regulatory measure that can directly affect the status of tenure, as it does whenever land forfeiture occurs because landowners cannot meet tax obligations. Police powers, usually expressed in terms of state or local governments, broadly influence the character and intensity of land utilization. Zoning, a controversial regulatory means, has assumed sweeping capacity to influence land values and to limit land uses to those sanctioned by the community. Although it does not strip one of tenure rights, zoning allegedly abridges use as the paramount property right, for it reduces the owner/user's prerogatives in the exercise of his rights in land. Proceedings in eminent domain, normally exercised only by government, but sometimes initiated by private parties where a public purpose can be demonstrated, abridge land rights by condemnation and seizure of land for a use deemed more beneficial to society than any use made by an individual or group. Escheat is another aspect of the controlling group's capacity to acquire back any land granted through public land laws. Land not utilized by members of a tribe, for example, may well revert back to the corporate body for reallocation (assignment) to another member.

Not everything in the lifestyle of a people stems from a land relationship. But certainly resources, living space, and homeland are parameters much identified with land, its use, and rights to it. If we think in gross terms, then no people functions in the environment without concepts of resource allocation, although sophisticated institutional structure based on land tenure principles may never have dawned upon some cultures, or may be entirely absent because there is no need to resolve conflict through the elaboration of property institutions. But the human utilization of any environment is worked out in the context of perceptions and views of nature and of how a given resource should be allocated among a people. Land tenure institutions may ultimately, through long-term utilization of a given locale or region, lead to an equilibrium in man's relationship to the physical base of his sustenance. Land tenure practices generally reflect a people's considerable efforts to utilize given resource situations and endure. Tenure structure tends to be in close balance with the vagaries of nature and therefore reveals clearly the strength of that endurance.

Yet no tenure system is apt for all habitats—one is appropriate for the forest, another for the plains, a third for the desert; nor is any system perfectly adapted to any one habitat. Which tenure pattern best approximates the most logical human organization of space to sustain a people and maintain the resource itself is only revealed in a larger context—that is, as part of a resource use system (cf. Firey 1960). To separate elements of tenure from the land to which it is attached, and from the technology and institutions that link members of the community or society governed by that form of tenure, is to fail to recognize that *any* land use predicates the existence of tenure and that tenure depends upon the entire realm of sociopolitical interactions within cultures.

This bibliographical endeavor seeks to demonstrate how land tenure permeates virtually everything identified as Indian. By means of a typological approach I have drawn together the pertinent literature and identified major themes and issues, and I have also attempted to reveal the intricacy of the relationship of land tenure to the Indian's past and the continuing interactions with white society. In many ways the approach is open-ended—that is, heuristic in nature—but if we accept the definition that Indian land tenure is a set of rights and practices subject to the jurisdiction of a body of federal law and treaties as well as to tribal customs and by-laws, we can draw fairly effective bounds for this study. Studies by Kinney (1937), for example, tend to emphasize the role of legislation and administration in ascertaining the scope of Indian land tenure. On the other hand, Washburn (1971b) and Price (1973) draw attention to the realm defined by case law, for so much of Indian land tenure today has been subjected to litigation that it is in the courts that the parameters of Indian landownership are being reshaped. What is important in defining terms is that the definition provides a locus around which to operate, to return to frequently in order to get one's bearings. In that sense, the typological diagram (Figure 1) should serve the reader as both a map and a compass, to orient him in the search for source materials, ideas, facts about events, and the like.

By generally referring to the reservation "system," which comprises both tribal and individual tenures in land, we identify a Euro-American construct based on treaties and laws administered by the federal government (i.e., the Bureau of Indian Affairs). But no typology could bound the realm of law since contact times and ignore the aboriginal past. The question arises, therefore, to what degree does the rubric of Indian land tenure comprehend aboriginal concepts of land rights? To the extent that there is a surviving element of aboriginal practice among the tribes—e.g., in the way they "assign" tracts of land to families—the rubric extends beyond law and administration to embrace traditional Indian views of land allocation and use. In its aboriginal context, Indian land tenure concerns what came before contact as has generally been reported by Europeans and later by Americans through informants and personal observations. Even though native customs of landholding no longer survive intact, their reconstruction by scholars has made this an illuminating and useful area of study. Put another way, Indian land tenure is not just a thing of the past or of the present, but a phenomenon along a continuum, varied and embellished by new discoveries or the reassessment of long-standing facts, or extinguished or expanded by the circumstances of law, economics, polity, and social change.

The breadth of the terminology depends upon usage, past or present. Land allotment, for example, created private property for individual Indians out of tribal land assets. As long as this property remains under the protective wing of federal trusteeship, it is *Indian* land tenure. But once taken in fee patent (i.e., an unrestricted title no longer held in trust), such lands held by Indians lie outside the meaning of this rubric. Scholars tend to construe Indian land tenure broadly, while public officials generally apply a narrower construction. To be sure, an Indian owning his land like any other citizen may still enjoy tenure in an aboriginal holding that is the subject of litigation before the Indian Claims Commission. By dint of membership in a tribe, that Indian may gain personally if the Commission awards a financial settlement for lands taken a century ago. Moreover, even an Indian holding an allotment in fee and now subject to local taxation, enjoys tenure in tribal resources. His patented allotment remains part of the reservation owing not only to its location within the boundaries of the reservation, but also to its legal relationship to the tribal holding as a corporate entity.

Only the land status of the descendants of Indians who lost all of their lands lies outside our consideration. Few of these Indians today hold land as members of tribes; thus, few enjoy sovereign immunities, tax exemptions, or special services. While there is considerable interest in the way land has entered into their livelihoods and lifestyles, their circumstances are nonetheless peripheral to our concern.

Readers should be wary of interpreting tribal tenure as being a single set of customs and practices subject to uniform administration by the federal government. Despite the existence of equivalent communal practices among many tribes in aboriginal times, tribal tenure varied across the continent. And because tribes have not only separate ethnohistories and distinct treaties and laws, but also a considerable body of case law pertinent only to their specific relationship to the federal government, contemporary tribal tenure also varies considerably. What tends to lead to universals in Indian land tenure is the similarity of the institutions that have been applied to all Indians: that is, parallel patterns of negotiation for treaties of cessions, similar histories of broken promises, relocation and the introduction of policies of land allotment, comparable problems of economic growth and stagnation on a finite and complex land configuration, and problems of litigation involving state and local government. The literature and my analysis attempt to distinguish universals from specifics, Native Americans in general from individual tribes.

There is both a time and a space continuum in the functioning of Indian land tenure. The reservation, for example, is a geographic reality lying within a state and subject to a specific body of federal, and in some cases state, law. It is also a historical link to treaty rights. Many tribal groups (for example, in Oklahoma) no longer hold tenure rights in an existing corporate estate, for the reservations went out of trust long ago; yet historical rights in such land now occupied by others do exist. Even more to the point is the survival, by dint of treaties of hunting and fishing rights on lands no longer tribal but once part of native territory, as in the Northwest. "In perpetuity," which appears in the wording of so many treaties, conveys the meaning of an indefinite time continuum within a specific geographical area.

This geographical locus of Indian land rights is unique in American experience with the allocation of land. A reservation as a piece of real estate presents no special problems of comprehension for the non-Indian neighbor; even the fact that quite different tenure practices exist within its borders can be generally understood. But that there may still persist some trace of tribal rights to lands that lie outside the external bounds of a reservation confounds the white populace; even more widely misunderstood is the potential "threat" that non-Indians owning land and residing within reservation boundaries may be subject to tribal government if the courts so interpret tribal sovereignty (see Section AC). However they may be rejected as a potential "third" government distinct from federal and state, reservations are political entities that some might liken to colonies and others to municipalities; and still others would regard them as federal districts or else as land units similar in status to public lands. Thus the Indian reservation is, depending on context, real estate, legal entity or jural place, or surviving homeland.

Land Tenure Literature and Relevant Indian Studies

Although the layman may experience difficulty in comprehending land tenure or in defining its parameters, scholars have long been studying its institutional basis, its functioning in society and its relationship to the use of the environment. In order to understand how the property institution and land tenure flourish in American society, one must recognize that they are fundamental to our economic system and to the source of its capitalization. One must also recognize the continuing influence of land tenure on rural lifestyles, agricultural production, and resource conservation (cf. Barlowe 1970; Bertrand and Corty 1962; Clawson 1968). In the more descriptive aspects of land tenure, especially as they bear on events in "taking up" the land, American historians have produced an astounding volume of writings. American land history has come to be identified, logically enough, with the history of public land law policy (Gates 1968; Robbins 1942; Hibbard 1924). The moving frontier of settlement and land speculation (Billington 1974; Dick 1970; Swierenga 1968) closely relates to the displacement of the Indian, and in fact it is hard to bypass the theme of Indian land dispossession in any account of the growth of the American West (Sutton 1970b). Gates is particularly careful to weave the analysis of Indian land tenure, especially its demise at the native level and its replacement by Euro-American institutions, into the historical discussions of land policy as background to further changes in laws governing public lands.

Land tenure attracts scholars of many persuasions. Although it is not a discipline—it is more akin to such interdisciplinary studies as conservation and ecology—land tenure is a "field"; but it is one that lacks a unitary set of theories or concepts. In Section A readers will note that the general discussion of the evolution of land tenure studies in anthropology (mainly triggered by Herskovits's 1952 conceptualization of land tenure as part of economic anthropology) cannot be separated from a discussion of the development of interest in, and analysis of, aboriginal tenure practices here and on other continents. Anthropological interest has focused on the administration of native peoples, and it has been better explicated for European involvement in Africa, southeast Asia, and the Pacific islands than for the United States or Canada. With reference to the geographical study of land tenure, Brookfield (1964) noted that "several [geographers] achieve a very close understanding of the relationships between social phenomena on the one hand, and the nature and mode of use of environmental resources on the other...." (p. 296); he nevertheless stressed the inadequacy of geographers' commitment to such studies, and the weaknesses inherent in those tenure studies that have been written. Those specializing in rural lifeways and land economics took up a sociological and economic interest; the Bertrand and Corty text (1962) sums up their interdisciplinary viewpoint.

The foregoing briefly suggests that all of the disciplines that might bring their methods and viewpoints to the study of land tenure have done so, and in fact have not ignored the Indian, although the greatest emphasis has been placed on private property institutions such as the family farm and on public land policy.

Indian land tenure literature represents but a fraction of that which has been written and published on the Indian. Probably anthropology and history dominate the literary production to date. As the editors of a symposium of writings in American anthropology suggested, the ready-made indigenous population appealed to the American preference for the empirical and inductive (Mead and Bunzel 1960, p. 2). Hallowell (1957) reinforced this point by asserting that "the continuing presence of the Indians on our frontiers or in our midst has given American anthropology a distinctive cast . . ." (p. 91). Unquestionably, the Indian has played a major role in the shaping of a distinctive American contribution to anthropological thought. But Bohannan (1963) contended that "American Indian studies, on which so much American anthropology was based, have deteriorated in the twentieth century; the able scholar in the field cannot begin to encompass the vastness of the subject" (p. 392). A large share of the literary product is ethnographic and ecological, and only a small portion effectively analyzes or examines land tenure in either its aboriginal context or in its form as modified by Euro-American institutions.

Not only have anthropologists done exhaustive fieldwork throughout the continent, but they have also contributed directly to the formulation of policy for the self-determination of tribes. In the late 1920s and throughout the 1930s, several anthropologists participated in governmental efforts to find suitable remedies to tribal problems, including those stemming from inadequacies of the land base.

> Out of this came a picture of the irrational, vacillating policies of land use and ownership which have marked American Indian policy, the relatively small degree of Indian utilization of their resources, and the almost total lack of real understanding by Indians of the techniques of an agricultural economy or the principles or motivations underlying successful agricultural enterprise in the American economic system. (Kennard and Macgregor 1953, p. 833)

These scholars began to draw from their studies of Indian tribes new inferences toward a theory of acculturation and culture change (cf. Keesing 1953). Until this time their preoccupation was with the still-functioning Indian patterns of leadership and social structure, rather than with new patterns and trends in social groupings and values. Some studies were made of systems of land tenure, experiences with irrigated agriculture, and tribal and subtribal boundaries (see Sections A and AB). Anthropologists engaged in the survey of the vital effects of dams on the relocation and lifestyles of tribes (cf. Missouri River Basin Studies in Section AC). Barnett (1956) further observed how anthropologists were extending to the Pacific islands this interest in land tenure and native peoples.

The theme of Indian-white relations has tended to dominate the interest of the historian of the Indian (cf. Hagan 1963). An earlier interest in colonial-period Indian affairs has now been revitalized. Indian removal and the cession of territory by treaty, while compelling themes, have been much overworked. The historian has, until recently, portrayed the Indian mainly as the antagonist in the story of westward expansion. Few historical accounts of the Indian avoid the land theme, although its interpreters seem largely preoccupied with the events of confrontation, dispossession, and cession by treaty. If traditional historical accounts of the tribes seem repetitive, those more ethnohistorical in approach (cf. Macgregor 1946; Wallace 1970) have offered new insights and explanations for past situations involving Indian-white interaction. Washburn (1971a) and Berkhofer (1971) have emphasized the contributions of ethnohistory to the study of the Indian. Sturtevant (1966) identified historical ethnography and historiography of nonliterate cultures as the two main interests of ethnohistory, and Washburn (1971a) talked of the emergence of the anthropologist-turned-historian. Other approaches to Indian historiography have been suggested by Howard (1969) and Prucha (1971), and in the report of a symposium on ethnohistory (Symposium 1961).

Unlike the work of historians or anthropologists, the major literary product of geographers ignores the Indian. The Indian has been a fruitful subject around which to build a theory of geographic determinism. Earlier curiosity arose among anthropogeographers or grew out of interest in economic activity on the continent. Haas (1925) urged his colleagues to investigate the Indian and use the reservation as a field laboratory; but he too saw in the Indians "a simple adaptation to environment" (p. 86). The anthropogeographers sought to relate the Indian to the cultural history of the New World and to Old World origins, diffusions, and migrations; the writings of several geographers under the influence of C. O. Sauer at Berkeley, often in conjunction with research by A. L. Kroeber and his colleagues, are typical. Reviews of geographic literature suggest that the total volume of writings is meager compared to that in history or anthropology and that land tenure receives little attention.

A recent symposium of geographers (Lazewski 1973) demonstrated a focused interest in economic studies of Indian lands, especially in relation to the location and the probability of acceptance and success of economic developments on reservations. Its participants pointed to perception studies as a means of evaluating native attitudes toward developments. The symposium also identified the study of Indian urban relocation as an area for continued research. With reference to culture change, they identified political, economic, and related issues as worthy of continued study.

It is my contention that all future research of Indian themes by geographers, even those bent toward the interpretation of the urbanization of the Indian, will depend on a thorough grounding in the institutions of land tenure that have determined and continue to determine much of the lifestyle of contemporary tribes. And although it is not readily demonstrated, land rights do figure in the circumstances, if not the decision, that lead Indians to seek urban relocation from reservations.[3]

THE TYPOLOGICAL APPROACH

The foregoing discussion has outlined how Indian land tenure has become an inextricable part of the fabric of American history, economy, and law. The themes, processes, and events that comprise the subject matter of Indian land tenure relate to several time periods, differing environments, and varying institutions. Moreover, the history of Indian affairs has involved the contact, confrontation, and interaction of two markedly different culture systems.

Had I organized the bibliographical information along simple historical or environmental lines, much of the interrelatedness of this subject matter would be obscured for the reader. Instead, I have chosen to organize a typology around the concept of change in Indian land status. This change is best observed by reference to those man-land relationships that have involved major cultural confrontation between Indians and Euro-Americans. The typology is organized into three sets that express these man-land relationships: (1) *autonomy and self-determination*, embracing the aboriginal past, surviving native institutions, efforts to reclaim aboriginal rights in land, and efforts to sustain or modify tribal autonomy; (2) *dispossession and termination*, including all processes of acquisition of Indian land by whatever means; adjustment of Indian-white differences in the occupation of reservation lands; reexamination of the motivations, justifications, and frauds in the taking of land; formulation of policies for ending trusteeship for tribes; and change in tenure wrought by the imposition of Euro-American land institutions upon the tribes; and (3) *protec-*

tion and reservation, encompassing the actual administration of Indian land law, problems of economic development posed by tenure complexities, implications of tenure adjustments for Indian livelihood and social expression, and legal issues in the persistence of tribes and their lands, especially in terms of jurisdiction.

Constant reference to Figure 1 will afford readers the opportunity to become more aware of the interrelatedness of the various aspects of Indian land tenure and will show that its subject matter cannot always be neatly sorted into discrete sets. It should be kept in mind that sets 1, 2, and 3 each contain a vast store of facts, events, and situations, and that each set can be examined separately from the others. Each set is divided into several subsets, which intersect in various ways. By simple analogy, we could identify set 1 as red, set 2 as blue, and set 3 as yellow; intersections AB (purple), BC (green), and AC (orange) constitute mixtures, containing elements of red and blue, blue and yellow, and yellow and red, respectively; ABC is a further subset (black), constituting a mixture of all of these colors. In this way I intend that the intersecting sets reveal the interrelatedness of the subject matter and that each of the intersections, determined mainly in legal terms, would have its own, separate subject matter. Although much of the literature falls into place with this scheme, one will still find numerous items that have been discussed in more than one subset for any of several reasons.

The primary discussions appear in subsets A (aboriginal occupancy and territoriality), B (land cessions and establishment of reservations), and C (land administration and land utilization). Subset AB (aboriginal title and land claims) deals with legal considerations such as litigious efforts to recompense tribes for lost lands; subset BC (title clarification and change) concerns, for example, extinguishment of title preserved in treaties of cession; and subset AC (tenure and jurisdiction) includes litigation to halt efforts to abridge the legal rights of tribes vis-à-vis the jurisdiction of states. Subset ABC (tenure and culture change) focuses on the dual questions of how changes in tenure have affected native culture and how changes in Indian culture have influenced tenure practices.

A chapter of this book is devoted to each of these subsets. A more detailed discussion of the typology—and thus of the structure of the book—follows. Finally, a sample area (California) is analyzed to demonstrate the utility of the typology as a reference tool equal to, but quite different in purpose from, the indexes. It will be fruitful, of course, to keep the structure of the diagram in mind. For example, it will prove difficult to comprehend the bases for land claims litigation and its adjudication (AB) without referring to land cessions and treaties (B), conditions of culture change, especially those affecting tribal persistence today

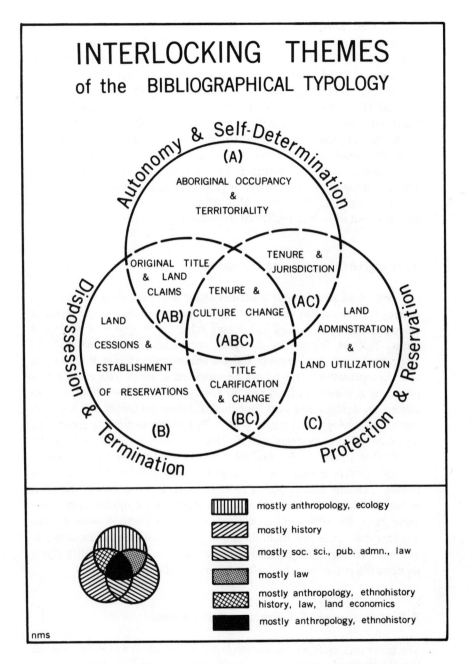

INTERLOCKING THEMES
of the BIBLIOGRAPHICAL TYPOLOGY

Autonomy & Self-Determination

(A)

ABORIGINAL OCCUPANCY
&
TERRITORIALITY

Dispossession & Termination

ORIGINAL TITLE
& LAND
CLAIMS

TENURE &
JURISDICTION

TENURE &
CULTURE CHANGE

(AB)

(AC)

(ABC)

LAND
CESSIONS &

ESTABLISHMENT

OF RESERVATIONS

LAND
ADMINSTRATION
&
LAND UTILIZATION

TITLE
CLARIFICATION
& CHANGE

(BC)

(B)

(C)

Protection & Reservation

	mostly anthropology, ecology
	mostly history
	mostly soc. sci., pub. admn., law
	mostly law
	mostly anthropology, ethnohistory history, law, land economics
	mostly anthropology, ethnohistory

nms

Figure 1

(ABC), and aboriginal territoriality (A). All of these contain elements important in the background research for, and the interpretation of, land claims. Similarly, the position taken by many tribes regarding territorial autonomy vis-à-vis the reservations (AC) will become clear when one refers to the discussion of aboriginal territoriality (A), the legal system that protects tribal lands (C), and the circumstances that have sustained the tribal quest for self-determination today (ABC). Finally, shifts in land title status (BC) after treaties were ratified must be seen from several perspectives: the intent of treaties and the circumstances of diplomacy (B), how title changes relate to the continued reservation of Indian land in trust (C), and the influence of such shifts in land tenure, for example, on Indian assimilation and acculturation (ABC). One example of this sort of issue is the allotment of land to individual Indians.

A. Aboriginal Occupancy and Territoriality

One may pose innumerable questions about aboriginal distributions with respect to how Indian culture perceived space as sociopolitical territory belonging to a given people who were subsisting within it in ecological terms. This set focuses on aboriginal occupancy, however defined and interpreted, and the literature reflects ethnographic accounts as well as later reconstructions, which have been derived as much from reevaluation of historical sources as from new ethnographic field observations. Studies seeking to describe and map aboriginal distributions combine interests in linguistics, ecology, and native polity. Part of my research questions the relevance of the methods and findings of studies in native linguistic distribution to the further understanding of territoriality and the role of the landholding group, whether that be tribe, tribelet, band, or community. Scholars hold opposing views of the political origins of the tribe, seeing it either as an aboriginal or as a post-contact organization; some argue that the tribe was articulated as an organization with a given territory only after the establishment of reservations (see the discussion in Sections AB and ABC). Tribal or band concepts of territoriality figure significantly in the litigation before the Indian Claims Commission.

B. Land Cessions and Establishment of Reservations

The historian's craft is diversely displayed in this subset and in BC, and the literature clearly reveals the ambivalent pattern of Indian affairs administration. Commencing with early colonial times, this subset raises a host of questions about the origins of the practice of land reservation, and the implications of religious involvement in securing land from the tribes. It also involves the mass of studies which reviews the events leading to, and the consequences following, treaties of cession, subsequent removals, and land reservation for various tribes. Its focus is cession, and it relates closely to the sweep of westward expansion from the enactment of the Northwest Ordinance in 1787 to the end of the treaty-negotiating period in 1871. Writers have examined the processes and the attitudes and values that led to the dispossession of the Indians from their lands; some have recounted what took place when tribes were regrouped into intertribal amalgams on reservations. The study of treaties and their aftermath has been a preoccupation of many historians; a continuing interest in land cessions becomes apparent, especially among graduate students at several universities in the Plains states. The newer colonial histories and historical geographies deserve special mention, for they not only shed new light on obscure events, but also reevaluate what many observers might consider incontestable facts of colonial contact. This applies particularly to the locational factors of Indian-white relations that older literature tended to ignore or misinterpret.

C. Land Administration and Land Utilization

When finally many tribes accepted their fate, settled down, and came to count on the trust protection of federal treaties, the government had to consider new policies aimed at the management and development of tribal resources. Many disciplines have contributed to the study of reservations and their economic and social change. On questions of administrative policy, most of the published and processed materials are government documents, some of which provide primary data, but most of which deal with interpretations useful for better understanding how Indian land tenure has been administered since the close of the treaty period. The literature examines, among other topics, the legal foundations of tribal and individual tenure and the need for tenure changes in order to implement development—as, for example, through the vehicle of specific laws designed to strengthen tribal government (e.g., the IRA, 1934). Prepared by land economists, rural sociologists, geographers, and Bureau of Indian Affairs (BIA) officials, land surveys and land use studies of reservations form an important body of literature, but only some of these documents, articles, and theses undertake to explore the intricate relationships between the use and tenure of land resources. Interesting work has been done by a handful of scholars relating to the treatment of the reservation as a land institution, especially as a microcosm surrounded by the white society with which Indians must interact in both social and economic terms. A few of these studies consider space/behavior relationships of Indians to nearby communities.

AB. Aboriginal Title and Land Claims

The Indian's day in court dawned feebly before the turn of the century. Early litigation centered on the legality of his dispossession from aboriginal territory and relocation on a reservation. Many court cases dealt with claims to lands taken after the negotiation and acceptance of treaties of cession: that is, by extinguishment of title to reservations, especially in conjunction with the granting of allotments to individual Indians and the opening of "surplus" tribal lands to entry under the public land laws. Since the establishment of the Indian Claims Commission in 1946, numerous tribes have gone to court to seek monetary judgments against the government for actions going as far back as the "time of taking." Many of the cases turn on a reconstruction of the events in an attempt to prove unconscionable actions in the dispossession of Native Americans of their aboriginal occupancy. While the analysis of aboriginal title or Indian title is essentially a legal historian's task, the interpretation of findings relating to native occupancy at the time of taking has depended mainly on the outlook of anthropologists and historians versed in things Indian. The specialized nature of the research that has gone into the preparation of expert testimony for the plaintiff (the tribes) and the defense (federal government) has demanded the energies of the ablest scholars, who have been obliged at all times to think in an interdisciplinary fashion about matters as far apart as the ecological factors of subsistent hunting and the economic forces contributing to historical land speculation.

BC. Title Clarification and Change

With the ink of the signatories hardly dry, demands for adjustment of the boundaries of reservations, as well as claims of fraud in the laying out of those lands, became fairly commonplace. In the Mexican Cession Area (the U.S. Southwest) confusion and litigation arose almost immediately because of differences in the interpretation of Spanish and Mexican law and U.S. administrative policy toward Indians' rights in land. Problems arose with cattlemen, land speculators, and railroad agents, and with squaw men residing on reservations. Land allotment created new problems for the tribes; individual Indians were confused as to the intent and legal status of lands held in fee patent, and now that individual holdings were subject to the inheritance laws of the states, federal trusteeship itself became suspect. Administration of the vast domain of the West was beyond the competence of the territorial governor, doubling as superintendent of Indian affairs, and the registrars of the land offices; neither could manage to see to the needs of Indians relocating on reservations scattered over several hundred thousand square miles. For example, land exchanges with the railroads were necessary because of conflicting descriptions of land parcels held by the tribes and the railroad companies, and similar circumstances arose with respect to bona fide entries by homesteaders. Allotment created new problems in the administration of individual holdings now subject to the laws of descent of the states. Ultimately, the process of termination of federal trusteeship continued to erode tribal confidence in the government; this policy has vacillated with changes in national administration. It was employed most recently during the 1950s.

AC. Tenure and Jurisdiction

Indians now better understand their rights in lands. They have secured able counsel on the interpretation of treaties and have recognized the power of the mass media and the courts to help achieve changes in the administration of their land affairs. Conflict over jurisdiction has become a major issue in the past two decades. State and local attempts to abridge the rights of Indians to their federally guaranteed immunities have angered the tribes and led to pan-Indian legal-political movements with the aim of securing greater recognition of tribal autonomy. Controversies have involved blatant challenges to the integrity of treaty protection of aboriginal hunting and fishing rights, claims of outright interference in the allocation of tribal water rights by state governments, and attempts to modify tribal or individual Indian tenure by means of local zoning ordinances. A major concern in recent years has been the far-reaching implications of federal laws that have permitted states to assume civil and criminal jurisdiction over reservations. Much of the literature reports case law.

ABC. Land Tenure and Culture Change

Historical events of contact and confrontation, the diffusion of differing cultural traits and institutions, and the very mixing of peoples of different stock and ethnicity all represent factors contributing to Indian acculturation in the past several centuries. With respect to land tenure, it is most inviting to assess, however incompletely, the effects of changes in tenure upon native culture or, conversely, the effects of changes in the composition of Indian culture upon tenure practices. It is easy enough to discover what facets of tenure have contributed, for example, to physical or geographical change, as in the relocation of tribes or the abandonment of villages upon the allotment of land in severalty. It is another matter to uncover the relationships between changes in tenure, especially the adoption of Euro-American property concepts, and Indian acculturation and assimilation. Fortunately, several symposia have explored Indian culture change and not only provide considerable insight into the interpretation of changes wrought by the intrusion of new institutions, but also suggest a certain methodology for the study of Indian acculturation. But I tend to conclude that what has contributed most to change in native culture has been the introduction of a differing legal apparatus, including land tenure institutions, governing Indian affairs.

I hope that, by focusing my conclusions on the changing nature of Indian land tenure over the course of 200 years, it will be possible to demonstrate the continuing importance of legal institutions in fashioning new legal instruments to protect tribal autonomy. In reality, the preservation of Indian culture depends upon the survival of the jural community, which owes its persistence to non-Indian legal institutions. Indians have discovered that through involvement in American legal practice—witness Deloria, Bennett, and Kickingbird—they can make great strides toward protecting the lifestyles they have come to identify as tribal, whatever the degree of change that has been wrought upon them.

The Typology Applied to California

California holds a prominent position in studies of the Indian, for it has been a proving ground for many methods utilized in ethnographic research. But unlike the Plains and the Northeast Woodlands, California does not figure importantly in histories of the tribes. One will readily discover a wealth of ethnographic materials (Section A); Gifford (1918), Kroeber (1925, 1962), and White (1963) represent studies that include considerations of aboriginal practices of land tenure. Although Indian affairs properly began with Spanish entry, the important land studies in Section B deal with treaty negotiations with the United States Government and the dispossession of California Indians (Ellison 1925; Lipps 1932; and Crouter and Rolle 1960). Note that Kroeber, Ellison, and Lipps reappear as background studies in land claims research (Section AB) along with several other studies (e.g., Harvey 1961 and Stewart 1961). In fact, the "Indians of California"—a legally defined entity for purposes of litigation—focused attention on the need to refine ecological and ethnohistorical methodologies, and one interesting result is the new ecological typology for native California by Beals and Hester (1956).

Although only a small total acreage within California has been held in trust, land administration has been particularly problematic in the half-century during which California has risen to urban-industrial prominence (Section C). Sutton (1964) and Travis (1968) deal with the relationship between land tenure and land utilization on specific reservations; most of the relevant literature appears as government documents not cited in this volume (for additional sources, one can examine U.S. Congress, House, 1953). Efforts to extinguish title or otherwise modify the trust status of Indian lands (Section BC) by means of land allotment or termination of federal trusteeship are discussed in several works (Dyer 1945; Kasch 1947; and Busselen 1962). Dale (1949) provides a historical review of Indian affairs administration in California, cutting across the typology—Sections B, BC, and C.

In recent years many California Indians, whether living on or off reservations, have asserted land rights or have opposed the intrusion of local law enforcement within their jural communities (Section AC). Indians, for example, occupied former military lands, and others took temporary possession of Alcatraz Island, gaining national prominence for their cause. Other Indians have publicly rejected the monetary award of 47 cents an acre for lands lost by their ancestors in the last century. Actually, little of the situation involving California Indians in litigation, land occupancy, and the like appears in major published works. The *Newsletter* of the California Indian Legal Services (Berkeley) reports most of the litigation. But Indian water rights (Sondheim and Alexander 1960), tax-exemption (Goodrich 1926), and allotment of land (Sutton 1967) have been variously discussed. Many legal problems of Indian lands come under review by Price (1969) and Cree (1974). Aside from the general review of acculturation by Downs (in Leacock and Lurie 1971) and a more detailed analysis of the relationship between land tenure and Indian culture change in the Mission area by Sutton (1964), such studies are generally lacking (Section ABC).

I have tried to demonstrate that California Indians are part of the discussion of each subset, and that it behooves the researcher to consider how each subset interacts with the others in determining what references should be further explored.

Notes

1. *Christian Science Monitor*, July 19, 1974.
2. On the application of Hallowell's theory to Indians, see Herman's 1956 study of the Huron.
3. The Indian and urbanization is a field in itself and cannot be treated fully in this volume. Especially useful is J. N. Kerri (ed.), "American Indians: A Bibliography of Contemporary Studies and Urban Research," *Exchange Bibliography*, nos. 376-7, Council of Planning Librarians (Monticello, Ill.). The current approach to the urban focus is well handled by J. O. Waddell and O. M. Watson (eds.), *The American Indian in Urban Society* (Boston: Little, Brown, 1971), two studies from which are reviewed in this book—Nagata (1971) and Jorgensen (1971).

Works Cited in the Introduction

Barlowe, 1970
Barnett, 1956
Beals & Hester, 1956
Berkhofer, 1971
Bertrand & Corty, 1962
Billington, 1974
Bohannan, 1963, 1965
Brookfield, 1964
Busselen, 1962
Castile, 1974
Clawson, 1968
Collier, 1949
Cree, 1974
Crouter & Rolle, 1960
Dale, 1949
Dick, 1970
Dukelow & Zakheim, 1972
Dyer, 1945
Ellison, 1925
Firey, 1960
Fried, 1952
Gates, 1968
Gifford, 1918
Goodrich, 1926
Haas, 1925
Hagan, 1963
Hallowell, 1943, 1957
Harvey, 1961
Herman, 1956
Herskovits, 1952
Hibbard, 1924

Howard, 1969
Kasch, 1947
Keesing, 1953
Kennard & Macgregor, 1953
Kickingbird & Ducheneaux, 1973
Kinney, 1937
Kroeber, 1925, 1962
Lazewski, 1973
Leacock & Lurie, 1971
Lipps, 1932
Macgregor, 1946
Mead & Bunzel, 1960
Neils, 1971
Price, 1969, 1973
Prucha, 1971
Robbins, 1942
Sondheim & Alexander, 1960
Stewart, O. C., 1961
Sturtevant, 1966
Sutton, 1964, 1967, 1970b
Swierenga, 1968
Symposium, 1961
Thomas, 1966a/b
Travis, 1968
U.S. Congress, House, 1953
Wallace, 1970
Washburn, 1971a/b
Whalen, 1971
White, 1963
Wise, 1971
Wissler, 1938a

SECTION A

Aboriginal Occupancy
and Territoriality

Introduction

Like all peoples past and present, Indian groups differentiated themselves
one from another in their occupancy of land. As identifiable kin groups
(clans, lineages, families, villages), or bands and tribelets, and with less
frequency as tribes, they expressed rudimentary or sophisticated concepts
of territoriality and land tenure. Despite gaps in our knowledge, it may be
said safely that all Indian peoples recognized bounds to their use of the
environment and mobility within it, and, whether as a corporate entity
(e.g., tribe) or as a smaller socioeconomic group (e.g. band), to our
knowledge all Indians allocated resources of their environment among
their own kind. Unfortunately, the cumulative literature, which is based
essentially on observations at and since contact and which relies mostly on
native informants and cautious anthropological reconstructions, not only
lacks many essential data about specific peoples and behavioral practices,
but has tended to occupy itself mostly with tribal distributions, however
arrived at. While countless ethnographies and ethnogeographies identify
particulars of village distributions, affix place names to generalized maps,
and in passing refer to property institutions, land tenure in general has not
constituted a main "field." Moreover, when we review the data of native
territoriality, we find, for example, that aboriginal distributions are often
expressed in terms of linguistic rather than ecological patterns. Lacking
sufficient ecological methodology, we cannot be altogether certain of just
how useful linguistic distribution data may be in the interpretation of
Indian territoriality.

It should not come as a surprise that many generalizations about native land tenure stand as relatively unsubstantiated assumptions that perhaps can never be adequately documented or verified through oral tradition. The source materials for later scientific interpretations were all too often committed to paper by persons uninitiated in the study of non-European cultures. In addition, basic historical data relevant to better reconstructions of tribal distributions and claims to territory lay unused in archives or were otherwise unknown to students until it was unearthed by recent research into tribal land claims as part of litigation before the Indian Claims Commission (see Section AB). To be sure, some sources misinterpreted and incompletely reported indigenous occupancy, perhaps because of the pressure of white covetousness of Indian lands. Perhaps too the earlier literature tended to gloss over the question of native landholding and territorial practices because, unlike the white intruder, "the savage's mind knew no such thing as absolute ownership of land by individuals" (Grinnell 1907).

That native peoples generally perceived the environment as a usufruct to be utilized without regard to ownership came to be a prevailing view. In fact, many of the earlier studies sought to demonstrate how the lifestyles of the Indians were fashioned by the environment. Often termed "environmental determinism," this argument overly stressed the restrictions of the environment and ignored the options open to differing culture groups. Innumerable assumptions about the Indian's cultural achievements arose from this view (cf. Fynn 1907, Huntington 1919). It was not until scholars turned to sedentary, agrarian Indian communities that they seriously considered indigenous land tenure institutions. Yet fairly stereotyped generalizations again resulted. Scholars quickly came to view communal landholding as the only major land institution, and thus oversimplified the relationship of Indian horticultural societies to their environment.

Fortunately, rigorous scholarship by specialists in several disciplines has filled the need for greater accuracy in reporting native landholding practices and territorial claims. In part, this has been stimulated by long-standing academic debates generated, for example, by continuing researches into the nature of the family hunting territory (see Section ABC) as conducted by Speck and Eiseley (1939), and Leacock (1954). In addition, the demand for legal clarity in claims litigation has necessitated a more rigorous examination of earlier findings, more exacting examination both of the quality of the map renditions and of the mappable data themselves in territorial studies, and a more critical questioning of the reliability, for example, of the information of native informants. Among anthropologists, however, professional reappraisal of findings dates back to numerous studies in the 1930s (cf. Ray et al. 1938; Park et al.

1938). Newer studies have benefitted from the growth of the field of ethnohistory (e.g., Leacock and Lurie 1971), and since this has occurred in conjunction with professional academic involvement in land claims cases, the ensuing discussion of aboriginal territoriality and land tenure will be divided into several phases. In the present section, the focus will be on the basic literature; in Section AB emphasis will be placed on the literature that has arisen in response to litigation.

Interpretation of Native Land Tenure

In relative terms, the land tenure literature is thin, whereas that dealing with territorial distributions and claims comprehends not only subject matter pertinent here, but also seemingly unrelated matters dealing with native languages and other customs. Were one to peruse most ethnographic studies of monograph size, fragments of land tenure and property rights would be found (cf. Dozier 1953; Forde 1931a; Hoebel 1940; Kroeber 1935; Singh 1966; Smith and Roberts 1954; Spier 1928, 1930). Some ethnographic studies suggest, for example, regional variations in the intensity of interest in property rights. Studies of California Indians, by examining the functions of clans and lineages, have modified earlier thinking about landholding among essentially sedentary yet non-farming Indians (Drucker 1937; Gifford 1918, 1926; Spier 1923; Strong 1929; White 1963). Most of these studies emphasize that despite a general pattern of communally held land, familial ownership, akin to private land rights, did exist more extensively than originally assumed. The clan's role as the fundamental social unit of landownership has been stressed in studies of agrarian communities such as that of the Hopi (Beaglehole 1936; Forde 1931b). Kroeber's (1951) pseudohistory of the Mohave epic reported on the role of the clan in territorial holdings at the time these Indians occupied the valley which bears their name. As a rule, the communal nature of land tenure reappears with considerable consistency in the study of agrarian Indians (Hill 1936; Haile 1954; Whalen 1971; Riley 1968; Spier 1928; Smith and Roberts 1954). In comparable terms, usufructuary practices are most often reported for bands of the Plateau and Great Basin (cf. Cappannari's review study, 1960), the Plains (Hoebel 1940), and the eastern forests (Snyderman 1951). Most relevant literature lacks observations about how individuals gained membership in various landholding and land-using groups or communities; presumably kinship ties formed the fundamental basis, although adoption of captives has been reported (e.g., among the Apache).

Relying heavily on the culture-area approach based mainly on the work of Wissler and Kroeber, Linton (1943) prepared a useful though brief summary for the continent, noting that "the linkage between ecologies and basic economies in North America is close enough to make a description of land tenure by culture areas fairly valid" (p. 44). Typologies similar to his—for arctic, subarctic, Great Plains, northeastern woodland, Pacific coast, California, Great Plateau, Southeast, and Southwest—find their way into many general ethnographic studies (cf. Oswalt 1966; Underhill 1953), thereby helping to relate basic lifestyles to particulars of landholding patterns. Linton concluded that aside from Canada and parts of our Southwest, the aboriginal systems of tenure no longer existed, for

> they were adapted to particular combinations of ecological and social conditions which are also extinct, and any attempt to reconstitute them has about as much chance of success as similar attempts would have with modern American farmers. (PP. 53-54)

Much the same typology forms the matrix of a chapter on property and land tenure in Driver and Massey (1957) and a discussion in Driver (1969), which is synchronically (topically) organized. While Driver attempts to partially update aspects of land tenure here and there, the only truly new item is a map (exhibit 29) which delimits regional areas of land tenure based upon relationships between kinship and residence (e.g., patricentered, bicentered, etc.). Driver, in restating much the same conclusions reached by former writers, noted that "with few exceptions the same alignment of relatives controlled multiple uses of land when they were controlled by groups of relatives at all" (1961 ed., p. 260).

Because of its cross-cultural context and emphasis on methodology, Herskovits's *Economic Anthropology* (1952) offers considerable insight into the nature of aboriginal land tenure in America. One can gain a useful perspective that suggests how the Indian fits into general conclusions about the lifestyles, landholdings, and territorial practices of non-European peoples. Herskovits emphasized that the ownership of resources was common rather than communal, and that it was not the land but what it yielded—that is, usufruct—that seemed to be fundamental in the ownership patterns of most Indian groups. He suggested, for example, that the Navajo concept of "inherited use ownership" seemed a more appropriate identification than "communal ownership" for many agrarian peoples among whom "use gives tenure the complexion of ownership" (1965 ed., p. 370). (See Aberle 1974a, which sustains these earlier observations and at the same time expands more fully on Navajo land tenure concepts.) In a diachronic study of selected societies, Forde (1934) also included comparisons of land tenure institutions, including those of hunting and gathering and horticultural Indians.

Despite the evidence of variety in aboriginal landholding practices, scholars have tended to examine tenure in terms of relatively autonomous populations. Just as Speck and Eiseley (1939) stressed the family hunting territory as a native institution, others have emphasized the importance of clan or other kin groups. Wissler (1938a) identified the family group in terms of land rights; he noted that individual ownership of land was foreign to indigenous practices, although exclusive use of certain plots of ground or of such resources as individual trees could be held by families, clans, or other socioeconomic groups. Kroeber's earlier writings on California (1925) focused on the village community and then on the tribelet as autonomous units. Gifford (1926) considered the lineage to be the representative political unit, as did Strong (1929).

Several studies of the Northwest have suggested that larger social configurations have linked Indians to their resource base. Studies by Suttles (1960, 1963, 1968) and other anthropologists (e.g., Elmendorf 1971) indicate that intervillage ties formed the basis for a social organization that governed access to resources and the sharing of surpluses against a future time of scarcity. Suttles's studies focused on the Coast Salish, for which he observed that

> By potlatching, a group established its status vis-à-vis other groups, in effect saying 'we are an extended family (or a village of several extended families) with title to such-and-such a territory having such-and-such resources.' (1960, p. 301)

He saw the Coast Salish, for example, as constituting a contiguous, "single population with a single social system that was in 1855 artificially split into political units by the reservation system" (correspondence, 11-1-74). Although he recognized extended family property rights in clam or fern beds and other resources, he stressed the communal basis of resource access and sharing, and suggested that this means made for greater efficiency in the exploitation of the environment.

Although Kroeber (1955, 1962) ultimately underscored the position that the landholding group in aboriginal America was always less than the tribe or nation, and more often a band or tribelet, this position has run counter to some views, especially in eastern Anglo-America, where the tribe is identified with aboriginal territorial domains (cf. Wallace 1957; Fried 1966; Helm 1968 and see Section ABC). More recently, the band has been reexamined and displaced by stronger emphasis, at least in Northern California, on semi-sedentary tribelets as autonomous political units "numbering into the hundreds" of people (Kunkel 1974). One conclusion, perhaps, is that land tenure and territoriality cannot be separated; the identifiable locus of land tenure rights in Indian communities has had very much to do with territorial bounds, which in turn relate to ecological factors in the pursuit of a livelihood.

Territoriality and Tribal Distributions

Territoriality and livelihood fundamentally coincide; that is, one can demonstrate marked relationships between the area occupied or utilized by a given people and their notion of a claim to paramount rights within that area. Since agrarian peoples are sedentary, the sites of their villages, even those known only through oral tradition or archaeological discovery, essentially fix the distribution of the landholding group on a map. It is more difficult to map adequately the land unit of a hunting and gathering population unless, as in the case of the "Indians of California," they too were sedentary. Thus ecological arguments that seek explanations for aboriginal distributions come into play when scholars attempt to reconstruct territorial domains among mobile bands or tribelets. For some scholars, perhaps, any distribution of an Indian population, whether explained ecologically or on the basis of linguistic associations, has some territorial significance in terms of claims to land and related resources. Oliver (1962), for example, in applying Kroeberian ecological premises to the Plains, conceded that ecological factors definitely contributed to native distributions. Here he emphasized how corporate responsibility was difficult to maintain among dispersed peoples; he pointed to the Cheyenne and Teton Dakota, who had abandoned the clan system, which was not well suited to necessities of Plains life. Even with reference to Athapaskan Indians in the far north, where Indians did not compose neat political or cultural units, the locus of territoriality was the village (Osgood 1936).

To date an amalgam of methods has been employed to ascertain and explain practices of territoriality in aboriginal America. Many of the newer researchers have benefitted immensely from more rigorous treatment of the subject of territoriality by scholars investigating land claims dating back a century or more. Such research has reappraised ecological data, archaeological evidence, and historical documentation. These and other scholars have examined, for example, the evidence for aboriginal tribal organization upon which much of the reconstruction of distributional patterns has depended (cf. Reeve 1956; Wallace 1957; Hoffman 1964; K. M. Stewart 1969; Tuck 1971b; and such older works as Swanton 1922; Hoover 1935; Oblasser 1936; Fenton 1940; and Hoebel 1940).

As a rule, reconstructions fall short of infallible accuracy, for they depend mainly for setting bounds on determining the sites of settlements at a given time, usually either the earliest period of contact or the time of taking. So-called "territorial" maps or those of village sites result from the synthesis of data of historical more than of archaeological evidence, as do the countless ethnographies and ethnogeographies that have grown out of the "Berkeley school," which has focused on California Indian studies. It is rather prophetic that as early as 1918, when Kroeber completed his *Handbook* (published in 1925), he observed that

> Over much of Southern California . . . the opportunity to prepare an exact aboriginal village map passed away fifty years ago. The numerous little reservations of today do in the rough conserve the ancient ethnic and local distribution; but not under the old circumstances. (P. 616)

One can persuasively argue on the basis of historic contact data that existing reservations represent the locus of original territory, and while this may be significantly true in the West, it is obviously invalid for much of the eastern United States (see Figure 2). But even on the basis of newer studies, I found (Sutton 1964) it nearly impossible to improve upon earlier findings by Kroeber and his students who had sought to determine the sites of villages and band distributions in Southern California (Strong 1929; White 1963).

Several specific studies for California (Barrett 1908; Loud 1918; Heizer and Hester 1970; Schenck 1926; O. C. Stewart 1943; Zigmond 1938), the Northwest (Ray 1936; Spier 1930, 1936; Waterman 1920), and for the Southwest, including the Great Basin (Forde 1931a; Kelly 1932, 1938; Spier 1928; Steward 1933, 1939) make important use of historical data, in several cases utilizing exploration surveys including those for trans-western railroad routes. However, linguistic factors, i.e., mainly native language distributions, also contribute importantly to accounts of native distributions. Loud, for example, in his study (1918) of Wiyot terrotory, defines its bounds along such linguistic lines, although he supports his conclusions with evidence of village sites. Ecological factors also enter into explanations of territoriality, as may be seen in his observation that "all of this prairie should be regarded as Wiyot territory, while the lower waters of Little River must be considered as Yurok possession" (p. 249). Stewart (1943) noted that Pomo language and tribal bounds cut across environmental provinces. Much earlier, Barrett had turned to similar linguistic evidence as the basis for mapping territorial boundaries of the Pomo.

Linguistic correlations played a considerable role in Aschmann's efforts (1970) to reconstruct the patterns of migration of Apachean peoples into the Southwest. The study attempts to show a correspondence between territorial movement and language affiliations among those Athapaskans who came to occupy parts of New Mexico and Arizona. Most of his study reveals the importance not only of linguistic research but of ethnohistoric reconstruction of tribal or band groups. Athapaskans, he noted, did displace some sedentary peoples (e.g., Pimas), but in general they came to occupy relatively unwelcome ecological niches or refuge zones; he characterized their migrations as *Unterwanderungen*, or the migrations of poorer folk into areas unattractive to others. He noted too that Pawnee, Kiowa and Comanche pushing provided "some of the impetus for Athapaskan expansion southward and westward" (p. 97). This study, like several others (cf. M. E. Opler 1971), emphasizes the importance of reconstructing both aboriginal patterns of movement and those occurring between contact and conquest.

The above sampling merely suggests how ecological, linguistic and historical data interweave in the many reconstructions of native distributions. These studies do not all ask, Just what territory did an Indian group or tribe occupy or lay claim to prior to contact? Many researchers question the accuracy of such contact studies; much of the literature perhaps depends too strongly on such sources. Certainly those cartographic reconstructions that base their boundaries on historical documentation come up with a more concrete rendition of "ownership" or claim area. Compare, for example, Bolton's treatment (1920) of the New York City area to that of Beauchamp (1900); the former relies upon contact information mainly, whereas the latter attempts a reconstruction back to A.D. 1600. Swanton's detailed, almost encyclopedic, reconstruction (1922) of Creek Indian settlement sharply points up the validity of historical records and maps in detailing sites of native villages and setting limits for tribal or subtribal grouping. Many of his maps are redrawn from older maps prepared as early as 1715. He had hoped that later study would display on maps of a smaller (he said larger) scale locations of both prehistoric and historic sites. Hoffman (1964) employed a similar method in reconstructing Indian occupancy of tidewater Virginia and North Carolina (ca. 1608); he correlated archaeological and historical data as a means of validating a conclusion that Iroquoians were located on the headwaters of the Potomac and upper Ohio drainage over 350 years. Even more revealing of the utility of the archaeological method is Tuck's monograph (1971b) on the settlement archaeology of the Onondaga. Here, instead of regrouping several proto-Iroquoian peoples in the general area in which they were encountered in colonial times, he argues that the tribe developed *in situ* in upper New York. The maintenance of local microtraditions (e.g., ceramics), by dint of the persistence of matrilocal residence patterns with female-owned and -worked horticultural lands, helped provide data that correlated village sites at different time periods. It is apparent that delimitation of the territory of a tribal grouping based on such archaeological evidence and reinforced by historical contact literature strengthens the Indians' arguments that a given area was their homeland for several centuries prior to contact.

Whatever their degree of reliability, map reconstructions based upon various data—archaeological, historical, and present-day empirical observations—serve a useful purpose in associating given areas with tribal names. Yet some studies point up the weaknesses of such reconstruction. Berreman, in his Oregon study (1937), asserted that such sources as accounts by travelers and missionaries already had distorted the picture of tribal distributions. He did find considerable value in linguistic and psychological inquiries of informants. For example, his discovery that the Sahaptin came to be found in an area outside their original territory owing to invasions by the Snake and Bannock revealed the utility of ethnohistorical methods. For earlier methodological discussions see Ray et al. (1938) and Park et al. (1938); the latter include criticisms of Berremen, Steward (1937) and Teit (1928).

As early as his *Basin-Plateau* study, Steward (1938) began to enunciate the development of an ecological approach to the distribution of bands in the arid West.[1] His was not the earliest study that correlated environment with given culture complexes. Steward came to stress that studies of the interrelatedness of culture, technology, and the quest for food, seasonal patterns of subsistence and human mobility could and did help to establish the size of an area needed by given groups when some approximation of numbers could be reasoned. He had noted that no group habitually and exclusively utilized a clearly defined territory. In his 1955a study, Steward continued to emphasize exploitation of habitats by one, two, or three families living together in isolation from others, and as he noted for countless examples of simple hunting and gathering peoples in the Great Basin:

> ... the arbitrary exclusion of territorially delimited groups of families from utilization of other territories would have caused starvation and death .... the absence of property claims of local groups to delimitable areas of natural resources upon which work has not been expended was the corollary of the fragmented nature of Shoshonean society. (P. 108)

Kroeber (1939) also explored the relationships between tribes and ecological factors throughout North America. Noting that Wissler's earlier efforts (1926) focused on spatial distributions of culture traits and complexes but did not take into account ecological theories, Kroeber set about construction of a tribal map of continental proportions, which by its compiler's own admission did not represent absolute conditions at any fixed dateline. It did attempt to lay out tribal territories as they were at the time of first contact by Europeans. To Kroeber, maps based on period of occupation were better than those based on time of discovery, since the dateline varied so markedly for aboriginal reconstruction. Aside from the more general maps of Wissler, Murdock, Voegelin, and Driver (Driver et al. 1953; Voegelin and Voegelin 1944; Sturtevant 1967), Kroeber's is the most comprehensive, although the Driver map (discussion of which is reserved for Section AB) reflects data that were not available at the time Kroeber prepared his map. Interestingly enough, Kroeber is the prime source for a series of covariant maps which depict comparatively aboriginal territory and surviving reservation areas (U.S. Congress 1953). Figure 2 adapts portions of those maps.

Swanton, in *The Indian Tribes of North America* (1952), provided an analysis of the factors that were considered in arriving at a better reconstruction of the geographical distributions of tribes. He was concerned with how to treat inexact, incomplete, and inconclusive evidence and how to apply the concept of "tribe" to native distributions. He questioned the effects, for example, of intertribal contact on native dislocation and mobility, and he found suspect those distributions based wholly on locations of tribes at first encounter. He abandoned such an approach in favor of locating each "tribe in the region with which it was most closely associated historically" (p. 4). Thus he chose a fairly stable dateline—ca. 1650 A.D.—for the eastern and southern United States and eastern Canada in order that the distribution might approximate aboriginal conditions. The Swanton volume does point up many of the problems that have faced scholars seeking definitive reconstruction of aboriginal lifestyles and patterns of occupancy.

The interface between territorial expression of an Indian people and the distribution of related languages forms the focus of Heizer's slim volume (1966) devoted to California research. Heizer has pulled together most of the substantive and methodological discussion dealing with the mapping of California Indian distributions. He reviews several earlier cartographic efforts such as those of Taylor (1864 [cf. Heizer 1941]), Powers (1877), and Powell (1891), and he reproduces Powers's map and a 1910 posthumous revision of Powell's tribal map. His emphasis, however, is on the Kroeber map in the latter's *Handbook of California Indians* (1925), which Heizer and Kroeber updated in 1955 in connection with land claims research (cf. O. C. Stewart 1961, in Section AB). Heizer also discussed the comparative efforts of C. Hart Merriam, a biologist-turned-ethnographer who also mapped native distributions in the state. The Kroeber and Merriam maps rely heavily on data related to language distributions. Baumhoff (1958) utilizes the cartographic approaches of both scholars in his discussion of methods applied to California Athabascan groups.

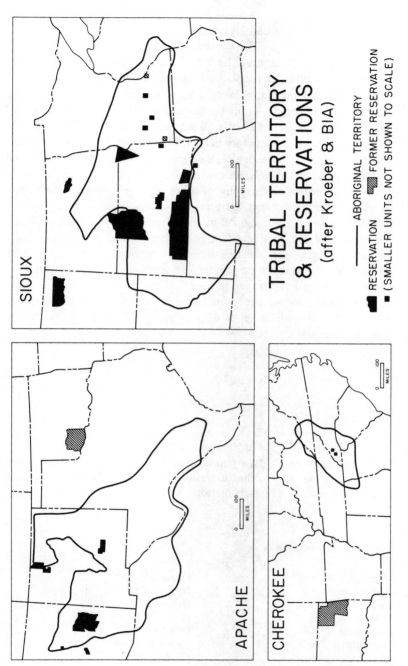

Figure 2[2]

A review of the foregoing studies indicates that to date no single method has led to a definitive reconstruction of aboriginal territoriality and practice of land tenure. The use of linguistic information, especially the gross distribution of people by language and dialect, has been a poor substitute for an integrated picture based on ecological, historical, and archaeological evidence. As further discussion of the role and function of the tribe will stress, it has often been assumed that the territory of a particular people is the territory occupied by a group that speaks the same language or dialect; consequently, the people as a tribal entity in space and the territory of that people are coextensive both physically and logically. Much of the earlier gross mapping of tribes relied on such linguistic data in the absence of verification against solid sociopolitical bases that might have yielded better mapping. All in all, if Kroeber's statement for California (1962) and the continent (1955) still has merit, then villages, bands, tribelets, lineages, and the like should be stressed in examining territoriality, for ". . . it was these smaller communities that were independent, sovereign, and held and used a territory" (1955, p. 313). If this were true, then to date one should expect to find that the status of current mapping of native distributions in terms of aboriginal territoriality is still incomplete and inaccurate.

Notes

1. See Thomas, 1973, for an empirical test of Steward's theories.
2. These maps adapt data from Kroeber (1939) and U.S. Congress (House) 1953. See further discussion of maps in the Bibliographical and Cartographical Sources section.

Works Cited in Section A

Aberle, 1974a   Dozier, 1953
Aschmann, 1970   Driver, 1969
Barrett, 1908   Driver & Massey, 1957
Baumhoff, 1958   Driver et al., 1953
Beaglehole, 1936   Drucker, 1937
Beauchamp, 1900   Elmendorf, 1971
Berreman, 1937   Fenton, 1940
Bolton, 1920   Forde, 1931a/b, 1934
Cappannari, 1960   Fried, 1966

Fynn, 1907
Gifford, 1918, *1923, 1926
Gilmore, *1928
Grinnell, 1907
Haile, 1954
Heizer, 1941, 1966
Heizer & Hester, 1970
Helm, 1968
Herskovits, 1952
Hill, 1936
Hinsdale, *1932
Hoebel, 1940
Hoffman, 1964
Hoover, *1931, 1935, *1941
Huntington, 1919
Kelly, 1932, 1938
Kroeber, 1925, 1935, 1939, 1951,
 1955, 1962
Kunkel, 1974
Leacock, 1954
Leacock & Lurie, 1971
Linton, 1943
Loud, 1918
Oblasser, 1936
Oliver, 1962
Opler, M. E., 1971
Ortiz, *1972
Osgood, 1936
Oswalt, 1966
Park et al., 1938
Ray, 1936

Ray et al., 1938
Reeve, 1956
Riley, 1968
Schenck, 1926
Singh, 1966
Smith & Roberts, 1954
Snyderman, 1951
Speck, *1928, *1940
Speck & Eiseley, 1939
Spier, 1923, 1928, 1930, 1936
Steward, 1933, 1937, 1938, 1939,
 1955a
Stewart, K. M., 1969
Stewart, O. C., 1943, 1961
Strong, 1929
Sturtevant, 1967
Suttles, 1960, 1963, 1968
Sutton, 1964
Swanton, 1922, 1952
Teit, 1928
Thomas, 1973
Tuck, 1971b
Underhill, 1953
U.S. Congress, House, 1953
Voegelin & Voegelin, 1944
Wallace, 1957
Waterman, 1920
Whalen, 1971
White, 1963
Wissler, 1926, 1938a
Zigmond, 1938

*Denotes works not actually cited, but relevant to this section.

SECTION B

Land Cessions and the Establishment of Reservations

Introduction

Most students of Indian affairs would agree that taking of Indian land by any and all means prevailed for most of two centuries. So widespread was this process that it is not surprising to find it pervades the literature, in which fiction has all too often intermingled with fact to confound the search for a true perspective on Indian-white relations over land. But historians, as well as some anthropologists and historical geographers, continue to reconstruct the events and motives of the past in hopes of achieving a more accurate picture of Euro-American efforts to dispossess Indians of their lands. Most general accounts of Indian-white history report the facts as best understood and underscore in one way or another how dispossession has affected the lifeways of tribesmen. Quite often these accounts seem apologetic for the actions of the white man (Macleod 1928; McNickle 1949, 1962; Hagan 1961; Fey and McNickle 1959, 1970; Debo 1970). Historians have been most prolific in their reconstructions of treaty negotiations for the cession of Indian lands. In fact, treaty studies tend to overwhelm the literature, each one exposing in some way elements of fraud and speculation. It should be recognized that while studies of land cessions involve the question of establishing reservations for the tribes, the taking of Indian land and the reserving of land for Indians constitute a dichotomous process, and so it is reported in much of the literature.

It is also true that the colonial and national periods receive separate treatment by historians, but Indian land cessions and reservations as dichotomous subject matter do not neatly divide at the end of the colonial period and the formation of a national government. Colonial experiences with the acquisition of Indian lands find parallels in later efforts to secure the cession of territory under the fledgling nation. Similarly, the reservation of land occurred in several colonies before it became policy under federal Indian administration. And while researchers relate policies and practices back and forth across the dateline of nationhood, it is not necessarily correct to assert that colonial experiences and solutions in Indian affairs were precedents in the establishment of national policies.

The dichotomy of cession and reservation may, in fact, be viewed as a dual process, cession of one place virtually predicating reservation of another. For had dispossession not led to the ultimate establishment of trust lands for the tribes, probably few treaties would have been consummated, hostilities toward and harassment of settlers would have persisted and led to greater bloodshed, and today perhaps few tribes would have survived as distinct cultural entities. What the literature stresses for the earlier years of treaty negotiation was a preoccupation with the means of legally securing Indian lands; what became of the tribes on reserved tracts often became a matter of secondary concern. After 1871, however, treaty-writing no longer constituted the main vehicle of policy, and the real issues centered on improving the human condition of the tribes now presumed to be peacefully settled on remnants of once-vast aboriginal holdings.

Discerning students may observe another kind of dichotomy in the literature, one created more by the interests and disciplinary orientation of scholars than by historical themes in Indian affairs. In a recent symposium scholars considered the efforts of historians and anthropologists writing in the Indian field. Berkhofer (1971) contrasted anthropological interest in the aboriginal past and the reservation present with historical interest in the time in between. Anthropologists, of course, have stressed the aboriginal past in an attempt to discern persistence or change of native social and material culture. For historians the focus has been on the fundamental changes wrought by Indian-white relations. And both disciplines have come to analyze the crucial Euro-American institutions that have circumscribed and intruded upon the activities of Indians. The advent of a common interest in ethnohistory, which Berkhofer describes as more a courtship than a marriage, has suggested new vistas for reappraisal of earlier findings that were interpreted mainly from a white viewpoint. Berkhofer referred to the work of Fenton et al. (1957). Fenton's own earlier observations recommended the joining of the two disciplines for mutual gain in studies of the Northeast (the idea has application to other parts of the country as well). Fenton, an anthropologist, observed that researchers who would meet the challenge will have to examine thoroughly the archives of the northeastern states, "for the Indian deeds of New

England hold the story of land tenure and tell a good deal about tribal organization" (1957, p. 11).

In a series of studies Jennings (1965-71) has accomplished this directive, but with emphasis on colonial Pennsylvania. And in some respects— but in broader terms—Jacobs (1972) has also attempted to meet this challenge. In fact, study of the colonial history of Indian-white relations has taken on new vigor and has led to many new and intriguing conclusions, although most of the new work has been prepared by historians working without the parallel input of historically oriented ethnographers.

Washburn (1971a), writing in the same symposium as Berkhofer, compared disciplinary approaches to the study of the Indian and characterized scholars belonging to two opposing schools of thought as "humanistically-oriented historians." He cited Jacobs, Hagan, and himself as seeing the government as the perpetrator of "unjust and unconscionable actions" (cf. Jacobs 1972; Washburn 1965), and conversely cited Prucha, Vaughan, and Leach (cf. Prucha 1969) as among those attributing "purer motives and more honorable dealings" to the whites. Berkhofer's and Washburn's review articles discuss a wide range of subjects of importance in Indian history, and students of Indian land tenure will gain considerable perspective by examining these methodological and historiographic studies.

The virtual absence of anthropological writings on the period of land cessions and reservations is probably owing to the fact that anthropologists have been less familiar than historians with documentary source materials. Until the recent growth of the ethnohistorical approach, historians have monopolized the field (cf. Section AB). The period in between, according to Berkhofer's observations, was mostly one of Indian-white confrontation that both disciplines can shed light upon, but land tenure focuses on land institutions, cadastral records, maps and the like. Not until the advent of ecological research in anthropology were anthropologists much interested in land per se, whereas historians have long been preoccupied with pioneer settlement, the westward movement, and, of course, the displacement of the Indian. Aware of their own ethnocentricities, recent histories of Indian-white relations reflect a revisionist view of what occurred, but some observers might want to suggest that until more Indian scholars participate in the reexamination of their own ethnic histories since contact, certain biases will undoubtedly persist. (Readers will find, for example, cogent criticisms of such biases, written by Indian scholars, in *The Indian Historian.*)

Colonial Land Policies and the Indian

Although colonial policies ultimately focused on the acquisition of land from the Indians, efforts at accommodation and "co-existence" in place did occur. Many would argue that early land acquisition for settlers was in the interest of preserving the peace. Recent studies have reexamined many facets of Indian-white relations along many frontiers where the land question was paramount. Two review articles should be cited here. Sheehan (1969) is particularly useful for its broad sweep of a diverse literature relating to culture difference between Indians and Europeans, missionary efforts and removal policies; his bibliography cites many studies reviewed elsewhere in this book. Jennings (1971b) focuses even more sharply on land matters, for he traces the conflicting attitudes toward the legitimacy of colonial officials' negotiating land acquisitions with Indians; and for the Northeast he observes:

> It was the *double* conquest by which Indians lost not only sovereignty, but commons and severalty also, that established the harshest possible terms for the Indian who might hope to assimilate into "civilization." Property and liberty were synonyms in the 17th and 18th centuries. When the Indian was dispossessed of his land, he lost all hope of finding any niche in "civilized" society except that of servant or slave. (P. 541)

Land acquisition policies and problems—e.g., settler covetousness of Indian land, land speculation, conflicting interests of colonial powers—figure prominently in numerous studies which focus on various colonial frontiers. (Cf., for example, Blunt's 1825 study of jurisdictional matters.) Evolving British land-purchase policies concerned Alvord (1917) and Buffington (1921). DeForest (1851) examined English acquisition of Connecticut Indian lands. F. H. Stewart (1932, 1972) included abstracts of deeds of land cessions by Indians in southern New Jersey. Such acquisitions throughout the colonies did not occur without incident as most studies suggest (Halsey 1901; Leach 1966; Nammack 1969; Trelease 1960; Vaughan 1965). Trelease, for example, in comparing British and Dutch land acquisition policies in colonial New York, noted that initially commerce rather than colonization was uppermost in the minds of the Dutch. He contrasted the advantages of sustaining the lucrative fur trade with the Iroquois with the effects land acquisition and farming by colonists had on the ultimate demise of that trade. He also reported how Indians first "discovered not only that hunting was destroyed by extensive settlement and the fencing of fields, but that the transaction was considered to be permanent" (p. 12). This suggested a major difference in viewpoints toward the holding of rights in land. Nammack suggested that in adopting land policies that protected the Indians from seizure of their lands, Britain alienated the colonists, and she cited this alienation as contributing to the growth of revolutionary sentiment.

Of special value in Leach's study is his chapter devoted to the history of land speculation in New York and Maine. Such speculation created conditions favorable to pioneer farming, and engrossment of vast acreage tended to discourage or curtail colonization on the frontier, but it did contribute to the deterioration of Indian relations. Chicanery and outright fraud contributed to friction and hostilities between Indians and white settlers. Leach also pointed out that land acquisition invoived not only purchase but also governmental consent, and it thereby subjected speculation to politics.

Several other studies examine land purchases and the taking of Iroquois lands within New York and adjacent areas (Turner 1852; Wait 1912; Parker 1925; Hill 1930; Manley 1947; Bauman 1960; Lankes 1962, 1964). Nash (1967) discusses colonial rivalries for lands of the Iroquois in the Susquehanna Valley, which served as a buffer between English and French trade interests. Weslager (1972) devotes one chapter to rivalry over lands of the Delawares and includes useful maps showing villages and reservations in the colonial period. Similar rivalries are discussed in Forbes's review (1936) of the antecedents to Indian removal in Creek territory, where the rivalry involved the English, the Spanish, and the French. Garrow (1974) deals briefly with treaties, allotments, and removal of Powhatans in the period 1646-1706. Rountree (1973) in a more definitive study has examined the colonial situation leading to the reduction of Powhatan holdings and the gradual dissipation of reserved tracts into the national period (cf. her briefer 1972 paper; the larger study, a doctoral dissertation, is being prepared for publication).

One of the most astute pieces of colonial reconstruction to date has been prepared by Jennings in a series of papers that revises many interpretations of fraudulent land acquisitions in Pennsylvania. Relying heavily on colonial documents, including records of deeds and related land papers, this ethnohistorian set out (1970) to demonstrate how the sons of William Penn proceeded to engross their landholdings. The study focused on the events leading to the "Walking Purchase," which sought to gain for the Penns clear title to the Lehigh Valley (cf. Jennings 1965a/b). In two other studies (1966, 1968b) Jennings also described the cunning property manipulations of James Logan, then secretary of the province, agent to the Penn family, and commissioner of property in Pennsylvania. In the 1966 paper, he observed that

> The 'fur-trade interest' in Pennsylvania, which was pre-eminently
> James Logan, was not a social and political factor protecting Indians
> from the encroachments of settling farmers, as has sometimes been
> alleged was the case in other colonies. Rather, in Pennsylvania, the
> trade was a means of accelerating settlement. (P. 420)

Logan apparently got Indians to clear land for his speculative purposes,
and he helped to displace them in efforts to gain additional land for
settlement, thus creating a land monopoly. Logan was especially culpable
in the events leading to the displacement of the Tulpehocken (a community of Lenni Lenape Indians) and embezzlement of Penn's properties
(1968b). In another paper (1968a) Jennings sought a newer interpretation
of the dispersal of the Susquehannock from their homeland, and found his
answer in the efforts of Lord Baltimore to annex the Delaware Bay colony
to Maryland. Here Jennings also reexamined inter-tribal relationships between the Iroquois and the Susquehannock, noting that the former tribe,
while extending its hegemony over the latter, did not secure landownership for themselves. The study appraised Dutch and English relations
with the Indians, and closed with an appendix on Lenape landownership.

Jennings in several papers reminds readers that we should reexamine
our "ethnocentric assumptions" about, for example, rights to the soil; his
colonial papers penetrate deeply into the motives and events that resulted
in the seizure or cession of Indian lands. In his study of the "Covenant
Chain," (1971) for example, he traced the institutionalization of relationships between various tribes and Europeans; he suggested that the Chain
served as a way of stabilizing these relationships even while Europeans vied
for advantages among the tribes; in this way it helped the English penetrate French holdings. The Chain also served as the agency through which
vast territories underwent gradual depopulation [by Indians] as well as
functional and political reorganization. The author noted too that the
Chain acted as a diplomatic mechanism prior to the creation of a frontier
between Indian and white settlement which came to represent a line
between hostile forces. Jennings's pending book (in press) explores
broader questions of European land dealings with Indians, concentrating
on New England rather than on the Middle Colonies; it expands upon his
shorter study that treats of the 'virgin land and savage people' theme
(1971b).

One historical geographer (Mitchell 1972) has asserted that "one can
describe land use in frontier areas without reference to the processes of
land acquisition, but analysis requires an understanding of these processes"
(p. 462). In recounting the British (Virginia Colony) interest in creating a
buffer zone to the west of their colony by settling the Shenandoah Valley,

Mitchell reported that the valley was virtually unsettled, owing to the fact that both the Iroquois and Cherokee treated the area as a hunting preserve. Because it constituted a human void, it represented a potential zone of conflict with Indians who allied themselves to the French. Knowledge of Indian perceptions of environment and their "tribal" distributions beyond the frontier can thus improve our reconstruction of the conditions under which Indian lands were sought. This is not the only study that underscores the fact that Europeans, and later Americans, considered habitats receiving only periodic migratory uses—such as for hunting or gathering—open for more permanent settlement.

The frontier theme in Indian-white relations has variously focused on treaties, wars, trade, and missionary activity, all of which bear some relationship to land (Alden 1944; Corkran 1967; Rand 1913; Uhler 1950). Uhler specifically examined William Penn's land acquisition policies (cf. Wallace 1961, who reconstructed post-cession Delaware migrations from 1600 to 1774). Kimmey (1960) outlined the justification for bartering Christianity for land. (It is rather interesting that at a later date many missionary organizations secured nominal acreage on reservations so that they could construct a church and residence.) De Vorsey, another historical geographer, went to great lengths to reconstruct (1966) the southern Indian boundary. Taking a position different from that of the many scholars who have argued that aboriginal concepts of territory were poorly defined because the tribe itself was not well defined as a political-territorial unit, De Vorsey noted the occasionally quite sophisticated notions of boundaries of those Indians who had participated in the setting of the southern Indian boundary. Jacobs (1972) carried the argument further by inferring that the boundary, which constituted an early attempt to segregate white from Indian colonial frontiers, was possibly an antecedent of the later development of the removal and reservation policies. For example, in the national period the Mississippi River for a time became a similar demarcation between white and Indian. One critic (Dunbar 1969) complimented the author by noting that "Prior to De Vorsey's work, no one had amassed all the data necessary to form an accurate cartographic depiction of the Southern Boundary Line" (p. 181). De Vorsey (1971) provided a further evaluation of the cartographic data for the reconstruction of Indian settlement in the South. For an interpretation of the northern Indian boundary line, see Farrand (1905) and the discussion of other relevant sources in Billington's bibliography (1974). A more elaborate attempt to present reserves and cessions over most of eastern North America, utilizing older maps and superimposed boundaries, was made by Narvey who examined (1974) the British Proclamation of

1763, today the foundational law governing Canadian Indian rights but also the forerunner of treaty provisions in the United States. (See Section AC.)

For an older but comprehensive discussion of the land-acquisition policies of all of the colonial powers, the colonies themselves, and the later policies of the United States, one should examine Cyrus Thomas's introduction to Royce's (1899) compilation of cession maps. For shorter summaries, see Harris (1953), who related land acquisition to the evolution of a national land system; Kinney (1937), whose historical analysis focused mainly on administrative developments; and Washburn (1971b), who reviewed attitudes and motives behind such acquisition. Harris especially noted that as our national land system evolved, Indian concepts of tenure did not survive into the American period. (See below for a discussion of the protection of Indian lands in colonial times.)

Westward Expansion and Indian Lands

The westward expansion of settlement occurred in advance of the cession of native "sovereignty"; it did not merely follow such cessions. In fact, pioneer thrust prior to the completion of negotiations for title to Indian lands constituted a problem in land administration for at least three-quarters of the last century. The cession of Indian lands was a prerequisite for the ultimate transfer of acreage to individuals, to railroads, and to the future states, and such transfers of tribal land came about under the disposal policies of the public land laws. Thus it is logical to examine how the history of public land policy has treated the theme of Indian land acquisition. It is also pertinent to suggest that the point of departure, time-wise, should be the enactment of two ordinances: the Land Ordinance (1785), because it advanced our national land system which, in turn, implemented land settlement; and the Northwest Ordinance (1787), because it enunciated a policy of recognizing Indian title and occupancy as a matter of "utmost good faith" (cf. Deloria 1971).

Several studies interweave accounts of the process of land settlement and westward expansion and at the same time examine public land policy as it related to Indian land tenure (Billington 1974; Bogue, Phillips, and Wright 1970; Hafen, Hollon, and Rister 1970; Foreman 1933, 1936). Billington provides an extensive bibliographical section. Malin (1921) stimulated considerable research on the importance of Indian land in the evolution of public land policies. He stressed that for an understanding of the pre—Civil War period and the history of the West, Indian policy represented a fundamental ingredient. In dealing with the cessions that made way for subsequent expansion into the Plains (Kansas and Nebraska), Malin revealed the intricate relationship that Indian land, once ceded, bore to the further disposal of public domain. Other studies also direct attention to how chicanery, fraud, and speculation, as well as bona fide homesteading and illegal but tolerated squatting, accompanied white entry into Indian country (Dick 1970; Chandler 1945; Gates 1968). Gates stressed that treaty-writing was important well in advance of white settlement and speculative activities on the frontier. In another study, Gates (1954) recounted efforts at private land acquisition on the Osage Reserve in Kansas. Sheldon (1936) examined cession developments in Nebraska relative to the emergence of private property within that state. Several studies consider the allotment policy as it triggered speculation over Indian lands (cf. Robbins 1942). Other relevant studies include Treat (1910), Padelford (1936), and Rohrbough (1968); the latter related land cessions to the administration of the General Land Office in the South.

Although speculation reappears in countless studies of Indian land history, Swierenga (1966, 1968) introduced a new methodological approach through the use of quantitative data. By utilizing the compiled cartographic materials in Royce (1899) and new evidence garnered in the land claims suit by the Sac and Fox Indians in Iowa, he could assert that land speculation in frontier America was more profitable—relative to other investment opportunities of the time—than previous observers had noted. The appraisal of the value of land at a particular point in the past, on the remote frontier, far from roads, rails, or land settlement, and especially where there had been speculative activity, assumed considerable attention in land claims research. Land claims awards granted by the Indian Claims Commission are in monetary terms—so much per acre—as based on land values researched for the period of "taking"; these figures had to account for what speculation had done to the market (see Section AB).

Expansionist policies, especially their ambivalent implications for Indian occupancy of the eastern United States, were sustained by the general view that white settlement and continued Indian presence were incompatible. Horsman (1967) observed that many interpretations of this period of American history held that the nation had no coherent policy toward Indian land rights. Such a view, of course, ignores the attempt of the government to work out a policy that respected aboriginal rights to land and that essentially favored the British practice of acknowledging title and negotiating formal purchase as the best means to effect a lasting removal (cf. Cohen 1947; Washburn 1971b). Prucha (1969) has tended to defend Jefferson's view that cultivators could justify taking over lands of those who mainly hunted or gathered for a livelihood, and this argument runs through much of the literature of the nineteenth century and reflects the theme of American manifest destiny (cf. Weinberg 1963).

Although several books trace the evolution of policies and refer to land administration, few examine land tenure for the early national period. Kinney (1937) is still a good statement, although he tended to focus mainly on the official record. Mohr (1933) limited his study to the pre-constitution period, during which time a federal system for the management of Indian affairs evolved. He observed how in the years prior to the land ordinance of 1785 the government reevaluated colonial policies, especially the function of the treaty in dealing with Indians, and he discussed the early protective role of the government in checking encroachment upon, and illegal purchase of, Indian lands. Prucha (1962) assessed the origins and results of the Trade and Intercourse Act, which laid down the rules of Indian-American relations until the advent of the removal policies of the 1830s. Harmon (1941) selected four time periods (1789-96, 1796-1812, 1812-25, and 1825-50) and looked at Indian affairs in New York, the old Northwest, and the South during each period. His discussion begins with early congressional efforts to formulate policy, spans the removal years, and ends prior to the establishment of the reservation system throughout much of the West. It also behooves readers to examine studies of continuing European Indian policies after the revolutionary period; for example, Berkhofer (1969) reviewed the reasons why the British kept military posts in the Old Northwest. He noted that there was some fear of Indian reprisals for the British cession of territory to the new nation, and he also recounted the British idea of establishing a neutral barrier state to check United States plans for settlement to the West.

Indian Removal

So much has been written about the events and aftermath of Indian removal (cf. Abel 1908a; Foreman 1932; Kinney 1937; Josephy 1961) that one can identify a definite body of literature on the subject and distinguish strongly opposing positions on the merits of the policy, especially with reference to the South and the Five Civilized Tribes. Virtually all of the eastern half of the country saw the removal and relocation of tribes to the Plains (see Figure 3). Proposals emerged for a separate Indian state or protectorate (Abel 1908b; Colgrove 1911; Foreman 1933; Walker 1874). Oklahoma was the chosen location of this effort, but by the late 1880s it was clear that the movement had failed. Some scholars have indicated that although this removal policy made its greatest thrust on

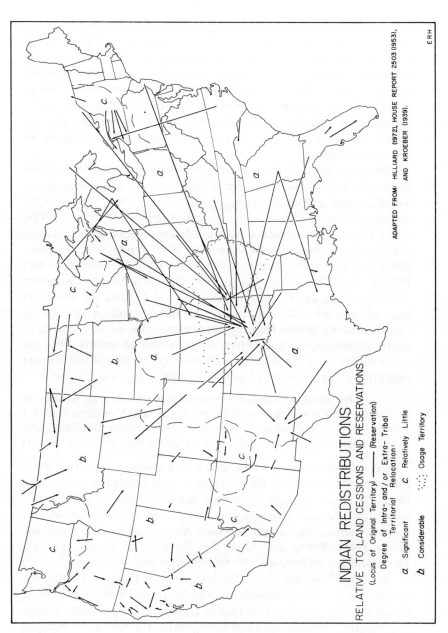

Figure 3[1]

Indians of the South and the East before 1840, it was still being conjured up as a solution to Indian-white relations into the 1850s in Texas, California, and the Northwest. The literature focuses as much on the aftermath of the policy as on its implementation; there has also been some reconstruction of frontier conditions and Indian land tenure prior to removal. In recent years removal policies have also been reappraised, leading to an exchange of views between scholars taking favorable and unfavorable positions toward its proponents. By and large, negative interpretations prevail.

The antecedents of the removal policy were policies governing land acquisition by colonists and rival colonial powers (cf. Forbes 1936), boundaries and cessions (De Vorsey 1966; Cotterill 1963; Halbert 1923), and the granting of allotments to members of various tribes (Young 1958, 1961). Considerable corruption and speculation occurred prior to, during, and following removal of Indians (Chandler 1945; Young 1955; Van Every 1966) and led to litigation, especially over Georgia's actions (Guttman 1965; Burke 1969). Perhaps Georgia's interference in federal management of Indian affairs was the first by any state, but Alabama and Mississippi soon followed suit. Allotment of land to half-breed Indians who demonstrated a love for private property was seen as a ploy to force removal of nearly all Indians, for few Indians would accept allotments. That the policy had in mind the relative ease with which Indians would alienate their title seemed apparent to Young (1958) who stated that

> The allotment treaties of the 1830's represent an attempt to apply Anglo-American notions of justice, which enshrined private property in land and freedom of contract as virtually absolute values, to Indian tribes whose tastes and traditions were otherwise. (P. 44)

Young and other observers have shown how allotments and treaties of cession sought to head off the problems of land speculation that plagued the removal process. Similar speculation, in much of the South, benefitting speculators and land companies more than they did individual settlers, occurred during negotiations for land cessions among the Chickasaw (Silver 1944). Young also noted that for the next twenty years the government was disillusioned with the allotment process.

In fact, if we may take the lead from McCluggage (1970), the antecedents of this disillusionment may be found in the departure of Congress from the Jeffersonian ideal of granting fee simple title to Indians as a means of civilizing and acculturating them. The Senate, for example, rejected the granting of patents to lands to either individuals or tribes; as McCluggage put it, the decisions of the upper house "show a consistent and clear determination to deny the Indians the security of fee simple title to land either severally or as a group" (p. 425). Any student of the history of private property among Indians must not only reassess colonial reports and practices, but also examine experiences with land in severalty prior to the Dawes Act (General Allotment Act, 1887). (Cf. Kinney 1937 and see Section BC.)

Many scholars have researched the genesis and ideology of the removal policy. Jacobs (1972) reminds us of the earlier proposal of Washington to relocate all Indians west of the Boundary Line of 1763. Jeffersonian and Jacksonian viewpoints have received considerable reassessment (DeRosier 1970; Prucha 1963, 1967; Washburn 1965, 1971b). Washburn particularly criticized the pro-Jackson interpretations of Prucha, who has accepted the removal practice as one that was necessary in the interest of the security of the West. Prucha has tended to take the government on faith and has played down the "cultural blindness" Washburn speaks of in terms of removal as a solution to a "racial problem." Those who saw removal as a just and honorable practice rather than as an unconscionable one, tended to suggest that removal created breathing-time for the Indians to adjust to the advance of white civilization.

Removal, of course, brought various tribes face to face in the Great Plains. Confrontation over claims to territory resulted from many relocations and led to separate negotiations for land cessions, this time to make room for incoming southern and eastern tribes. The issue was one of the rights of "nomadic" Plains tribes versus the forced intrusion of the sedentary Five Civilized Tribes. However, as Chapman (1933) reported, efforts were also made to persuade Chickasaws and Choctaws to cede lands only very recently granted them, in order to allow Plains tribes to relocate within Indian territory. Foreman (1933) observed the conflict between these two quite different cultures—hunting vs. agrarian—and noted the profound influence exercised by immigrant tribes who, he said, hastened the advance of civilization in the West and thus paved the way for later white occupancy. Rister (1936) recounted the unsuccessful experiment of bringing the more sedentary Choctaw into common grounds with Comanche and Kiowa; Jones (1966) discussed the conditions and outcome of establishing separate reservations for various Plains Indians. Anson (1964) examined what happened when sedentary and nomadic tribes came together, especially where the introduction of the horse had stimulated an exaggerated demand for land and increased the competition for buffalo. Anson alluded to the deterioration of the Osage, Pawnee, and other Plains Indians following contact with eastern tribes.

When the literature about a single tribe is examined more closely, it is possible to reconstruct a better picture of the role land tenure played in the removal policy. For the Cherokee one finds several ethnohistorical and geographical accounts that span the period from before removal to contemporary settlement in eastern Oklahoma. Wilms in a recent doctoral study (1973) has reconstructed Cherokee land use in Georgia for the period 1830-38, noting how they underwent considerable acculturation during that time. These Indians had abandoned nucleated villages in favor of individual farmsteads and presumably could lay claim to all improvements made in clearing unoccupied lands. The improvements, but not the land itself, which remained tribally held, could be sold. This suggests a native capacity to adopt or modify Euro-American land institutions and at the same time hold on to traditional customs. Wilms has since published some of these findings (1974a/b). More than one scholar has pointed to the Cherokee capacity to embrace western culture even while whites were encroaching upon their lands, and more than one study (Malone, 1956; Gulick 1960) reflects favorably on native adaptability. Ballas's brief accounts (1960, 1962) of the Cherokees who escaped removal and relocated in North Carolina discussed this adaptability and reported on the persistence of communal tenure. Hewes (1942b) also treated favorable land settlement adjustments made by Cherokees in eastern Oklahoma, where utlimately communal tenure gave way to private holdings (see Section BC).

Preoccupation with the Five Civilized Tribes has partially obscured the parallel plights experienced by countless tribes farther north. For example, the Menominee moved over to make room for the Stockbridge-Munsee (Kowalke 1956), and several Indian groups of New York that were obliged to emigrate to the Lake States were later moved again to Indian Territory. Speculation appeared as a strong motive in the Sioux and Winnebago relocations from Minnesota (Lass 1963; Stewart 1964). Other studies have included the cessions and relocations of the Miami (Anson 1970), the Indiana (Gordon 1950), various Iowa tribes (Aumann 1906), the Kansa (Unrau 1971), the Potawatomi (O'Connor 1942), and the Delaware (Weslager 1972); and the cessions of title in Ohio beyond the Greenville Treaty line (Leidy 1929) and in the Old Northwest (Smith 1956-57). A good many of the books and articles that deal comprehensively with the history of a particular tribe include discussions of relocation from areas of the East; because of greater scholarly interest in the later developments of these people within the Plains, however, these studies receive attention in Section BC.

Treaties and Land Cessions

An Indian treaty may be likened to a literary work (cf. Wroth 1928), and the events surrounding its negotiation and signing often read like theater. But it is, of course, the legal and political significance that the treaties bear to land that makes them so important more than a century after their ratification. Logically enough, historians have devoted considerable attention to all aspects of Indian treaties—the background to their negotiation, treaty-writing assemblages, Indian oratory, broken promises and the violation of treaties, and more recently, land claims dating back to treaty provisions. In Indian affairs, treaty-writing implied recognition of the tribes as nations. Actually, colonial powers engaged in treaty-writing (DePuy 1917; Historical Society of Pennsylvania 1938; Holmes 1969; Washburn 1971b), but the real thrust of such negotiations did not come until the national period.

Often field surveys and contacts took place with tribes at some distance from white settlement; field observers gathered information and so better informed officials as to the predisposition of tribes toward treaty parleys. Few surveys were as comprehensive, for example, as those by Morse (1822) and Schoolcraft (1853); the latter, which is available in a modern reprint, documented a considerable amount of information on acreage, boundaries, claims, titles, and related land matters for the tribes visited. Ultimately, the Congress became disenchanted with the treaty-making practice and in 1871 brought it to an end, but because of the provisions written into treaties, their impact continues to be felt. Many Indians today, as part of the national Indian movement, call for revision of outstanding treaties and demand that the government live up to the conditions set down in treaties more than a century ago.

Students not familiar with treaties of land cession will find several legal volumes useful as sources of treaty lists and interpretations (Bledsoe 1909; Cohen 1941; Connelley 1925; Fay 1967, 1970; Kappler 1903-38; Price 1973; Thwaites 1900). Kappler prepared the definitive compilation; this work was reprinted in several recent editions. Cohen is still the recognized authority on federal Indian law (see Section C); Price updates Cohen and provides a typology for the analysis of relevant federal Indian law and cases. The other studies deal with specific tribes or states. In addition, treaties are reviewed in various historical contexts by Kinney (1937), Leupp (1910), Manypenny (1880), Schmeckebier (1927), and Washburn (1971b). Leupp and Manypenny were Commissioners of Indian Affairs. The Schmeckebier volume is an administrative history of the Office of

Indian Affairs. Finally, one will find treaty abstracts, references to treaties, related Indian responses, and other land matters compiled in several useful anthologies (Deloria 1971; Forbes 1964; Washburn 1964, 1973).

While every history of a tribe has its map or maps, all too often they represent reproductions or redrawings of existing maps, or compilations based on treaties, other original sources, or the renditions of cession areas prepared by Royce (1899). The Royce volume, which has been reprinted, contains not only cession maps by states but a comprehensive listing of all actions leading to cessions or to the establishment, adjustment, or extinguishment of reservations, whether by treaty, statute, executive order, or administrative decision. Most land claim cases and many published studies cite cession numbers such as "Royce 262" which constituted, for example, the subject of Swierenga's study of speculation over Indian lands in Iowa (1966), and the Royce renditions of land cessions have proven useful in land claims litigation. More recently Hilliard summarized much of the data contained in the Royce volume in a series of maps that formed part of an article dealing with the trans-Mississippi West (1971), and in a map supplement to the *Annals of the Association of American Geographers* (1972). The latter effort depicts land cessions in a series of five multi-colored maps that span the period 1784-1972. On each map Hilliard utilizes the same color—dark brown—to depict unceded lands; thus, with the sweep of the eye one can estimate the retreat of the Indian frontier.[2]

Treaty-writing in Indian affairs has its own history and literature. Lindquist (1948-49) prepared an analysis of treaty-writing and sorted treaties into categories: those of peace and friendship, perpetual annuities, allotment, and so on. Although many studies make reference to the assemblages, oratory, and related negotiations, historians do not always report in great detail the events of negotiation in such a way as to show how boundaries, for example, were determined. Lindquist's analysis provides a chronological and topical discussion of such matters as language difficulties in the wording of treaties, the commutation and renewal of treaties, fulfillment of treaties, and outmoded treaties still in force. An appendix lists his numerous categories.

Historians consider the personages involved in Indian treaty negotiation and in Indian affairs administration as important. Certainly at the treaty level personalities played a crucial role on both sides in the actual negotiations, or "forest diplomacy" as it has been called for the earlier period. The Indian himself proved an able diplomat—for example, Red Cloud and the negotiations for a Sioux treaty (J. C. Olson 1965). Perhaps the problems that impeded progress toward acceptable compromises resulted from the ineptitude, unwillingness, or ignorance of negotiators (cf. Crouter and Rolle's 1960 discussion of treaty commissioners in California). Neil (1956) showed how the understaffed and overworked territorial governor, doubling as superintendent of Indian affairs, had to negotiate treaties and implement policy at a great distance from Washington. Often the problems on the frontier were caused by land-hungry settlers and speculators or railroad agents who would not wait for the completion of treaties of cession and Indian withdrawal. To appreciate fully the problems of administering Indian affairs during the territorial years, one should peruse Eblen (1968). (Cf. Prucha's 1967 study of Lewis Cass as territorial governor.) At various times the soldier (cf. Bender 1952), the Indian agent (cf. Unrau 1964), the squaw man (cf. Hagan 1971a; Brown 1930; and see Section BC), the missionary, the trader, and land speculators and settlers interacted with the tribes for better or for worse, and influenced not only treaty proceedings and the final wording of these documents, but also events and administrative actions in the years that followed the enactment of treaties. Curiously enough, little appears in print or manuscript on the role of the special allotting agent who did the actual work of subdividing reservations (cf. Prucha 1971 and see Section BC).[3]

The bulk of the treaty and land-cessions literature deals with state or regional land units or specific tribes, and as one should expect, the Great Plains region has received a great deal of attention because so much happened there. Every tribe and every state or former territory has come under investigation (cf. Abernethy 1913-15; Chapman 1933, 1943, 1946; Cory 1903-04; Danziger 1973; Foreman 1941; Gates 1937; Humphreys 1971; Mattison 1955; Meyer 1964; Nelson 1946; Utley 1963). One finds too that graduate programs in history have taken considerable advantage of the Plains as a field area (Akright 1924; Brown 1930; Flekke 1935; Jackson 1909; Neuhoff 1922; Richards 1922; Townsend 1939; Whitten 1950). These studies deal with specific treaties, cessions, and reservations, and examine problems of settlers and railroads and the general agitation for Indian removal from areas in which they were established as part of their relocation from the East. For example, Cory recounted in the cession of Osage lands in Kansas the role of the Settlers' Protective Association, and Brown, in her examination of the Cherokee neutral-lands controversy, reviewed the activities of the "Land Leaguers" or "Neutral Land Home Protection Corps," which intimidated and threatened Indians in order to get them to sell out. Gates examined the means by which Indian land—e.g., the Christian Indian tract in Kansas—often passed directly to individuals or railroad companies, bypassing the usual process by which land became public domain and thus subject to entry rules under the public land laws. Humphreys's study is one of those that have examined intertribal conflicts at the time of treaty-negotiation; in this case, there were Crow and Sioux counterclaims, and the former were ultimately displaced. More than one student has undertaken to study the land cession known as the Platte Purchase, located on the edge of the Plains in northwestern Missouri (Neuhoff 1922; Whitten 1950).

Because of its unique status on entering the Union, Texas should be discussed separately. Not only was Texas a separate sovereign with its own Indian affairs policies, but at statehood it did not turn over a "public domain" to the federal government or include a disclaimer clause in its statehood act; consequently, a special state-federal situation over Indians ensued. A pair of published masters theses which complement each other focused on the policies of Republican Texas (Muckleroy 1922-23) and on Texas as a state (Koch 1924-26). Both studies dealt comprehensively with events, treaties, and policy developments. Harmon's paper (1930-31) covered the same time period as Koch's, and Foreman (1948) dealt specifically with the Comanche treaty of October 18, 1865. Reeve (1946-47), Richardson (1933), Rister (1936), and Chapman (1933) all focused on efforts to establish a reservation within Texas, variously defined as lying along the Brazos River, or south of the Arkansas River and west of the 98th meridian, or simply in the northwest (panhandle) of the state. Reeve also reviewed Spanish occupation of Texas.

Similar studies reviewed the treaty period and the advent of land reservation in other parts of the West. In a four-part study Reeve (1937-38) examined federal policy in New Mexico and later recounted Navajo land problems (1946). For the Southwest in general Spicer (1962) has provided the comprehensive culture history of Indian-white contact with an emphasis on acculturation; his brief paper (1959) discusses the enclavement of southwestern tribes and anticipates the later book, which is discussed more fully in Section ABC. For the Far West during the years when the nation acquired Texas, the Northwest, and the Mexican Cession, Trennert (1969) fills a gap in the historical analysis of the creation of a reservation system twenty years before the abandonment of the treaty-making practice. Several relevant studies span the periods explored in this section and in Section BC (e.g., Colley 1973; Delaney 1971).

California figured prominently in the establishment of the reservation policy. As early as 1861 Browne reported on small reservations. A special report on the needs of the Mission Indians, including a proposal for a large reservation in Southern California, was prepared in 1852, but it did not appear in an available publication for another century (Wilson 1952). Ellison (1922) outlined the basic Indian policy during the 1850s.

Hastings (1971), in reviewing the Indian laws of California, recounted the conditions of land-hunger that led to restrictive and prejudicial legislation that circumscribed Indian activities and abridged their land rights. Knoop (1941) and Leonard (1928) examined that policy as it was applied in the Sacramento and San Joaquin Valleys, respectively. Ellison (1925) and Crouter and Rolle (1960) reexamined the bases for the rejection of the unratified treaties of 1852; Kelsey (1973) has offered a revisionist view of the Senate's actions. My historical analysis (Sutton 1964) pulls together most of the events leading up to the cession of Indian land and the establishment of 31 small reservations in Southern California. Price (1973) includes a section on the California treaties citing relevant official letters and an extract from Sutton. The demoralized state of Indian leadership by the time of negotiations attested to the downfall of many tribal groups. However, with reference to Southern California, Phillips (1973) indicates that Indian leadership was exceptionally assertive, leading to a major uprising that must have accounted in some part for pro-Indian provisions, including a vast land reserve, in the two treaties affecting the southern half of the state.

Oregon similarly experienced a rejection of treaties by Congress and the later establishment of several smaller reservations (Coan 1920, 1922; Robbins 1974). However, the Klamath did enter into an important treaty in 1864, the events of which Stern, an anthropologist, has explained (1956). He suggested that the early contacts with Euro-American culture, either through Williamette Valley white settlement or through association with the Kalapuya and Columbia River tribes, led to a brief florescence of Klamath culture, akin to that experienced by the Plains Indians in the late eighteenth and early nineteenth centuries. In a later work, Stern (1965) continued his assessment of the Klamath from contact times to the advent of termination of federal trusteeship in the early 1960s (see Section BC). Ratcliff (1973) deals with the Kalapuya in the pre-treaty contact period.

The aforementioned states or regions have been the subject of far too many Indian history studies to review all of them here. The Geographical Index to Authors will provide access to the relevant material.

The Reservation Idea

Did the creators of reservations have humanitarian purposes in mind? Did they conceive of a separate land unit for the tribes as a home base for the exercise of tribal tenure and law? It is likely many colonials, federal officials, even settlers, missionaries, and speculators saw the reservation as a counterforce to the sweeping take-over of the continent. Certainly in retrospect it seems a logical by-product of evolving land policy. Perhaps ultimately it could be considered as a replacement for the earlier policy, which acknowledged the tribes as sovereign entities or nations. By the 1880s their autonomous status would no longer be tolerated. Reservation of land seemed, then, to represent an effort to create a land institution that, while compromising tribal autonomy and shrinking native territory, nevertheless largely freed the tribes of interference from the local populace.

It is too simple, of course, to take seriously Macleod's (1928) pronouncement that "incompatibility of groups makes for segregation" (p. 383); yet his review of the origins of the practice of segregating natives on reserves is worthwhile and carries the reader back to antiquity. It identifies segregation, for example, in ancient India and describes its later application by the English in their spreading conquest of Irish and Scottish tribes during the later Middle Ages. James (1894), Kawashima (1969b), Harris (1953), and Pomeroy and Yoho (1964) all refer to the practice in colonial America. The James study suggested that a system of reservations developed in conjunction with land purchases in almost all colonies, and that various forms of self-government were advocated for the tribes. Kawashima more thoroughly researched its origins and practices in one colony—Massachusetts. He recounted the establishment of reservations or plantations, and the exercise of home-rule and exclusive territorial rights within villages under the supervision of white guardians. Kawashima suggested that the "reservation was not an integral part in the political system of the colony . . . [and] authorities did not intend the [reservation] system to be permanent" (p. 56). He noted too that at first the reserves were defined as tribal units, but that they became ethnically mixed; this sequence occurred elsewhere on the eastern seaboard and, for that matter, over much of Indian Country. Ultimately one colony after another abolished the practice, since land reservation was seen as an expedient and its gradual extinction seemed a logical outcome of the assimilation of Indians. (MacFarlane 1933 is cited as a chief source for a summary of the reservation practice in colonial New England.)

In a later study Kawashima (1974) demonstrated that all of the southern colonies made explicit efforts in legislation to protect the land rights of both independent and non-tribal Indians. As he noted, North Carolina "considered Indian-white land disputes as an urgent problem, that might lead to fatal consequences to the colonial peace and welfare . . ." (p. 11). Laws in some states specifically sought to check the alienation of native land by prohibiting purchases by whites. He suggested that such land laws were mostly concerned with trade in the case of independent tribes in South Carolina and Georgia, but mostly concerned with land in Virginia, Maryland, and, to a lesser degree, North Carolina. Kawashima suggests that colonial legislation quite clearly was, in his words, "an instrument of social change rather than a means of maintaining the status quo" (p. 15). Such research lends strength to the view that the reservation idea has its roots in colonial experiences with Indians.

Although colonial policies toward land reservation, including the practice of land allotment, seem in retrospect to be the forerunners of later national practices, and although land originally set aside for Indians in the colonial period continues to be occupied by their descendants to this day, it should not be supposed that the new nation immediately embraced this colonial institution. During the long treaty era, reservation of land represented the withholding *by* the tribes of lands from cession. But by mid-century, in the Far West reservation came to mean that in creating reservations out of public domain, the national government was setting aside land *for* the tribes. This shift in the meaning of reservation came about essentially as a result of a sequence of events that led the Senate to refuse to ratify treaties, with the consequence that Indian lands became part of the public domain, as happened in California, Oregon, and other parts of the Northwest and the Great Basin. Trennert (1969) noted that the new policy emerged when it was no longer possible to create a separate Indian country as a homeland for various tribes; it made better sense to establish enclaves for Indians within developing white settlements (many were garrisoned). Such a policy, others had noted, did not come easily, for many officials and settlers expressed renewed interest in the removal practice in order to create, for example, a large Indian protectorate in the desert.

Reservation, so Trennert reported, led to a strong effort to encourage agriculture, especially among formerly "nomadic" (i.e., hunting) tribes. Although the intentions were good, the policy of segregation to protect the tribes from degrading influences was hampered by westward expansion. Moreover, the reservation system depended on the integrity of field agents, on the cooperation of settlers and railroad companies as well as of the tribes, and on administrative practices in Washington, where efforts to subvert this policy were fashionable for several decades. (Many of the events that led to the undermining of this new land policy are discussed in Section BC.)

After 1871, when treaty-making with tribes was abrogated by Congress, the executive branch could no longer negotiate by that means for the establishment of Indian reservations as residual tribal holdings. Consequently, the President made wider use of the executive order to create reservations, which left the question of tribal title to some lands in doubt. The existence of two dissimilar instruments—treaties and executive orders—may account, in part, for some popular misunderstanding as to the "ownership" of reservations. While in Indian affairs parlance the distinction is now essentially moot, at one time treaty reserves were clearly tribal, whereas executive-order reserves were thought to have been carved out of the public domain and therefore to constitute "public" rather than tribal lands. Of course, as Section AB points out, however they were established, reservations did not quiet Indian claims to the continent.

Notes

1. This map is intended more for graphic display than perfect accuracy; it suggests the dynamics of tribal movements under duress and otherwise. Areas on the map identified by (a), (b), or (c) relate to numbers of Indians relocated; *significant* relocation (a), for example, connotes the removal and/or migration of whole tribes, to the point of reducing the Indian presence in a given area to a very small number relative to the number at the time of relocation; in contrast, *relatively little* (c) implies that most of the tribes present in the area at the time of relocation to reservations are still living within the area; *considerable* (b) suggests an intermediate situation. The obvious concentration occurred in the central Plains, largely within what has been identified as originally Osage territory. The map adapts Hilliard (1972) (whose work is reviewed in the Bibliographical and Cartographic Sources section, and in Section B), Kroeber (1939), and U.S. Congress, House (1953).
2. For more details, see my review in *Pacific Historical Review*, vol. 42, no. 1 (Feb., 1973), p. 108.
3. On the teaching of treaties in history, as applied to the Chippewa, see Keller (1972).

Works Cited in Section B

Abel, 1908a/b
Abernethy, 1913-15
Akright, 1924
Alden, 1944
Alvord, 1917
Anson, 1964, 1970
Aumann, 1906
Ballas, 1960, 1962
Bauman, 1960

Bechham, *1971
Bender, 1952
Berkhofer, 1969, 1971
Billington, 1974
Bledsoe, 1909
Blumenthal, *1955
Blunt, 1825
Bogue et al., 1970
Brown, 1930

Browne, 1861
Buffington, 1921
Burke, 1969
Chandler, 1945
Chapman, 1933, 1943, 1946
Coan, 1920, 1922
Cohen, 1941, 1947
Colgrove, 1911
Colley, 1973
Connelley, 1925
Corkran, 1967
Cory, 1903-04
Cotterill, 1963
Covington, *1951
Crouter & Rolle, 1960
Danziger, 1973
Debo, 1970
DeForest, 1851
Delaney, 1971
Deloria, 1971
DePuy, 1917
DeRosier, 1970
Deutsch, *1956
De Vorsey, 1966, 1971
Dick, 1970
Dunbar, 1969
Eblen, 1968
Ellison, 1922, 1925
Farrand, 1905
Fay, 1967-72
Fey & McNickle, 1959, 1970
Fenton et al., 1957
Flekke, 1935
Forbes, G., 1936
Forbes, J.D., 1964
Foreman, 1932, 1933, 1936, 1941, 1948
Garrow, 1974
Gates, 1937, 1954, 1968
Gordon, 1950
Gulick, 1960
Guttman, 1965
Hafen et al., 1970
Hagan, 1961, 1971a
Halbert, 1923
Halsey, 1901
Harmon, 1930-31, 1941

Harris, 1953
Hastings, 1971
Hewes, 1942b
Hill, 1930
Hilliard, 1971, 1972
Historical Society of Pennsylvania, 1938
Holmes, 1969
Horsman, 1967
Howard, *1972
Humphreys, 1971
Iden, *1929
Jackson, 1909
Jacobs, 1954, 1972
James, 1894
Jennings, 1965a/b, 1966, 1968a/b, 1970, 1971a/b, in press
Jones, 1966
Josephy, 1961
Kappler, 1903-38
Kawashima, 1969b, 1974
Keller, 1972
Kelsey, 1973
Kimmey, 1960
Kinney, 1937
Knoop, 1941
Koch, 1924-26
Kowalke, 1956
Lankes, 1962, 1964
Lass, 1963
Leach, 1966
Leidy, 1929
Leonard, 1928
Leupp, 1910
Lindquist, 1948-49
MacFarlane, 1933
Macleod, 1928
Malin, 1921
Malone, 1956
Manley, 1947
Manypenny, 1880
Mattison, 1955
McCluggage, 1970
McNickle, 1949, 1962, *1973
Meyer, 1964
Mitchell, 1972
Mohr, 1933

Morse, 1822
Muckleroy, 1922-23
Nammack, 1969
Narvey, 1974
Nash, 1967
Neil, 1956
Nelson, 1946
Neuhoff, 1922
O'Callaghan, *1951
O'Connor, 1942
Olson, J.C., 1965
Padelford, 1936
Parker, A. C., 1925
Parker, T. V., 1907
Phillips, 1973
Pomeroy & Yoho, 1964
Price, 1973
Prucha, 1962, 1963, 1967, 1969, 1971
Rand, 1913
Ratcliff, 1973
Reeve, 1937-38, 1946, 1946-47
Richards, 1922
Richardson, 1933
Rister, 1936
Robbins, R. M., 1942
Robbins, W. G., 1974
Rohrbough, 1968
Rountree, 1972, 1973
Royce, 1899
Ruttenber, 1872
Satz, *1974
Schmeckebier, 1927
Schoolcraft, 1853
Sheehan, 1969

Sheldon, 1936
Silver, 1944
Smith, 1956-57
Spicer, 1959, 1962
Stern, 1956, 1965
Stewart, F. H., 1932, 1972
Stewart, O. C., *1966
Stewart, W. J., 1964
Sutton, 1964
Swierenga, 1966, 1968
Thwaites, 1900
Townsend, 1939
Treat, 1910
Trelease, 1960
Trennert, 1969
Turner, 1852
Uhler, 1950
Unrau, 1964, 1971
Utley, 1963
Van Every, 1966
Vaughan, 1965
Voegelin, *1955
Wait, 1912
Walker, 1874
Wallace, 1961
Washburn, 1964, 1965, 1971a/b
Weinberg, 1963
Weslager, 1972
Whitten, 1950
Wilms, 1973, 1974a/b
Wilson, 1952
Wroth, 1928
Wylie, 1905-07
Young, 1955, 1958, 1961

*Denotes works not actually cited, but relevant to this section.

SECTION C

Land Administration
and Land Utilization

Introduction

Given the fundamental premise that land utilization depends upon the effective synthesis of many factors, of which land tenure structure is only one, it is instructive to draw attention to the nature of the infrastructure in which Indians have had to function as users of land resources. One should remember that land tenure structures may inhibit or facilitate land resource uses. Anglo-Americans developed the structure to which Indians have had to adapt their lifeways, whether they choose to remain on reservations or to go elsewhere to gain a livelihood. This is another way of saying that for individual Indians or tribes to succeed in the American economy they ultimately have had to comprehend the market system and the flow of capital, and they have needed access to mortgage credit. But it is also true that even those Indians who turned their backs on the system have not really escaped its institutions.

Two institutional orderings of the land resources of this country have played immense roles in Indian land utilization—private property in land in the form of allotment and corporate property in the form of tribal ownership. The policy change expressed in the replacement of the General Allotment Act (1887) by the Indian Reorganization Act (1934) placed emphasis on the tribe and on corporate resources. Tribes and individual Indians have moved increasingly into the mainstream of American economic activity and consequently will continue to feel the influence of basic land tenure structures and economic externalities (e.g., marketing conditions and mortgage rates) that formerly had no bearing on the utilization of trust lands (cf. Demsetz 1967; Sorkin 1973).

The establishment of the reservation system, then, predicated a federal commitment to helping Indians make the best economic use of their lands. The reservation as such amounted to an institutional effort to stabilize the land base as the locus of both economic and sociopolitical life for the tribe and its members. But the selection of reservation lands did not in itself provide an effective plan for the economic future of the tribes. Radical changes in Indian livelihood accompanied tribal displacement from traditional pursuits to the economic activities possible on a more limited space. Clearly, the establishment of a reservation did not bring with it an ordered system of land use appropriate to the resource base, notwithstanding the introduction of plows, draft animals, and seed, and the employment of resident farmers to train Indians in the ways of agriculture. Although unable to return to older ways of surviving—many unsuccessful attempts of Indians to return to hunting, for example, are reported in the literature—they did not quickly embrace the new means of subsistence. The introduction of agriculture, especially among pre-agrarian tribes, brought a double cultural shock because it occurred together with allotment, an alien land institution.

Voget (1961-62) has shown that where economic continuity could be sustained, and where Indians could adjust more slowly and choose for themselves from among new opportunities, a more viable social and cultural life was achieved. Yet he noted too that

> rapid disruption of the economic system seemingly has stimulated turbulence in individual lives as the effects have spread to other aspects of the social and cultural system, and the mounting stress has induced hostile, apathetic, and anxious reactions to government efforts at developing a new economic base. (PP. 157-8)

Kinney has observed (1950), for example, how late was the arrival of new legislation which "heralded an entirely new day in the administration of the forested lands on Indian reservations" (p. 263). Little of the Indian resource was adequately assessed in terms of its capabilities until 1910 or after. Nearly two decades later the "Meriam Report" (1928) noted well the continuing situation: "Even under the best conditions it is doubtful whether a well-rounded program of economic advancement framed with due consideration of the natural resources of the reservations has anywhere been thoroughly tried out" (p. 14).

While the literature tends to be effective in the examination, for example, of those facets of tenure that have led to complexities of ownership based on inheritance, it has not as thoroughly considered means by which Indians as individuals and families could achieve a modicum of success in land use. The consensus on the effects of land in severalty has been negative; however, a few studies do report on more successful aspects of individual or family leasing of farm or ranch lands, despite the bad name associated with "unearned" income acquired through land-leasing. The fact is that neither a reservation nor an allotment has ever really constituted a viable economic unit or a natural (ecological) unit for resource management. Reservations, as irrationally bound land units, have had all the conservation problems that have beset most land users in this country, but the problems have been more acute because of the higher density of families dependent upon a limited—all too often, marginal—land base.

Scholars recognize that it is not possible to find perfect parallels between Indian and non-Indian land-use patterns. The application of trusteeship has postponed, as it were, the need for Indians to cope with adverse market conditions and other external business factors that land users must consider in any economic enterprise (cf. Demsetz 1967). A number of the studies that relate land use to land tenure demonstrate how land leasing has provided a partial solution to dealing with economic factors beyond the control of the tribes or individual Indians. That is to say, the non-Indian understands the marketplace for which the allotment constitutes just another available piece of land (although often at lower annual or seasonal rental rates). Even with the possibility of mortgaging under new federal regulations and with careful guidance of the Indian landholder, credit, taxes, and expenses are not fully comprehended by most Indians (cf. the discussion of Stern and Boggs 1971 in Section BC). Most critics of the reservation system of course identify leasing as another scheme designed to allow whites to get at Indian land, for while it may put considerable acreage into production, leasing does not realize much financial gain for Indian owners.

Most studies emphasize that allotment of land has led to two structural problems for Indians with respect to the general economy: (1) Allotment created land units too small to be successful; rural economics in this country have reached a point where large units have become essential for economies of scale. In this sense the tenure structure has frustrated the resolution of problems and has caused new ones. Fragmentation of allotments has aggravated this situation. (2) On the other hand, the IRA, as a means of enabling tribes to achieve a corporate economy partially through incorporation of allotted lands in consolidation schemes, suggests a change in tenure structure that could help to resolve land use problems and at the same time sustain the tribe as a working unit.

The Indian Land Base

In order for readers to put the following discussion in perspective, it may be instructive to set out here a few facts about the Indian land base. Roughly 50 million acres, of which at least 39 million are tribal, remain in trust today; in 1873 the acreage was three times what it is now. But the figure of 50 million acres, or approximately 78,000 square miles, has little meaning until compared to the national totals. Indian lands today account for just over two percent of the national territory, a total area larger than New England and equivalent to South Dakota in size. The Navajo Reservation—the largest, at more than twelve million acres—roughly equals the combined areas of New Hampshire and Vermont. Even when authorities spell out the native Alaskan land claim in specific geographical terms and other acreages are added to the reservation "system," as suggested by Kickingbird and Ducheneaux (1973), Indian lands will comprise less than five percent of gross national area. As Figure 4 portrays the pattern, the western states contain almost all of the Indian lands, a fact that is not surprising, given the westward progression of land cession. The crucial fact that readers should recall is that most of the West is dry or arid. Small wonder that water issues (discussed in Section AC) demand considerable expertise in this region. Thus, while a modest amount of farmland persists on many reservations, by far the most important resource by percentage of land area and by activity of the tribes is grazable forage. A few reservations are more valuable for their timber or minerals, and several others have notable scenic or recreation resources, encouraging tourism. But by and large, the tribes occupy a meager land base, and for many reservations the best resources are developed or exploited under lease by non-Indians (cf. Haas 1957; Hough 1967; Sutton 1970b).

Figure 4 and its accompanying key have been updated, so far as it has been possible, to 1974. Not all reservations have been named, only those that receive some textual treatment or are otherwise especially notable. In areas with many terminated land units—such as northern and central California—specific land units are not identified; readers should refer to the key. Most recently the Menominee Indian Reservation was restored to the trusteeship of the BIA by law, so that number 23 is the only notable restoration. Alternating black and white rendering of reservations is intended only to distinguish land units from one another.

The Condition of the Indians

The problems that continue to beset the tribes and individual Indians today (cf. Kickingbird and Ducheneaux 1973, the most recent review of the land base) have historical frames of reference, which in my estimation begin logically with the survey of the "conditions" of the tribes, that being a popular term before the turn of the century.

Periodic review of policies and practices has characterized the history of Indian affairs as a governmental responsibility. Many of the survey studies are landmarks along the arduous course toward a constructive pro-tribal policy in land utilization. Among the earliest studies that examined the Indian land base (cited in Section BC) was Jackson's *A Century of Dishonor* (1881), the most persuasive such work of its time; among other studies were those published by the Indian Rights Association and the several books written by former Commissioners of Indian Affairs (Walker 1874; Manypenny 1880; Leupp 1910). Few offered analytical evaluations of tenure structure; they seem, in retrospect, very unsophisticated in their understanding of native concepts of territoriality or land tenure. Walker, for example, was a strong advocate of the idea that one or two large reservations would serve the needs of indigenous people better than small enclaves scattered among non-Indian settlements; his view was that the larger configurations would more successfully resist encroachment at a time when policy favored maintenance of a separation between Indian and white. However, despite this advantage, consolidation of bands and tribes ignored the importance of cultural differentiations by throwing together not only Indians unfamiliar with each other but many who had been long-time enemies competing for the same territories (cf. Cohen 1937). Manypenny, writing at the time allotment first became popular, urged this change in tenure, and Leupp, writing after the policy had been in operation for more than two decades, was its most ardent defender. His volume devotes at least five chapters to relevant land tenure issues (cf. his shorter paper of 1909). Writings by non-officials often tended to express anxiety over the Indians' plight but shed too little light on institutional solutions (cf. Humphrey 1905; Moorehead 1914).

Not until the 1920s did serious review of Indian affairs come of age. The Twenties became a decade of ferment, by the end of which land management policy would swing 180 degrees from the prevailing pro-

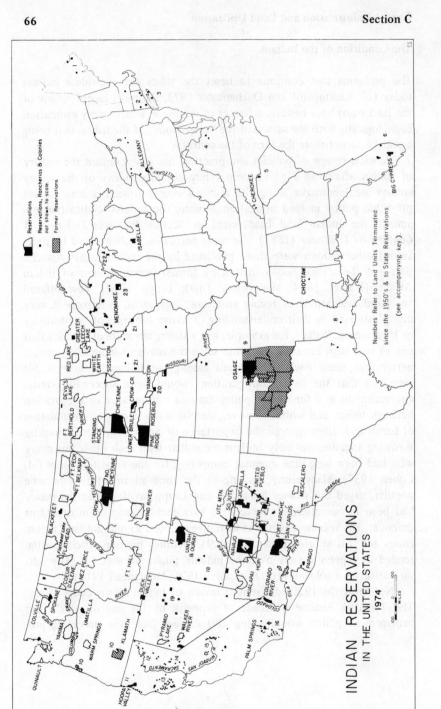

Figure 4[1]

Table to Figure 4

State Reservations

1. (Maine): Penobscot, Indian Township, Pleasant Point.
2. (Connecticut): Scaticook, Panguesett, Pequot; (Massachusetts): Nipmuc.
†3. (New York): Upstate—St. Regis, Oneida, Onondaga, Tuscarora, Tonawanda, Cattaraugus, and Allegany; Long Island—Poosepatuck, Shinnecock; (Pennsylvania): Allegany, Cornplanter.
4. (Virginia): Mattaponi, Pamunkey.
5. (South Carolina): Catawba.
6. (Florida): Miccosukee, Seminole.
7. (Texas): In east—Alabama-Coushatta; in west—Ysleta Tigua. (68 Stat. 768).

Terminated Reservations, Colonies, or Rancherias:

8. Coushatta (Koasati).
9. Modoc, Ottawa, Peoria, Wyandotte (70 Stat. 718ff.).
10. Grande Ronde, Siletz (68 Stat. 724); Klamath (68 Stat. 718).
*11. Blue Lake, Elk Valley, Ruffeys, Rohnerville, Table Bluff.
*12. Greenville, Likely, Quartz Valley, Redding, Smith River, Taylorville.
*13. Alexander Valley, Big Valley Cache Creek, Cloverdale, Graton, Guidiville, Hopland, Lytton, Mark West, Paskenta, Pinoleville, Potter Valley, Redwood Valley, Robinson, Scotts Valley, Upper Lake.

*14. Auburn, Buena Vista, Chicken Ranch, Chico, Mooretown, Nevada City, Shingle Springs, Strawberry Valley, Wilton.
*15. Big Sandy, Indian Ranch, North Fork, Picayune, Strathmore, Table Mountain.
*16. Laguna, Mission Creek.
17. Uintah & Ouray (mixed bloods only) (68 Stat. 868).
18. Cedar City, Indian Peaks, Kanosh, Koosharem, Shivwitz (68 Stat. 1099).
19. Austin, Beowawe, Carlin, Eureka, Wells.
20. Ponca (76 Stat. 429).
21. In east—Wabasha; in west—Pipestone.
22. Beaver, Hog, Fox Islands.

Restored from Terminated Status:

23. Menominee terminated by 68 Stat. 250; restored by P.L. 93-197, December 1973.

† Jurisdiction to New York via 62 Stat. 112 and 64 Stat. 845; portion of Allegany and adjacent Cornplanter Reserve in Pennsylvania severed for Kinzua Dam project (see Section AC).

* California Rancherías terminated pursuant to 72 Stat. 619, 78 Stat. 390; item 16 reservations once part of Mission Indian Agency (Riverside). Rancheria data updated by BIA, Sacramento, January 1974.

allotment position (cf. Downes 1945). This period, its antecedents and its after-effects as they related to the Southwest were ably treated by Dale (1949). Debo (1970) treated this same sweep of time, but in grosser terms and for the nation in general, whereas Washburn (1971b), within the legal-historical framework, better assesses the main institutional issues contributing to new land policy in Indian affairs. Further reflections on the evolution of the problems leading up to the IRA appear in the writings of another former commissioner, John Collier (1932, 1949).

Two volumes that mark a cadence in Indian administration appeared in the late 1920s (Schmeckebier 1927, reprinted 1972; Meriam 1928). Taken together, the volumes provide a fairly comprehensive picture of the historical, legal, administrative, economic, and social problems facing the tribes during the half-century following establishment of the reservations and during their later opening-up as part of land allotment schemes. Schmeckebier reviewed the long era of treaty-making, the formation of the Indian agency under the War Department and its transfer to the Interior Department, and the evolution of land policies up to 1927, whereas the "Meriam Report" paid attention to the relationship among Indian economic resources, land tenure, and socioeconomic well-being, and emphasized the erosion of the Indian's rights and lack of adequate management of his property. This report represented the first major statement of a new policy that emerged with the Collier administration (1933-45)—a policy that insistently attacked the allotment process as a failure and inaugurated activities directed toward the consolidation of tribal efforts as a way to improve the "conditions" of Indians. In his 1932 paper Collier had stressed the need to place greater emphasis on Indian corporate business and on the tribe's capacity to assign land among its own members without the deleterious effects of alienation or encumbered heirship. (Collier's administration has been appraised in at least one doctoral study—Philp 1968.)

Despite the innovations and progress initiated by the Collier administration, the Indian land situation has not altogether been bettered in the past 40 years, largely because of considerable vacillation in policy since 1945. A number of writings appeared too soon after the inauguration of new programs to evaluate the impact of changing land policies; instead they tended to focus on events leading to the changes (cf. many papers in LaFarge 1943). Indeed, the bulk of Kinney's impressively entitled volume (1937) precedes the IRA, but it reports semi-officially on the legislative record and constitutes the chief source on the background leading to the enactment of the IRA other than the documents themselves. Its author, a forest and range expert in the BIA, had worked closely with the management of Indian lands.

Over the years other studies have appeared (Loram and McIlwraith 1943), quite often in reaction to policy shifts that have undermined the trusteeship of Indian lands (Simpson and Yinger 1957; U.S. Congress, Senate 1958; Tyler 1964a; Brophy and Aberle 1966; Cahn 1969). Simpson and Yinger brought together a number of specialists in the Indian field who reviewed the effects of changing policy, especially toward the termination of federal trusteeship over tribes (see Section BC). Brophy and Aberle, coming as it did after the shelving of the termination policy but not soon enough to offset its real impact, might be considered a successor, in some ways, to the "Meriam Report," because of the broad scope of its survey of Indian affairs and its recommendations. In a much briefer, but widely distributed report sponsored by the Citizens' Advocate Center, Cahn (1969) put together a bolder statement—partly an indictment, partly an assessment—of such matters as the role of land in tribal life, complexities of land tenure, and resource problems that have not yet been resolved even after nearly a century of government responsibility for the economic and social well-being of the tribes. (Two shorter papers take strong positions on the state of Indian affairs in the mid-50s: Cohen 1953 and Van De Mark 1956.)

Here as in other sections of the typology it should be stressed that fully half of the published and manuscript materials pertinent to Indian land tenure are government documents, papers, and reports; the more important are cited in Snodgrass (1968). Although they deserve careful review along with archival source materials, it is beyond the scope of this volume to do more than cite a number of relevant examples. It is unfortunate that the documentary materials are not utilized more in published studies, especially in those that attempt comparative analysis of land problems. To date no one has prepared a concise bibliography of state documents in Indian affairs, although several listings for individual states do exist. Just as I would point out the value of statements and speeches made by Indians and others in the course of treaty negotiations, I would recommend the examination of the hearings in Indian affairs. They are of value because they report the vocal responses of Indians and the interplay of ideas, politics, and other factors that precede legislation; and also because they include reports submitted to subcommittees that have met in both Washington, D.C. and in regional centers near Indian populations. The gross differences in viewpoint, for example, between legislators and Indian spokesmen come alive in the dramatic dialogue of these hearings, and cross-examination of expert witnesses very often reveals the political motivations behind Indian land legislation. In my own experience I have also discovered a useful source of tenure-related discussions in reports filed in agency offices; from time to time specialists from outside the BIA have been called in to prepare a study, and all too often such manscripts have ended up lost in a file (unless by chance the expert has sought its publication in another form). Since so many states now have committees, commissions, or offices within other bureaus to manage Indian affairs, the available documentary materials may be expected to expand and make the chore of land-related research even more demanding. For example, in Wisconsin there is a special Menominee Committee with a staff officer in the state capital, and some years ago the California state legislature created an Indian subcommittee which for a decade released a series of biennial reports before it became defunct by law. In other states, agencies or branches of universities conduct Indian research projects—for example, the Institute of Indian Studies of the University of South Dakota (cf. Schusky 1959) and the Bureau of Ethnic Research of the University of Arizona (cf. Kelly 1953).

Legal Facets of Land Administration

A good deal of federal Indian law pertains to land rights and to those land institutions that make it possible for varying land-use patterns to function on reservations. Various studies seek to clarify the status of Indian land rights within a state, and thus review treaties and related laws, without dealing specifically with land utilization (cf. Haas 1957 for a general review; Kelly 1953 for Arizona; Manley 1960 for New York; Semple 1952, McArthur 1949, and Mills 1919 for Oklahoma). Other studies focus on laws in a historical-geographical context, relating land to legislation without actually conducting legal discussions (Anderson 1956; Bach 1937; Bounds 1971; Bourne 1953; Laidlaw 1960). Most of these studies are in manuscript and of limited distribution. Laidlaw's published thesis dealt with the Bannock-Shoshoni of Fort Hall, weaving legislation into a historical and contemporary account of land problems. Loomer's (1955) study of Bad River, Wisconsin includes considerable legal-administrative discussion as well. In fact, many of these studies include discussions of laws and procedures.

However, the only comprehensive treatments of law, land tenure, and land utilization deal with the entire field (F. S. Cohen 1941, 1971; Price 1973). These volumes are treatises on federal Indian law; Cohen's is the classic work that brought together all relevant legislation, case law, regulations, articles, and books. Cohen, a practicing attorney and legal historian as well as a staunch supporter of Indian rights, researched almost all facets of the Indian field (see L. K. Cohen 1960 for a collection of his related writings). Some controversy attended the publication of a "revised" edition of his work (FIL 1958), which was also later reprinted under the aegis of the Association on American Indian Affairs in 1966. Many scholars, including some Indians, have assessed the revision as an expurgated version of the original, intended in part to place greater stress on the capacity of the federal government to regulate or supervise the activities of the tribes, and thereby to diminish their autonomy as granted under treaties. As a result of this controversy, the American Indian Law Center of the University of New Mexico sponsored a reprinting of the original text (1971). It included an introduction on the life of F. S. Cohen and a bibliography of sources utilized in the earlier editions. Of course much has been added to Indian law since the 1940s, and significant case law has modified the body of legislation reviewed by Cohen.

Price (1973) pulled together the bulk of relevant laws and case citations in the form of a large case book with readings. Its size attests to the enormous amount of legislation and litigation that has arisen since the Cohen volume was first published. While it does not review the legislation and administrative policy as Cohen did, Price, in Chapter 4, reviews more or less sequentially the important legislation pertaining to land tenure, and includes abstracts of various studies, reports, and decision that pertain to these laws. It is the most comprehensive treatment to date. In another study, Price (1969), in the course of his association with the Office of Economic Opportunity, prepared an instructive statement on the role lawyers might play in furthering the purposes of tribal government and aiding in resource development. While many aspects of his study concerned tribal or individual Indian matters not related to land, he noted the conflicts that arose within tribes over the division and allocation of resources; he observed too that it was necessary to extricate "resources from legal and political snarls that render them virtually useless" (p. 200). Lawyers, he felt, could provide the catalytic ingredient to assist tribes toward patterns more in line with new planning concepts in land utilization. Other studies that treat facets of law, land tenure, and administration include Kinney (1937), which was almost an official administrative review, Schifter (1970), Bennett (1960), O'Reilly (1970), and Nash (1971), which focuses on the ethics of federal trusteeship.

Another group of legal studies attempts to unravel the complexities of leasing Indian resources; of especial concern for the last two decades has been the need for clarification of laws and regulations that affect mining on Indian lands. Commercial interests in this period of economic expansion have increasingly coveted Indian mineral resources. Legally sophisticated and often designed for the specialist, this literature has essentially emanated from a single source—the Rocky Mountain Mineral Law Institute (Berger 1968a/b; Gibbons 1965; Radloff 1966; Sonosky 1960). The Radloff study considers leasing policies on Indian lands from the perspective of public land-leasing. Berger and Mounce (1971) have evaluated the implications of state conservation laws for the development of Indian mineral wealth. Two other volumes deal specifically with leasing procedures: McLane (1955) and Schlesinger (1967). The latter deals with non-mineral land leasing on the Palm Springs Indian Reservation in California. (Cf. Kelly 1963 on Navajo oil and Glasscock 1938 for several chapters on oil wealth of Indians in Oklahoma; both studies are mostly historical accounts.)

The Reservation as a Land Institution

More than one scholar has sought a useful definition of "reservation." Legal interpretation and classification of the reservation appears in several sources (Schmeckebier 1927; Cohen 1941; FIL 1958), but much of the discussion concerns differences among the various bases for their establishment: treaties, statutes, and executive orders. For reasons that are largely political (territorial, jurisdictional, and so on), to identify a reservation simply as a large landholding acknowledged to be "owned" by a tribe and held in trust by the federal government does not mean very much. Certainly a reservation is more than a place where Indians hold special tenure rights. Cohen (1937) defined an Indian reservation as an administrative unit, stressing that all too often it was not a cultural or social unit because members of several tribes whose social organization differed came to be domiciled on the same land unit under a single administration. Berger (1968a) said of the reservation that it is ". . . part of the public domain set aside by proper authority for use and occupation by a group of Indians" (p. 91). The reference to "public domain" might well lead to erroneous conclusions, since the idea that the reservation is set aside out of the public domain suggests that its status is the same as that of a national park or forest. And of course this is untrue. Inasmuch as public land laws have little or no bearing on Indian lands, it is perhaps wiser to seek a definition that avoids reference to the public domain. Historically, of course, executive-order reservations did not have the standing of those established by treaty or law, but this situation has been rectified (see Anonymous 1960 in Section BC).

Citing a decision from a noted case, Price (1969) restated the judge's view that

> An Indian reservation . . . is in the nature of a school, and the Indians are gathered there, under the charge of an agent, for the

purpose of acquiring the habits, ideas, and aspirations that distinguish the civilized from the uncivilized man. (P. 202)

Price further compared a reservation to a campus, one which would cease to exist when all Indians had attained sufficient degrees of civilization.

It should be noted that the preceding observations all reflect an effort to interpret the meaning of "reservation." What it suggests is that no definition can exclude legal or social intent. Social scientists, however, seek more than a legal definition. Stern, for example (1965), offered some advice:

> For many Indian peoples reservations are a highly significant reality, constituting the only familiar homeland, the major continuity with the past, the sole real property, and the principal token of the government's resolution to honor pledges made long ago. (P. 266)

Rountree (1972), one of the few scholars to examine eastern reservations under state trust, sustained this viewpoint by noting how a reservation "validates and continues their [Indian] distinct identity" (p. 94). She noted, moreover, that "reservated" Indians do not consider non-reservation Indians as truly Indian because they live on land which was bought from whites and for which they pay taxes.

Walker (1971) emphasized the importance of the size and configuration of a reservation as factors determining the degree of conservatism or susceptibility to Euro-American influences. Hoffmeister (1945) was concerned with compactness in comparing the Ute Mountain and Southern Ute Reservations. He surmised that because of unclear boundaries and lack of social integration, reservations may be unfit units for social or cultural analysis. Another excellent statement of what a reservation means to Indians was prepared by three anthropologists (Diamond et al. 1964).

By dint of the unique body of law that governs its existence, the reservation is many things—a homeland, an ethnic place, a legal place bounding a jural community, an administrative unit, a form of property incorporating both post-contact aspects of native land tenure and modifications wrought by law and administrative practice. In theory its internal order is inviolate and its people autonomous, but since the days of land allotment and the opening of surplus lands to homesteading, we must distinguish "open" from "closed" reservations (compare the Dakotas with the Southwestern states).

Studies that emphasize the lack of separateness of reservations and thereby tend to stress the interaction within a county or region (Calef 1948; Loomer 1955; Longwell 1961; Sutton 1964, 1967; Ballas 1970;

Jorgensen 1971, 1972) would question any definition that isolates the Indian reservation from its socioeconomic and political surroundings. In reality, they suggest, a reservation is a microcosm within a larger human occupancy. Thus it is also necessary to distinguish the reservation per se from Indian Country, which is legally defined as "country within which federal laws relating to Indians and tribal laws and customs are applicable" (FIL 1958, p. 13; Cohen 1941, p. 5). Indian Country at any particular time must be viewed in relation to the then-existing body of law and to the status of the "moving frontier"; along this frontier settlement and socioeconomic relationships between tribes and Euro-Americans have been subjected to changes. Such laws prevailed beyond the external boundaries of reservations for various purposes (e.g., prohibition on sale of liquor). But because of modifications in federal laws, some states have assumed considerable authority to regulate law and order on reservations (see Section AC). Consquently the effective meaning of "Indian Country" has changed, and the parameters of tribal autonomy have been modified, so that it is true to say that (1) even within the same state, no two reservations necessarily enjoy exactly the same legal-political status, and (2) in no two states do reservations possess the same legal-political protections. Finally, extreme views of the definition of reservation either imply or suggest "prison," or "refuge" (cf. Hertzberg 1971) or, as in Embry's (1956) title, "concentration camps."

Few land units thus masquerade under as many aliases as the Indian reservation. To those non-Indians living in close proximity (especially the residents of the county in which a reservation is located), immunities from local taxes and police powers seem to contradict the ideas that states have plenary jurisdiction over all territory within their borders. Yet, though the trusteeship function extends a general blanket of federal immunity over reservations, that immunity is not uniform, and its effect varies from state to state. As bounded, of course, the reservation may at one time have defined a social or ethnic community; the contexts of Nurge (1970) and Walker (1971) suggest that the reservation more than anything else is a cultural entity, a social phenomenon occupying specific geographic space. Similarly, the kinds of studies Levy and Kunitz (1971) have conducted among the Navajo and Hopi view the reservation as a cultural milieu akin to ghettos and related urban neighborhoods. Colson (in Walker 1971) emphasized that as a social system or a geographical entity the reservation is only part of a larger system, and that external forces setting it in motion perpetuate it (Macgregor in the Nurge volume spoke of two systems — Indian community and government agency). Colson noted that

All reservations are land reserved by the state for a particular purpose and therefore not open to private ownership until it can be demonstrated that the public purpose is no longer being served by the reservation in question. (P. 9)

Such statements suggest the intent of the government to stimulate social and economic change for which the reservation constitutes a special medium. One facet of culture change suggested by some observers bears on the effectiveness of reservation land uses: the suggestion is that the establishment of the reservation stimulated the growth of true tribal government, which certainly has become significant in economic development in recent years (cf. Wilson 1961; Fonaroff 1971 and see Section ABC). Of course in its historical sense the reservation is tied to treaties and laws and embodies aspects of land tenure and policy understood by tribal members. In sum, borrowing from a more general study of micropolitics, "Only confusion will be created by trying to draw too sharp and exclusive a line between political and other forms of organization" (Burns 1961, p. 9).

By far the most interesting analysis of the reservation's relationship to economic growth is that of the metropolis-satellite theory, which considers the cession of land, encroachment on Indian resources, and legal acquisition by non-Indians of the favored use of these resources. As employed by Jorgensen (1971), who evaluated the approach in terms of the Northern Utes (Uintah-Ouray Reservation), the theory suggests that non-Indian control of urban markets and political activity as well as of immediate rural economies and local governments has subordinated most reservations to urban-oriented economic activity. Non-Indian economic interests have benefitted first from the expropriation of Indian land resources, now part of the hinterland of urbanization, and secondly by acquisition of the use of these resources by dint of low rent, tax allowances, and other benefits. The Jorgensen paper, published as part of a symposium on the urban relocation of Indians, provides another way to examine the context in which it has been necessary for younger Indian families to migrate or commute to find a new opportunity away from reservations. The author also contends that the lack of access to political power over their strategic resources is a discouraging consequence of the metropolis-satellite situation for the tribes. (Cf. Thomas 1966a/b; Thomas describes reservation administration as colonialism.)

A major concern among researchers has been the description of how the reservation, as a base for livelihood or residence, has related Indians to the surrounding areas. These studies focus on quite different considerations. Although they rarely emphasize land tenure per se, they nonetheless seek to identify the reservation as the locus of livelihood and settlement for many resident Indian families and sociocultural identity for many non-resident families. They firmly state that reservations neither confine Indians nor necessarily drive them away to find a new life in the white society. Waddell (1969), for example, showed that Papago residing off the reservation, including some who had migrated to Tucson, continued to identify themselves with reservations. He likened the situation to the Papago's indigenous patterns of dispersion, and noted that

> It is difficult to support the proposition that familiar kinship units and relationships are drastically disrupted by the exigencies of off-reservation occupational environments and thereby make Papago adaption to jobs more difficult. (P. 143)

To Waddell, kinship boundaries are "sentimental domains" that extend over considerable spatial areas and that can still function even when greatly modified; but establishment of a reservation within an area of extensive nonindigenous settlement tends to aggravate a precarious subsistence economy with the result that the Indian is less able to support himself.

Another interpreter of Papago occupancy (Hackenberg 1972) has shown that the "boundary-maintenance mechanism" of the reservation permits the Papago to seek employment in nearby rural or urban communities without affecting the integrity of their lands. Nagata (1971) and Nielson (1967) have also stressed the magnetic attraction of the surrounding areas for Indian economic pursuits; these still turn, in part, on the ability of the Indian family to reside on or return to tax-free land among persons of their own ethnic background.

Weightman (1972) carried even further the analysis of how Indian mobility within a larger non-Indian area is closely related to the reservation as the locus of activities. In examining a small reservation, an enclave within an area of urbanization (Vancouver, B.C.), she distinguished between legal place and social space; she observed that the former, by segregating a social system, has preserved its economic base, group functions, and ethnic identity, while the latter has continued to be perceived in terms of old patterns of intervillage relationships. Although Indians seek employment within the social space, very few cross-cultural ties have evolved. (On the persistence of intervillage ties in the Northwest, see Suttles 1963.)

What Weightman has identified in a limited sample has application in other parts of Indian Country. I discussed Indian socioeconomic activity (Sutton 1964), for example, with respect to 30 bands of Mission Indians in the urbanizing environment of Southern California. Here, we also find that Indians, although working mostly in the larger geographic area external to the reservations, tend to interact mostly between the homes of non-resident Indian families and the reservation communities. Because so few of these reservations are allotted, and because only limited acreage has been readily available in the marketplace for non-Indian developments, they are relatively isolated even within an urbanizing environment in which speculative land sales have approached the outward limits of freely available land (cf. Steiner 1966). Only the Palm Springs Indian Reservation shows a strong interaction with its immediate urban area, and even here the possibilities of development have been limited (Sutton 1967).

Thus the reservation has been interpreted as a system unto itself and as a small part of a larger socioeconomic milieu. Literature, especially land-use literature, documents well the greater spatial interaction of reservations within the surrounding area, although this is probably more true of the uses of allotted lands than of those held by the tribe. The reservation as a jural place has come to manage its resources in terms of the external marketplace, changing the Indian's relationship to the reservation and to the surrounding socioeconomic space.

Land Policy, Management and Tenure

The literature of Indian economic development reflects the continuous efforts of the government to further land utilization, whether by encouraging land allotment or by strengthening the tribal corporate resource. Early literature of course enthusiastically endorsed agriculture as a family institution (cf. Leupp 1909; Sells 1917; Kinney 1937); more recent studies share the mood and sentiment of the tribes, which seek increased autonomy in order to develop forest, grazing, mineral, or touristic resources (cf. Hunt 1970; Deloria 1970; Sorkin 1973). Those who advocate turning economic and other affairs over to the Indians (cf. Kickingbird and Ducheneaux 1973; Forbes 1965) have urged the strengthening of protections to ensure tribal autonomy and to create stability in the land base on which the tribes count for their income. Forbes, for one, recommended the creation of tribal regions or community service districts, even counties, out of reservations; he argued for integration of tribes into the national political structure while protecting their separate rights. He also advocated an Inter-Tribal Development Corporation, asserting that there should be an increase in land for the tribes, in light of the work of the Public Land Law Review Commission (whose report appeared in 1970). Forbes recommended that "all further alienation of the public domain be halted until native land needs are met" (p. 160). The Commission, however, did not consider it within their jurisdiction to examine land policy relative to Indian rights.

Many tribes continue to need to acquire land, not only by purchase or grant from the public domain (cf. Hooker 1972), but by consolidation, to straighten out the hopelessly tangled maze that has resulted from multiple-heirship problems (see Section BC). Gilbert and Taylor (1966) provided data on the status of land-purchase programs first undertaken in the 1930s under the provisions of the IRA. Their analysis, while brief, included a tabulation of the status of land acquisition programs vis-à-vis restrictions within certain states based on federal appropriation legislation. States have exerted considerable thrust to prevent expansion of the external boundaries of reservations, but under the IRA tribes could purchase encumbered allotments and consolidate these lands for tribal purposes. Unfortunately, data showing how consolidation has really worked are hard to come by in any single compilation. Gilbert and Taylor focused only on the Southwest, and no nationwide account exists. (For a more general treatment of tenure and resource management see Goding 1958 and Province 1956.)

Several other economic studies touch upon land tenure as a critical factor in making Indian resources work for individuals or tribes. Dorner (1961) offered a general prognosis for Indian economic growth; Taylor (1970) examined the role of education and the character of the labor force in reservation economic activity; Voget (1961-62) reviewed specific tribal developments; and Hough (1967) compiled a handbook of useful discussions on all aspects of Indian economic activity, including considerations of non-Indian leasing of reservation resources. Kinney (1950) wrote an analysis of Indian resource management focusing on tribal rather than individual resources. Since so many of the case studies cited below deal with how tribal governments may impede or encourage economic growth, the discussions chaired by Bennett (1970) at a national convocation of Indian scholars should prove informative, especially considering the desire of tribes to increase their autonomy in land management. Bennett, himself an Indian, a former Commissioner of Indian Affairs, and a lawyer, has filled in the gaps in the Indians' scholarly competence to understand how the bureaucratic structure tends to interfere in the logical and progressive growth of reservation economies. This dialogue among Indians widens one's appreciation of the problems posed, for example, by the introduction of non-Indian capitalization of industry and commerce on reservations; it becomes apparent that much of the income from such activities goes off the reservation.

Another useful volume is Sorkin's survey (1971) of Indian economic conditions. Discussing industrialization, property and income management, and related problems, Sorkin outlines the causes behind Indian poverty, including weaknesses in land tenure structure. He suggested that allotments were economically unsuitable for farming, owing to their small size, and that the limited size of flocks, as among the Navajo or San Carlos Apache, limited the success of a ranch economy. In noting the perplexing problems of heirship for utilization of much Indian land, Sorkin asserted that state, not tribal, laws limited the capacity to render such lands useful to Indians. And he emphasized that tribal enterprise was proving successful mainly because it permitted tribes to enjoy more financial resources and left the lands unencumbered for future development. Less useful to the study of land tenure and land use, but offering a similar discussion, is Levitan and Hetrick (1971). Tuttle (1971) spoke for a growing consensus that the tribes should have more freedom over land title, but referred to a constant fear of alienation of tribal or individual lands should titles fall into the hands of Indians who are as yet ill prepared to utilize land titles as collateral for the acquisition of credit.

The preceding discussions clearly indicate that the government's involvement in resource development on the reservations relates more to tribal or communal tenure than to individual rights in land. This emphasis, of course, has evolved in the decades since the passage of the Indian Reorganization Act in 1934. Many of the provisions of the IRA have directly affected the role of tribal authority over land and other resources and have led to the emergence of strong constitutions and by-laws, written by the tribes but reviewed and authorized by the government. With the IRA came the virtual abrogation of the allotment policy (see Section BC; cf. Brophy and Aberle 1966; Price 1973, Chap. IV; Tyler 1973), maintenance of tribal acreage in trust, and the indefinite extension of the trust period, necessitating the strengthening of tribal government in order to maintain a communal resource for the preservation of tribal identity and lifestyles. While much of the current literature evaluating the status of governmental jurisdictions in Indian affairs concerns itself with the federal-tribal-state interaction (see Section AC), discussions of tribal constitutions and by-laws only allude to the matter of land tenure. The constitutions and by-laws themselves are, of course, most useful to the pursuit of the study of tribal tenure. Fay (1967-72) has compiled a nearly complete set of these documents. Perusal of them suggests a number of observations. Nearly all of them include sections spelling out the tribal authority to allocate and regulate tenant-in-common use of assignable lands. Moreover, tribal authority over matters of leasing such resources to non-Indians is assured. Taken together, these documents shed light on how the tribes have embraced Euro-American legal institutions under the tutelage of the government, and because of their similar origins, they very often contain the same provisions and even the same wording. Most of them express a broad tribal responsibility ". . . to protect and preserve the property, wild life [sic] and natural resources . . . of the tribe, and to regulate the conduct of trade and the use and disposition of property upon the reservation. . . ." Some set the condition that preference in leasing shall be given to tribal cooperative associations (as in grazing) or to individual Indian members of the tribe. Most of the documents emphasize the tribe's power to assign and regulate individual uses of land for various purposes.

No general assessment of the land tenure content of the documents in other than their legal-administrative context has been made. Since these documents reflect the government's repudiation of the allotment policy, the "land code" elements of tribal constitutions and by-laws express the government's policy toward those tribes that voluntarily embraced the law in the 1930s or had it thrust upon them by later legislation (cf. Tyler 1973). As for the tendency in the documents to reinforce the functions of the tribe as a political and economic organization, there is no doubt that this assertion of authority coincides with congressional policy, although as various discussions below will indicate, tribes have responded in very different ways to their powers under the IRA.

Case Studies

Of the vast store of case studies (or type studies) too few provide analytical discussion of the role of land tenure in the utilization of Indian resources. Studies of specific reservations, while many of them include observations about land uses and resource development, tend to recount historical factors of Indian-white relations, stressing treaties, laws, and administration. Discussion of several studies that significantly interpret the relationship between land tenure and changes in Indian social and economic behavior will be reserved for Section ABC.

In fact, no discipline has approached the problem of reservation land utilization in a definitive way. A wealth of information may be found in numerous graduate theses, accompanied by fairly immature analysis and conclusions. Few of these have gotten into print. Theses of budding geographers examine the land relation, but they tend to bog down in historical-legal discussions no less than those of history students, whose knowledge of land is less adequate. The traditional stresses in each discipline have influenced the direction of such thesis or dissertation research. Several studies offer useful cartographic compilations, some revealing considerable originality. But most studies, in manuscript or in print, rely heavily on the official source materials in documents and in agency files. It is left to field observations by anthropologists to provide useful and poignant commentaries on the views held by Indians. Rarely in the literature does one encounter a study that amply and effectively synthesizes the data and methods necessary to transcend disciplinary limits.

Historically oriented case studies (Anderson 1956; Bourne 1953; Harner 1965; Hill 1930; Laidlaw 1960; Mobley 1970; Murray 1953; Sorensen 1971) represent some of the graduate efforts. Laidlaw's published study deals with Shoshone-Bannock land tenure from aboriginal times to the present and traces reservation history from its inception through land allotment and the IRA. If utilized in conjunction with related studies (e.g., Liljeblad 1958), it would provide a good view of an ethnohistorical treatment of a common theme. Sorensen's emphasis on changing livelihood ecology considered the influence of policy changes and of non-Indian property concepts. His study of the role of land allotment among the Shoshone-Bannock, for example, reveals how white private property concepts have led to economic stagnation among Indians who prefer to live by communal tenure concepts despite the perpetuation of poverty (cf. the discussion of land allotment in Section BC). Bourne recounted the history of Palm Springs as it evolved as a tourist resort and showed how Indian land problems related to growth problems of that city.

Other historical studies include Kelly (1968), Lurie (1969), and Shane (1959). Kelly, in reconstructing the growth of the Navajo reservation as a legal entity up to the time of the IRA, prepared a background study that is useful for the further interpretation of current Navajo land problems. His study examined efforts, checked by the Taylor Grazing Act and the unfavorable reaction of the states, to expand the reservation eastward into public domain area (cf. Fonaroff 1963, 1964). Lurie provided a general examination of Indian-white relations in Wisconsin but little on land utilization. Shane discussed some implications of land use, considering, for example, the relocation of Indians at Fort Berthold owing to the construction of Garrison Dam. (For a broader discussion of dams and Indian lands see Section AC.)

Many researchers have interpreted the role of the tribe in economic development (Getty 1961-62, 1963; Herbert 1962; Rietz 1953; Fryer 1942; Hunt 1970; Roberts 1943; Ballas 1962, 1970; Sherman 1962; Stern 1961-62). Getty reported that for the San Carlos Apache, cattle-raising and marketing represented a non-Apache activity in which they had achieved considerable success. The reservation was organized into several cattle associations and divided into roughly equal ranges on which members had rights to graze individually-owned cattle. This arrangement led to more efficient range utilization and greater individual involvement. The reservations became legal corporations under Arizona law, in order to be able to borrow money from local banks. In evaluating the relative merits of the cattle enterprise, Getty noted, however, that traditional values have worked against the Indians' becoming successful cattlemen. For example, attempts to stimulate cooperative efforts within extended families have been nullified by the fact that many members of a group come to depend upon the efforts of one person because "cooperation distributes responsibility irregularly" (1961-62, p. 185).

Stern's review of the potential political power of a tribe can apply to many reservations where tribal endeavors in economic activity and in government have been encouraged under the aegis of the IRA. In the case of the Klamath, his analysis concerned shifts in membership loyalty during an earlier period of out-migration and on the eve of termination. Roberts observed how the Red Shirt Table community of Sioux in planning the development of their reservation had had to recognize the common interest and at the same time avoid disturbing existing tenure, since to do so would have alienated individual landowners. Rietz's review of the Fort Berthold Indians noted that they did not tend to apply themselves wholeheartedly to long-term development efforts involving collective participation, for the stock associations had ceased to function; he reflected on the sense of dependence felt by tribal members, the government having assumed most of the decision-making for so long. Hunt suggested that collective enterprises can be furthered so long as there are sufficient resources—timber and scenic attractions in the case of the Warm Springs Indians—and funds for their development. Sherman noted that the Red Lake Chippewa, who, unlike the rest of the Chippewa in Minnesota, have never taken allotments, run both a sawmill and a commercial fishery as cooperative enterprises. Sherman supported the view that where allotments were rejected, the possibility of succcessful tribal enterprises exists. He noted that because the band owned its forest resources in common, the government did not have to deal with numerous individual owners or fragmented holdings.

Even in the historical record there is considerable evidence that where tribes rejected allotments, tribal leadership has been more successful in economic enterprises. Burrill (1972) recounted that the Osage of the 1880s had chosen land not suited to farming, hoping thus to discourage non-Indian covetousness of their lands. Strong tribal control of land use was important, for by keeping land units large, they could interest cattlemen in leasing their holdings for a considerable time (see the discussion of cattlemen on reservations in Section BC, and cf. Hewes's 1942a, b and 1944 discussions of Cherokee occupancy).

Tribal leadership in economic enterprises still bears the influence of elements of pre-reservation concepts of property and resource rights. The interplay between the tribe as a corporate entity and its members as individuals and families constitutes an important process by which native and Euro-American institutions have been variously exercised and modified. Although legalistic and organizational distinctions between tribes and members have been noted (Cohen 1941 spoke of tribal ownership vs. tenancy-in-common; Deloria 1970 referred to corporate and conglomerate ownership), such clearcut distinctions are often hard to apply to specific tribal bodies. Forde (1931b) identified the persistence of communal tenures among the Hopi. His findings have been reinforced by those of Page (1940) and Willey (1969); the latter noted the emphasis on use rather than title in the Hopi outlook toward land rights.

Downs (1964) noted that among the Navajos, despite use-ownership concepts generally ascribed to that tribe, feelings of proprietorship by family or homestead group over grazing land could be distinguished where allotment had not occurred. Fonaroff (1963) revealed that Navajo rejection of the IRA was the result of fears of herd reduction as well as of opposition to the establishment of a central agency at Window Rock. Stock reduction was indeed the policy of the government in the 1930s, during which time they organized the reservation into land-management districts. The thrust of the program was to create "genuine localized function mechanisms" to force the few large stockholders to reduce herd size by holding them up to public ridicule. Fonaroff's study shows how tribes can exert a counterproductive force and how use rights of a member (in this case, a Navajo stockholder) may actually frustrate efforts at conservation. As he put it,

> As long as he [the Navajo stockowner] is using the range, other families will not normally infringe on his right, even though the section could carry many more sheep units. If his range is not in use, anyone may claim "ownership" by stocking it. (P. 222)

Furthermore, he observed, "this ownership-in-use peculiarity of the Navajo property concept was never broken by the Indian Service." (For further views on Navajo attitudes and government policy, see Fonaroff 1964; for a newer historical interpretation of the stock reduction problem, see Boyce 1974.)

Gilbreath's recent (1973) analysis of Navajo economy inferred that clumsy procedures for making tribal lands available under lease have served to discourage indigenous economic development on the reservation. All leasing, for example, is arranged between private parties and the Navajo Tribal Council, and considerable delays normally occur; even individual

Navajos must themselves follow these procedures in order to lease tribal land for business ventures. Since Navajos generally oppose white concepts of property, they equate leasing arrangements with an alien culture. Because of this, the Indian business sector is inadequate and most of the tribe continues to rely upon agriculture and animal husbandry.

For the Havasupai, Martin (1968, 1973) has reassessed and updated earlier interpretations of land tenure practices (Service 1947). Noting the out-migration of younger families, Martin explained how private claims—the result of a tourist economy dependent on horses and the need for pasturage—had come about on a non-allotted reservation. In actual practice, certain families have laid claim to the best lands, while some non-resident landless families, through better education and skills, have returned to hold commanding positions on the tribal council. This has created conflicts between the tribal government and those who would monopolize the land; as a result, the tribal government tends to remain unstable. In his more recent paper he sought to explain the reasons for Indian non-use of available farmland during a period of privation on the reservation in the early 1960s. His explanations suggest that for the Havasupai, a radical transformation of family organization and land tenure is as much a prerequisite for full cultivation of arable land as the availability of capital and heavy machinery.

Although the studies of Indian land use in print or in manuscript—other than government documents—are few in number, those available take a variety of approaches. Aside from the older ethnographic account of the operations of land tenure in the matrilineal society of the Hopis (Forde 1931b) and similar studies that stress the subsistence orientation and the inward-looking view of Indians toward land (cf. Section A), many of the studies attempt to identify those characteristics of land tenure that draw reservation economic activity into the surrounding non-Indian socio-economic and political milieu. These studies consider the reservation within a larger context and demonstrate how individual reservations participate in the activities of the dominant society. Loomer's analysis (1955) of the Bad River Indian Reservation provides, for example, a concise outline of the kinds of problems and policies imposed upon a reservation by its mixed tenures and its association with state and local government. Hoffmeister (1945) contrasted the two related Ute reservations—Ute Mountain, which has maintained tribal tenure, and the Southern Ute, which accepted partial allotment. And in two earlier works (Sutton 1964, 1967) I contrasted the role of allotment and assignment under tenancy-in-common for reservations in Southern California. Figure 5 displays the land tenure patterns described. Loomer is especially useful because he relates mixed tenures of an open reservation to taxation and land ad-

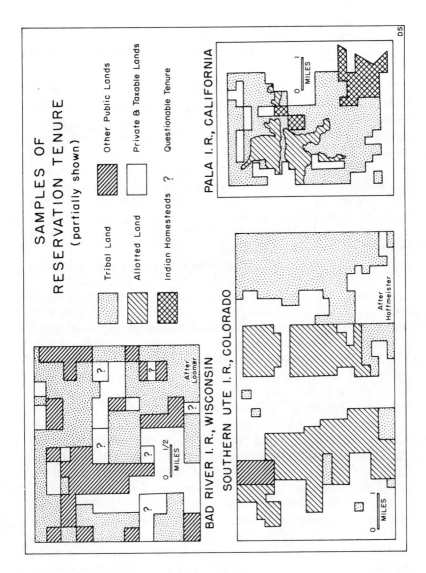

Figure 5[2]

ministration (cf. Platt's brief field observation, 1959). In the Hoffmeister study this poignant observation is made:

> The limits of the reservation were established with a total disregard for the physical relationships of the region. The boundaries cut across both physical and economic unit areas; furthermore, there is no nucleus or center of gravitation to give cohesion. Only the unity of race and federal administration holds the reservation together. (P. 603)

Rectangular configurations in boundary-setting, in general, can be noted as a function of the land-survey system. My 1964 work further discussed the resulting problem relative to the cutting up of drainages, which affected the allocation of water rights shared by Indians and non-Indians; the latter have often gained allocations that have exceeded the total flow of a stream. For a great many allotted reservations, land units were laid out according to the township system, not unlike homesteads; this led to disjointed land-use patterns. With sale or lease to non-Indians, it becomes clear how the land system encouraged a highly irregular configuration, bringing Indians and non-Indians in close contact as neighboring owners or users.

Other studies reveal similar or contradictory patterns of ownership and related problems in actual land use. Ballas (1970) studied Todd County, one of four counties in South Dakota in which Rosebud Sioux Indian Reservation is located. Unlike the other three, Todd County is "closed" in terms of the relative percentage of non-Indian landholdings allowed within the bounds of the reservation. Despite the dominance of Indians within this one county, Ballas discovered that the considerable fragmentation of land and the lack of capital and managerial experience have tended to frustrate Indian farming and ranching. The tribe has purchased land and attempted to consolidate land units in order to implement programs for the development of industrial parks and recreation areas and for other uses. He finds then that among Teton Dakota, inadequacies of tenure and capitalization, more than historic rejection of farming, explain the difficulty of commercial success at ranching or farming. Again one sees the role of tribal government as encouraging development of tourism and industry as a source of employment on the reservation. Longwell (1961) compared Indian and non-Indian utilization of lands in the three counties in Nebraska in which the Omaha Indian Reservation lies. By comparison at three levels—county, township, and sample areas including allotments—he was able to assess a land tenure structure that has mostly served to enable non-Indians to lease Indian lands for agricultural purposes. Wilson (1972) revealed that ranching as a tribal enterprise has achieved considerable success on tribal lands because most of the irrigable land on the Wind River Indian Reservation has been alienated, whereas some allotted land within grazing ranges has been purchased by the tribe as a means to implement animal husbandry. Janke (1967) attempted to compare reservations in Montana, where allotments have been dominant, with those in Arizona, where tribes have rejected allotment; he went on to examine the tribally-held Menominee reserve in comparison to the allotment of all other reserves in Wisconsin.

Many land-use studies of reservations do not elaborate fully or sufficiently on tenure structure. While Jensen's (1964) land survey of the Turtle Mountain Indian Reservation in North Dakota is useful for its maps, including those that depict allotments and fee patents, its author fails to analyze his data that pertain to land utilization. A sampling of the studies of the Missouri River Basin Investigations Project (cf. Ward 1956; see Snodgrass 1968 for a larger list) produced useful though limited tenure and land economic data, noting that Indians tended to lease their lands and showed a preference for the use of tribal resources. Bounds (1971) reported on the circumstances of the Alabama-Coushatta, who were given a tract of land under Texas state law and who, finding it too small to meet tribal needs, have become farm laborers or loggers, or have migrated to cities to find employment; only more recently have they developed a tourist enterprise to improve their economy. Hoover's (1930, 1936) land-use articles on tribes in the Southwest say little of land tenure, yet they are now historically useful as field studies.

In a larger study of the human ecology of the Colorado River delta—a study growing out of land claims research—Aschmann (1966) examined the effects of allotted lands and the entry of non-Indian settlers on surplus tracts of the Fort Yuma Indian Reservation. He showed how for lack of capital Indian allotments came to be developed under lease and how heirship complicated land use even though Indians had been granted 40-acre farms, once deemed more than ample. Unlike the Indians who work seasonally for the non-Indian lessees in the Umatilla area of Oregon (Stern and Boggs 1971), here few of the resident Indians provide farm labor to those renting the land, so that Mexican immigrants (braceros) are brought in. Aschmann has summarized the impact of heirship, anticipating its increase in geometric progession; he found that inheritance rules and prohibition of land sales are rapidly destroying the basis for individual land ownership; only through common tribal ownership would the land once again be available for Indian use. Yet this multiplicity of inherited ownerships does seem to provide a fairly even distribution of rental income (see the discussion of heirship in Section BC).

Upstream on the Colorado River Indian Reservation, Travis (1968) has examined Indian allotments, heirship, and leasing, predicting that eventually the Indians will be no more than a group of absentee landlords and that their primary concern will be the distribution of assets and not their relationship to the ancestral land base. Fragmentation of land through heirship had encouraged the tribe to seek a land-leasing program as early as 1963, together with efforts to consolidate holdings, and led to an emphasis on "unearned" or lease income.

Among other studies are those by Debo (1951) which includes brief chapters on land purchases for the Five Civilized Tribes and on the management of individual Indian property. Aberle's study (1948) of the Pueblos also considered land purchase problems following the quieting of title by the Pueblo Act of 1924. A more general survey of land problems in the Southwest was prepared by Gilbert and Taylor (1966). The most timely treatment of the Indian's land base, dealing especially with the further acquisition of lands to meet long-term per-capita needs, is Kickingbird and Ducheneaux's hard-hitting commentary (1973) on current land status. The authors reviewed the status of existing holdings, the submarginal land acquisition program begun in the 1930s, questions of Indians' acquiring surplus federal land, and the restoration of lands such as Blue Lake (Taos). Kickingbird and Ducheneaux spoke of restoring the original ratio of one million Indians to 135 million acres as stable acreage dating back to 1871 (before allotment took another 90 million acres). They suggested that today's 800,000 Indians times 135 acres per capita would result in about 100 million acres, nearly double the current figure (excluding the Alaska settlement). They would like to see the restoration of all Indian lands within federal field departments, full tribal jurisdiction over fishing and hunting areas, and a program of land acquisition to be instituted for all non-federal Indian tribes that are now landless.

There remains, of course, a continuing need to assess the strengths and weaknesses of land tenure on most reservations, where native and Euro-American institutions intermingle in complex ways and where the long history of allotment has taken its toll in farm fragmentation, unworkable consolidation schemes, and out-migration of Indian families. On the other hand, further studies of successful individual or corporate enterprises are essential if researchers, tribal leaders, and administrators are to discover better ways to make land tenure work for Indians.

Notes

1. Sources include: BIA, "Indian Lands and Related Facilities as of 1971," (map); *Idem.*, American Indians and Their Federal Relationship," (March 1972); *Idem.*, "Federal Trusteeship Terminated or in Process of Termination as of June 30, 1964"; Economic Development Administration, "Federal and State Indian Reservations: An EDA Handbook," (January 1971). This last source did not prove to be comprehensive, so that other items on the map have been based on correspondence.

2. Several reservations do not contain allotments; these are generally located in the Southwest. Those partly allotted form various configurations; lands allotted were arable at the time of allotment even though, in the samples and in other cases, much acreage remained uncleared or poorly utilized simply because water was unavailable or the cost of development prohibitive. Quite a number of studies contrast farming and ranching on allotted reservations; allotted land that had not been cleared for farming generally constituted obstacles to group use. Sources include: Hoffmeister (1945), Loomer (1955), Sutton (1964).

Works Cited in Section C

Aberle, 1948
Anderson, 1956
Anonymous, 1960
Aschmann, 1966
Bach, 1937
Ballas, *1960, 1962, 1970
Bennett, E. F., 1960
Bennett, R., 1970
Berger, 1968a/b
Berger & Mounce, 1971
Bounds, 1971
Bourne, 1953
Boyce, 1974
Brophy & Aberle, 1966
Burns, 1961
Burrill, 1972
Cahn, 1969
Calef, 1948
Cohen, F. S., 1937, 1941, 1953, 1971
Cohen, L. K., 1960
Collier, 1932, 1949
Colson, 1971
Dale, 1949
Debo, 1951, 1970
Deloria, 1970
Demsetz, 1967

Diamond et al., 1964
Dorner, 1961
Downes, 1945
Downs, 1964
Embry, 1956
Fay, 1967-72
FIL, 1958
Fonaroff, 1964, 1964, 1971
Forbes, 1965
Forde, 1931b
Fryer, 1942
Getty, 1961-62. 1963
Gibbons, 1965
Gilbert & Taylor, 1966
Gilbreath, 1973
Glasscock, 1938
Goding, 1958
Haas, 1957
Hackenberg, 1972
Harner, 1965
Herbert, 1962
Hertzberg, 1971
Hewes, 1942a/b, 1944
Hill, 1930
Hoffmeister, 1945
Hooker, 1972
Hoover, 1930, 1936

Hough, 1967
Humphrey, 1905
Hunt, 1970
Jackson, 1881
Janke, 1967
Jensen, 1964
Jorgensen, 1971, 1972
Kelly, L. C., 1963, 1968
Kelly, W. H., 1953
Kickingbird & Ducheneaux, 1973
Kinney, 1937, 1950
LaFarge, 1943
Laidlaw, 1960
Leupp, 1909, 1910
Levitan & Hetrick, 1971
Levy & Kunitz, 1971
Liljeblad, 1958
Longwell, 1961
Loomer, 1955
Loram & McIlwraith, 1943
Lurie, 1969
Macgregor, 1970
Manley, 1960
Manypenny, 1880
Martin, 1968, 1973
McArthur, 1949
McLane, 1955
Meriam, 1928
Mills, 1919
Mobley, 1970
Moorehead, 1914
Murray, 1953
Nagata, 1971
Nash, 1971
Nielson, 1967
Nurge, 1970
O'Reilly, 1970
Page, 1940
Philp, 1968
Platt, 1959
Price, 1969, 1973

Province, 1956
Radloff, 1966
Rietz, 1953
Roberts, 1943
Rountree, 1972
Schifter, 1970
Schlesinger, 1967
Schmeckebier, 1927
Schusky, 1959
Sells, 1917
Semple, 1952
Shane, 1959
Sherman, 1962
Simpson & Yinger, 1957
Snodgrass, 1968
Sonosky, 1960
Sorensen, 1971
Sorkin, 1971, 1973
Steiner, 1966
Stern, 1961-62, 1965
Stern & Boggs, 1971
Suttles, 1963
Sutton, 1964, 1967, 1970b
Taylor, 1970
Thomas, 1966a/b
Travis, 1968
Tuttle, 1971
Tyler, 1964a, 1973
U.S. Congress, Senate, 1958
Van De Mark, 1956
Voget, 1961-62
Waddell, 1969
Walker, D. E., 1971
Walker, F. A., 1874
Ward, 1956
Washburn, 1971b
Weightman, 1972
Willey, 1969
Wilson, H. C., 1961
Wilson, P. B., 1972

---

*Denotes works not actually cited, but relevant to this section.

SECTION AB

Aboriginal Title and Land Claims

Introduction

A number of scholars have asserted that Native Americans have fared better under our system of government than have their counterparts in other colonial and post-colonial countries (Cohen 1947; Horsman 1967; Washburn 1971b). More often than not, this view is derived from the treatment accorded these indigenous peoples by the invading culture in the process of acquiring their lands, rather than from any interpretation of subsequent relations or administration. Although Cohen observed that "... the keynote of our land policy has been recognition of Indian property rights" (pp. 36-37), judicial efforts to set the record straight by proper recompense for land taken by unconscionable means attest to our collective feeling that the Indians did not fare well in the long run. Characterized as "belated justice" (Washburn), these efforts have sought to purge our society of past inequities and restore faith in our system of government. Indeed, recognition of the right of an indigenous people to sue a government over the misdeeds of its predecessors is a consideration that few conquerors have ever accorded a subjugated people.

Indian land claims predate of course our government's willingness to be sued (suits have been accepted essentially since the 1880s); but the litigation that has involved the participation of scholars as well as members of the legal profession basically commenced with the passage of the Indian Claims Commission Act in 1946. Early cases heard by the U.S. Court of Claims (see Wilkinson 1966), while germane to this discussion, came before scholars took a direct interest or were sought out to participate in the development of background research for the prosecution of claims against the federal government. A number of these earlier cases pertaining to the land rights of Indians in the South (cf. Summers 1937; Chapman 1936, 1944) or in the Plains (cf. McNeely 1939), have received attention from historians writing special accounts of the tribes removed to or displaced within the Plains.

Readers should recognize that the published literature represents but part of a vast store of documentary and other archival material bearing on Indian lands, and that a significant part of the literature cited in Sections B and BC discusses the circumstances and legal provisions under which tribes relinquished their territories. Anson's generalizations (1970) about the Indians' plight in negotiations reveal clearly the substance and mood of historic accounts:

> It was probably impossible to negotiate equitable treaties from 1778 to 1870. In spite of official federal benevolence, no Senate would have ratified a treaty that penalized the federal government for the benefit of Indian tribes. At the same time, every Indian treaty penalized the political and cultural structure of the Indian party. However, there remains the legal fact that the treaties were made with tribes or political bodies, not with individual Indians, and the Indian Claims Commission findings seek to rectify injustices, no matter how far in the past, to tribes which still exist . . . . (PP. 302-3)

However, it is also important to recognize that a distinct legal literature on land claims exists, along with a body of methodological literature to which historians, anthropologists, and geographers have contributed.

In using this literature, it is necessary for the researcher to sift out much of the purely legal material—e.g., discussion of qualifications of expert witnesses, determination of which aspect of the law cases will be heard under, etc.— and focus on those implications of the litigation that bear on land tenure. Clearly, the Indian Claims Commission Act, which created the Commission and which established the parameters of litigation against the government, must be examined, along with the literature about the cases that have been tried under its provisions. We should also consider several questions that bear on the grounds for litigation and the problems faced by the researchers presenting appellant and defendant arguments.

In many of the cases before the Commission, tribes have sought compensation for the loss of lands to which they claimed "aboriginal title." Much emphasis will therefore be placed here on such problems of demonstrating aboriginal title as proving use and occupancy of a definable area and showing that such a holding was exclusive. Many related academic questions have arisen in connection with such issues as the meaning of "time immemorial," the conditions for recognizing an identifiable group with legal standing, and the problems of determination and verification of fixed boundaries marking exclusive holdings. Scholars have also examined the variable meaning of "tribe" and the difficulty of defining in Euro-American terms a native political unit and its territory. Just as the court cases have brought appellant and defendant adversaries together, so too they have pitted resourceful scholars against one another, though both sides have turned by and large to the same basic documentary, historic, ethnographic, and cartographic sources.

Outside of the legal arena, those who seek to understand how theory and practice can be brought to bear upon a legal matter that is very real to contemporary tribes will continue to be interested in this literature. The publication of the journal *Ethnohistory* is a major event that has resulted from scholarly involvement in these cases and the resulting developments in the methods of ethnohistory.

The Indian Claims Commission and the Law

Indian claims litigation can be approached from various angles, and the law has enumerated several categories under which a case can be tried. The bulk of the cases have ultimately been argued under the terms of the first category under the Indian Claims Commission Act, which deals with claims in law or equity arising under the constitution, laws, treaties, or executive orders of the United States. These cases have generally turned on the payment for lands acquired by treaty, by statute, or otherwise prior to the allotment act, or through the opening of reservations after allotment.

A second category concerns claims in law or equity involving torts. A third involves fraud, duress, and just compensation; a number of studies have discussed the interpretation of "unconscionable consideration," which is given in the law as a grounds for compensation. Selander (1947), in reviewing the scope of the I.C.C. Act, pointed out that although there was no formal prohibition against going behind the treaties to determine if any frauds or duress had been committed, the courts and the Commission were reluctant to do so; in one case the courts noted that "the power to make and unmake [treaties] is essentially political and not judicial . . ." (p. 411). A fourth category concerns claims against treaties of cession without compensation and involves the interpretation of rights of occupancy. This category seeks a clear interpretation of such rights in terms of later compensation (cf. Oliver 1959). A final category, which has been acknowledged as a somewhat innovative provision in Indian claims litigation, concerns "fair and honorable dealings," turning mostly on moral rather than legal questions (cf. Kelly 1971).

Barney, head of the Indian Claims Section of the Land Division of the Department of Justice from 1946 until his death in 1974, examined (1955, 1960) the problems of defining the claimant and what has been allowable. He found, for example, that the claims of Western Cherokees and Creeks who had not relocated were allowed, but not those of the Chippewa and Ottawa Nations. He also outlined the arguments over the meaning of "immemorial possession," questions of definable territory and exclusive occupancy, and problems in determining market value (Barney 1963) and the interpretation of treaties. The functions and performance of the Commission have been interpreted (1960) by Barker, a lawyer involved in land claims before the Commission since its inception and by Vance (1969), one of the commissioners. Of especial interest has been the interpretation given by the Commission to the determination of aboriginal title. Only after the decisions of the Commission were recognized by the Court of Claims, which has appellate jurisdiction, did the grounds for aboriginal title begin to become clear; until then the Commission had tended to hold to a narrower view of its jurisdiction. Previously, the grant of investigatory power, which is a provision of the I.C.C. Act, had lain unused. Vance most particularly criticized the Commission's failure to expedite cases, but he urged changes that were not regarded as necessarily the best by the legal profession or by anthropologists.

These legal considerations take on meaning only when we examine how historians and anthropologists were able to work under the law to provide expertise for the reconstruction of original title based on exclusive use and occupancy by Indians. Several other papers should be cited here: O. C. Stewart (1958) effectively traced the steps involved in land claims litigations, as seen from the viewpoint of a participating anthropologist; F. S. Cohen (1945) offered a brief legal evaluation of the earlier claims litigation; and LeDuc (1957), expert witness, reviewed the evolution of the Commission and its functions during its first decade.

A more recent study of the Indian Claims Commission should be singled out for its sweeping and largely critical review. Danforth (1973) has able updated the legal history of the Commission in several important ways. While her study overlaps earlier ones in reviewing the Court of Claims and early efforts to create an Indian Claims Commission, she comes to examine procedural problems, conflicts in the application of the enabling law, and moral issues. She reinforces Vance's findings (1969) that the Commission has overly stressed one of its two authorized functions—adjudication—to the disparagement of the other—investigation; in fact, she demonstrates that this unifunctional emphasis has led the Commission to operate mostly as a court in which litigants are pitted against each other, and she notes,

> Had it been accepted that claims-settling dealt rather with finding facts on cases which in principle have been acknowledged as valid, it would not have been necessary for both the Indian groups and the Department of Justice to conduct separate investigations. (P. 376)

Danforth is sensitive to the fact that legal-bureaucratic procedures have been a failing of the Commission, and in a legal atmosphere ethnological facts and advice lose some of their meaning; this is supported by heavy reliance on the writings of Prof. Nancy Lurie (1955, 1956, 1957), which are also discussed below. Danforth shares with many other observers the idea that thanks to the academic expertise brought to land claims litigation, many tribes have felt they received a fair hearing. Interestingly enough, she also noted in passing that one area of unresolved land claims remains to be litigated: fraudulent or unethical acquisition of Indian allotments. Regrettably, this problem lies outside the jurisdiction of the Commission, since it deals with individual Indians rather than tribes.

Aboriginal Title

Who owned America before the coming of the Europeans? Although it is seemingly self-evident that the indigenous peoples held the land, this answer tends to oversimplify the situation insofar as questions of international law are concerned, especially in the application of Anglo-American legal and property traditions. Thus the distinction between aboriginal title and Indian occupancy is not semantic; rather it is a legal consideration that came to involve numerous scholars in new kinds of historical and ethnographic research. The record of treaty-making demonstrates that the United States as a sovereign did negotiate and purchase—that is, transfer the title of—Indian lands (cf. Washburn 1971b), despite the arguments that we secured the continent through a "dual conquest" over land tenure and over polity, as asserted by Jennings (1971b).

In spite of the fact that Fried (1952) saw Indian-white land relations as a contest between two quite different social systems—tribal and Euro-American—over the control of territory, many of the ablest legal minds have maintained the position that the United States followed a policy of respecting the Indians' land rights. In this view, in the absence of treaties, executive orders, or statutes, the U.S. upheld the native right of occupancy and indeed secured land mainly by purchase. F. S. Cohen (1947) cited

California and the 18 unratified treaties as a major exception to the land purchase rule. Cohen's view was that the creation of a reservation was the withholding of a tract of land from cession by the tribes and originated with them; it was not a grant by the government. Furthermore, he suggested that the policy of land acquisition by purchase rather than by conquest ultimately benefitted realty and economic practices, for by our conscientious acquisitions we achieved better title security. That is, legal recognition and payment for Indian lands assisted, rather than hampered, land development; for the government, he asserted, could not later merely give the land away. As he put it, "Because land which the government had paid for had to be sold to settlers for cash or equivalent services, our West has escaped the fate of areas of South America, Canada, and Australia . . ." (in L. K. Cohen 1960, p. 283). F. S. Cohen also reviewed (1941) the origin of many of our ideas about aboriginal or native title. In his study of Spanish origins of Indian title (1942) Cohen suggested that our federal Indian laws owed much of their content to Hispanic origins; his conclusion was that our policies and administration tended to conform to human legal ideals of sixteenth-century Spanish theological jurisprudence, especially as expressed in the thinking of Francisco de Vitoria. Although such discussions seem tangential, readers might refer to Pennington's (1970) re-evaluation of the position taken by Las Casas, who influenced the evolution of native policy in both Americas. Las Casas had held that the Indians' *dominium* was legitimate and just and that the Spaniards had no right to usurp that title; he argued that the Pope could not grant the Spanish king *dominium* in the New World without the consent of the Indians; that the Spanish could gain just title only if they secured the consent of the Indians to being under Spanish rule. It is interesting that studies of Vitoria and Las Casas suggest that much of our diplomacy and dealings with Indians seem, in part, to stem from early thinking about international law. (Related studies include Bourke 1894; Dart 1921; Ezell 1955; Kappler 1903-38, Vol. IV, 1929; M.K.M.B. 1942; Price 1973.)

Other researchers have sought explanations of the native rights to land or justifications for taking that land on the basis of natural law. For example, it has been claimed that the rights of agriculturalists are superior to those of "savage" hunting tribes, and that Indians are entitled to that land which they had subdued or improved; essentially, this is the bias in favor of farming. Other studies ask whether sovereigns had the power to extinguish a title, and what powers the colonies had prior to nationhood, and the states thereafter, to extinguish title or assume jurisdiction over Indians and their lands. Snow (1921), Kinney (1937), and Washburn (1971b) are good examples of sources that delve into colonial and national precedents; Snow's study is especially useful as a comparative interpretation that deals with other colonials and native peoples. Washburn sought to dispel the impression that Indians were treacherous wanderers deserving to be dispossessed of their lands; he considered, in the ethico-legal terms of the times, the differences between natural rights and aboriginal title, summarizing the view that prevailed in the early nineteenth century as the country embarked on a half-century or more of treaty-writing.

> The "natural" rights of the Indians had to be seen in terms of the "speculative" rights of the earlier European Monarchs, the "juridical" rights of their successor American states, and the "practical" economic demands of the millions who now populated the continent. (P. 66)

Not far afield from the discussion of aboriginal title and land purchases is the literature that discusses the justification for taking Indian lands. Moralistic arguments, like those presented by Kimmey (1960)—that the Indians were more than repaid, for they gained Christianity in exchange for whatever lands they lost—have had little place in the courtroom. Rejection of native land institutions (e.g., Nichols 1970, who observed that Euro-Americans found communal ownership unworthy) has also been of little relevance to the litigation. In any event, much of the literature that examines the concepts of manifest destiny and natural rights, or considers the roles, for example, of missionaries and squawmen, was written as part of the background to determining original title and exclusive use and occupancy. In a pair of studies (1957, 1959) and in his book (1971b), Washburn examined the range of arguments that concerned ethical, legal, moralistic, and other positions taken on the matter of Indian land dispossession. Many of these views are aired in Pearce (1967), Eisinger (1948), Sheehan (1969), Schifter (1954), and briefly recounted by Fey and McNickle (1959, 1970).

The Indian's views of his land rights, of course, must be taken into account. Contrasting and in some ways complementing the contributions of native informants to ethnographic reconstruction of tribal territoriality and aboriginal occupancy, are the statements and speeches to be found in Indian oratory. Although hardly "expert testimony" in the courtroom sense, they reflect Indian response under duress to white aggression, especially to the doctrine of discovery that allegedly gave Euro-Americans a "right" to extinguish Indian title. To the extent that individual Indian leaders reflected their culture, their statements about their view of nature, earth, and land rights are important indigenous documents. Many of these speeches, and similarly much Indian correspondence, may be found in historical studies, legal testimony, anthologies, and even fiction. It is significant that in his introduction to an anthology of Indian oratory,

Frederick W. Turner III (in Armstrong 1971) states that "From Henry
Hudson to [General] O. O. Howard, the major theme of these documents
is land: who owned it, what title meant, and how much of it could be
sacrificed without destroying the sources of life itself" (p. xiv). He notes,
too,

> how in responding to advancing whites the Indian was compelled to
> move from strong assertions of his natural rights to appeals to what
> he could only hope was common humanity. . . . how the arrogance
> of the whites grows as they move ever westward . . . until we come
> to the very end of the long trail there on the westward-most rim of
> the land. . . . (P. xiv)

Indian oratory demands that we examine important Indian messages,
many of which respond, or react, to white arrogance and spurious justifications for the taking of the land. The realm of Indian oratory constitutes
an almost untapped and largely unsynthesized source of the Indian's
perception of territoriality and his interpretation of his rights. In addition
to the collected speeches and written statements of Indian leaders, one
should, in this "new environmental era" of the 1970s, consider the recent
interpretations of the Indian land ethic in writings on property perception
in America. For example, Dukelow and Zakheim (1972) and Large (1973)
turn to Indian conservation ethics and perceptions of rights to resources in
order to contrast them with Euro-American attitudes of dominance over
the environment, especially as expressed in the function of private property in our society. They cite various literary works as sources of statements and interpretations that sensitively comprehend Indian views of
earth. Among them are the writings of Frank Waters, John Neihardt, Dee
Brown, and Tom McLuhan. In addition, Juergensmeyer and Wadley
(1974) turned to the Indians' communal tenure orientation toward resources to find a suitable parallel to their argument that the "commons" is
a viable concept for the conservation of land and other resources. I would
also add the somewhat mystical essays by John Collier (1949, 1962),
Commissioner of Indian Affairs from 1933 to 1945, who attempted to
capture in print the Indians' perception of man's relationship to nature.

Readers will profit from the perusal of several anthologies which
include expressions of native concern over cession and dispossession, as in
the speeches of Seneca, Potawatomi, Flathead, Sioux, Hopi, and Kickapoo
Indian leaders (cf. Armstrong 1971; Forbes 1964; Moquin and Van Doren
1973). Similar oratory on land purchases by Sioux, Shawnee, Yakima, and
Miami Indians and reactions to the removal of the Sauk and Apache may
be found in Armstrong and in Vanderwerth (1971). Forbes reports the
Pyramid Lake Indians' position on protection of their lands and waters;

Deloria (1971) and Vogel (1972) include statements or interpretations of Indian reaction to the taking of tribal lands for reservoirs by eminent domain. Pleas to sustain treaty rights to hunting and fishing for the Nisqually and Yakima appear, respectively, in Vogel and in Moquin and Van Doren. On this same problem, other intepretations include Indian statements or interpreted views: Wilson (1959), Macgregor (1949), and Coffeen (1972). This sampling by no means exhausts available documentation of the Indians' views of their land rights. Since Indians in recent decades have testified before congressional committee hearings on proposed legislation that would modify land rights or take their lands, this testimony and "forest diplomacy" oratory provide a body of ideas, perceptions, and facts that will prove instructive in the pursuit of belated justice.

Use and Occupancy

Scholars entered the litigation before the Indian Claims Commission when they were asked by the litigants to find evidence for or against tribal claims to the aboriginal use and occupancy of specific territories. This request related to the fourth class under Section Two of the Indian Claims Commission Act and concerned the question of exclusive use. Barney (1955, 1960) emphasized that both use and occupancy were matters of inference drawn from the facts as interpreted by the Commission or by the courts. The requirement that exclusiveness be determined made it necessary to define the claimant group and to argue the facts of aboriginal subsistence. Under these terms, many areas could not be shown to have been exclusively occupied by any one of the claimants; often utilization of an area by a given band or tribe was not continuous but seasonal or even periodic. The literature deals with the methodological problems of proving or disproving exclusive use and occupancy by a particular tribe, and it demonstrates the validity of ecological and ethnohistoric reconstructions. For example, it was possible to fix boundaries by determining who comprised the landholding unit and what constituted the tribe, and to decide whether historical, ethnographic, linguistic, or other bases for the construction of territorial maps were the proper means of fixing boundaries.

More than one scholar has noted that to make an award to one tribe is to diminish another's claim to an adjacent area. Manners (1956) stressed that a determination that an area had joint use meant, in terms of the law, that nobody would be compensated. Steward (1955b), in questioning the validity of applying to Indians the Euro-American concept of exclusive rights to land, said that it was unlikely, though not impossible, that some Indian societies claimed such rights to a territory. Lurie (1955) warned of the danger that the lawyer's concern with precedents might lead to overgeneralizing the ethnologist's findings:

> ... the ethnologist may see his concepts of land ownership as derived from one society interpreted as firm precedents in another case. ... extreme and explicit boundary-consciousness in one tribe may not be repeated in another. Superficially it appears that in the latter case the evidence of use, occupancy and extent of range is not as "strong" as in the former case. (P. 364)

Furthermore, in mapping tribal territories, she felt that data on aboriginal occupancy and resource development were equally valid, no matter whether informants were conscious or unconscious of the extent of their activities. In attempting to reconstruct original territories as claimed, the Commissioners have tended to be most interested in clear statements on use and occupancy at the time land was ceded or lost, rather than those attempting to prove possession since "time immemorial." Lurie reinforced her position on the time of taking in another paper (1956) in which she noted that the Commissioners, because they tended to focus on exclusive occupancy, more often rejected claims to areas utilized by more than one tribe. Such problems arise in the effort to make logical facts and concepts understood by a legal audience immersed in Anglo-American property traditions and land law which emphasize definitive boundaries and nearly exclusive rights to resources within those bounds.

The most interesting and perhaps most exciting aspect of the cases was the claims for compensation for cessions of aboriginal domain. Questions of compensable interest came up in numerous cases, in which aboriginal title had to be proved. In the absence of treaties, or where treaties were contested, the proof of use and occupancy has depended upon historical and anthropological evidence and its admissibility in court. Here, archival data, historical documents, chronicles, and the general fusion of the historical and anthropological methods, as well as the refinement of ecological methodology, aided the efforts of scholars on both sides of the cases. The best general summary of the cases, role of law, and anthropological participation was prepared by Lurie (1957), but an updated interpretation of land claims, considering theory and specific cases, appears in Washburn (1971b). Anthropologists entered land claims litigation mainly in response to the need to validate claims to exclusive aboriginal use and occupancy, and O. C. Stewart (1961), who had served as an expert witness, emphasized that despite the efforts of the defense, ethnographic accounts have tended to substantiate the claims (cf. Ray 1955a).

The literature on California and Intermontane litigation is of especial interest because so much of these cases has turned on attempts to prove aboriginal use and occupancy. It is here that one sees how anthropological research has paid off. Stewart (1966a) applied various aboriginal land-ownership theories to the investigation of Great Basin territoriality and presented arguments for and against a finding of exclusive use and occupancy of definable areas. In his study (1961) of the California land claims case, he examined the opposing views: the argument for complete aboriginal use offered by the plaintiff team headed by Prof. Alfred Kroeber and the ecological theory of partial use offered by the defense research team headed by Prof. Ralph Beals. Stewart tended to equate the ecological theory advanced by Beals and his team with the nuclear area or primary subsistence area as defined by many ethnologists. He also discussed the decision of the Commission, which incorporated the testimony of the petitioners's expert witness. The Indians of California case generated a tremendous amount of lively ethnographic interest in aboriginal California; it also led Kroeber to reexamine (1962) the aboriginal bases of landownership. Furthermore, it served as the background for a new ecological typology of California Indians (Beals and Hester 1956). Thus both plaintiff and defendant expert witnesses published academic studies based upon their research into aboriginal use and occupancy.

Application of a more general nature also resulted from anthropological participation in claims research. A much-quoted paper by Kroeber (1955) attempted to generalize on the nature of the landholding unit for tribal America, contending that the unit had to be smaller than the tribe. Partly on the basis of his interpretations of the role of the band and tribelet in aboriginal California in contrast to the role of the tribes in the East, he tended to equate tribe with a larger nationality, which would be ethnic and nonpolitical. Kroeber asserted that the Indian Claims Commission tended to construe cases in tribal terms; the tribe, he and others suggested, became a factor only after contact, especially after federal treaty negotiations (cf. Cohen 1942). O. C. Stewart referred (1970) to the identification of the Shoshoneans as a tribe as an "anthropologist's fiction," although Wallace (1957) made a strong case for saying that true political tribes had held territory in the Northeast. Manners (1957) supported the argument for smaller land units in his analysis of the political geography of the Walapai, for he found that these Indians did not express any true tribal unity in aboriginal or early contact times. Kroeber's reconstruction (1951) of the Mohave epic of the occupation of the Mohave Valley and K. M. Stewart's later observations (1969) on Mohave land claims data tend to reinforce the view that these Indians, like most agrarian peoples in the Southwest, had tribal organization. On the other hand, Opler (1971b), in reconstructing Jicarilla Apache territory, rejects the notion that these people were a tribe.

Since "virtually every acre of land west of the Mississippi River was subject to at least one claim" (I.C.C. 1968), delineation of exclusively defined territories of use and occupancy raised methodological questions. Clarification of the landholding unit did contribute to a better interpretation of the historic and ethnographic literature, and it assisted in determination in the field of just what areas should be bounded and how they might be rendered on maps. Barney (1960) alluded to the anthropologist's inclination to outline general areas of tribal domain on the basis of linguistic differentiation; he noted that this criterion would not necessarily establish that an Indian group used or occupied such areas within specifically defined external boundaries. At least one scholar has demonstrated, however, how linguistic data can provide a good picture of tribal mapping in the intertribal zone of Tonto Apache and Yavapai; Brugge (1965) utilized historical records of Indian scouts and their linguistic affiliations.

Lurie (1957) observed that the Commission had accepted the "Indians of California" as an identifiable group, even though the landholding unit was the band or the tribelet whose aboriginal bounds did not conform to state boundaries. Yet the Commission refused to recognize the Chippewa Nation as a distinct entity occupying territory. These distinctions as to which group constituted a tribe or tribelet and which should be a legally-identified group represent, for example, the kind of problem in interpretation that ethnologists and lawyers found in case after case. In discussing tribal boundaries, Lurie contrasted the interpretations of contiguous territories offered by plaintiff tribes to the Justice Department's theory of land use based on "nuclear areas," which assumed much unused or sparsely occupied land. Lurie asserted:

> As far as anthropologists are concerned, the question remains open whether the traditional techniques of tribal mapping are simply an established convention convenient for academic purposes, or whether such maps reflect the empirical conclusions of many independent researchers in regard to the proper designation of territoriality of human groups generally considered. (P. 66)

The Justice Department emphasized intensive economic utilization as the basis for proving use and occupancy, whereas the plaintiff tribes, in laying claim to territory, emphasized seasonal use as well as such noneconomic factors as social and religious uses, all of which tended to suggest more extensive occupancy.

As Section A demonstrated, the mapping of tribal territories is a venerable practice among ethnographers in this country. Yet the accuracy of the delineations produced by the methodology of such mapping has been incompletely evaluated, especially with regard to the soundness of linguistic information as a basis for demonstrating the distribution of Indians in precontact or early contact times. As for ecological approaches, they have illuminated the livelihood basis for distributions, but not the political or tribal. Such studies as Hickerson's (1965), which analyzes the "debatable" buffer zone created by intertribal competition and warfare between Chippewa and Sioux Indians, demonstrate an ecological fact (in this case, the distribution and habits of the Virginia deer) and its influence on boundary perception as well as non-use of the zone. Certainly land claims research triggered even greater interest in earlier mapping efforts. Even more important, it led modern scholars to scrutinize the older maps anew.

Researchers have turned to available cartographic sources as well as to linguistic and ecological data. O. C. Stewart (1966a), with observations by d'Azevedo (1964), supported the academic merits of fixed boundaries based on ethnographic and historical literature. In his Great Basin study he provided a valuable series of maps reconstructing the territories of various landholding units, based upon the work of numerous scholars. Superimposing some 13 separate sets of data on one map (his no. 8), he found a marked tendency for the different criteria to conform to the same definite locations; on another map (his no. 9) he showed the claims area of tribes in the Basin cases. Similarly, in his Bannock study (Stewart 1970) he demonstrated that ". . . the device of indicating a separate territory for the Bannock in Idaho appears to be completely improper. It is much better to show the Bannock and Shoshoni as jointly occupying the area where the Bannock are identified" (p. 191). Here again, Stewart made available a series of maps on a common base, and defined his own determined bounds of Shoshoni Indians, revealing the approximation of Bannock to the area of Shoshoni through covariant research. This method, well known to geographers, consists in the mapping of comparative data on a common base map or on a series of such maps drawn to the same scale. Covariant research may confirm a specific configuration of tribal areas by multiple representation of dots or lines, or simply of names of villages for which exact site locations are not known. Few land claims in print utilize such data, but the methodology has no doubt been employed in court. (Cf. Ruby and Brown 1970, and see Figure 6, which is a composite of the tenures that have existed or now exist; as such the diagram synthesizes findings in dozens of sources.) Ultimately Stewart showed how closely the Bannock and Shoshoni were interwoven before and during contact times. He consistently supported the fixed-boundary delineation of tribes and argued that it was an established practice among anthropologists at least since the work of Wissler. The fact that so many Great Basin cases—turning on determination of original title based on exclusive aboriginal use and occupancy—have been decided in favor of the plaintiffs, he suggested, vindicated this methodology for mapping tribal areas. Such maps and cartographic methodology have revealed the significance of otherwise obscure data and have clarified information that had never been seen in ecological perspective by earlier researchers.

Review of tribal maps has proven useful in evaluating their utility in claims reconstruction. Heizer (1966) brought together most of the published studies and two important maps on native territoriality in California (see earlier discussion in Section A); as a source book, it is especially useful in relating language and territory, but Heizer does not fully deal with the relationship of this study to claims cases. Driver's earlier map (1953) of tribal territories came under sharp criticism from both Ray (1955b) and Wheeler-Voegelin (1956). It was an effort to depict cartographically the distribution of racial, linguistic, and cultural data on various tribes, and it brought together some new and hitherto unpublished materials. But his critics observed that tribal boundary lines were not so definitely represented, despite his apparent emphasis on boundaries. Wheeler-Voegelin criticized Driver and his colleagues for assigning what purported to be boundaries to specific areal occupancy in cases where the tribes may never in fact have been there. Ray, discussing Driver's potential influence on claims litigation, summed up the argument:

> . . . it is unfortunate that a work of such a character should appear at a time when the welfare of the Indians may be affected by such uncritical and unprofessional use as may occur in litigation before the Indian Land Claims Commission. (P. 146)

If the determination of exclusive use and occupancy proved difficult, so did the process of estimating what the tract finally decided upon was worth a hundred or more years ago. Many appraisers have assumed that because the environmental and economic conditions at the time of taking differed considerably from contemporary conditions involving the realty market, so should the principles of land valuation differ, but the Indian Claims Commission set the fair market value of the tract as a whole at the time of taking as the criterion (Barney 1963). Barney noted the contribution of economic history to these historical appraisals, although he acknowledged that land appraisers have generally had little of the background needed for these special valuation studies. Among his many observations, Barney indicated that appraisers working on land claims cases have found it difficult to adequately appraise the value of vast tracts of

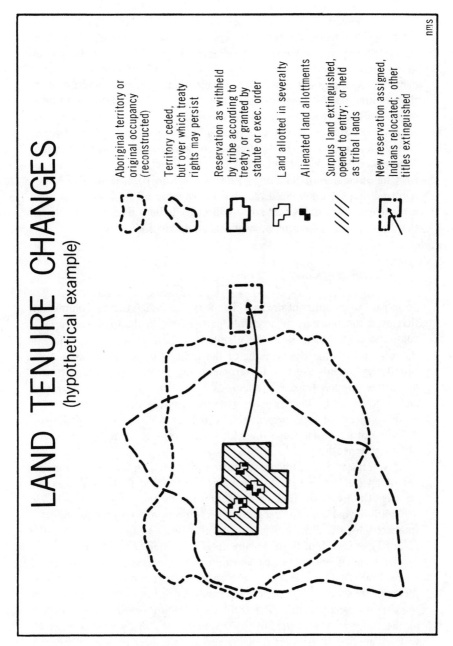

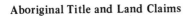

Figure 6

land located at considerable distance from adequate transportation. Lacking comparable historical data about the value of similarly remote tracts on the frontier, they have tended to overemphasize the role of transportation as a catalyst influencing land values. In his study, Barney noted land size and the time-period involved, and stressed the factor of demand, especially the demand for cheap public land, and the character of the resource itself (for example, it was assumed that only land with timber on it could produce crops). Given the limitations of present-day knowledge of conditions at the time of taking, it was difficult to appraise accurately. To throw light on the facts of land speculation on the various frontiers, at least one historian has utilized claims data to good advantage (see the discussion of Swierenga 1966, in Section B). Inasmuch as Barney reported that the generalized valuations have ranged from $.40 to $3.75 an acre, it is small wonder that some California Indians have recently stated that they would not accept an award calculated at $.47 an acre.[1]

A Sampling of Court Testimony

So large is the number of dockets filed with the Indian Claims Commission that even the research of academic participants in the litigation forms a voluminous literature. Both the plaintiffs—tribes, bands, or other identifiable groups within the meaning of the Indian Claims Commission Act—and the defendant—the U.S. Government, represented by the Department of Justice—prepared sizeable documents as each case was in preparation and in court. O. C. Stewart wrote good step-by-step analyses (1959, 1961) of this process of legal preparation, which he followed in the Chippewa and California Indian cases in which he served as expert witness and observer, respectively.

Two classes of documents submitted to the Indian Claims Commission are of special interest to the researcher: proposed findings and expert reports. The proposed findings are submitted by the plaintiff in each case and are followed by a varying pattern of "objections to proposed findings" (prepared by the Justice Department), "answers to objections" (by the plaintiff), etc. Each of these documents is submitted with a brief.

The reports are submitted as exhibits in the cases, and the principal researcher often appears in court as an expert witness. Such reports prepared by scholars have often appeared in print in modified form once the case has been decided. The scholarly literature has not made wide use of the findings or reports, but it is expected that this wealth of research will be applied to broader projects such as the preparation of the new Handbook of North American Indians, and will provide background to new ethnohistories of the American Indian.

Most of the original documentation of land claims research prepared for litigation is housed in the files of the I.C.C., the National Archives, and various law offices and universities. Much of this material is available in microfiche form, with indexes in hard cover (Ross 1973b), and a number of expert reports have been reprinted in book form. The Commission's decisions are also available, both on paper and on microfiche, together with index volumes (Native American Rights Fund 1973a; Ross 1973a).[2]

Two petitioners' findings will be examined here, Lower Pend D'Oreille (1957), prepared by J. W. Cragun, and Goshute Tribe (1971), prepared by R. W. Barker, both of the law firm of Wilkinson, Cragun and Barker. The former study concerned the question of Indian title as based on use, occupancy, and possession; it dealt with reconstruction of data on territory and considered criteria of linguistic boundaries and village sites in determining territory. For example, researchers made considerable use of the earlier writings (see Section A) of Teit, Chalfant, Ray and Spier and others who prepared territorial maps and linguistic-area maps for the Northwest; expert witness A. H. Smith, who also worked in this field, testified in court. In the case for exclusive occupancy, for example, the specific observations of ethnologists, in print and in the testimony, formed an important part of the evidence. The petitioner's lawyers argued that they had demonstrated exclusive use and occupancy both by proving the facts of such use and occupancy through ethnographic reconstruction, and by showing that government recognition of aboriginal title was implicit in the efforts of the territorial governor to negotiate and to map Indian territory; these efforts were demonstrated through examination of historical documents.

The other study—by attorneys for the Goshute Tribe—concerned a subsequent Commission hearing to determine the value of the land at the time of taking in 1875. This heavily documented testimony demonstrated the step-by-step procedures used in documenting the classification and values of land resources. Since nearly half of the claim related to mineral values, the bulk (pp. 43-190) of the document was devoted to a careful historical reconstruction of mining activities. The study utilized not only mineral literature but also government reports, contemporary journal articles, and newspaper stories to help reconstruct production and value, mine by mine and district by district. Although it is not the most readable text, it is nevertheless a superb historical study. It was necessary to restrict attention to the period of taking, and some observers will note how closely the study approximates the methodology of historical geography espoused and practiced by Ralph H. Brown. Brown was a geographer who emphasized a reconstruction of the geography of the past on the basis of contemporary writings and statistical and other data available, subject to selective supplementation by examination of later publications and fieldwork.[3]

The Quechan Tribe of the Fort Yuma Reservation, California, Petitioners (U.S. Department of Justice 1964) is a defendant's proposed finding in published form and contains similar carefully prepared testimony including data on the physical environment, historical evidence of occupancy, and arguments against the Quechan Tribe's claim of aboriginal title. It too includes a volume of historical and ethnographic data and reprints significant passages from laws and documents; thus it demonstrates the validity of utilizing historical, ethnographic, and administrative source materials.

The methodologies of the Berkeley School in anthropology, geography, and history come to the fore in the preparation of background studies variously identified as ecological, ethnohistorical, ethnological, or historical (see Stewart 1961 for observations on Kroeber's contributions). One will note that cross-disciplinary means were developed in order to provide suitable testimony. While each of these studies was directed to a specific, practical application, they are academic endeavors standing on their own merits, and while it may not be true in every case, many of these works grew out of or led to doctoral studies in their disciplines. Harvey [n.d.] is a good example of a doctoral study that became the raw material for ethnohistorical research as part of the Indians of California case, which was heard under the provisions of part 5, section 2. The author examined settlement and social organization and provided a wealth of historical and ethnographic data. His study of the Yuma (1961) explored the nature of aboriginal use and occupancy at the time of contact by means of detailed ethnobotanical and ethnozoological analyses. Aschmann (1966) is a spin-off of original claims research relating to the same Yuma cases. In an older work by Stanley (1954) the Yuma figure importantly in a historical geographic study of the lower Colorado. Aschmann (1963) is a study similar in method to his 1966 article; it dealt with the Tonto Apache and demonstrated more fully the applicability of the ecological approach to the reconstruction of aboriginal occupancy and use patterns. Here historical materials served to identify place and event relationships and to corroborate informants' data and ethnographic accounts.

Related Published Studies

Land claims litigation is reported and interpreted in numerous histories of Indian tribes (Anson 1970; Rockwell 1956; Ruby and Brown 1970; Wallace 1957) and is the subject of various papers and manuscripts dating back to the last century. Chapman (1965) and Johnson (1966) are among the few book-length studies. The Chapman study of the Otoes and Missourias demonstrated the range of competence of a historian who has specialized in Indian-white relations in the Great Plains (cf. his 1957 and 1962 papers and see Sections B and BC). The Otoe and Missouria case affirmed the principle that when aboriginal title is proved, the taking of the land is compensable under the Indian Claims Commission Act. Several chapters explore the litigation, the nature of the award, and the recovery under aboriginal title. In reconstructing the circumstances of preparing and arguing the merits of aboriginal title, Chapman showed how, for example, the defendant sought to change the claims law so as to exclude aboriginal title from its coverage (this was in 1956); the plaintiff's reply was that such exclusion would eliminate more than two-thirds of the claims without a trial. There is much methodology in this study, describing the working relations of tribe, attorney, and expert witness.

Chapman's shorter study of the Kiowa, Comanche, and Apache (1962) traced the litigation through the jurisdictional act and set forth the issues of historical valuation and the discrepancy between plaintiff's determination (in this case, $3.75 an acre) and the defendant's ($.50 an acre). Chapman looked at the variable and often regrettable role of the Indian agent in securing treaties that a century later have become objects of much criticism and litigation. Chapman's Nemaha Half-breed study (1957) was part of the Otoe and Missouria litigation, for which Chapman testified, and it is discussed in the larger volume (1965) as well.

The Johnson volume (1966) is devoted to the California claims case and is mostly a historical analysis of the case and its background; it depends heavily on statutes and other documents. The California land claims issues have invited many scholars to explore various ramifications of the unratified treaties. For earlier discussions see Ellison's study (1925), Lipps' thin volume (1932), and two studies by O. C. Stewart (1961 and *in press*). Several manuscripts also examine the background to the loss of title to Indian land within California (Dyer 1945, Sutton 1964).

More recently there has been intense interest in native claims in Alaska prior to and since the establishment of the Land Settlement Act (Arnold 1967; Block 1971; Goldschmitt and Haas 1946, which preceded most of the agitation for a settlement; Federal Field Committee 1968). The latter volume, an enormous government document, is the last word in the study of Alaskan natives and their lands. Several interpretations now have the advantage of perspective (Nathan 1972; Kickingbird and Ducheneaux 1973; Lysyk 1973). Contained in the Nathan study are two papers that examine native rights in Alaska relative to other federal resource issues within that state.

It can hardly be said that the plaintiff tribes have won all of the cases decided by the Indian Claims Commission, or that all potential cases have been permitted in court. The legal record of the cases heard and decided is available (see note 2). However, too few cases have been subjected to the careful examination that Chapman has given to the Otoe and Missouria case. An increase in the number of land claims histories will certainly not glut the market, nor will additional investigations into land speculation, utilizing land claims documents, go unread. With the revitalization of studies in colonial history and historical geography, land claims research will go a long way toward redressing the complaints of the many Indian observers who have found Indian-white ethnohistory wanting. It may be hoped that Indian scholars, especially those who combine a legal and historical bent, will undertake to explore further the question of aboriginal title and tribal claims to territory.

Land Claims and Alternative Means of Redress

Thus far, claims litigation has focused on the recovery of a determined monetary value for all lands taken by fraud, duress, or similar means. The recovery of the land itself, as recently seen in Alaska, has been considered a legitimate matter for adjudication, legislation, and executive action. One might also note, for example, the administrative transfer of Blue Lake back to the Taos Pueblo (Bodine 1973; Whatley 1969) and the similar restoration of Mt. Adams as a sacred land to the Yakima Indians. Additionally, Congress did authorize the establishment of a forty-acre reservation in California for the Bridgeport Indian colony of Paiutes.[4] Prior to these events, Indians have rarely received land restorations despite all of their pleading and the intervention of friends. Even during the Collier years (1933-45), when the government was most supportive of new land programs for the tribes, efforts to secure submarginal lands through purchase realized very little acreage (cf. Gilbert and Taylor 1966; Kickingbird and Ducheneaux 1973).

Recent Indian entry onto "surplus" government lands, including the island of Alcatraz and several unoccupied military reserves, and the Kootenai declaration of "war" at Bonners Ferry, Idaho, suggest that Indians are going to pursue more volatile means for the recovery or the acquisition of land. Perhaps it has been the few gestures of land return already enumerated that have spirited many Indians to become more active and vocal in the matter of land acquisition. The Indians also have support from several advocates of a policy recommending that the government consider restoring surplus public domain to the tribes (cf. Kickingbird and Ducheneaux 1973, Chap. 4; Hooker 1972; Hodge 1973). Reservation and relocated Indians, frustrated by trying to eke out an existence on meager land resources or disillusioned over BIA efforts to assist them in finding urban employment, have good cause for seeking land increments. Even Indians who have not been identified with reservations for a generation or more have enlisted the support of fellow Indians and white allies in efforts to secure land as a base for Indian identity.

A most recent event, still pending as I write, demonstrates how this might work to the betterment of the Indian. Congress has prepared a bill that would restore some 186,000 acres to the Havasupai Indians by removing acreage from both the Grand Canyon National Park and the adjacent Kaibab National Forest. Writing in the *Sierra Club Bulletin* (the Sierra Club has openly opposed such restoration), Watkins (1974) has pointed out that these Indians originally accepted litigation as the means to redress their grievance, and now they would ask that the judgment awarding them millions of dollars be set aside in favor of a return of land. According to law, as discussed earlier, the Indian Claims Commission cannot hand down a land claims judgment award in other than monetary terms. Watkins and others contend that the Indians have no special expertise to manage these lands now held in public trust and administered by conservation agencies. They feel that ultimately such a land return would lead to development of the area in ways contrary to the purposes for which both national park and forest lands were set aside. As an example of this concern, Watkins cites the fact that both the Havasupai and their neighbors, the Hualapai, are on record as supporting the construction of a dam on the Colorado River, one that would lead to the inundation of a portion of the Grand Canyon National Monument. Arizona has had an interest in such a dam ever since that state won a decision in the *Arizona vs. California* water rights case in 1963. Of course, Congress has the legislative prerogative to transfer public lands to the tribe, or to any tribe for that matter, but such an act might seriously erode public confidence in current national environmental efforts. Moreover, were the land transferred by enactment of this pending bill,[5] there is every reason to believe that the Department of the Interior will still continue to oversee much of the management of former public lands. While many observers feel a certain anxiety over the possibility that the Havasupai will become the owners of former Grand Canyon lands, others may indeed feel that the Indians will be as dedicated to preservation as is the National Park Service.

Dukelow and Zakheim (1972) have suggested another alternative to the tribes—the land patent annulment suit, which represents a new legal tactic in land claims. Although the authors raise the usual arguments—that

"Indians would establish a dangerous precedent casting a cloud upon title to vast areas of land," and that "the probability of recovering a particular area of land will be inversely proportional to the value of that land to the present title holder" (p. 223)–the land patent annulment is nonetheless based on the doctrine of aboriginal title, which is an equitable title based on actual, exclusive, and continuous use and occupancy of a definable area until loss of the property. The land patent annulment therefore turns on the issue of invalidating a patent held now by non-Indians and the demonstration that aboriginal occupancy would invalidate any patents issued to another if the chain of private title flowing from such a patent raised questions of fraud. Since the claims legislation forbade the return of land, it should be noted that the danger of placing a cloud over existing titles does perhaps preclude any approach that would return lands long held in other tenure. But certainly the events at Alcatraz and Wounded Knee raise again the question of the return of lands, especially those considered part of the public domain, as were Blue Lake and Mt. Adams. Nielsen (1973) also recognized the problems posed by the restoration of Indian title to land now held in private ownership; he observed that thus far only lands held in public ownership, parts of national forests, for example, have been restored to tribes.

Notes

1. California Indian Legal Services *Newsletter*, 5, no. 2: 3-6 (June 14, 1972).

2. Clearwater Publishing Co., New York, with the cooperation of the Indian Claims Commission and the law firm of Wilkinson, Cragun and Barker (Washington, D.C.), has published the Decisions of the I.C.C. (including abstracts) and a nearly complete collection of written expert reports submitted to the Commission; each collection has been indexed in a printed volume (Ross 1973 a/b). Clearwater has also announced publication of three additional collections: Transcripts of Oral Expert Testimony, Briefs (including petitions, defendant's answers, proposed findings of facts, etc.), and GAO reports on disbursements to tribes under the terms of 19th-century treaties. The Native American Rights Fund distributes bound copies of the Commission's decisions and has also produced an index (Native American Rights Fund, 1973a). Garland Publishing Co., New York, has begun publication of a series of hard-cover volumes from the Expert Testimony (e.g., Manners 1974 and Steward 1974). These volumes contain photo-offset reproductions of original manuscripts by ethnographers who served as expert witnesses in the cases—in this example, Manners for the Southern Paiute, Steward for the Ute. Included in both

volumes and no doubt in the introductory sections of the entire series, are preliminary comments on the series, on the Indian Claims Commission, and on the ethnohistorical reports. The Steward volume also contains data reprinted from government documents. Aschmann (1963) was reprinted (1974) by Garland as Vol. II of its Apache series. The ethnohistorical reports parallel in content and method those discussed in this section.

3. Cf. discussion of *Mirror for Americans: Likeness of the Eastern Seaboard*, 1810 (New York: American Geographical Society, 1943) as discussed in J. K. Wright, *Geography in the Making, 1851-1951* (New York: American Geographical Society, 1952) p. 290.

4. American Indian Law *Newsletter* 5, no. 5: 74-75 (April 30, 1972), and *Wassaja* 2, no. 9 (Oct.-Nov. 1974).

5. Passed and signed as the Grand Canyon Park Enlargement Act, January 4, 1975.

Works Cited in Section AB

Anson, 1970
Armstrong, 1971
Arnold, 1967
Aschmann, 1963, 1966
Barker, 1960
Barney, 1955, 1960, 1963
Beals & Hester, 1956
Block, 1971
Bodine, 1973
Bourke, 1894
Brugge, 1965
Chapman, 1936, 1944, 1957, 1962, 1965
Coffeen, 1972
Cohen, F. S., 1941, 1942, 1945, 1947
Cohen, L. K., 1960
Danforth, 1973
Dart, 1921
Deloria, 1971
Driver et al., 1953
Dukelow & Zakheim, 1972
Dyer, 1945
Eisinger, 1948
Ellison, 1925
Ezell, 1955
Federal Field Committee, 1968
Fey & McNickle, 1959, 1970
Forbes, 1964
Fried, 1952

Gilbert & Taylor, 1966
Goldschmitt & Haas, 1946
Harvey, 1961, n.d.
Heizer, 1966
Hickerson, 1965
Hodge, 1973
Horsman, 1967
I.C.C., 1968
Jennings, 1971b
Johnson, 1966
Juergensmeyer & Wadley, 1974
Kappler, 1903-38, vol. IV, 1929
Kelly, 1971
Kickingbird & Ducheneaux, 1973
Kimmey, 1960
Kinney, 1937
Kroeber, 1951, 1955, 1962
Large, 1973
LeDuc, 1957
Lipps, 1932
Lurie, 1955, 1956, 1957
Lysyk, 1973
Macgregor, 1949
Manners, 1956, 1957, 1974
McNeely, 1939
Moquin & Van Doren, 1973
Nathan, 1972
Native American Rights Fund, 1973a
Nichols, 1970
Nielson, 1973

Oliver, 1959
Opler, M. E., 1971
Pearce, 1953 [1967]
Pennington, 1970
Price, 1973
Ray, 1955a/b
Rockwell, 1956
Ross, 1973a/b
Ruby & Brown, 1970
Schifter, 1954
Selander, 1947
Sheehan, 1969
Snow, 1921
Stanley, 1954
Steward, 1955b, 1974
Stewart, K. M., 1969

Stewart, O. C., 1958, 1959, 1961,
    1966a, 1970, 1974, in press
Summers, 1937
Sutton, 1964
Swierenga, 1966
U.S. Department of Justice, 1964
Vance, 1969
Vanderwerth, 1971
Vogel, 1972
Wallace, 1957
Washburn, 1957, 1959, 1971b
Watkins, 1974
Whatley, 1969
Wheeler-Voegelin, 1956
Wilkinson, 1966
Wilson, 1959

SECTION BC

Title Clarification and Change

Introduction

For numerous reasons the establishment of the reservation system did not succeed in ending the contest for tribal lands. Despite treaties and legislation designed to confirm tribal rights to given tracts of land and to assert federal supremacy and protection over the tribes, intrusions upon Indian lands and pressure for their acquisition continued almost unabated for another half century, that is, into the 1920s. Perhaps, as Hagan suggested, "the reservation system would have functioned better if Americans had been prepared to subsidize the experiment properly" (1971b, p. 355). But the fact remains that the government was as culpable as many of the transgressors. The government and many private citizens encouraged "opening" the reservations, that is, further diminishing tribal lands by allotting individual tracts to tribal members and declaring the remainder a surplus open to homesteading under public land laws. Allotment became the major vehicle of a land policy aimed at assimilation; the concommitant reduction of total tribal landholdings intended the virtual demise of tribal lifeways.

Conflicts also arose over other circumstances, deliberate or accidental; indeed the encroachments by cattlemen and railroad interests provoked their own set of conflicts and litigation. Moreover, the government continued its policy of terminating tribal status for many groups in the Plains. Although this policy was relaxed during the decades prior to and during the Collier administration (1933-45), it was renewed with vigor in the

1950s and early 1960s and caught in its net the Klamath and Menominee as well as several smaller Indian groups.

This section, then, reports the circumstances that led to the need for greater clarification of Indian title once land reservation became the policy. It also assesses the interpretation of the allotment policy that was essentially abrogated in 1934 when the Indian Reorganization Act became law. Finally, it examines the termination policy of the more recent period in the light of the consequences of ending the trusteeship of various tribes and their lands.

Opening of and Encroachment upon Indian Lands

The cause of encroachment upon Indian lands may be found in the uninterrupted confrontation of Indians and whites in the settlement of the Midwest and Far West, for land reservation coincided in time with what Abel (1904) termed continual "waves" of migration that led to the extinguishment of reservation titles in Kansas. Encroachment also occurred as railroad promoters secured land grants across the Plains and Intermontane regions, including territories of the Pueblo, Navajo, and other nearby Indian tribes. Already cattlemen had entered these regions and moved cattle onto lands later determined to lie within reservations. But conflicts also arose because it was difficult to administer properly the vast addition to the public domain that came with the acquisition of the Mexican Cession and the Northwest (Dunham 1937, 1941). Many reservations established by means of executive order (after the abrogation of the treaty power in 1871) had boundaries that were not fully substantiated in the field; rather, they were drawn on maps only by reference to range and township. Many bona fide homestead entries lay, then, within reserves, and in numerous cases such entries were made under questionable circumstances that were upheld later on. Presidents widely employed the executive order to change boundaries without congressional approval until it was determined that such executive-order reservations carved out of the public domain conveyed the same legal protections as those created by treaty or statute (Anonymous 1960; U.S. President 1912).

Preoccupation with the opening of reservations in the Plains and commensurate interest in land values will be apparent from the abundance of studies (cf. Condra 1907; Davis 1919; Fielding 1952; Gates 1954; Haley 1940; Moore 1952; Rhodes 1920; Williams 1922; see also Section B). Stewart (1933) reviewed the evolution of Indian Territory and the creation of Oklahoma as a territory and then as a state, and discussed the ceded lands of almost all of the tribes that held reservations in eastern

Oklahoma. His study provides useful maps showing the changes in the status of the territory and its Indian lands (cf. Morris & McReynolds, 1965). The opening of reserves in the Plains was intended to make room for relocated tribes, for according to Summers's explanation (1937), the leased district of the Choctaw and Chickasaw was to accommodate Kiowa, Apache, Comanche, Cheyenne, and Arapahoe (cf. Berthrong 1956). Several scholars have interpreted the problems of relocating tribes in Indian Territory and settling them among the Five Civilized Tribes as part of the extinguishment of part or all of Kansas (Rainey 1933; Gates 1937; Abel 1904; Gittinger 1917; Gibson 1963). Other problems included keeping Omaha Indians on their original reservations (Warner 1970) and getting the Pawnee to vacate ceded lands. Few studies seek to assess the impact of post-Civil War policies on the Five Civilized Tribes; this is the theme of Bailey's study (1972) of reconstruction in Indian Territory and its effects on land policy that led to the further loss of their lands. (See the historical atlas discussion in the Bibliographical and Cartographic Sources section; cf. Morris and McReynolds 1965; Socolofsky and Self 1972.)

Similar problems of title extinguishment, reduction in acreage, and dissolution of reservations occurred elsewhere in the Plains and in the Far West. Koch reviewed (1924-26) how political agitation led to the dissolution of a reservation in Texas and the relocation of Comanche, Apache, and Kiowa within Indian Territory. Many observers have commented on the erosion of Indian land rights in California, although to date no one has attempted a full-length history of Indian affairs within that state. Crevelli (1959) focused on problems of encroachment, trespass, land purchases, land claims, and termination issues on some 40 rancherías in the northern part of the state. Kasch (1947) reported on the clarification of title to one ranchería. Anderson's (1956) study concerned one of the more important surviving reservations, the Hoopa in northwest California. Seymour (1906) offered a contemporary interpretation of the conflict over Indian and railroad lands as well as an account of early land allotment in Southern California. Hill (1927) included a discussion of the ejectment of Indians from former rancho lands and their relocation among another band of Indians.[1] I attempted to provide (Sutton 1964) a broader historical geography of the Mission Indians and the establishment of a reservation system, including observations about the contributions of Helen Hunt Jackson, who served as an Indian commissioner reporting on the plight of the Mission Indians. Otis (1947) examined the similar problems of adjustment and changes on the Klamath reservation in Oregon.

Several studies examine policy issues and problems of land administration for the period under review. In the process, they often provide useful comparative discussions. For example, Dale (1949) examined the

Southwest from the establishment of reservations to the end of the Collier administration. Rushmore (1914) demonstrated in a review of the Indian policies of President Grant how the abolition of treaty-making helped abate pernicious abuses, bringing to an end the practice of treating Indians as nations. Grant was in office during the critical years when tribes were first adjusting to reservations and when the clergy was called in to assist in field administration. Burney (1936) focused on land tenure in the review of policy developments once the reservation system took shape in the West. A rather more crusading approach was taken by Humphrey (1905), much along the lines of Jackson's more effective and better well-known volume, *A Century of Dishonor* (1881).

Because of the close correlation between the history of Indian reservations and the changing status of the public domain, there are frequent references to Indian lands in reports on public land administration. Donaldson's compilation (1884) of public land statistics and related information, for example, includes maps of Indian reservations and data on the extinguishment of Indian titles. Westphall (1965), in his study of the public domain in New Mexico, included, all too briefly, observations about Indian boundaries, surveys, and restorations. LaManna (1934) reviewed briefly illegal uses of Indian lands, and Green (1939) dealt with reservations, cessions, and allotment in the history of public land administration in South Dakota.

The emphasis in land tenure literature has been placed on problems in the Midwest and Far West. Nevertheless, studies of eastern tribes and their land problems are not lacking, although this literature is often obscured by the tendency of the relevant studies to focus on the larger historical themes in which the Indian plays a relatively small role. Houghton (1920) traced the history and fate of one reserve in New York that eventually was extinguished to make way for non-Indian settlers; he noted the problems of relocating homeless Indian immigrants who came to settle on the poorer lands of the Cattaraugus and Allegany reservations that were held in common by the Seneca Nation. Congdon (1967) reviewed the history of the Allegany (or Allegheny), and Deardorff (1941) discussed the Cornplanter grant; both areas in recent years have been affected by the impoundment of the Allegheny Reservation as part of the Kinzua Dam project (see Section AC).[2] Scaife (1896) reported on the Catawba Indians of South Carolina, who ultimately secured a small reserve under state trust. Indeed, most of the reservations along the eastern seaboard are held in trust by the states. (See Figure 4.)

Cattlemen

Many of the studies that relate how cattlemen sought to check the establishment of reservations or succeeded in entering reserved lands treat all of the many issues that ultimately led to extinguishment of title or reduction in acreage. This was the era of relatively free use of the open range; this freedom began to be regulated only in the 1920s, and was permanently restricted in terms of the public domain after 1934. Hagan (1971b) noted that treaty writers generally provided that reservations would be closed to any entry, but officials could not foresee the difficulty of enforcing these provisions against cattlemen. Unlawful occupancy and encroachment occurred, in part, because Indians did not fence their lands and did not adhere to reservation boundaries in the movement of their own livestock. Rustling on reservations also contributed to Indian-white difficulties. In addition, as Oliphant suggested (1950), white juries were not likely to punish whites for utilizing Indian rangelands, especially where Indians were absent from the land. Land-hungry settlers confronted officials, arguing that Indian holdings were too large. In the early reservation years cattlemen tended to forestall the allotment of land among some tribes (cf. Berthrong 1971; Hagan 1971b; Buntin 1932; Monahan 1967-68). Many studies thus include observations about cattlemen, the allotment process, and the leasing of Indian range (Cornett 1954; Savage 1972; Dale 1942; Wallace and Hoebel 1952; Burrill 1972; Ewers 1958). Hudson's more recent reconstruction (1973) of the opening of the Sioux country effectively shows how cattle interests triggered both the entry of cattle onto the reservation in Dakota Territory and subsequent homesteading. His maps reveal the sequential reduction of Indian lands by these two processes.

The processes considered here involved personal interaction between certain whites and the Indians; the Indians could see by the mere presence of cowboys on the land how cattlemen's interests were defeating the basic reasons for establishment of reservations. Chapman described (1942-43) how whites married into the Osage tribe in order to secure property interests, and showed how agents, in order to check the influence of land-hungry cattlemen, urged Indians to move. He also noted the interference of real estate agents who "helped" Indians select allotments with an eye to their leasing by cattlemen. The growth of towns nearby ultimately led to the demise of the cattle interests in favor of farmers, who saw Indian lands as potentially leasable (Hagan 1971b).

Railroads

The checkerboard observable on land tenure maps of western states became a familiar configuration on the land as railroad companies secured land grants consisting of alternate sections (each 640 acres) on both sides of a proposed right-of-way. Most of the lines traversed regions of sedentary tribes whose lands lay partially or wholly in the path of a railroad. This was especially notable for the Santa Fe grant through Pueblo, Navajo, and Hualapai country south of the Grand Canyon region. Where railroad grants intersected tracts reserved by treaty, statute, or executive order, promoters and company officials sought to exchange grant lands for tribal lands so long as the companies and the government (speaking for the tribes) found it mutually beneficial. Moreover, in other instances, as prior to the granting of lands for a railroad right-of-way, promoters stimulated land speculation to encourage settler interest, hence encourage Congress to make a grant to them, and thus reduce the potential size of a reservation. Billington (1974) and Gates (1968) considered various problems of railroads in their expansion across western America. Rae (1952) reviewed the Northern Route in its relation to Indian lands; Mosk (1944) and Greever (1954) reconstructed the circumstances of land adjustments along the Santa Fe right-of-way; Clark's dissertation (1947) discussed Indian Territory and railroad growth; and Prather (1943-1944) examined the purchases and treaties engendered by a railroad in Michigan. In Oregon, even wagon-road grants led to conflicts over Indian lands (O'Callaghan 1952).

Both Clark and Gates noted that railroad interests materially influenced policies leading to dissolution of tribal lands and the creation of allotments. They suggested that speculators, railroad promoters, and settlers tended to unite against the tribes in hopes of securing railways through newly settled or potentially developable farm lands. In Kansas, for example, treaty-writing ultimately led to the acquisition of Osage, Kickapoo, and Potawatomi lands for railroad rights-of-way. In fact, as Gates pointed out, such acquisition meant bypassing the transfer of ceded Indian lands to the public domain, which would have made such lands subject to general entry laws. As a consequence, by 1871 Congress was being urged to bring the treaty-making powers over Indian affairs to an end.

Few scholars have examined the relationship of railroads to Indian lands as closely as Greever and Mosk. Greever described the desire of the Santa Fe Railroad Company to acquire equivalent lieu sections where the right-of-way encountered established Indian reservations. The cattlemen's opposition stemmed from the fact that they were then making use of lands adjacent to those of squatting Navajos and did not want to see them given to the railroad. Navajos had apparently wandered eastward off the reservation onto the public domain, where they were urged to take allotments. Had there not been opposition to a grant to the Santa Fe in this area of western New Mexico, the government might have enclosed a larger tract for the tribe, thus diminishing even more the area the cattlemen might utilize. Mosk discussed indemnity selections in the exchange between railroads and Indians. With reference to lieu selections in Arizona—those acquired by the state rather than the railroad—Gladen's study (1970) of school lands reveals how prior withdrawals for Indian reservations (and the railroads) led to a blocking-up of state lands. Navajo nomadism, by dint of its mobile nature, conflicted with the interests of the railroad; alternate landownership through any part of the reservation would give the railroad a right-of-way, but it would create conflicting tenure patterns and lead to the Indians crossing railroad holdings, as Hoover reported (1931b). (For an interpretation of the litigation between the Hualapai and the Santa Fe Railroad, see M.K.M.B. 1942.)

The checkerboard of the Southern Pacific Railroad led to some confiscation of Indian lands by simple manipulation of the executive order. I have examined (Sutton 1964) the implications of the checkerboard for the distribution of reservation lands, specifically in connection with Palm Springs, California, where former railroad lands and Indian sections alternate even today. This situation has created numerous municipal problems and conflicts over civil and criminal jurisdiction, and more recently has involved an investigation of the legal practices of the guardians of these Indians (cf. Ainsworth 1965, and the comments on the *Riverside-Press Enterprise* in the Bibliographic Note).

Other Boundary/Title Issues

Lands within the Mexican Cession that later became the territories of Arizona and New Mexico and the state of California presented additional title-clearance problems to the Indians because of misconceptions about the intent of Hispanic law. Hispanic tenure practices with respect to Indians' land rights under both Spain and Mexico were never well understood by U.S. officials (cf. Ezell 1955, Hutchinson 1965-65). Consequently, in the American period, the government did not turn for guidance or precedents to Hispanic law in determining what exactly Indian title should be. In California, for example, the tendency was to disregard or ignore Hispanic law. Cohen (1942), however, in assessing the Spanish legal background for Indians' rights under the United States, amply demonstrated that the Spanish respected the sanctity of Indian land titles and the Mexicans subsequently sustained this position. He suggested that in fact "the relevance of Spanish law was formally recognized in treaties by which the United States undertook to recognize property and other rights enjoyed by the inhabitants of the ceded territory under the prior sovereignty" (in L. K. Cohen, 1960, p. 249) It was Cohen's contention that the humane principles that have guided our own legal approach to Indian affairs stem from prior Spanish practices. (See also Pennington 1970 and Price 1973; see Kappler 1903-38, Vol. IV, 1929, pp. 1166-75 on differences between U.S. and foreign recognition of Indian land tenure.)

The controversy over Pueblo land titles, which ended in legislation in 1924, stemmed from confusion over entry rights of 3000 or more non-Indian claimants prior to and during American acquisition of New Mexico. These claimants (representing some 12,000 persons) had entered Pueblo lands then confirmed as grants under Spain and reaffirmed by the Mexican government. Also involved were efforts to encourage the alienation of Indian land by regarding the tribes as autonomous political units under Spanish-Mexican law. But the courts came to treat the Pueblos as a dependent people under federal law and placed their lands in trust. These claims issues and much of the litigation are reported by Brayer (1939), Quail (1937), and Troiel (1914). Seymour (1924) reviewed the case *Sandoval vs. U.S.*, which led to the court interpretation of the legal status of Pueblo Indians, whereas Long (1949) focused on the activities of Senator Bursum, who attempted to promote legislation favorable to the settlers. Aberle (1948) recounted the land-acquisition problems of the Pueblos following the enactment of the law that quieted title to their lands, but that did not restore acreage then held by non-Indians. In the larger context of how land was acquired from the Pueblos, Carlson (1971) traced the practices for the upper Rio Grande Valley. Deloria (1974) nicely summed up how the Pueblos secured favorable legislation despite the options open to settlers. Ultimately the claimants were removed from the disputed land.

Kelly (1963) demonstrated how the interpretation of an executive order affected Navajo efforts to expand the reservation after 1900. The discovery of oil helped to stimulate some areal expansion of the bounds of the Navajo reservation, mostly within Arizona, although oil was of minor significance as a resource. When the government sought to extend the reservation by executive order, adjacent non-Indian landowners objected, even though the land was to serve those who had "wandered" out of the reservation eastward into New Mexico. Indians saw the land as traditionally theirs. When non-Indians wished to lease Indian lands, the question arose as to which law—the general leasing act or special Indian leasing acts—should be invoked for executive-order lands. Congress had equated such reserves with those under treaty or statute, but it was still possible by executive order to restore Indian lands to the public domain, often depriving Indians of good resources set aside for them in favor of non-Indians. Indeed, the indiscriminate use of the executive order modified many reservations between the 1850s and the 1920s. Consequently in 1927 Congress, in passing the Indian Oil Leasing Act, took away the presidential power to restore any executive-order reservation to the public domain (Anonymous 1960; Cohen 1941). Legal interpretations have generally asserted that equitable title to executive-order reserves belongs to the tribe, though legal title remains in the United States.

Indians have also asserted claims to lands held by other tribes. The Navajo-Hopi land conflict has perhaps received the most attention because of its unique political geography. Jones (1950) clearly portrayed how cultural differences in perception have helped to make the boundary conflict:

> The laying out of the reservation as a rectangle bounded by latitude and longitude was obviously a swivel-chair job by someone with a map and a ruler and little knowledge of the area and the problems. To the Hopi and the Navajo, longitude . . . and . . . latitude meant nothing whatsoever. Such boundaries were artificial ones without regard to topography, natural landmarks, land nature and utilization, or ethnic boundaries. . . . The lack of realism in setting up the reservation became manifest in the difficulties of its later operation. (P. 22)

Neither tribe has sufficient land for all of its needs, and since Navajo population growth has been phenomenal, they have continued to encroach upon Hopi lands. Hopi claims, Page noted (1940), are based upon traditional occupancy, for they were among the few tribes whose lands were retained throughout the cession period, and, indeed, the boundaries do surround their original homeland. At one time the government encouraged Hopis to leave their mesa villages and spread out in order to make effective use of arable lands as a means to check the intrusion of Navajos. But encroachment continued onto their cleared lands, and the Hopi rejected taking allotments on these communal holdings. Range management problems on the Navajo Reservation during the 1930s, when the government created a grazing district that included the Hopi Reservation, further aggravated the conflict, for it firmly established the boundary between the Hopi and the Navajo. As it happened, this necessitated that the Hopis secure permits from the Navajos in order to graze their livestock in the area identified in the land dispute (Stephens 1961).

More recently the boundary dispute has led Congress to undertake an inquiry into the problem, and both sides have sought favorable legislation to resolve the conflict. Besides brief legislative reviews in print

(ILIDS 1972; Anonymous 1973), which examine the Hopi proposal for the transfer to them of more than one million acres from the Navajo Reservation and the counter-proposal by the Navajos for the transfer of 35,000 acres of Hopi-occupied lands to the Navajos, few other studies have examined the problem. Especially useful are two papers (1974a/b) by Prof. David Aberle, an anthropologist who has served as a consultant in the case mainly as an advocate in behalf of the Navajos (correspondence October 25, 1974). Aberle carefully reviews the character of Navajo concepts of land tenure, arguing that any relocation of these Indians would mean displacement of their fellow tribesmen. Because of the nature of use-rights under Navajo customary procedures, Aberle says that there is no unoccupied land within the reservation onto which relocated Navajos could be settled; to so relocate them would be tantamount to taking use-rights from other kin-groups without compensation. He sees current legislative proposals as punitive toward the Navajos; his alternative proposal would grant to the Navajos within the disputed area permanent rights to stay, and to the tribe an opportunity to purchase the acreage. In turn, the Hopis would be granted some territory near Moencopi, long occupied mainly by their tribesmen. Aberle's study implies that, in historical review, the Hopis have not demonstrated by occupancy a claim to the disputed area since 1700. Before this time there is no doubt as to their claim, but since then they have not effectively held the land. One might point out the quite different positions taken by Page more than 35 years ago and by Aberle today, leaving perhaps for others the task of resolving two quite opposing views of tribal rights to the disputed area.

Another aspect of the Hopi-Navajo problem, concerning resettlement of members of both tribes on the Colorado River Indian Reservation, has also been studied (Fontana 1963; McIntire 1969). Fontana reported that the Mohave and Chemehuevi tribes felt intimidated into accepting Hopi and Navajo settlers on surplus farm lands, for they were threatened with the possibility that their lands might be thrown open to non-Indian settlement. Land speculators and developers, eager to expand agriculture under the reclamation laws, had urged the state of Arizona to secure congressional approval to open the reservation; the state legislature, in 1915, did memorialize Congress to that effect, but to no avail. The few studies reviewed here suggest the possibility of further examination of problems of relocating Indians who wish to remain on the land as farmers where land capacity has been exhausted. There should be considerable interest in how resident tribes accept newcomers and in how they integrate them into the tribal organization, especially in terms of tenure rights. In the case of the Colorado River Indian Reservation, despite initial qualms, the newcomers were ultimately accepted and accorded full rights in the lands they cultivated. (Another facet of the agrarian problem at the Colorado River Indian Reservation is discussed in Section C; see Travis 1968.)

During the decades of land adjustments several organizations defended the Indians' rights to the land. The Lake Mohonk Conferences in New York were among the first to bring together persons interested in reforming the administration of Indian Affairs, but the work of the Philadelphia-based Indian Rights Association has been the more lasting. (For brief comments on this organization, see Dale 1949; see Fritz 1963 for an evaluation of the activities of the Lake Mohonk Conferences.) Organized in the early 1880s, the association was particularly effective in the Indians' behalf into the 1920s; afterward its role was less spectacular. Its officers and members had been especially active in fieldwork, in negotiations of various sorts, and in the preparation of numerous publications. At least one of its leaders, Charles C. Painter, conducted several field surveys in the Far West, mostly in California; another, F. E. Leupp, became a commissioner of Indian affairs. (Cf. Brosius 1924; Bonnin 1924; Harrison 1887; Meserve 1896; Painter 1883, 1887, 1888; Scaife 1896.) Both organizations published annual reports.[3]

Land Allotment

The allotment of land in severalty, which is analogous to the granting of a homestead, has received more criticism than other land policies in Indian affairs. The object of most of the criticism has been the goal of assimilating individual Indians and of thereby separating them from tribal ways. Allotment could be likened to a homestead; it embodied the family farm tradition; therefore, it was sugggested, it would cause Indian families to abandon villages and move out onto the soil. Gates (1936) suggested that the passage of the General Allotment Act was undoubtedly supported by western pressure to have Indian lands made available for settlement through purchase of surplus tracts in excess of *pro rata* allotments of arable lands. And certainly the results of the act bear out this interpretation, for more than 100 million acres were sold out of reservations. Yet for many years before its enactment and for several decades thereafter, even the Indians' champions had supported the high-blown objectives of land allotment (Fritz 1963; Gates 1886; Leupp 1909; Meserve 1896; Mardock 1971; Priest 1942; Painter 1887). Interestingly enough, Painter, Meserve, and Leupp, who wrote for the Indian Rights Association, were staunch supporters of the objectives of land allotment; Leupp, writing nearly 25 years after the act was passed, still sang its praises. Prucha

(1973) reprints many of the papers and lectures that supported the land allotment program, including those by Senator Henry Dawes, who wrote the law, Charles C. Painter, who was the most active officer of the Indian Rights Association, and Merrill E. Gates, a leader of the Lake Mohonk Conferences. Later studies reflect a growing disenchantment with, or even outright rejection of, the policy, and offered alternative answers to the problems of Indian land administration (Debo 1940; Harper 1943; Kinney 1937; Meriam 1928; Otis 1934). Another volume taking a critical position on the allotment policy has been written by Washburn (in press).

Land allotment and its alleged socioeconomic benefits to the Indian harked back to practices in colonial times. Much of the earlier discussion had claimed that private property in land would befit a praying or Christian Indian, and thus there is considerable reference in this early literature to allotments, although they were often identified simply as "reservations." Allotments were granted to individuals or groups who lived among or adjacent to white settlement, but not to tribes (Harris 1953; Knoepfler 1922). The granting of allotments also encouraged the bribing of chiefs and influential Indians into signing treaties. At least one source indicates that even Spanish policy sought to integrate Indians into white society by permitting non-Indians to purchase land and settle among Indians (Hutchinson 1964-65, 1969). We have already reviewed other implications of allotment as a means to cede the homelands of the Five Civilized Tribes in the South (e.g., Young 1961; see Section B). Historians have also researched the allotment practices elsewhere prior to the General Allotment Act (Dawes Act) of 1887 (Gates 1971; Paulson 1971). And several studies examine the evolution of this land policy for various time periods (Burney 1936; Burns 1954; Cady 1926) or with reference to Senator Dawes and the act itself (Hey 1939; Murray 1945; Thayer 1888). Hagan (1956), Fey and McNickle (1959, 1970), Washburn (1971b), and Tyler (1973) summarized the important historical aspects of the policy and such implications as the decline of Indian land use and the alienation of trust holdings, while Haas (1957), Kinney (1937), and Cohen (1941) evaluated the legal basis for Indian private property in land. The definitive study of the adverse effects of the half-century of land allotment was prepared as a government report (U.S. National Resources Board 1935).

The literature has reported on how allotments opened up reservations, led to the extinguishment of title to "surplus" tracts and created, through homesteading, a mixed Indian country. It has shown how the government has sought to stimulate Indian farming and has urged Indians to move out of villages and construct farmsteads on their lands. Yet the thrust and conclusions of most studies suggest, as Harper (1943) ably pointed out, that allotment was failing and that contrasts between tribal and allotted land use patterns revealed how the latter was destroying tribal life and creating indigent and landless Indians.

Not all of the studies are purely negative. In reading Fritz, Hagan, Kinney, or Priest, for example,one finds mixed feelings about the intent, effectiveness, and equivocal goals of the allotment policy. Hagan, for example, tells us that it was to be regretted that the policy was first applied to the Plains Indians, who were less experienced in farming, whereas the relocated Five Civilized Tribes, who knew far more about agriculture, were the last to receive severalty in the Plains. He and others also noted that the movement came unpropitiously in the post-Civil War period when farming was hit hard by the need for more land per operating unit. In fact, Indian allotments, even where equivalent in acreage to homesteads, have proven grossly inadequate through the changes in land economics during most of this century.

Criticism of government land policy has taken other forms. Priest's study (1942), written after many of the provisions of the Indian Reorganization Act had become effective, expressed disapproval of the new policy that, to him, had retreated from its commitment to cultural assimilation. Noting that policy-makers never conceived of the reservation as permanent and that allotment did create the necessary contact between Indians and whites, Priest stressed that not enough land had been set aside for allotments and that opening to non-Indian homesteading and the like curtailed the allotment of land to later generations of Indians. He also recounted that Dawes himself grew fearful that abuses of the law would minimize its effectiveness.

Otis's somewhat obscure study (1934, reprinted 1973) of the effects of the Dawes Act to 1900 offers a better-balanced appraisal of that legislation. According to Prof. Francis Prucha, editor of the 1973 reprint, Otis made heavy use of documents, hearings, and proceedings—for example, those of the Lake Mohonk Conferences—which strongly supported the allotment of land in severalty. The Otis volume reexamined the organizations associated with allotment and their goals, and offered comments on Indian attitudes and capacities to deal with private property. He also examined how the allotment process came to the reservation, referring especially to the work of Fletcher. Prucha notes that Kinney, Priest, Fritz, and Mardock, whose works all appear in print at later dates, all seemed to be unaware of Otis's carefully documented research.

Many historians have pointed to inequities that outweigh much of the idealism expressed in the literature. Debo (1940) described how scheming lawyers and speculators sought to separate Indians from their allotments and suggested that the real intent was to destroy communal lifestyles. Shepard (1935, 1943) stressed the actual loss of the land and the dele-terious effects of allotment on continued land use, through breakup of larger units that were best held communally (e.g., grazing and forest resources). He was especially critical of the fact that allotment made many Indians landlords. Hagan (1961) lamented the entry of regular law-enforcement personnel onto reservations, and the resulting decline in the number of Indian policemen and judges, following the advent of land allotment. Green (1923), Meyer (1967), and Trenholm and Carley (1964), like Hagan, reported on the evils of the leasing that soon followed the allotment policy, aiding white grazing and farming and making indigent landlords of the Indians.

Considering the importance of the allotment policy in federal Indian affairs administration, it is surprising how little has been said about the actual process of subdividing tribal land; Prucha, in fact, asserted (1971) that the process has been neglected by historians. He urged a review, for example, of the writings of Fletcher (1885) who reported favorably on the Indians' selection of appropriate parcels of land and asserted that Indians were not concerned with monetary values in their choices, for they did not think in terms of later land sales. Just how much of a contribution, good or bad, white encroachment and presence on reservations had on the allotment process can only be surmised. Hagan (1971a) suggested that squawmen were often at the heart of factionalism on reservations and that they perhaps encouraged land allotment. There can be no doubt that missionaries working on reservations urged Indians to select individual holdings.

How Indians came to select particular parcels is described in only a handful of studies. Brown (1944) reported on the survey and appraisal of allotments among the Choctaw and Chickasaw. Hewes (1942a/b, 1944), in studying Cherokee settlement after removal to Oklahoma, reported that most allottees tended to choose sites that included their pre-allotment homes, but that many sought an opportunity for new free land. But, when taking old farmstead sites, they had to select the rest of their allotted acreage elsewhere, thus creating noncontiguous holdings. Many found themselves owners of unfamiliar plots in poorer parts of the Ozarks or Prairie Plains. He also revealed how restricted Indians (half-blood or more) received poorer allotments than the "white" Indians (less than half-blood) or freedmen. Most restricted Indians took allotments in the eastern half of the Cherokee nation in Oklahoma. As Hewes put it,

> The allotment of land in severalty had the effect of anchoring the restricted Indians in familiar localities, since most of them

selected their old farms or neighboring land or were allotted such land by the commission in charge if they refused to make a selection. (1942a, p. 280)

A corollary to these observations by Hewes are those by Graebner, who reviewed (1945) the persistence of communal tenure practices among the Five Civilized Tribes after settlement in Oklahoma. Here one stratagem for preserving communal land among the tribes was to defer the allotment process through the creation of a landed aristocracy which tied up the land by leasing it to cattlemen. Ultimately, allotment of land did end the cattlemen's hold and led to the opening of reservations in Indian Territory and elsewhere, both in the Plains and Far West.

Many additional works have been written on the cattlemen's influence on land allotment and later utilization of Indian lands. Cattlemen figured prominently in the history of the Osage Reservation (Burrill 1972). They generally opposed land allotment, since it would break up large browsable tracts of land, and their interference frustrated many efforts to allot land. It was reported for the Osage allotment program (Chapman 1942-43), that cattlemen and locators, in helping Indians pick suitable lands, mainly had their eyes on potentially leasable tracts. Cattlemen, for example, wanted allotments in compact form regardless of the character of the land. Agents, on the other hand, compelled Indians to take allotments adjoining homesteads, partly as a means to defeat the efforts of cattlemen, who sought to secure large blocks of pasturage under long-term leases. Burrill noted that the Osage in the earlier years opposed allotments and encouraged cattlemen to lease their lands.

Indians have not been seen as knowledgeable in the proper selection of arable lands. Agents considered Indians simple-minded in such matters as inheritance and the allotment process (Forbes [quoting Wovoka] 1967). Many problems faced the "civilizing" agents, who were often confronted with requests for allotments by tribal exiles (cf. Ruby and Brown 1970); agents did seek to allot land to absentee Indians, often over the objections of other tribal members. The question of the rights of those Indians who left reservations in pre-allotment times has been debated many times. When efforts were made to grant additional allotments on the Klamath reservation intratribal division resulted—mainly because it would have meant dividing up the tribal timberlands, which were the only lands left (Stern 1965). It is also reported that disputes arose whenever a tribe was settled on a reservation already allocated to another tribe; a good example of this situation involved Spokane Indians settled on the Coeur d'Alene Reservation (Cotroneo and Dozier 1974). Other Indians, as among the Navajo, even feared that the government might take back allotments after they had made improvements (cf. Sasaki 1960). Lang (1953) reported on Indians who claimed they did not know what lands were theirs.

In general, attitudes toward allotment tended to divide Indians within most tribes. A rich store of data awaits the researcher interested in utilizing Indian informants and archival sources, especially letters between allotting agents and either superintendents or Washington officials, as I have pointed out elsewhere (Sutton 1964). Such data often reveal the existence and nature of rifts among tribal members, especially those arising over the division of land units already long occupied by particular families. In Southern California, for example, a major cause of dissension was the attempt to break up family orchards and to divide grazable tracts among a few resident families and several off-reservation members.

The letters received by the Office of Indian Affairs between 1824 and 1880 are available from the National Archives as Microcopy 234. (Hill 1974 provided brief historical sketches of the field units of the Office of Indian Affairs, together with indexes keyed to the microfilm.)

Although many scholars allude to the fact that many tribes insisted upon allotments at the time of treaty-writing, resistance to this land policy led to the failure of many programs. In many cases we can piece together, albeit somewhat incompletely, what took place, from the recollections of older tribal members or from archival documents and letters, for such sources often reveal the day-by-day confrontation of agents and Indians (cf. Chapman 1948). Many scholars have inferred that Indians feared that procedures would not be democratic on the one hand, or, on the other, that leadership would be disrupted by the fact that headmen would lose status by the reduction of their landholdings. No doubt there was much more resistance to land allotment than there was support, and further research would shed light on both Indian leadership and the reaction to Euro-American institutions. That a correlation existed between allotment and off-reservation migration by dissident Indians has also been inferred, without sufficient evidence to determine the cause. But no doubt, too, allotting agents ignored or rejected Indian pleas to keep families together in order to protect vested interests in land developments.

Lurie's (1966) observations on the contribution of Alice Fletcher, an early American anthropologist who worked zealously in behalf of Indian land rights, provide an instructive view on the degree of individual involvement in the allotment process. Fletcher, who was apparently strongly committed to securing private property for Indians, promoted the allotment of land and was personally involved in the allotment process among the Omaha, Winnebago, and Nez Perce; in fact, it is suggested that her experiences among the Omaha helped in the writing of the Dawes Act. Fletcher, like many of her contemporaries, saw tribal ties as obstacles to progress. Of course, in the early years scientists were rarely involved in the Indian field, and this makes Fletcher's work and later writings all the more interesting. Lurie notes, however, that Fletcher in her zeal did not accurately assess the outcome of allotment among the Omaha Indians. (On this situation and later events see Mead 1932 and Bohannan 1963.) One should also peruse the reminiscences of Tibbles, written in 1905 at the end of a long career in behalf of Indians, and published in 1958. It is quite likely that Tibbles, who worked with the Ponca and Omaha Tribes—he described Fletcher's visit among them at the time when they were concerned over title to land—was even more instrumental than Fletcher in fashioning an effective allotment act.

While the intent of the allotment program may be deemed laudable—for it sought to curtail the influence of tribalism only in order to abet the assimilation of individual Indians—it is surprising that so many allotment efforts were cold and calculating. Indeed, all too often allotment seems to have been thrust upon, rather than offered to, the tribes. Altruistic as the motives for allotment seem in retrospect, officials in their zeal to "do good" lacked whatever perspective was essential to gain the Indians' cooperation, which was a necessary prerequisite to the success of the program. Considered as schemes to resettle indigenous peoples for whatever reasons, we find parallels in two other situations—Indian relocation to permit the construction of dams that have inundated Indian lands (see Section AC) and similar relocations on a grander scale elsewhere in the world, where scholars readily identify the same colonial behavior of officials toward indigenous peoples. (For a discussion of general literature on this theme, see Sutton 1970b and the epilogue to the present volume.)

Land allotment has achieved some success, although too few case studies are available for review. Stern and Boggs (1971) have demonstrated that allotment, when fully understood, can work on a selective basis in a mixed society. Indian-white interaction on the Umatilla Reservation shows that Indian landlordism there has become a viable alternative to Indian farming, and that income under lease arrangements can be worthwhile, although it would never make an Indian well off. While elsewhere land-leasing by Indians is regarded negatively, here the symbiotic relationship of non-Indian lessees to allotted landlords has proven workable; the whites' entrepreneurial ability, their access to credit, and their farming skills all point to leasing rather than to Indian attempts at farming. The working relationship here has gone beyond simple business arrangements. However, since the most valuable farmland is held by the lowest-income Indians and this is the acreage leased, it is somewhat difficult to call this a successful alternative. In a qualified sense, it is better than letting the land lie idle, earning no income. (For related discussions of allotment land use, see Section C.)

Some studies do compare the success of the allotment programs to that of land utilization under tribal assignment, that is, by some means other than the allotment procedure, which has the force of law behind it. Hewes's Cherokee papers (1942a/b, 1944) provide contrasts in land use between holdings of restricted and non-restricted tribal members; thus Hewes identifies the effects of land alienation and leasing. Ballas (1960, 1962) very briefly noted that Eastern Cherokees in North Carolina, in rejecting allotments, chose assignments with modest success. An earlier work of mine (Sutton 1967) assessed the outcome of land allotment in Southern California where rural land is today at a premium for various non-Indian land uses, and found that tribally assigned tracts, whether on non-allotted or allotted reservations, were comparable in use to allotted lands: private property in land has had little meaning for several hundred allottees and their heirs. I showed that little land had ever been farmed, much of it had never been cleared, and only a small portion, perhaps two to three percent of total arable land, was at any one time leased for agriculture. Moreover, as many homes had been constructed on assignments as on allotted land, despite the fact that the former would not, in the context of American realty practice, seem secure in title. But it may be argued that Indians here and elsewhere do not necessarily feel there is more title security in an allotment than in an assignment.

It is enough to say that more research needs to be done on allotments as private property in Euro-American terms. Research into the realty side of "civilizing" the Indian has been dominated by review of the defects of the allotting process, the relative ease by which land could be alienated and encumbered, and the negative effects of land-leasing. Just how much we may say the Indian has learned about the role of real estate in economic activity will depend upon further investigation of his participation in those enterprises involving the use of individual or corporate lands. One limiting factor on our comprehension of how Indians have understood the allotment process is the fact that few Indian observations are reported and interpreted in the literature; even when scholarly studies include Indian narratives, the amount of significant commentary may be small or inconclusive, as in the example of Jim Whitewolf, the Kiowa Apache whose life-story is reported by Brant (1969). This book, in most ways, is more useful for Brant's observations on problems of tribal acculturation under the allotment program. (Several other studies examine facets of land allotment: Barrett 1926; Buffalohead 1964; Cotroneo and Dozier 1974; Johnston 1948; McNickle 1946; Meserve 1933; Madsen 1958; and Sweeney 1924.)

Land Leasing

A brief four years after the passage of the General Allotment Act (1887), Congress further opened the door to the encumbrance of Indian lands by enacting a leasing act. Although much debated, and years later highly criticized on the grounds that it led to what has been termed "unearned" income, the leasing of Indian land resources made some funds available that might otherwise not have existed. Yet the long-range effects of the leasing of Indian land may be summed up in Kinney's (1937) chapter title, "Allotment Purpose Defeated by Lease and Sale."

Historically, non-Indians have sought leases on an annual or, at any rate, a short-term basis, and the laws so limited such agreements. Before they were formalized, leasing for such purposes as the grazing of cattle on reservations or intermittent farming of allotments was concluded in oral agreements, the terms of which were often unknown to officials. Some leases merely legitimized former encroachment by cattlemen. After allotment, lands on many reservations stood idle, either because Indians had no interest in farming or because the lands had finally become so over-burdened by heirship complexities that co-heirs argued among themselves, bringing use of the land to a virtual standstill. Indians lacked capitalization, and indeed many of the supporters of allotment in severalty frowned upon non-Indian utilization, for they thought it would encourage indigence among Indians. Leasing for farming, grazing, timber-cutting, and mining, for the earlier period, did not make serious inroads upon Indian title. If land was encumbered at all, the term was from one to five years. Developmental leases, however, came to involve longer periods, normally for 25 years with renewal options for a similar period; in other instances leases ran to a total of 60 years. But in the past few decades interest in Indian land has generally increased as land speculation has become a national pastime. Some developmental leases on tribal lands, for example, have yielded considerable income and led some tribes to flex their political muscles. Although none of these leases alienates tribal or individual land, what happens to such trust lands when the terms are unfavorable to Indians is tantamount to alienation, for little can be done until the lease runs its course. It has meant in the past that individuals and tribes have been led by poor advice or outright chicanery to lease their birthright "down the river."

Lands in close proximity to non-Indian settlements, and therefore in much demand, are of special interest. Only rarely does one find urban developments directly affected by the existence of a reservation. Historically, several towns in the Midwest and West came to occupy Indian lands, often prior to cession; with cession, sufficient room to grow became available. Palm Springs comes to mind as a current example of a city that has not always gotten along well with its Indian neighbors (cf. Sutton 1967). Here, on alternate sections of land—owing to the checkerboard pattern created by an original railroad grant—Indian and non-Indian developments have progressed at different rates, leaving Indian tracts idle in the midst of the city. Commercial leasing, leading to both business and housing developments, has occurred on some Indian lands in the past fifteen years, but not without court cases, a legal scandal, and strong Indian expression of disdain for how the U.S. Government has failed to fulfill its trust obligation. Much litigation arose over jurisdiction to zone or tax non-Indian developments on leased Indian land, and much of the story may be found in the newspapers or in law reporters. But the story of the collusion in the handling of court appointments of guardians and the corruption in their management of Indian lands has more effectively been told in Ringwald's Pulitzer Prize-winning series of articles, selections from which have been reprinted (Ringwald, n.d.). (For a favorable picture of the court's role in the administration of Indian land at Palm Springs, see Ainsworth 1965.)

Few studies of urban use of Indian lands exist, although references to non-Indian leasing or purchase of some Indian parcels for urban purposes may be found scattered in the literature. Recent reference to suburban housing developments on Pueblo lands near Santa Fe or within driving distance of the Albuquerque metropolitan area point to the heightening interest in trust lands. Similarly, lease developments involving long-term agreements now affect the growth of some reservations more distant from large cities, such as the Colorado River Indian Reservation. But urban encroachment is bound to come as the Seattle and Phoenix-Tucson areas and parts of Southern California expand (cf. Steiner 1966). Currently one town stands alone in its legal basis of existence: Salamanca, New York, fully eighty-five percent of which lies within the Allegany Reserve of the Seneca Nation. The history of this situation goes back a century or more to the time of the expansion of railroads, which in this instance passed through a portion of the reservation. After a period of conflict and some confusion over land titles, Congress provided legislation that placed leasing in the hands of the corporate body of the tribe, affecting Allegany and nearby Cattaraugus reserves. As Hogan (1974) points out, these leases come up for renewal within less than twenty years, and the town's anxiety over the matter has become obvious. Presumably, the tribe holds the trump card: by an agreement in law, decided in 1875, the tribe must grant renewal, but the monetary arrangements will be different. While financially the Seneca cannot lose, a lease that will run perhaps two hundred years must surely be almost tantamount to land alienation. Not even the complex problems of Palm Springs can compare to the legal situation at Salamanca, although there seems to be closer accord between city residents and Indians in the New York community. (Another facet of this reserve's tenure problems involves the inundation of tribal lands owing to the construction of Kinzua Dam; see Section AC.)

Leasing of reservation lands—whether of allotments or of tribal tracts—involves legal issues that relate to several other sections of this study. Readers should also refer to the discussion of leasing in Section C; the discussion includes a review of case studies of land-use practices that reflect efforts at tribal resource management as well as the leasing of allotments to non-Indians. Leasing also appears as a significant factor in the discussion of state and local jurisdiction over reservations where considerable acreage, monetary investments, and physical developments have taken place through non-Indian capital. The discussion in Section AC raises questions about the power of state and local government to intervene in developments on Indian lands or to encumber these developments in what must be regarded as a direct challenge to federal supremacy in Indian affairs. Land leasing should also be considered in the context of title change or encumbrance, inasmuch as it has often betrayed the Indian or even the tribe, virtually tying up his patrimony in a way that may be viewed as tantamount to outright alienation through land sale (cf. Jones 1974).

Heirship and Alienation

Although federal policies restricted or postponed the transfer of title—that is, a fee patent—to Indians, a tremendous acreage very quickly changed hands, so that over the years land alienation has represented a serious weakness. Moreover, lands held in Indian ownership all too often passed on to heirs several times in a very few years. It is true that at the outset of the allotment process, many Indians died before they received land parcels, and their shares, as a rule, went to heirs determined intestate. Of course, heirship then as now did not deter efforts to encourage alienation of Indian lands. And alienation has also been encouraged by the termination of federal trusteeship over individual Indians (cf. Fey and McNickle 1959, 1970). The sale of land, as a cause of the loss of the base for freehold farming among Indians in Oklahoma, concerned Forbes, who examined (1941) the role of guardians and state laws governing Indian estates. Forbes concluded that "the Indian's hereditary disregard for and inexperience in private land holdings was an important cause in the rapid alienation of allotments" (p. 193). In the case of Oklahoma Indian lands, the presence of oil deposits encouraged non-Indian land acquisition. Alienation has also resulted from the sale of inherited tracts as part of a land cession (Loper 1955). It has led in some cases to the loss of some of the finest farmland within reservations necessitating a shift to animal raising (cf. Wilson 1972). Cotroneo and Dozier (1974) note how early fee-patents among Coeur d'Alene led to landlessness through sales, or to mortgage indebtedness and subsequent loss of land rights.

Heirship problems require for their full understanding a knowledge of law and administrative practices. Indian lands are subject to the inheritance laws set down by the states, although tribal customs may be invoked under specific circumstances. Most of the older literature is in the form of government documents, which go to great lengths to provide statistical and other data that make clear how complex heirship can become when land is left intestate. Older documents that should be examined include the special tenure studies made by the U.S. National Resources Board (1935) during the early years of the Collier administration. The passage of the Indian Reorganization Act with its emphasis on the role of the tribe by no means eliminated the heirship problem, even though little or no land allotment occurred in the years following the act. Heirship or land fractionation has continued as a problem into recent decades, as witness the several sets of hearings that reported on the problem (U.S. Congress, House of Representatives 1960, 1966; U.S. Congress, Senate 1961; and other studies, as cited by Snodgrass 1968).

Other recent studies offer several solutions to the heirship confusion. Langone (1969), for example, suggested that the government limit the number of those who may inherit land. His study considered how to assign costs of administration, how to effect consolidation schemes, and how to protect mineral and other rights in land. Williams (1970, 1971) went beyond administrative matters to evaluate laws and cases. Her study probed the basic question of why land sale, consolidation, partition, and leasing become so complex when multiple owners hold an allotment. She noted that officials tend to spend more time administering lands with fewer owners, with the net result that many Indians become "helpless absentee landlords." She also discovered that some heirship problems have arisen because of an "inflexible adherence" to probate procedures laid down in law.

Since the days of the IRA, efforts have been made to assist the tribes in their acquisition of allotted lands in multiple heirship (usually meaning five or more heirs), but this practice has progressed slowly, partly because of a lack of funds (cf. Gilbert and Taylor 1966). Williams suggested that there was a need for legislation to grant tribes the power of eminent domain as a relatively inexpensive way to clear title when grossly encumbered. Implementation of a policy that would assist the tribes in gaining ownership of allotments suffering from heirship complexities would at least keep the land in trust. The literature is unfortunately thin on analysis of individual cases correlating, for example, land configuration with land utilization under heirship and after the implementation of consolidation or purchase schemes.

Just how kinship and related social organization among Indians may have affected the probating of inheritable Indian land cannot be fully evaluated because so little of the literature explores the relevant ethnographic data (cf. Shepardson and Hammond 1966 and see Section A). However, a study of the Pima Indians at Salt River, Arizona (Munsell 1967) suggests how a kinship network may influence inheritance today. Munsell reports that lease income, which is less than that from wage-labor, is derived from non-Indian utilization of allotments held both by surviving allottees and heirs. Since tribal capacity enters into the rules governing who can inherit, the extended kinship network selectively eliminates those who do not maintain proper behavior toward kinsmen. Those Indians who moved off the reservation have come to expect an unfavorable evaluation of their eligibility. In general, the BIA does rely on statements of survivors as to who is kin. But if wills are written, the influence of the family network declines relative to that of the individual holding the land. This expression of kinship associated with an introduced tenure institution is regarded not as being derived from traditional patrilineal patterns, but rather as having arisen only in the past decades in response to land allotment. Williams (1971), in discussing the Yakima, supplies an additional example of how tribal rules may govern intestate succession. One should examine applicable state laws as well as the General Allotment Act in order to become fully conversant in the heirship issues (cf. Newkirk 1928; Brophy and Aberle 1966).

Perhaps Cohen (1937) made the most telling observation about the relationship between the white man's laws and the need for ethnographic competence:

> In imposing state inheritance laws upon certain Indian reserves we inevitably read into Indian social life the concepts upon which white inheritance is based, i.e., marriage, divorce, ownership and property, etc. To what extent these concepts represent anything actual in native Indian social organization we do not know. (P. 219)

Termination of Trusteeship

The termination of a tribe from federal trusteeship, the final step, so to speak, toward assimilation, legally ends significant protections over land tenure. Once a stated transition period has elapsed and certain conditions have been met, an Indian reservation ceases to exist as a federal instrumentality or as a jural place. Depending on the provisions agreed upon, a former reservation may remain real property held by the tribe as a corporate entity, or part of it may be divided up and distributed among the membership and the remaining land sold, or, as uniquely in the case of the Menominee Reservation, it may be made into a county with the land then "publicly" held (Hart 1959). It should be kept in mind that such property after termination generally remains subject to the jurisdiction within which it is located, i.e., the state and local governmental units.

While the termination policy has been a tool of Indian affairs at various times and has ushered numerous tribes out of federal trusteeship in the past, it was never so severely criticized as during the 1950s. Actually, of course, the trusteeship of more tribes was terminated in the period 1880-1915 than during the recent period. However, the public had became more fully knowledgeable of Indian affairs in the post-war years, when, too, the champions of tribal rights saw the motives of termination as a counterblow to all the efforts of the Collier Administration (cf. Tyler 1964b, 1973). The policy has, of course, always had its advocates and its critics, and the arguments pro and con parallel those voiced during the era of land allotment. A staunch supporter of termination was Senator Watkins, whose position (1957) resembled that of many promoters of the allotment policies in the last century. LaFarge (1957) offered an able retort to the Watkins position. Later studies addressed themselves to a review of the legislation and administrative problems that termination has produced (Brophy and Aberle 1966; Fey and McNickle 1970; Peterson 1970; Washburn 1971b; Tyler 1973). The studies by Brophy and Aberle and by Tyler were written in conjunction with the work of the Commission on the Rights, Liberties and Responsiblities of the American Indian. Hyde, in a brief seminar paper (1971), suggested ways in which a tribe might retain partial trusteeship after termination. Some of the interpretations of the intent and effects of the termination of federal trusteeship emphasize the shift of jurisdiction from federal to state (cf. Debo 1970). It can be argued that the lifting of the trust status of Indian land is a political modification over tribal property more than a change in its tenure structure. Certainly the increase in influence of state and local laws once the reservation ceases to be a federal instrumentality demonstrates how closely tied are our political and property institutions where Indian land tenure is concerned. (Cf. Price's 1973 discussion and see Section AC.)

Although the termination policy affected the land status of several tribes before it was shelved as an inappropriate measure, only two—the Klamath and the Menominee—have received any real scholarly appraisal; and the latter has become a *cause célèbre*. The definitive work on the Klamath is an ethnohistory (Stern 1965) that very sensitively examines Indian-white relations and the function of the reservation. Stern, in collaboration with Vincent Ostrom, prepared a background paper on Klamath termination for the volume edited by Brophy and Aberle (cf. Fey and McNickle 1970 ed.). Despite the many problems that beset the tribe during the ordeal of termination and since its consummation, the division of land and the sale of a portion of the reservation to the government has not been seen as disruptive, for much of the tribe accepted termination, having been essentially assimilated years ago. Nonetheless, several studies have pointed critically at shortcomings of the policy as applied to the Klamath. Singled out for special criticism was the fact that in order to pay individual Indians their cash share of tribal resources, the Klamath were forced to sell a sustained-yield forest that had been netting a fair annual income for the tribe. The fact that much of this forest was acquired by the Forest Service, which has been operating under sustained-yield principles, does not alter the basic issue of the Indians' alienation of their landed patrimony (cf. Hood 1972). A further indication that Klamath termination was not a happy event consented to by all of the tribe is the recent lobbying effort to bring about a restoration bill akin to that won by the Menominee (December 1973, P.L. 93-197).

Menominee termination has triggered a mass of writings that has helped to draw attention to the ill effects that this policy has had on a tribe not fully prepared to take up land management and civil government as defined by the white man's laws. Conversion of a reservation to a county under state law led to much of the financial difficulty the tribe has experienced. Indians have feared that their lands would be alienated and that the lumber mill, operated by Menominee Enterprises and representing the only corporate means of livelihood, would fail, and for a time the county approached bankruptcy. The several studies of the earlier years of planning for termination (Sady 1947; Ames and Fisher 1959) were updated by Orfield (1966), who noted that termination had failed to provide real ownership and to stimulate individual initiative and that

> The ultimate goal of the legislation was not merely to grant control of property but to stimulate economic development. From all indications, however, the transfer of tribal assets to a strictly

> regulated form of private ownership has succeeded only in under-
> mining the precarious basis of the tribal economy and in seriously
> damaging the economic self-sufficiency of the Menominee people.
> (P. 801)

Both Orfield and Ames and Fisher provide careful analyses of the provisions of the law and the Indians' reaction to termination. More recently,
Orfield (1973) has evaluated the movement for restoration.

Lurie, an anthropologist, has published two provocative statements
(1971, 1972) concerning recent efforts at land development and the active
position taken by DRUMS (Determination of Rights and Unity for
Menomineee Stockholders), which in 1972 sought new legislation to
restore the tribe to federal trusteeship. She equated Menominee County to
a colony subordinated to the laws of Wisconsin.

In these and other studies scholars have also evaluated such related
matters as tribal water rights, taxation, and governmental jurisdiction.
Neumann (1953) and Busselen (1962) provided evaluations of the impact
of termination on Indians in California, where the government allegedly
planned to test the policy. By the time the policy was contested and
finally shelved, some 40 rancherías upstate had been terminated. Schusky
(1959) evaluated fiscal, psychological, and cultural effects that attended
the planning of tribal adjustment to land inundation behind the Fort
Randall Dam on the Lower Brulé Reservation in South Dakota. In the
early planning it was suggested that compensation for the loss of land
would enable the Indians to move toward termination of federal services
by 1975. Yet Schusky observed that it was doubtful that the tribe would
have reached economic capacity to be severed; in fact the legislation never
incorporated a provision for termination. And despite considerable urging,
neither the Turtle Mountain Chippewa nor the Eastern Cherokee accepted
termination (Fey and McNickle 1970 ed.; Delorme 1955).

The pair of studies of Narragansett detribalization by Boissevain
(1956, 1959) points up how in certain specific situations remnants of
tribes in the East have accepted termination, in this case under the
provisions of Rhode Island state law in 1880. Boissevain suggested that
detribalization could be successful, provided that the Indians initiated the
transfer of status, that they had become fully integrated into the community, and that their desire for tribal cultural continuity was respected
by non-Indians. In addition, it seemed important that the legislative body
pay just compensation prior to the marketing of Indian land. In the case of
the Narragansett, the tribe organized under the IRA even without a land
base, and they have persisted as a distinct people despite the termination
of the trust status of their land nearly a century ago. However, it should be
pointed out that the Narragansett had never been supervised by the federal

government; that is to say, their termination did not shift jurisdiction to a traditionally anti-Indian government, as has so often been the case in the West.

In recent years conflicts over Indian reservations have seemed to stem more from jurisdictional issues than from questions of actual ownership of land. Yet both subtly and overtly the effects of local governmental laws and ordinances impinge upon or encumber the exercise of rights in property. Section AC focuses on many of these relationships.

Notes

1. *Ranchos,* not to be confused with *rancherías,* were large land grants during the Spanish days in the Southwest; many of these grants passed to Anglos through purchase or other means even while Indians still resided, for example, in their villages. The Spanish referred to the villages as rancherías. In later years, the term "ranchería" came to be applied to smaller Indian reservations in upstate California.
2. From time to time *Akwesasne Notes* (published at the St. Regis Mohawk reservation in upstate New York) includes articles that recount the land problems of the Seneca and other tribes in New York and New England.
3. The annual reports of the Lake Mohonk Conference of Friends of the Indian have been published on microfiche by Clearwater Publishing Company. A printed index volume, containing an introductory essay on the history and significance of the conferences, has been announced. A microfiche edition of the Annual Reports of the Indian Rights Association has also been announced by the same publisher.

Works Cited in Section BC

Abel, 1904
Aberle, D., 1974a/b
Aberle, S. D., 1948
Ainsworth, 1965
Ames & Fisher, 1959
Anderson, 1956
Anonymous, 1960, 1973
Bailey, 1972
Ballas, 1960, 1962
Barrett, 1926
Berthrong, 1956, 1971
Billington, 1974
Bohannan, 1963
Boissevain, 1956, 1959
Bonnin, 1924

Brant, 1969
Brayer, 1939
Brophy & Aberle, 1966
Brosius, 1924
Brown, 1944
Buffalohead, 1964
Buntin, 1932
Burney, 1936
Burns, 1954
Burrill, 1972
Busselen, 1962
Cady, 1926
Carlson, 1971
Chapman, 1942-43, *1946, 1948
Clark, 1947

Cohen, F. S., 1937, 1941, 1942
Cohen, L. K., 1960
Condra, 1907
Congdon, 1967
Cornett, 1954
Cotroneo & Dozier, 1974
Crevelli, 1959
Dale, 1942, 1949
Danziger, 1974
Davis, 1919
Deardorff, 1941
Debo, 1940, 1970
Deloria, 1974
Delorme, 1955
Donaldson, 1884
Dunham, 1937, 1941
Dyer, 1945
Ewers, 1958
Ezell, 1955
Fey & McNickle, 1959, 1970
Fielding, 1952
Fletcher, 1885
Fontana, 1963
Forbes, G., 1941
Forbes, J. D., 1967
Fritz, 1963
Gates, M., 1886
Gates, P. W., 1936, 1937, 1954,
    1968, 1971
Gibson, 1963
Gilbert & Taylor, 1966
Gittinger, 1917
Gladen, 1970
Graebner, 1945
Green, C. L., 1939
Green, E., 1923
Greever, 1954
Haas, 1957
Hagan, 1956, 1961, 1971a/b
Haley, 1940
Harper, 1943
Harris, 1953
Harrison, 1887
Hart, 1959
Hewes, 1942a/b, 1944
Hey, 1939
Hill, E. E., 1974
Hill, J., 1927
Hogan, 1974
Hood, 1972
Hoover, 1931b

Houghton, 1920
Hudson, 1973
Humphrey, 1905
Hutchinson, 1964-65, 1969
Hyde, 1971
ILIDS, 1972
Jackson, 1881
Jefferson et al., *1972
Johnston, 1948
Jones, G. T., 1974
Jones, V. H., 1950
Kappler, 1903-38, vol. IV, 1929
Kasch, 1947
Kelly, 1963
Kinney, 1937
Knoepfler, 1922
Koch, 1924-26
LaFarge, 1957
LaManna, 1934
Lambert, *1973
Lang, 1953
Langone, 1969
Leupp, 1909
Long, 1949
Loper, 1955
Lurie, 1966, 1971, 1972
Madsen, 1958
Mardock, 1971
McCullar, *1973
McIntyre, 1969
McNickle, 1946
Mead, 1932
Meriam, 1928
Meserve, 1896, 1933
Meyer, 1967
M.K.M.B., 1942
Monahan, 1967-68
Moore, 1952
Moriarty, *1973
Morris & McReynolds, 1965
Mosk, 1944
Munsell, 1967
Murray, 1945
Neumann, 1953
Newkirk, 1928
O'Callaghan, 1952
Orfield, 1966, 1973
Otis, D. S., 1934
Otis, H., 1947
Page, 1940
Painter, 1883, 1887, 1888

Paulson, 1971
Pennington, 1970
Peterson, 1970
Prather, 1943, 1944
Price, 1973
Priest, 1942
Prucha, 1971, 1973
Quail, 1937
Rae, 1952
Rainey, 1933
Raymer, *1974
Relander, *1962
Rhodes, 1920
Ringwald, n.d.
Ruby & Brown, 1970
Rushmore, 1914
Sady, 1947
Sasaki, 1960
Savage, 1972
Scaife, 1896
Schusky, 1959
Seymour, C. F., 1906
Seymour, F. W., 1924
Shepard, 1935, 1943
Shepardson & Hammond, *1966
Snodgrass, 1968
Socolofsky & Self, 1972
Steiner, 1966

Stephens, 1961
Stern, 1965
Stern & Boggs, 1971
Stewart, 1933
Summers, 1937
Sutton, 1964, 1967, 1970b
Sweeney, 1924
Thayer, 1888
Thompson, *1972
Tibbles, 1958
Travis, 1968
Trenholm & Carley, 1964
Troiel, 1914
Tyler, 1964b, 1973
U.S. Congress, House, 1960, 1966
U.S. Congress, Senate, 1961
U.S. National Resources Board,
    1935
U.S. President, 1912
Wallace & Hoebel, 1952
Warner, 1970
Washburn, 1971b, in press
Watkins, 1957
Westphall, 1965
Williams, E. J., 1970, 1971
Williams, M. C., 1922
Wilson, 1972
Young, 1961

*Denotes works not actually cited, but relevant to this section.

SECTION AC

Tenure and Jurisdiction

Introduction

Of the mechanisms available for redress of grievances, the courts have proven the most responsive to the Indians' pleas for justice. A growing literature, largely legal in character, attests to the frequency with which Indians have taken their grievances to court, especially in the last two decades (cf. Cohen 1941, 1971; Price 1973; Sabatini 1973). This is not because litigation always resolves issues in favor of the tribes; such is certainly not the case. Rather, it is that the executive and legislative branches of government have all too often disappointed the Indians.

Conflicts—between the Bureau of Indian Affairs (BIA) in Washington and sister agencies (such as the Bureau of Reclamation); between the Department of the Interior, parent agency of the BIA, and other departments; and between federal agencies and those states in which reservations are located—have diminished the effectiveness of the federal trusteeship over the tribes (cf. Chambers 1971). Legislative efforts in Congress to augment tribal self-determination are often outweighed by other legislation enabling states to extend their jurisdiction over Indians and their lands. Ambivalence in federal Indian policy, added to increased state and local intrusion into Indian affairs, have made tribes both cautious and demanding. The courts have had a considerable effect on tribal outlook, as has the rise of Indian lawyers and legal organizations (cf. Washburn 1971b).

Unique in its political and legal status, the Indian reservation at times defies clear definition, and this has given rise to numerous difficulties. A reservation, as a federal instrumentality, normally remains immune to state and local jurisdiction; yet because it does lie within the boundaries of a state, and because states do have plenary powers over their own territory, the reservation may be variously subjected to state laws or jurisdiction in the broadest sense. Confusion and conflict are as old as Georgia's intervention into the affairs of the Cherokees in the 1830s (cf. Burke 1969), and as recent as attempts (1969) by the state of Oklahoma to secure custody through extradition of a Cheyenne Indian who had moved onto the Navajo Reservation in New Mexico (Nash 1970). Many states have openly flouted the intent of federal trusteeship within their boundaries by attempting to adjudicate Indian water rights, abridge treaty provisions that govern tribal fishing and hunting, and regulate non-Indian land development on reservations. Confusion may well arise from misinterpretations of the intent of various laws, as in the case of the allotment acts that require the devise of property left intestate to be reckoned according to state laws. Moreover, the unique status of the reservation as both a real property unit and a political-administrative area confounds many analysts; in the absence of clear-cut jurisdictions over land tenure and polity, the tribes are caught in the middle of a conflict among federal, tribal, and state governments.

In actual fact, the limits of state and local jurisdiction have been spelled out in earlier legal interpretations (Cohen 1941, Chap. 6; FIL 1958, Chap. 7), in part updated and modified by court decisions and legal opinions within the past twenty years or so (Oliver 1959; Brophy and Aberle 1966; Cahn 1969; Ericson and Snow 1970). It is of course an oversimplification to suppose that federal supremacy leaves no room for enforcement by the state civil, criminal, real estate or other codes with respect to either Indian or non-Indian utilization of reservation resources. Such a supposition is impossible today, in part because of the considerable vacillation of federal Indian policies over termination (see Section BC). Moreover, when the government passed enabling legislation to help the states assume civil and criminal jurisdiction over Indians and their lands (P.L. 280, 1953), more ill will and litigation resulted than were anticipated. Often issues have turned on the interpretation of the rights and immunities of the tribes; for while they are on the reservation, they are immune from the powers of the states, yet when individual Indians migrate to cities or work in the rural community beyond the bounds of a reservation, they lose such immunity. Thus it is the legal position of the tribe in its "extra-state" autonomy, which is sustained by the federal government in treaty and law, that forms the basis for continued confrontation and litigation.

Aside from the involvement of federal agencies in the controversial taking of Indian land for reservoirs, most of this section deals with conflicts and litigation in which states and local governmental units play dominant roles. Yet we have noted that more than one agency in carrying out federal responsibilities to the tribes has found itself confronted by another agency pressing the perfectly defensible demands of non-Indian interests. Often where the states are involved in the conflict, the federal government and the tribes argue from essentially the same vantage point. In general, it is state and local interests that continue to attempt to secure water rights that, if allocated to non-Indian uses, would unfairly curtail Indian land development. Several states have openly denied the free exercise of treaty provisions that guarantee that Indians can choose to hunt and fish according to tribal traditions in aboriginal territories (cf. American Friends Service Committee 1970).

Yet the states' arguments seem very appealing, for quite often they turn on the execution of state conservation policy, which many observers would at first argue is in the best interest of all concerned. State interference in the allocation of waters shared by tribes comes about because of confusion over the interpretation of tribal rights to water resources flowing within or through reservations. Such activity has led to the loss of Indian waters vital to tribal economic and social wellbeing. This interference in the exercise of treaty rights is in direct violation of the intent of federal supremacy over Indian affairs. The whole range of issues, in part triggered by the enactment of P.L. 280, has raised questions about the capacity of tribal autonomy within the states and the sanctity of the reservation as a jural place. Efforts have emerged to circumvent tribal immunities by attempting to tax, zone, or otherwise regulate non-Indian development of Indian resources. As is often the case, the literature reveals here that there are many points of view regarding the relationship between state jurisdiction and Indian land tenure. Moreover, some authorities would caution against reading too much into the intent of P.L. 280.

Chambers and Price (1974) have recently focused on the subject of leasing relative to tribal sovereignty within the states. They recognize, for example, that the powers of the Secretary of the Interior over leasing limit tribal self-government and may frustrate economic development on reservations. They examine the government's role both in protecting tribal autonomy and land ownership and in advising the tribe when lease arrangements will incur conflicts over jurisdiction with state and local governments. The authors outline the Secretary's function with respect to lease negotiations, whether dealing with agricultural or grazing resources, minerals, or business, industrial, or realty developments on reservations. They point out, for example, that the free-market situation into which certain tribal lands and allotted lands are projected makes for difficulties in securing the participation of non-Indians, many of whom feel that a broader non-Indian jurisdiction should exist over the area. Often state intervention in zoning, taxing, and related matters ensues. Chambers and Price argue, for example, that the Secretary has allowed jurisdictional conflicts to persist, and also that Congress and the courts have not definitely clarified the questions of jurisdiction that arise when non-Indians enter reservations under lease agreements.

This definitive paper sees governmental administration of leases as an overly protective role of the BIA limiting self-expression by the tribes; it recommends that short-term leases be unqualifiedly approved, as a reflection of the wishes of tribes, but that leases that tend to tie up tribal tenure in given resources for 50 years or more—tantamount to alienation of the resource—be more carefully supervised. Chambers and Price see much of the jurisdictional conflict as beginning in the Secretary's office, where non-Indian interests come into sharp conflict with those of the tribes (cf. Chambers 1971). They also refer to the question of jurisdiction in environmental matters, the National Environmental Protection Act of 1969 (NEPA) and the role of the states.

Other studies have examined aspects of these jurisdictional questions, including the role of the NEPA. For example, Moore (1973) has analyzed the potential of federal leasing of Indian tribal lands for resource preservation. Applying the precedent set by mineral leasing of Indian lands, the author sees the leasing of such lands by the National Park Service as a possible way to protect them from untoward economic development. However, some tribes express suspicion that such leasing will amount to acquisition by eminent domain. Another study (Anonymous 1972) comprehensively reviews grievances relating to Indian resources and evaluates the various means—governmental and judicial—open to tribes seeking redress. Finally, Schaab (1968) noted, in discussing the relationship between the courts and Indian industrial development, that

> The judicial objective should be to make business relations with tribes comparable to those with ordinary municipal corporations. Doing business in "Indian country" should not involve the exotic legal risks created by erroneous interpretation of the leading cases. (P. 330)

However governmental intent is explained, questions of federal or state jurisdiction raise doubts among the tribes about later return of land or the possible further incursion of local government into tribal affairs. Further obfuscating these problems of jurisdiction is the confused legal status of the reservation within the state.

The Indian Reservation as a Political-Geographical Place

An imponderable mass of research suggests the need for a thorough analysis of the reservation in its political-geographical milieu. Almost all the studies reviewed that deal with federal, state, and tribal jurisdiction imply that a special set of circumstances—legal, historical, and geographic— surround the existence of the Indian reservation. Yet no study to date has been devoted to showing how the combination of aboriginal occupancy, federal treaty or law, and administrative practice has created a *tertium quid* in American political geography, although a few works touch on this question as part of a larger chapter on the reservation as a tenure type (cf. Sutton 1964). Nowhere does this land institution appear in the carefully prepared analysis by Elazar (1968 and 1974) of land space and civil society in this country, for example, nor is it ever discussed as a political unit in standard texts on state and local government. Cohen, the legal theorist in Indian affairs, once aptly noted (1942) that "the political conception of the tribe is thus the origin of whatever is distinctive about the legal position of the Indian in the law of the United States" (p. 4). That reservations have become semi-autonomous land units, jural places distinct from surrounding municipalities or counties that are subject to state laws, is the result of a unique set of legal problems that Indians themselves cannot often fully explain or resolve. It is easier to understand what happens to the status of Indian land tenure when a tribe is terminated and its reservation becomes a proprietary unit within a state, or else becomes a territorial unit like Menominee County, Wisconsin (cf. Lurie 1972). Many of the problems that have led some states to seek jurisdiction over Indian reservations and their residents stem from the frustrations of public officials who can see no other way out of this paradox.

Little did people realize, when reservations were opened and surplus lands extinguished, that the proximity of whites to Indians would incur political and legal problems nearly a century later. The changing meaning of "Indian Country" is what makes the Indian reservation an enigma to almost everyone concerned. Not only do local inhabitants misconstrue the reasons for a separate set of laws governing tribes and individual Indians living on the reservations, but they also find it difficult to understand how a reservation can constitute a separate political entity from the state in which it lies, and yet neither elect representatives to the federal government as states do, nor sit on county-wide councils or municipal governments. The most assertive protest, of course, has singled out the tax immunities enjoyed by the tribes; in fact, the alleged loss of tax revenues is a specious argument to protest the continued autonomy of tribal Americans.

Autonomy and its Relationship to Land Tenure

Tribal autonomy is another way of defining Indian self-government. The assertion of the right to self-government has depended upon historical and judicial links to treaties, even though more than a century has passed since the government has treated the tribes as nations. Although Congress retains plenary powers to regulate the affairs of any tribe, in general it has not interfered in this internal "sovereignty" (cf. Oliver 1959; Kerr 1969). Kerr, for example, points out that the converse situation—external sovereignty of the tribes—ended with the Jacksonian era and Indian removal policies (see Section B). It was asserted, however, during the Civil War when certain tribes chose to ally themselves with the North or the South.

As so many scholars suggest, the notion of internal sovereignty, or autonomy over tribal affairs, is limited in its scope and effectiveness and subject to congressional review, but it has been reinforced by the Indian Reorganization Act (1934) and the Civil Rights Act (1968). (Cf. Burnett 1972; Smith 1973.) Cohen and Mause (1968), in a very comprehensive analysis of the tribes, the courts, and Indian administration, considered the tribe in terms of its land base, noting how land has remained the locus of tribal unity. They emphasized especially the issues of autonomy as they affect the future of many reservations where today corporate development of gross acreage may be the only opportunity for tribal members. For example, tribes have sought under the IRA to consolidate land in order to improve the corporate land resource (cf. Gilbert and Taylor 1966). These efforts must be protected from diminution of tribal autonomy. Many tribes, no doubt, recall the opposition of state and local interests, which formerly blocked acquisition programs designed to expand tribal resources (cf. the Navajo situation reported by Kelly 1963, Mosk 1944, and others; see Section BC).

Several views of tribal autonomy or internal sovereignty may prove useful to the researcher. Oliver (1959) questioned the validity of equating the position of the reservation as a legal-political entity with county or municipal status, but rejected as a legal fiction the idea that internal tribal sovereignty was based on aboriginal title. In this view he countered the long-held position of the famous legalist Felix Cohen, who had argued (1953) that internal sovereignty was based on rights of occupancy granted by the sovereign, the United States. And in fact, Cohen's view no longer receives much attention from jurists. Despite the fact that Congress has not granted the same deference to the idea of tribal sovereignty as the courts have, it has nevertheless acknowledged sovereignty as a good policy (Anonymous 1966). As another study suggested (Anonymous 1969),

An Indian reservation must be seen as an ethnic community banded together under the pressure of compact geographical areas, and allowed a great measure of self-government. Separation has been fostered by the desire to retain—and has in turn fostered the retention of—a traditional culture. Poverty due to the loss of ancient means of livelihood and the inability of the Indians to participate productively in the American economy has reinforced separation and affected tribal life. (P. 1356)

Even better stated is Oliver's (1959) point:

Indian tribes are curious enclaves, in some respects a third force within the Federal system. Whether tribal autonomy exists because of inherent sovereignty or a courteous regard for the past by the courts, it is a force of some importance to the tribesmen, enough to set them apart from their fellow Americans. . . . (P. 234)

But he went on to ask, "Is this a good thing? Should any minority be the subject of even voluntary *apartheid*?" (ibid.).

In essence, then, the literature seems to delineate two reasons for preserving tribal autonomy or limited internal sovereignty, both markedly related to land rights. The first is the maintenance of tribal integrity in order to develop reservation resources and administer land and funds with minimal interference (cf. Anonymous 1968a; Fretz 1966; Deloria 1970). The second is the protection of the rights of tribal members. Fretz, however, considered the obligations of the tribe in terms of the rights of its membership, by examining how a tribe may in effect sacrifice the rights of individuals to the corporate interest. As he put it, "the equitable or legal title might be determined to give a tribe plenary power over the distribution of its land despite the fact that use holders have treated the land as their own for generations" (p. 607).

However, such plenary power of a tribe would, no doubt, be modified with respect to the rights of individual Indians were they to invoke the equal protection clause of the Constitution. In part, the tribes are faced with a conflict between their plenary powers over reservations and the rights of individual Indians to seek protection under the provisions of the so-called Indian "bill of rights" act, that is, the Civil Rights Act of 1968.

Deloria, an Indian lawyer, commented (1970) on the corporate vs. conglomerate nature of a tribe and cited the issues of fishing and hunting in the Northwest. He noted that one problem has been that tribal members have asserted an individual right under treaties, and suggested that this has been a decided weakness: the tribe acting corporately would get better results in their conflict with the states involved. Obviously, assertions by the tribe as a corporate entity carry greater political force, and this capacity of the tribe may be politically effective in issues other than land tenure.

The recognition that a tribe has the power to accept or reject a state's request for extradition should be further proof of the tribe's internal sovereignty; the example of the Navajo Tribal Council's refusal to extradite a Cheyenne Indian back to Oklahoma indicates that the tribe recognized that it was exercising one of its sovereign powers. Oklahoma, in frustration, turned to the state of New Mexico, and by so doing sought to negate its recognition of tribal sovereignty, only to be defeated by a court case that declared that New Mexico had overextended its capacity to fulfill the request for extradition by apprehending the Indian (Nash 1970). If other tribes were to assert this power of extradition, internal sovereignty might be better understood by the states. Furthermore, were some reservations elevated to statehood or commonwealth status, they would be able to function on an equal basis with the states and further demonstrate the capacity of tribal autonomy. As for the Navajo, the most effective tribal unit in this country, Stucki (1971) advanced the theory that the size of its population recommended it for statehood; it is notable that heretofore population size has been a factor in statehood in our civil history.

Much of the material discussed above has been ably reviewed in a single study by Ericson and Snow (1970), and issues of jurisdiction and tribal autonomy within the states have been discussed by Pritchett (1963) and Kane (1965). Except in those eastern states which long ago assumed full or partial jurisdiction over tribal Indians and those few western states that have done so recently, it is apparent that federal Indian law and case law reinforce federal supremacy over Indian lands except where Congress has demonstrated intent to the contrary. For example, Pritchett reported the findings of a case in Oregon that interpreted P.L. 280 to include jurisidctional extension of state fish and game laws over tribal domains, only to have the federal district court hold that such was not the intent of Congress. Despite evidence that states have consistently intervened in tribal affairs, the fact is that most states which include reservations within their borders have since the mid-1950s created agencies to serve as liaisons with the Bureau of Indian Affairs and the tribal councils. This suggests an attempt by the states to begin a dialogue in the management of tribal resources in relation to the non-Indian majority in the states.

Public Law 280 was in effect from 1953 until 1968, when the Civil Rights Act essentially superseded it. While it did not actually abrogate the intent of P.L. 280, the Civil Rights Act provided the legislative mechanisms whereby the tribes could, in a sense, contest prior state assumption of jurisdiction, and it also gave the states the option to abrogate any authority they had assumed under the law (see Figure 7). In effect, P.L. 280

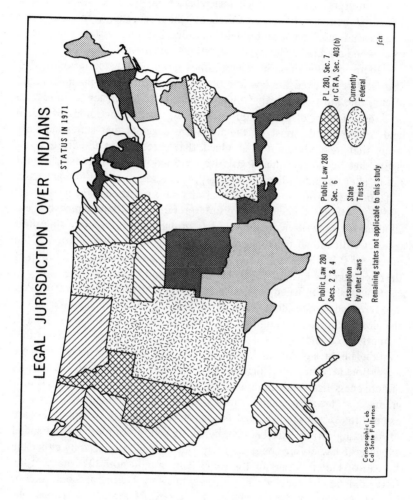

Figure 7[1]

intended only to grant the appropriate states the authority to assume jurisdiction in civil and criminal affairs. As it reads, the law does not give any state reason to assume that it has the power to regulate land tenure or land use on Indian reservations, whether or not the land is used by non-Indians, for the law concerns governmental, not proprietary, questions. Interpretations of disclaimer clauses in state constitutions and statehood acts should be consulted on those questions, for it is these clauses that must be appropriately modified before any state can extend its civil and criminal codes over reservations and tribes.

Where, despite these legal conditions governing the adoption of P.L. 280, a state invoked the law as authority for intervention in Indian land affairs, one must assume that that state considered this new authority to be a federal grant of permission to intervene in the functioning of Indian land tenure. While most of the literature suggests that states are fully aware that treaties cannot be abridged, that states cannot adjudicate water rights that lie outside their legislative jurisdiction, and that states cannot tax or alienate Indian land in any way, it is a fact that all too many cases of state intervention in reservation affairs have occurred since the passage of P.L. 280. It is likely that misinterpretation of the meaning of "encumbrance" as written in the law has brought more than one state into conflict with Indian tribes; for a more thorough legal interpretation of the impact of P.L. 280, see Price (1973), and for a more recent evaluation of the encumbrance question, see Hacker, Meier and Pauli (1974).

Obviously confusion over, and dissatisfaction with, the intent of P.L. 280 have led to considerable review of the law and its applications and to the desire for its amendment, as reflected in the Civil Rights Act (cf. Burnett 1972 and W. F. C., Jr., 1965). In fact, not all of the states that contain important Indian lands and populations have enacted suitable legislation to assume jurisdiction. In those that have adopted the law, its effectiveness has been minimized by confusion over what jurisdiction it grants a state. Also, many tribes reacted almost immediately to state assumption of jurisdiction, and in one or two instances, states were wary of assuming jurisdiction because by doing so they would have the added expense of law enforcement formerly financed and managed by either the Bureau of Indian Affairs or the tribes. One should note that many of the states did not immediately move to assume jurisdiction, and only one or two states have seemingly abused the intent of the law. For example, various issues of the *Newsletter* of the Berkeley-based California Indian Legal Services have discussed how that state has interpreted the authority. California, along with Minnesota, Nebraska, Oregon, and Wisconsin (and Alaska, by amendment five years later), were named in the act and thus immediately assumed jurisdiction with passage of the law.

The literature reflects the problems various states have had with interpretations of the law. State-tribal relations in Arizona, which has the largest number of Indians in the country, have been discussed in a number of reviews which have explored the problems of state assumption of jurisdiction (Kelly 1953; Houghton 1945; Angle 1959; Davis 1959; Shepardson 1963). Neighboring New Mexico has received parallel attention, including reviews of its state constitution (Ransom and Gilstrap 1971; Pease 1969; Nash 1970). In light of the fact that neither Arizona nor New Mexico ultimately enacted laws to assume state jurisdiction under P.L. 280 (Arizona did extend its broad air and water pollution legislation by dint of P.L. 280 to tribal lands[2]) Pease's discussion of revisions in New Mexico's constitution vis-à-vis Indians suggests the kind of legal problems that follow where the state assumes governmental jurisdiction over the tribes. Most of the studies deal with the implementation of law and order in various states—South Dakota (Dykshorn 1972; Abourezk 1966; Jackson 1938); North Dakota (Koons and Walker 1960); Washington, most outspoken on matters of treaty interpretations of aboriginal fishing and hunting (Newman 1970); Minnesota (Cain 1917-18). Many other states are also treated in various government reports emanating from special committees or research bureaus.

The literature does not deal exclusively with existing or pending legislation that would grant states limited powers in Indian affairs. For example, O'Toole and Tureen (1971) discuss the fact that while Maine does not have the right to exclusive power over Maine Indians, the federal government has apparently not exercised its constitutional prerogatives in behalf of those tribes. Their study examines treaty violations in their relation to the enforcement of state conservation laws governing hunting and fishing rights on reservations. The authors claim that "the federal government has never surrendered its powers over Maine's tribes" (p. 39).

Similarly, Gunther (1958-59) reexamined New York's powers over its resident tribes. Reviewing important historical events involving treaties and legislation, Gunther attempted to clarify federal-state matters leading up to the passage in 1948-50 of criminal and civil jurisdiction acts granting New York wide powers, with the proviso that state laws exempt reservation lands from taxation. In light of events in upstate New York in 1974 (the Onondaga reaction to state powers to intercede in tribal decisions to oust non-Indian residents on their reservation), it appears that some Indians do not recognize the state as their trustee. Yet, while they are designated as reservations under state trusteeship, federal paramount powers have not been completely abrogated (cf. Pounds 1922; Parker 1924).

State-tribal relations differ markedly from state to state, as they did among the colonies, and historical events in Indian-white relations have reflected the attempts made by states in recent years toward securing increasing prerogatives to intervene in tribal affairs. The range of problems becomes apparent in reading, for example, Loomer's study (1955) of the Bad River Indian Reservation in Wisconsin, where multiple ownerships within the reservation have involved problems of local tax assessments, title clarification, and related tenure issues. Similar problems have beset other reservations subsequent to the opening of surplus Indian lands to entry under public land laws. And, owing to land tenure configurations in the checkerboard region of the Navajo reservation in New Mexico, inter-ethnic conflicts have arisen there from time to time (Dietrich 1950-51). In her study of the Indians of Oklahoma, Debo (1940) reflected on the mutual adjustments that have been made in accepting unusual situations as a permanent feature of Oklahoma life, and on the Indian's acceptance of an alien economic system and a sociopolitical order in which the Indians are greatly outnumbered (cf. Wax 1970 for brief observations on the Cherokees today).

At the other end of the spectrum are Boissevain's observations (1956, 1959), which suggest that if Indians—in this case, the Narragansett of Rhode Island—can become part of a community in which they no longer feel the desperate need to perpetuate the legal place as a means to survive culturally, they may even accept detribalization.

Few studies have examined the question of jurisdiction in the colonial period, and Kawashima's evaluation (1969a/b) of Massachusetts policy is therefore useful for perspective. Although many of the studies that examine the legal history of state or federal jurisdiction over tribes in the eastern United States dip back into relevant colonial data, to date no one has brought together the whole story of the entire region or its several parts for either the colonial or the national period. In fact, it is not inappropriate to note that historians have been preoccupied with the colonial period, and it is time that more definitive studies explore the history of Indian land tenure under state jurisdiction within this region. Thanks, in some ways, to *Akwesasne Notes* (published at the St. Regis Indian Reservation in upstate New York), the land problems of the tribes throughout the East are being communicated to others; that newspaper, for example, reprinted a Boston *Sunday Globe* article on the struggle for recognition and aid that has confronted eastern Indians.[3]

Taxation, Zoning and Real Estate Development

Although attempts to tax Indian lands have a long history, they have become important only in recent years as Indian lands have attracted new capital for economic development. Tribal lands, however, are not subject to state and local taxation, and disclaimers in statehood acts and constitutions in most western states very clearly recognize the nature of Indian land immunities. P.L. 280, which transferred the authority over civil and criminal jurisdiction, did not lift this immunity. But lands taken out of trust—individual allotments for which the Indian has obtained a fee patent or reservations that have been terminated—fall within the purview of state and local taxing authorities. Most authors agree that questions of taxation of Indian lands and income—however it may be earned from the use of the land—turn on the issue of infringement on tribal self-government and the continuing intent of federal trusteeship. Several papers review the various cases, the historical evolution of tax-exemption, and problems of taxation, some with specific reference to Indians in certain states (Goodrich 1926; Brown 1931; Sharum 1947; Zimmerman 1955; Davies 1966; Faulhaber 1970; Babbitt 1971; White 1972; Cuykendall 1973; Johnson 1974).

Efforts to assimilate the tribes, such as the granting of land in fee simple, assumed that Indians would develop a Euro-American sense of responsibility and become members of the local community. Davies (1966), for example, emphasized that the states have long sought to separate Indians from their tribes and assimilate them, and he suggested that if the interest on the part of the states is so strong, they should shoulder the burdens of any costs. He searched for answers by noting that direct taxation would be impractical but that use of the privilege tax would reach primarily profit-producing property. He also debated the validity of a program involving payments similar to those made to local governments and states in lieu of public land exemptions from taxation.

Babbitt (1971) compared the exclusive jurisdiction concept in Indian affairs to similar practices that involve federal functions within the states. He suggested that it paralleled, for example, the intergovernmental immunity doctrine or similar doctrines of federal instrumentalities that operate within states; he further observed that exclusive jurisdiction over Indians finds its counterpart also in the disclaimer clauses by which states themselves acknowledged federal supremacy.

In all instances it is the tribe as an immune body politic in federal Indian law that cannot be taxed. Faulhaber (1970) notes that no court decision has yet maintained that the states can impose an income tax on tribal members residing on, and deriving income from employment on, a reservation. And presumably this immunity, even if the income is not earned from utilization of trust lands, is an extension of the right of self-government.

Of course, as Babbitt noted, "states still perceive a great disparity between state expenditures for services for Indians and amounts received in turn from Indians" (p. 357).

School funds, regrettably, fail to meet all needs. Aid under the federally impacted areas program and under the Johnson-O'Malley Act provide some funding for Indian education. Local governmental units and school districts that embrace the areas of Indian reservations apparently do not feel the funds are sufficient to compensate for the lack of taxation of Indian property (cf. Rosenfelt 1973). Babbitt has also interpreted P.L. 280 as having had adverse effects in easing the burden of the federal government by disrupting tribal life and frustrating tribal self-government. But the law, nonetheless, did not grant powers of taxation to the states. Non-Indian development of tribal resources, however, has encouraged local imposition of taxes on possessory or *ad valorem* interests. A Palm Springs, California, case involving county efforts to tax lease-holders was upheld in part because the statehood act did not expressly exempt Indian land from state jurisdiction.[4] Other interpretations of Palm Springs include those by Reynolds (1974) and Sparks (1968), both of which examine other cases of zoning and taxing relative to urban proximity to Indian reservations. Off-reservation holdings of a tribe are not considered part of the federal instrumentality as in the case of Mescalero Apache holdings[5] (cf. earlier studies: Anonymous 1955; Knoepfler 1922). On the other hand, even earnings on allotted Indian lands are exempt from federal income tax (Ellis 1974).

The demands of urban growth as several metropolitan areas expand into the rural environment, and of recreation in more remote areas, have drawn attention to Indian lands in selective parts of the West—notably in the Southwest (cf. Steiner 1966). Here land developments are the result of non-Indian capital investment and seem destined for non-Indian utilization; consequently several states have begun to challenge the nonintervention "policy" implied in the idea of a federal instrumentality. This is notable in California and the southwestern states (cf. Sutton 1967; McFeeley 1972; Olson 1972; Gilbreath 1973), where fairly recent land developments involving non-Indian capital have taken place. Sutton reviewed issues at Palm Springs, California before the court's decision; Gilbreath discussed the position taken by Arizona in its attempt to tax lease-holdings on the Navajo reservation. McFeeley listed several categories of state and local involvement that tend to interfere with federal purposes in helping tribes develop their resources—possessory use taxation, *ad valorem* taxation, subdivision and zoning powers, and licenses. States, of course, have good reason to protect their citizenry from fraud, as well as from untoward environmental developments, even within reservations. Just how they can enforce their laws or make them felt indirectly remains an open question. McFeeley recommended that all interested parties get together to promulgate regulations relating to every aspect of leasing in which state and local involvement suggests a need for clarification.

Olson, in his examination of P.L. 280 and the disclaimer clause relative to real estate development in New Mexico, noted that there has been a discrepancy in the interpretation of disclaimer clauses in that only proprietary and not governmental jurisdiction has been restricted. He took the position that New Mexico could not intervene or impose regulations over realty developments without consent of the Pueblos or of the federal government. Matthews (1973), however, challenged the recent court decision affecting the Colonias de Santa Fe development; he argued that the state has a basis for interference in the development of tribal lands—that the zoning, platting, and planning of local land use is a state prerogative that does not preempt federal supremacy in Indian affairs. But Keith (1974) provided a definitive reply to this by restating the conditions under which tribal autonomy flourishes and laying out the limiting circumstances under which states may function governmentally over reservations. For example, states are prohibited from exercising jurisdiction in the absence of specific federal legislation granting them such power; unless a state has properly exercised the options under P.L. 280, an existing disclaimer clause in a statehood act prevents a state from assuming jurisdiction. In general, states may not assume jurisdiction over reservations if by so doing they interfere with reservation self-government (i.e., internal sovereignty) or impair any tribal right granted or reserved by federal law.

Schaab (1968), in examining the role of the courts in adjudicating the interests of Indians or lessees, supported the expansion of federal policy to require the courts to uphold the principle that constitutional guarantees are available to non-Indians who enter into commercial relations with the tribes. In examining the potential strengths and weaknesses of the defunct Indian Resources Development Act of 1967 (actually a bill), he felt that tribes should be more amenable to judicial powers and that "the integration of Indian tribes into the mainstream of national commerce and the industrial development of Indian reservations . . . requires that the courts be available to construe and enforce tribal leases and agreements" (p. 318). The increase in jurisdiction of state courts over Indian land questions, of course, would bring the regulation of such matters within the purview of state laws, even if exemption from taxation did not change as a policy.[6]

Treaty Rights: Hunting and Fishing

Indian property rights extend back in time—that is, they are historical; treaty provisions exemplify this time factor in Indian land tenure. Treaties with the tribes include a multitude of provisions, and where the agreements they record grant tribes aboriginal hunting and fishing in "usual and accustomed" places long after the tribes have ceded vast tracts of land, they tend to produce marked inter-ethnic conflict. Tribes defend the need to perpetuate aboriginal rights to hunt, fish, and trap in certain territories or waters as fundamental to tribal lifestyles and traditional livelihood. Burnett (1970) and Hobbs (1964, 1969) have prepared studies that explore fully the ramifications of these aboriginal rights. Burnett traced the evolution of state interference in tribal hunting and fishing in relation to the grant of authority to states in other civil or criminal areas, and he structured his discussion around the four major types of disputes which most of the other literature examines: (1) federal regulation of hunting and related activities on trust lands; (2) state regulation of such activities on these lands; (3) federal regulation of ceded lands; and (4) state regulation of these lands. The main concern is the attempt of several states, mainly in the Northwest, to regulate Indian hunting and fishing on ceded lands. Hobbs's 1964 paper, a treatise that encompasses the whole field, could serve as an addendum to the *Handbook of Federal Indian Law*, which to date does not adequately treat this field (cf. Price 1973, Chap. 2). His 1969 paper updates the litigation and parallels Burnett's outline of the main areas of concern.

Numerous case studies have appeared in the past decade. Baenen (1965) reviewed the Nez Perce in particular; Wallen (1970) and Aschenbrenner (1971) devote most of the discussion to the Northwest. Clemmer's (1974) observations on Indian and non-Indian resource uses in northern Nevada show how conservation may be administered in such a way that as a resource is depleted, the Indians' right is diminished. McLoone (1968) and Anonymous (1955) apply treaty provisions to the implications and restrictions of P.L. 280.

Particularly useful is Phillips's (1972) analysis of the "vanishing Indian" theory as it has been interpreted in the cases of treaty hunting and fishing. In theory, treaty provisions were considered temporary as a means of protecting traditional subsistence until a tribe became "civilized." Phillips observed, "adoption of this theory, in effect, penalizes the Indians for failing to assimilate into the dominant non-Indian culture" (p. 253).

The state of Washington has received by far the most attention, for there state and local intervention in Indian treaty fishing and hunting activities has created conflict dating back several decades (cf. Buchanan

1915). The American Friends Service Committee (1970) prepared a book-length analysis of the problem which has been distributed widely. Other studies, including Anonymous (1968b) and Sanchez (1972), offer briefer pro-Indian interpretations, and Eastvold and Broz (1954) prepared a state document covering much the same ground. As a rule, intervention has occurred because of misinterpretation of treaty provisions and because of the lack of clear understanding of what powers the states hold in matters governing the tribes within their borders. And, indeed, it has been noted that the problems persist because states are not inclined to write regulatory measures restricting non-Indian sport or commercial fishing and hunting in favor of Indians. Thus, many states have argued that conservation of wildlife is a state affair, and that in the interest of such conservation, the Indian's utilization of wildlife resources must be regulated no more and no less than the non-Indian's. Unfortunately, the states have tended to regulate Indian utilization more stringently, even when it has proven to be marginal in terms of the total wildlife resource, that is, even when Indian use could not appreciably diminish the resource for other interests.

Indians respond to state and local intervention by claiming immunity and by asserting that enforcement of treaties by Congress is consistent with federal commitments to the tribes, which agreed to cessions on the understanding that they could continue to hunt, fish, and trap in "usual and accustomed" places in perpetuity. Yet, as Aschenbrenner observed, the needs of conservation must set an upper limit to Indian claims on resources, and the demonstrated needs of Indians must set a lower limit to such claims. Obviously two incompatible interests have been seeking the utilization of a limited resource, and in more recent cases the definition of those property rights expressed in the treaties has turned on the phrase "in common." State conservationists suggest that some regulation of Indian utilization can be demonstrated to be in the interest of the general preservation of wildlife. The question, as Burnett reviewed it, involves determination of how much utilization is "reasonable and necessary," considering how meager the Indian harvest is every year. Burnett has underscored not only the economic need of the Indians—that is, their need to discover "viable and indigenous industries"—but also the social and cultural needs that are vital to tribal life.

It is regrettable, from the viewpoint of conservation, that one must reject the general objectives of wildlife conservation as asserted by several states—laudable in themselves—in order to sustain the Indians' historical rights. But the government is obligated to protect aboriginal rights set down in treaties, especially when the states attempt to "emasculate the Indian's treaty rights" (Burnett 1970, p. 71) by reasoning that there is no intrinsic difference between the hunting and fishing rights enjoyed by Indians and those exercised under license by other citizens.

Water Rights

In nature, water is a unifying resource that ecologically relates land, soil, and biotic phenomena. In human terms, water is all too often just the opposite of a unifying force; nothing has led to greater divisiveness than the competition for the use and ownership of finite supplies of water as are found in the West. Allocation of such waters raised few questions under state laws until competing demands were asserted for waters that arise within, or course through, Indian reservations. Like state wildlife conservation laws, state water codes have tended to preempt the field of resource allocation, and it has been state courts that have adjudicated conflicts over water rights. In order to understand a conflict that has been an explosive issue involving tribes, states, and the federal government, one must realize that most resource rights of the tribes are often, if not usually, expressed as "implied reservations" accompanying the land, whether the land has been withheld by treaty provisions or set aside by statute or executive order. Such implied reservations include the rights to fish and hunt and to utilize certain waters, and they suggest the additional reservation of sufficient water to make possible the kinds of land uses intended at the time a reservation was established. Unlike the land itself, which can be set aside and defined by specific bounds, water and wildlife are fugitive resources; that is, they cannot be geographically bound. In order to be utilized by Indians, both water and wildlife that also traverse non-Indian properties, predicate the existence of some interaction between Indian and non-Indian users, whose claims to such resources normally run counter to each other. Since the resources are limited in supply, it is necessary that the two groups of users get together and understand what rights are paramount.

In the general scheme of water rights, eastern states tend to uphold the riparian doctrine with its emphasis on location, and the western states— especially in the arid intermontane region—sustain the appropriation doctrine, which determines allocation of water on the basis of the history of use. The riparian doctrine holds that the landowner whose lands lie adjacent to the water has first priority to divert and utilize the water so long as he does not impair its flow. In general, the tribes are exempt from state riparian doctrines and are not normally obliged to fulfill the provisions of the prior appropriation doctrine. Historically, the conflict over water rights arose over non-Indian entries onto Indian lands, some valid and some invalid under public land laws. One found—and still finds on many reservations today—enclaves of non-Indian holdings dependent upon the same waters that Indians depend on to maintain land use. Non-Indians have successfully filed suits not only for waters coursing through reservations, but also for upstream sources that were diverted before they entered reservations. In addition, large-scale water projects planned and developed by the government have often impounded waters upstream of Indian lands; these waters are no longer available to the Indians, in part because they have been allocated to other agricultural purposes.

The determination of tribal water rights has been complicated by the government's antipodal position in water matters. The government is seen as divided in its defense of tribal water rights because it is a party to other water interests and finds that it must allow the tribes to seek counsel elsewhere than from the solicitor's office of the Department of the Interior whenever there are conflicts of interest, as is often the case (Veeder 1969, 1973; Chambers 1971; Berkman and Viscusi 1973; Martone 1974; Weatherford 1974). Indian lands in the western states invariably lie within river basins administered in part by the Bureau of Reclamation, a sister agency of the BIA. Chambers discusses pertinent water situations involving the Yellowtail Dam across the Bighorn River on the Crow Indian Reservation, Pyramid Lake in Nevada, and Pueblo Indian rights on the Rio Grande.

In any interpretation of Indian water rights, the implications of the Winters doctrine are critical (Veeder 1965, 1971, 1972). Often defined as the "reservation" doctrine, based upon a famous case involving public interest in western water resources, the essential meaning of the doctrine is that the federal government holds plenary power over the public domain, and that an implied reservation of water rights is manifest in any land withdrawal—national park, forest, Indian reservation, or the like. This doctrine and other legal aspects of water rights are more fully outlined by Sondheim and Alexander, who noted (1960) the major differences between federal reserved Indian water rights and appropriative rights in western states. They emphasized that the prior appropriation doctrine underscores legal protections for the fruits of diligent enterprise, whereas Indian rights are based on need, not achievement; this seems logical for a people long deprived of the opportunity and sufficient capitalization to take advantage of the implied reservation of water. The Winters doctrine enunciated this implied reservation on the grounds that when lands were set aside for tribes by statute or executive order, and when tribes reserved tracts of land in the wording of treaties of cession, land policy directed the Indians to settle down and become farmers, and this depended upon ample and continuous supplies of water.

The Winters doctrine has been invoked in behalf of the tribes in several instances. Dellwo (1971) saw the doctrine as extending to matters of environmental quality, especially to the question of water pollution. In this instance, the doctrine would apply to more than just irrigation conditions; it would mean that land users must maintain water quality for waters shared by tribes. Decisions in favor of Indians seem to be exceptions to the general federal policy of recognizing the supremacy of state water laws over non-navigable streams. The Pelton Dam (Warm Springs Indian Reservation) decision raised the question of the applicability of state law vs. the Desert Land Act of 1877. In this instance, federal legislation was upheld as binding on decisions governing the location of a dam whose site abuts Indian lands and other public lands (Miller 1957). It was found, when the Winters doctrine was applied to water rights on the upper Rio Grande, that the question of legality of water rights did not arise until New Mexico came under United States land laws after the Mexican Cession (Clark 1971). Clark's study provides a good comparative picture of the existing water rights status of pre-Anglo grant lands, Indian lands, and lands withheld as part of the public domain.

Ranquist (1971) has asked,

> Is the tribe's use of the water restricted to that use impliedly contemplated at the time of the creation of the reservation, or may the Indians change the place and nature of use of their reserved water the same as other water users? (P. 35)

Citing the well-known decision in *Arizona vs. California* (1963), he emphasized that the amount of water reserved for tribal use may be based on the agricultural and related uses at the time of reservation, but beneficial use within reservations is not restricted to these uses. Although he showed that state laws cannot apply to reserved water rights, he did express concern over the effect of this legal situation on users other than Indians. While most legal analysts realize that there is need for cooperative use in a watershed where inconsistent practices may adversely affect quantity and periodicity of a supply much needed by both Indians and non-Indians, states and local water districts are helpless if they try to impose the appropriation doctrine with its emphasis on continuous use, for Indian water rights cannot be forfeited for non-use or abandoned (cf. Sondheim and Alexander 1960). Ranquist expressed some doubt that a proper body of law exists that can be invoked for the protection of all parties; he also doubts that a single regulatory agency would be acceptable to all parties.

Despite the disparate positions taken by the tribes in defense of their water rights and by non-Indian landowners making beneficial use of reserved waters, there is potential room for agreement over how best to adjudicate Indian water rights. Campbell has recently enunciated (1974) a less than popular proposal that the quantity of water allocated to the tribes be determined by their present use of and need for water, but that such use not be limited to agricultural pursuits. This position is advanced, in part, to counter the traditional view that water allocations under the reservation doctrine for tribes should be based upon "irrigable acreage," as ultimately also argued in *Arizona vs. California*. Noting that considerable litigation over Indian water rights has stemmed from uncertainties over just what is reserved for the tribes, Campbell reviews the entire realm of arguments for and against the quantification of such water rights in the interest of all parties. The author suggests, of course, that clarification of such rights would benefit non-Indian water users who would once and for all know what waters could be tapped and what quantities must be held in reserve for tribes but could be leased or sold out of trust. She also suggests that in clearing up uncertainties even the tribes would benefit: "An inventory and quantification may go a long way toward eliminating the insecurity of the Indians' water rights and diminishing evils of the dual roles played by both the Interior and Justice Departments" (p. 1308). It is her view that uncertainty has encouraged wide governmental discretion in the administration of tribal water rights, often to the detriment of Indians. Yet clarification of water rights under the reservation doctrine would give Indians a defensible claim, even if, in some instances, it would lead to some frustration in the development of their resources. Hitherto, quantification has been either neglected in the literature or bypassed because the government had always been reluctant to quantify Indian water resources, feeling that it would reduce their flexibility in allocating tribal rights. Campbell does not share this view, but rather argues that the government has seen the unspecified water right as a form of compensation for past wrongs.

The studies mentioned above report the issues in litigation and in administrative practice that relate to the allocation and use of water. Other legal conflicts involving water have come up in connection with access and wharfage rights on bodies of water and the taking of land for reservoirs. Normally, local law prevails in determination of the title to land below high-water levels, and in general it has been federal practice to be uninterested in submerged lands beneath navigable waters once a state enters the union. In the case of Flathead Lake in Montana, the state had acknowledged that owners of land bordering on navigable waters could take title below the low-water mark. Consequently certain submerged lands became part of the reservation, which the treaty alone would not have guaranteed. But the Indians' fishing rights, since they were based on a treaty, were said not to be dependent on the ownership of the lake bed (Haddon 1965). Haddon referred also to the Red Lake Indian Reservation in Minnesota, to show that an implied reservation of land containing navigable waters might have existed. In the latter case, lands along the lake shore had been allotted, but Congress had apparently not extinguished the tribal trust in the lake bed. The author concluded that the state law of riparian rights to land at low-water mark upheld the Indians' title to the bed of the lake. Rarely is a state law invoked for the benefit of Indians as happened here; usually it is federal policy which is overriding.

Reservoirs and Indian Lands

In the summer of 1972, as notable a figure as Arthur E. Morgan, first chairman of the Tennessee Valley Authority (TVA), openly urged that agency to shelve plans for Tellico Dam on the Little Tennessee. His reason was the potential destruction of archaeological sites of the Cherokee Indians.[7] Once again the government was seeking to inundate cherished Indian ground for the sake of flood control and land reclamation. Dams in many places around the world, at the same time that they elevate living standards, also depreciate the environment. Indians have been most vocal in opposition to the inundation of their finite and often marginal resource. A dozen or more dam construction projects have affected Indian lands in the United States (cf. Berkman and Viscusi 1973), and in most instances the federal government has instigated these projects (see Figure 8). All too often, although the potential disruption has led to litigation and injunctions against the project, construction has ultimately been completed and the Indians relocated. The taking of bottomlands within reservations has invoked outspoken anger and hostility by Indians and their allies. Morgan, who spoke up against Tellico Dam, also sought to assist the Allegany Senecas in their efforts to stop the construction of Kinzua Dam. The dam ultimately inundated parts of the Cornplanter Reserve in Pennsylvania, including the grave of Seneca religious prophet Handsome Lake, and parts of the Allegany Indian Reservation in Pennsylvania and New York. Morgan's own analysis (1971) discusses the Kinzua Dam and such similar projects as the Garrison and Oahe Dams. In a slightly more journalistic vein, Edmund Wilson wrote (1959) of the problems of land severance for dams for the St. Lawrence Seaway in New York which affected the Tuscarora, St. Regis, and Allegany reservations.

The Kinzua Dam, located on the upper Allegheny River, drew considerable attention in its planning stages because it reawakened old hostilities between Indians and the government. Here the Army Corps of Engineers was bent on the construction of a flood-control project to protect downstream urban-industrial developments in the Pittsburgh area. Morgan (1971) reported, on the basis of his independent survey, that a

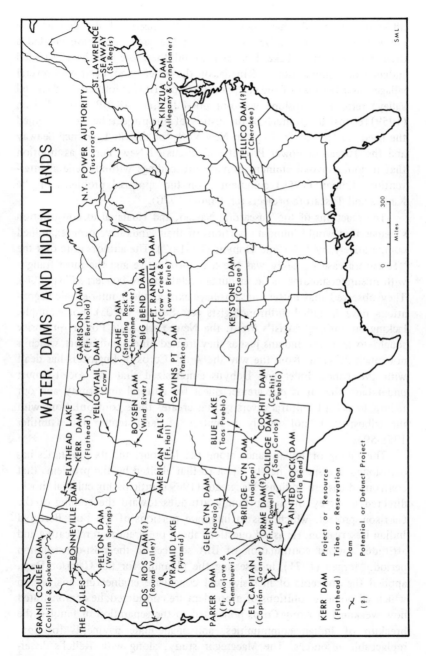

Figure 8[8]

different site would have better served the needs of the downstream population. The alternative site would at the same time have created a discharge path into Lake Erie and would therefore not have affected Indian lands. Inundation at Kinzua, on the other hand, destroyed several villages, and because of the steepness of slopes (it was formerly a glaciated valley) relocation upslope was not possible (see MRBIP 1963). Wilson (1959) reconstructed much of the history of this project; he also examined the need for land at St. Regis in New York for the St. Lawrence Seaway and the Tuscarora Power Project and discussed New York's assumption that it could invoke eminent domain proceedings without federal intervention. Edman (1959) commented on the appraisal problems of the Kinzua and Tuscarora projects (cf. Painter 1970).

The reactions of the Tuscarora, Navajo, and Hualapai to construction schemes that would inundate portions of their lands have been examined comparatively by Euler and Dobyns (1961-62). The authors note that the "Tuscarora case certainly was the least productive and the most fraught with misunderstanding as far as human relations are concerned" (p. 206). They observed that better relations have existed where inter-ethnic negotiations have included anthropologists (cf. Sutton 1970a). For example, lacking an anthropologist's input, the New York State Power Authority sought to treat the Indians just as they treated other landholders, which is not much different from the way the Army Corps of Engineers has dealt with the tribes. Euler and Dobyns emphasized that our society must understand that it is our greater quest for cultural uniformity and our failure to accept cultural diversity that creates these confrontations with the tribes; it is not simply a matter of land tenure (cf. Gunther 1958-59).

The taking of Indian lands along the Missouri and its tributaries has occasioned a response nearly equal to that elicited by the problems that confronted eastern Indians. Macgregor (1949), anticipating cultural shock, directed a survey of Indian family attitudes toward the coming of the Garrison project, which was to inundate portions of the Fort Berthold Indian Reservation. He asked questions about preferences in relocating and attitudes toward continuation of BIA services in the post-construction period. Morgan (1971), in assessing the planning for the Garrison Dam, applied the concepts of inclusive and conclusive engineering analysis, in which all possible solutions of a problem are considered; he demonstrated how weakness in Army Corps policy led to the separation of familes, the breakup of Indian communities, and inadequate payments for non-replaceable resources. The Macgregor study, along with Reifel's dissertation (1950) and article (1952) reveals efforts to ameliorate the plight of Indians faced with flooding by consulting their own counsel on how they would adjust. It was apparent that the bulk of the tribal membership did not want to leave the reservation or give up federal services for state services. Yet, since local non-Indian peoples were opposed to the purchase of lands in lieu of those to be inundated, another form of compensation had to be worked out. Nearly 75 percent of the Indians said they would utilize their lands, or would like to if land consolidation could come about, since they were interested in raising cattle. That Indians responded favorably speaks well for the survey and the whole idea that they can be enlisted to help make decisions in land use planning. Deloria (1971) includes tribal reactions to the Garrison Dam project (cf. Shane 1959; Meyer 1968; Glassner 1974).

Indians also made plans for themselves on the Lower Brule Indian Reservation in connection with the Fort Randall project (Schusky 1959). Schusky provided a good ethnological analysis of a people involved in directed culture change; he reconstructed the history of Indian-white relations in the area before he examined the problems confronting the tribe as it prepared for inundation of some of its lands. The tribe arrived at its own program for the utilization of repayment funds—a program including, for example, a land-consolidation scheme. Problems elsewhere in the Missouri drainage have produced related studies on the relationship of the Oahe Dam project to the Standing Rock and Cheyenne Reservations (Morgan 1971; MRBIP 1952). A small portion of the Crow Indian Reservation was inundated by Yellowtail Dam. Bruner (1961) reported on the relocation of Mandan to less desirable uplands and other areas unsuited to farming, after inundation of agricultural bottomlands on the Fort Berthold Indian Reservation in North Dakota.

Dams in the Northwest have also inundated reservation lands and portions of treaty territories. In noting that the Warm Springs Indians in Oregon had achieved some success in corporate enterprises through the use of compensation funds, Hunt (1970) recounted the loss of traditional salmon fishing grounds owing to the construction of the Dalles Dam on the Columbia River. Hobbs (1969) examined hunting and fishing and the Bonneville Dam, and Madsen (1958) discussed the inundation of lands of the Fort Hall Indian Reservation by the construction of the American Falls Dam on the Snake River. Equally important to the whole discussion is Lazarus's (1960) analysis of the legal conditions under which Indian lands can be taken by eminent domain for power development. He noted that while the Federal Power Act prohibits taking tribal lands without federal consent, tribal land in fee lies outside the restrictions of the law and may be condemned for power projects. Lazarus observed that arguments against the appropriation of Indian land turn on the fact that such action is inconsistent with the purposes for which reservations were established; he suggested that all too often this point has failed to stop development. Lazarus cited two cases approved by the Federal Power Commission—the Kerr Dam on the Flathead Reservation and the Pelton Dam on the Warm Springs Reservation; both were approved by special legislation (cf. Miller 1957).

Other authors have discussed the taking of Indian land for dams in parts of the Southwest and California. Sutton (1964) included historical observations on the construction of Capitán Grande Dam on the San Diego River to improve San Diego's water supplies. This project, dating back to the early 1930s, necessitated the relocation of two village communities and the purchase of two small ranches that later became new reservations. Morgan (1971) reviewed the Painted Rock project at Gila Bend.[9] Two Indian reservations in Arizona will be affected by the construction of Orme Dam—Fort McDowell and Salt River (Coffeen 1972). This dam is part of the general plan for the Central Arizona Project. Coffeen noted that the main issue has been the failure to seek Indian involvement in its planning and in the decision to construct it. As in Plains examples, here too Indians were confused and fearful or felt uncertain about the project, although officials assured them that recreation economy would offset the loss of bottomlands. Furthermore, it was feared that the Orme Dam project would frustrate the fulfillment of a community development plan that once consummated might lead to the release of award monies from a claims judgment in 1965.

There are of course too few Indians to speak for the archaeological treasures that have been or will be flooded by the various construction schemes. Fortunately, many major dams in the West back up water into remote canyons where few people, Indian or white, have ever lived. No contemporary Indian lands were involved, for example, in the creation of Lake Mead behind Hoover Dam, although there were Indian archaeological sites that were only partially salvaged prior to inundation (cf. Sutton 1968). Of course, while resident Indians are most directly affected by inundation of existing reservation lands, there is no reason to doubt that Indians holding a treaty right can protest, and even demand recompense for, losses of their cultural heritage. The Eastern Cherokee did voice objections to potential inundation of lands outside of their present reservation in North Carolina but within their aboriginal territory (see Figure 2).[10]

All in all, of course, scholars feel they must bear witness to the socioeconomic and cultural destruction that is brought down upon contemporary Indian communities by the construction of dams and other waterworks. Three anthropologists expressed this concern well in a statement first appearing in congressional hearings related to the Kinzua project; their comments (Diamond et al. 1964) have general application.

They stressed that the fundamental criterion in protecting Indian lands from such projects should be cultural, specifically the maintenance of continuity between ancient traditions preserved on, and symbolized by, the reservations, and the identity of the tribe as a community in the modern world. They emphasized, like others who have examined reclamation projects, that inundation and the ensuing relocation disturb tribal continuity between ancient traditions preserved on, and symbolized by, the reservations, and the identity of the tribe as a community in the These arguments revolve around a "fair cultural exchange," i.e., not the mere replacement of acreage by some monetary means, but the provision of community facilities and housing or the essentials for the perpetuation of tribal life. The key idea is expressed as "intangible damage," for which monetary recompense is never quite adequate.

Minerals and Mining

The question of state powers over minerals and mining on Indian reservations has been clarified mainly through the efforts of the Rocky Mountain Mineral Law Institute, which has sponsored several related studies (Berger and Mounce 1971; Berger 1968a/b; and see also Section C). Federal preemption of mining regulations on public and Indian lands normally overrides state laws. So long as state laws do not threaten federal policy or intent, however, they may govern exploration and mining. Berger and Mounce have asserted that the uncertainties and intricacies of Indian interests and leasing procedures discourage lessee developments, and that the Indian situation must be fully understood before sound negotiations can take place. Laws governing mining on public lands are inapplicable to Indian lands. Berger and Mounce discussed the Omnibus Tribal Leasing Act (1938) and other provisions, and analyzed the Wind River Indian Reservation case in Wyoming. Here the arguments followed from the principle that law does not allow for two sovereigns to govern identical subject matter simultaneously. Moreover, the researchers found that the Public Land Law Review Commission opposed extending the application of state mining laws to cover federal lands; presumably this would apply to Indian lands as well. They also suggested that the existence of a disclaimer clause in Wyoming's statehood act precluded the state from assuming jurisdiction over oil or gas resource development on or beneath trust lands. (For comparative interpretations of minerals and the Navajos, see Kelly 1963; Gordon 1973; and further discussion in Section BC; and for a discussion of intertribal conflicts over minerals, see Branam 1974.)

Some Conclusions

It is my feeling that researchers have only begun the study of state relations to tribal affairs. If one compares the scope and subject matter of Price (1973, Chap. 2) and Taylor (1972) to the parallel discussions in Cohen (1941), the FIL (1958), and the summary discussion in Brophy and Aberle (1966) on the powers of the states and the question of jurisdictions, it is evident that state involvement has greatly expanded over the past three decades, and its ramifications take one in many directions other than those that have been outlined in this section. For example, Indian political representation may increasingly assert itself toward changes beneficial to the tribes in counties where Indian population is relatively large and where local governments have sought to dominate school policies, levy taxes, or otherwise attempt to zone the development and use of Indian lands. To date there is almost no study of Indian political or electoral behavior in such counties—in Wisconsin, Minnesota, New Mexico, Arizona, and South Dakota—to suggest how Indians elected to local government might have long-term influence on the status of Indian affairs. While the immediate implications would be political, they could lead to a dialogue that might result in greater autonomy for the tribes. There is also a need for full-length studies of the history of various states in terms of Indian land relations, such as several colonial histories have achieved (cf. Wallace 1961; Trelease 1960; Huber 1933). Aside from the focus on Oklahoma, Indian Territory, and the adjacent Plains states and their involvements (cf. Debo 1940; Gates 1954), and a few studies that have focused on Indian administration in a given state (cf. Kelly 1953 for Arizona), the field is wide open.

What questions remain unanswered that bear on Indian land tenure within the context of state and local boundaries? For one, those that deal with potential state attitudes toward the expansion of Indian land or towards its consolidation into larger units that would further tribal economic enterprises. The issues over taxation and zoning are not at an end, and developments by and for non-Indians will invite continued scrutiny by researchers. Issues over eminent domain and the capacity to take Indian lands will always raise the standard question: how do agencies continue to justify taking Indian land for public purposes? Probably potential statehood does not loom as a major question, even for the Navajo, although commonwealth status may come sooner than we think. For we must be reminded that few persons probably expected the Congress to restore the Menominee tribe to trusteeship, a situation that now will invite new inquiries, especially with respect to the effective force of outstanding agreements made while under state jurisdiction.

Will we indeed expect to find a lessening of conflict and a decrease in litigation if the government arrives at a permanent land-base concept for Indians, as suggested by Kickingbird and Ducheneaux (1973)? I would sustain their recommendation (p. 231) that the Indian Claims Commission remain a permanent court for Indian land litigation. On the other hand, I am unsure that Deloria's provocative "contractual sovereignty" (1974, Chap. 8) is really the way to finally resolve conflicts. He sees such a possibility that would once again grant the kind of sovereignty held by tribes in the early nineteenth century; in its contemporary counterpart, the tribes would continue to receive United States economic assistance but would sustain a form of autonomy that exceeds the current situation. In any event, it is apparent that the tribes are moving more and more into the mainstream of economic and political activity; it will not be possible for them to retreat to the sanctuary of trust status if they hope to become involved in local, regional, or national economic or political activities. Yet the trust status of their lands continues to be a foundation upon which to build new institutional means to sustain self-government, and through it to continue to protect land rights.

Notes

1. Figure 7 represents an attempt to show for each state the federal laws currently in effect that govern civil and criminal jurisdiction over Indians. Although litigation continues to challenge state capacity to extend such jurisdiction to Indian trust lands, land in a proprietary sense is not the issue. But land is very much the issue! Only those states which include tribal lands are covered by the legislation cited on the map. P.L. 280 (1953) provides for the transfer of most civil authority in at least three different forms—much of which is probably moot, now that the provisions of the Civil Rights Act supersede the conditions under which many tribes embraced P.L. 280. Conditions have also changed in the last few years so that the map may be, in part, obsolete; yet the pattern suggests the kind of problem discussed in the literature and reviewed in this section. States covered by sections 2 and 4 were specifically named in the act (Alaska was added in 1958); states covered by section 6, under legislative or constitutional provisions, could elect to embrace the law (for example, by abrogating a disclaimer clause in the state constitution); section 7 provided for special means by which states could embrace the act; the Civil Rights Act made it mandatory that the tribes be consulted, that they vote on adoption, and that they then put it in writing to the governors. "Assumption by other laws" means, for some states, transfer by dint of termination legislation covering all or most tribes within a state; for

other states, it means laws such as those governing New York or Florida. One will readily note the other states that have assumed full jurisdiction since statehood or earlier (cf. Koch and Muckleroy studies with reference to Texas). For all practical purposes, reservations in remaining "reservation states"—all but Mississippi are in the West—are governed by internal sovereignty or tribal jurisdiction, except where the federal government has legislated supremacy for itself. The area in white represents states without tribal lands. All sources are the laws themselves and relevant legal articles cited in this section.

2. *Arizona Statutes* (1969) *suppl.*, title 36: 215, 223.

3. "Those non-Indian Indians," reprint in *Akwesasne Notes*, Spring 1971 issue, p. 15. See also Tamarin 1974.

4. *American Indian Law Newsletter* 4, no. 5 (April 15, 1970); 51

5. *American Indian Law Newsletter* 4, no. 15 (April 20, 1971): 152

6. For a comparative picture of real estate booms on reservations relative to general land speculation and development in the nation, see Wolff 1973.

7. *Akwesasne Notes*, late August ed. (1972): 18.

8. One can find a government document—mostly hearings—for virtually all of the projects shown on this map. As can be readily seen, dams impound great stretches of the nation's major rivers which course through or traverse Indian lands. The Missouri is most notable from the viewpoint of land severance and human dislocation. Three projects shown may already have lost status—Tellico on the Little Tennessee, Orme on the Verde, and Dos Rios on the Eel. But other projects of long standing may have been overlooked in this necessarily selective compilation.

9. One should distinguish permanent inundation or severance of Indian lands for various purposes from the practice of granting rights-of-way through reservations, which does not always involve questions of land appraisal or relocation of communities, or necessarily lead to litigation (cf. Frison 1965).

10. Baldwin, Gordon C., 1966 *Race Against Time: The Story of Salvage Archeology* (New York: Putnam's Sons) provides a useful statement about salvage archaeology, but neither his study nor others on this theme really examine the inundation of Indian lands in its historical or archaeological context.

Works Cited in Section AC

Abbott, 1960
Abourzek, 1966
American Friends Service Committee, 1970

Angle, 1959
Anonymous, 1955, 1966, 1968a/b, 1969, 1972
Aschenbrenner, 1971

Babbitt, 1971
Baenen, 1965
Benge, *1960
Berger, 1968a/b
Berger & Mounce, 1971
Bergman & Viscusi, 1973
Boissevain, 1956, 1959
Branam, 1974
Brophy & Aberle, 1966
Brown, 1931
Bruner, 1961
Buchanan, 1915
Burke, 1969
Burnett, 1970, 1972
Cahn, 1969
Cain, 1917-18
Campbell, 1974
Chambers, 1971
Chambers & Price, 1974
Clark, 1971
Clemmer, 1974
Coffeen, 1972
Cohen, 1941, 1942, 1953, 1971
Cohen & Mause, 1968
Currie, *1957
Cuykendall, 1973
Davies, 1966
Davis, 1959
Debo, 1940
Dellwo, 1971
Deloria, 1970, 1971, 1974
Diamond et al., 1964
Dietrich, 1950-51
Dykshorn, 1972
Eastvold & Broz, 1954
Edman, 1959
Elazar, 1968, 1974
Ellis, 1974
Ericson & Snow, 1970
Euler & Dobyns, 1961-62
Faulhaber, 1970
Feit, *1973
FIL, 1958
Fretz, 1966
Frison, 1965
Gates, 1954
Gilbert & Taylor, 1966
Gilbreath, 1973
Glassner, 1974
Goodrich, 1926
Gordon, 1973

Gunther, 1958-59
Hacker, Meier & Pauli, 1974
Haddon, 1965
Hobbs, 1964, 1969
Houghton, 1945
Huber, 1933
Hunt, 1970
Israel & Smithson, *1973
Jackson, 1938
Kane, 1965
Kawashima, 1969a/b
Keith, 1974
Kelly, L. C., 1963
Kelly, W. H., 1953
Kerr, 1969
Kickingbird & Ducheneaux, 1973
Knoepfler, 1922
Koons & Walker, 1960
LaFontaine, *1973
Lazarus, 1960
Loomer, 1955
Lurie, 1972
Macgregor, 1949
Madsen, 1958
Martone, 1974
Matthews, 1973
McFeeley, 1972
McLoone, 1968
Meyer, 1968
Miller, 1957
Moore, 1973
Morgan, 1971
Mosk, 1944
MRBIP, 1952, 1963
Nash, 1970
Newman, 1970
Oliver, 1959
Olson, 1972
O'Toole & Tureen, 1971
Painter, 1970
Parker, 1924
Pease, 1969
Phillips, 1972
Pounds, 1922
Price, 1969, 1973
Pritchett, 1963
Ranquist, 1971
Ransom & Gilstrap, 1971
Reifel, 1950, 1952
Reynolds, 1974
Rosenfelt, 1973

Sabatini, 1973
Sanchez, 1972
Schaab, 1968
Schusky, 1959
Shane, 1959
Sharum, 1947
Shepardson, 1963
Smith, 1973
Sondheim & Alexander, 1960
Sparks, 1968
Steiner, 1966
Stucki, 1971
Suttles, 1963
Sutton, 1964, 1967, 1968, 1970a
Taylor, 1972

Trelease, 1960
Tyler, *1973
Veeder, 1965, 1969, 1971, 1972,
    1973
Wallace, 1961
Wallen, 1970
Washburn, 1971b
Wax, 1970
Weatherford, *1974
W.F.C., Jr., 1965
White, 1972
Wilson, 1959
Wolff, 1973
Zimmerman, 1973

---

*Denotes works not actually cited, but relevant to this section.

SECTION ABC

Land Tenure and
Culture Change

*If the dominant society can control land
tenure, it can control the shape of the civilizing
process. While it is clear that the control over
land tenure has had an enormous effect on cultural change on Indian reservations, it is far less
certain that the effect has been as desired.*

(Price 1973, p. 526)

Introduction

However central land tenure has been to Indian-white relations over the
past several centuries, few scholars treat it as an engrossing phenomenon to
which they can turn again and again for new evidence and new interpretations. Yet most observers of the American Indian have not let the events
of Indian-white land history escape them. Territorial displacement, relocation on reservations, allotment of land to individuals, alienation and
heirship of such lands, and the resource factors which contribute to rural
poverty and urban relocation are all emotionally charged subjects that find
their way into countless studies. Much of this literature repeats similar
events and themes, yet on occasion new viewpoints or methods present a
fresh perspective. Such has been the case with the new vogue of colonial
history, for these studies make land a fundamental issue as they reexamine
colonial attitudes toward the Indians as one aspect of European occupancy
of the eastern seaboard. Earlier discussion (Section AB) underscored the

contribution of ecological and ethnohistorical research. But in general the bulk of ethnographic and historical studies focus on other themes. While there is a preoccupation with Indian land history, it is event-oriented, and although there is considerable ethnographic analysis, little of it places land in the foreground (cf. Wissler 1940; Hagan 1961; Spicer 1969b; Debo 1970). To be candid, it seems that many scholars who include brief discussions of land tenure feel it somehow belongs but do not feel at home with the subject. When seemingly most critical to an argument, it is often skirted or aborted as a topic. This is an especially critical problem of many studies that purport to interpret Indian acculturation.

What seems apparent is that few interpreters have been urged to pull together the diverse and often obscure data that would permit them to see land tenure as a critical economic institution that directly influences the lifestyles of the tribes and individual Indians. In part, perhaps, this synthesis awaits the more complete mining of a lode of information and the interpretation of countless other cultural factors contributing to Indian acculturation; certainly land tenure does not function independently of other institutions in society. Since the 1930s, when anthropologists began to focus on "time-dimensional studies" and to give considerable thought to the methods of acculturation research (cf. Keesing 1953), the body of literature that has specifically examined culture change has expanded beyond the competence of any one interpreter. Many of the writings in the pre-war years were speculative and directed toward methodological inquiry, and this continued to be the case for at least a decade into the post-war period (cf. Steward 1955a). And while there is a plethora of theoretical discussion of acculturation and much innovation through borrowing from sister disciplines such as geography, history, and sociology, little of it advises the interested student of how to examine pertinent tenurial practices in their role as factors leading to, or growing out of, culture change.

For example, Linton (1940) and Spicer (1961) edited symposia in the comparative study of Indian acculturation; but although their contributors did draw upon relevant historical events involving land and even made some instructive observations, neither editor selected land tenure as a topic for comparative review, and in neither case did the discussion of land profoundly influence generalized conclusions about Indian acculturation. Eggan's two volumes (1955, 1966) considered social change and referred to the fact that changes in social structure have continued throughout the historical period, not only as a result of direct acculturative processes but also as a consequence of internal adjustment to new conditions of social and cultural life. Nevertheless, because he did not correlate changes in social organization with relevant changes in land institutions, it cannot be determined whether or not these social changes are derived from modifications or extinguishment of aboriginal land institutions. Driver, however, reported (1969) the breakup of matrilineal systems owing to the assignment of land to men as heads of nuclear families among some Southeast tribes, and he noted that changes in kinship organization came in response to altered ecology and economy, as well as to contacts between peoples of differing systems. (For an earlier treatment of the role of descent and residence in land tenure, see Murdock 1949.) In almost all of the perspective studies in Leacock and Lurie's historical symposium (1971), land tenure receives selective review and is at times even treated as a key factor whose changes are cited as contributing to the decline, poverty, relocation, and other problems of Indians.

The methods of acculturation studies are of course comparative, whether the subject matter is laid out along a time or space dimension. Much of the interpretation takes the form of a time-space continuum which scholars must establish by turning to relevant historical events. Essential for such study is a reference plane from which to observe and measure culture change. Earlier focus on the distribution of culture elements and culture areas adapted in many ways the ideas on areal differentiation and the regional views of man and space held by geographers. But the notion of a time-space continuum and the importance of spatial concepts in the evaluation of a culture in place, though seemingly basic to geography, were still in a formative stage when anthropologists were seeking to establish an acculturation theory and apply it to Indians. Similarly, we find that human mobility in social space evolved as a behavioral concept independent of the study of acculturation; only later was it incorporated into the methodology of the study of Indian culture change. The study of acculturation has depended mostly upon the contributions of anthropologists.

The Linton and Spicer volumes, for example, drew attention to the application of the concepts of directed or enforced culture change and nondirected culture change among the tribes discussed. Many of the essays in these volumes reveal the contrasts among the deliberate and purposeful efforts to intervene in tribal lifestyles as a way to make Indians adapt to new conditions (e.g., land allotment); they also examine how, for example, policy has moved steadily away from enforcement of Euro-American values upon the tribes and toward allowing Indians to encounter our culture on their own terms, as by relaxing rules governing the free movement of Indians on and off reservations. The present way tribal governments function in general should be seen as an example of nondirected culture change. Other scholars have given different labels to much the same thing; for example, Barnett (1956) spoke of "reactive adaptation" or progressive adjustment and stabilized pluralism. But Lurie more recently (1971) preferred to refer not to cultural pluralism but rather to articulatory movement in the changing Indian situation, for in describing the vitality of Pan-Indianism, she asserted that "pluralism often occurs without the positive effort and contractual features that seem to characterize the Indians' endeavors" (p. 418).

These conceptual tools have been applied to reservation Indians in various ways. Spicer, an astute student of cultural continuity and change, considered the Indian reservation to have played a coercive role in the structural reorganization of tribes, with the definite intent of remaking Indian culture (1961). He observed the conformity that was achieved in reproducing the isolated farmstead wherever the policy was fully carried out, and he noted the cultural losses that resulted, for the Indian who participated in this process tended to assimilate readily. In his Southwest volume (1962) Spicer contended that the reservation has been a major force in maintaining the sacred relationship of man and land for those Indians who have resided in the United States (in contrast, for example, to Indians south of the border). A basic factor affecting group identification in the Southwest has been the maintenance of residences within traditional territories, which has tended to promote tribal cohesion. Thus he and others (cf. Beals 1953) have reported the capacity of "resistive acculturation" that has enabled tribes to reject certain intrusions by Euro-American culture.

Some observers contend that the reservation has been an ambiguous medium for the preservation of tribal lifeways through the maintenance of an autonomous land base. Dozier, Simpson and Yinger (1957) suggested, for example, that the reservation has not hindered assimilation (nor, they felt, had termination or relocation ended tribal identity). In their view individuals, but rarely tribal groups, assimilate. One might conclude that so long as the autonomous base—or jural place—persists, it is at least a hafl-way house, whose tenure structure and federal trust protections allow considerable latitude in how tribes may sustain traditional culture even as they adopt Euro-American economic or tribal institutions. Lurie (1971) felt that "left to their own devices, tribal communities could persist indefinitely as distinctive and dynamic combinations of local tradition, Pan-Indian elements and different selections from the larger society" (p. 420). She viewed the reservation system as having helped Indians to articulate, though not create, attitudes, and based this view on the fact that there are many distinctly Indian communities neither under federal jurisdiction nor benefitting from special services. Boissevain's views (1956, 1959) of the persistence of the Narragansett who detribalized nearly a century ago tend to sustain this position.

Yet, as Hallowell (1957) suggested, "one effect of the reservation has been the conservation of those aspects of native culture that had survived all the vicissitudes of previous contacts . . ." (p. 237). In the context of the Southwest, where tribes have retained more residual holdings, this observation may have considerable substance. Yet Spicer suggested (1961) that it was difficult to assess the effect of the reservation on the persistence or change of tribal culture, just as it was hard to identify the effects of the reservation in attempting to determine what is aboriginal and what has changed. Fenton's (1940) interpretation of the effect of the reservation in parts of the East was that while it preserved native language, much of the Indian culture had changed.

These methodological issues led Steward (1955b), in presenting a review of the work that anthropologists contributed to land claims research, to contrast two approaches to the study of acculturation. One approach was concerned with differentiating those elements of economy, society, leadership, and territoriality that were aboriginal from those that were post-contact in origin. Here he expanded upon the normative theory in anthropology, "which conceives culture change as an all-or-none proposition" (p. 295); he suggested how Indians at first maintain and reinforce aboriginal ways despite the acquisition of Euro-American culture but are eventually overwhelmed by outside influences and become assimilated. This approach leads, he suggested, to the assumption that what is not strictly Euro-American must be aboriginal. But he pointed to a contrasting approach, often termed "developmental" or "evolutionary," which holds that "special acculturating influences" (p. 296) may have dynamic effects on cultural change; here he argued that even limited contacts may have profound impact on native culture. Steward felt that scholars have tended to underestimate the extent of white influence. His essay underscores the importance of the second approach in acculturation studies and its relevance to land claims and culture change.

What is perhaps needed in the study of how land tenure relates to culture change is a set of questions encompassing all possible relationships between native and Euro-American institutions. Even more sorely needed is a model by which the institution of land tenure can be effectively analyzed as it functions relative to Indian-white history. The literature directs us to characterize much of the relevant culture change among Indians as institutional: that is to say, the cultural changes in question are changes in social, political, and economic concepts and practices that virtually Americanize the tribes in the process of adapting them to the dominant society. Perhaps this is the most instructive feature of Washburn's illuminating legal history of the Indian (1971b), for he stresses the importance of such institutional changes in the evolution of the Indian's status in our society. Spicer (1969b) also provides an approach that emphasizes institutional changes. Less effectively, Debo (1970) and several historians have pointed to the major institutional changes that have led to alterations or modifications of native culture (Hagan 1961 includes a chapter entitled "Acculturation under Duress"). But those studies that are concerned with economic or political activity do not necessarily focus on elements of acculturation that result from changes in land tenure. For example, the practice of farming or ranching does not in itself imply the successful incorporation of the imposed land system. Many scholars have repeated what Stafford (1971) reported for Crow culture change—that Indians have sold or leased land not primarily for economic gain, but largely because of their reluctance to farm.

Yet if scholars examine the common body of institutions that have been introduced into tribal life, they should be able to identify examples of Indian culture change set in motion by the conflict of values, perceptions, allocations, and uses of land and natural resources. These common institutional factors, which are found in quite different post-contact tribal histories, emanate from similar applications of federal land policies. They represent a common set of causes triggering changes both in how Indians identify the role of reservation lands in their external relations with non-Indian communities and the general society, and in how they organize land use and rights to resources internally. Those scholars who examine the market orientation of individual and corporate resources come closer, perhaps, to the issues in Indian acculturation than those who persist in restudying land allotment per se. Those who study the success or failure of tribes that have organized grazing associations and districts as a means of improving the utilization of tribal resources are studying institutional economic activities that differ from aboriginal practices or in some ways modify them. Others identify crucial factors in reviewing how, in their effort to ranch rather than farm, Indians have found land units designed for farming inadequate as management units for ranching. This suggests that Indians have begun to see land tenure as part of a larger economic scheme. Thus some preoccupation with the role of the tribe as a corporate entity since the days of the IRA seems justified.

What some of the scholars are saying is that observers should be wary of being misled by certain evidence. Indians seem to reject farming: so many historians and anthropologists have reported. There never was any good reason to assume that because people have rural roots and would prefer to live away from urbanizing influences, they have a competence or desire to farm. But the rejection of farming does not necessarily emanate from rejection of the idea of private property in land. Too many samplings do point to the need, for example, for a synthesis of observations about the nonuse of allotments as evidence for a rejection of the agrarian lifestyle. Because the subject matter of culture change takes the researcher far beyond the problem posed here, it is useful to outline sets of changes in livelihood, settlement, mobility, and related organization as a means of narrowing the field to those changes that are likely to have arisen from the introduction of Euro-American land tenure practices:

> *new configurations*—e.g., reduction or loss of territory; subdivision of finite resources, often into unworkable land units that are further divided by multiple heirship or alienated; etc.

> *new livelihood expressions*—e.g., shifts from traditional forms: from hunting, gathering, fishing, trapping to farming/ranching; from a subsistence to a wage-earning or market-oriented economy; from on-reservation subsistence to on-reservation commerce or industry; etc.

> *new locus of residence*—e.g., shifts from village or camp to agency town or nearby town or city—at times ghettoized—or to homestead or other rural residence; etc.

> *new sociopolitical and economic identities in place*—e.g., shifts from distinct bands or tribes to amalgams of tribes on reservations and from tribal entity as ethnic-territorial to jural community; the rise of mixed Indian-white communities on reservations, the market-oriented corporate entity, the Indian-white lessee relationship, Pan-Indian associations, grazing associations, local school districts, the conversion of the reservation to a county (i.e., Menominee); etc.

Most Indian communities have experienced many of the shifts in economic and political orientation outlined above; the locus of livelihood and residence and changes in land configurations and allocations have been noted repeatedly. Increased mobility toward both nearby and distant urban places has now probably affected upwards of half of all Indians. The following discussions will demonstrate that changes in native culture that are related to changes in land tenure are often accompanied by evidence of the persistence of aboriginal traits, although these are no longer as apparent as in the past. The response of individual Indians to land allotment over the past four generations reveals more acutely how resistive acculturation has tended to nullify private property in land, just as it is evident how the IRA in general abetted the objectives of tribal self-determination by returning to Indians a greater voice in land-tenure and land-use matters.

Despite Witthoft's tendency to overgeneralize from evidence garnered from the experience of eastern woodland Indians, he succinctly summarized (1961) what reservation cultures have become in the course of time and exposure to the "system" and the dominant society. In his judgment they represent neither the perpetuation of native cultures nor their dilution with European culture traits; nor should they be considered blends of native and European culture or the replacement of the former by the latter. In his view, reservation cultures result from an unconscious but selective process of adoption, interaction, and invention of culture traits, leading to a "live, adaptive and highly integrated system of behavior, belief and technique well fitted to life in a specific environment or age . . ." (pp. 74-75). Since he applied this view to the region least representative of the reservation system, one must challenge its validity outside the eastern woodlands—that is, in the Great Plains and the Far West, where there are larger, more permanent reservation communities.

Euro-American Institutions and the Indian

As was suggested in the introduction, land tenure derives its substance and practice from the property institution. But no institution is isolated from the functioning of others in a society, and when two differing cultures interact, an institution such as property will differ perceptibly in the body of law and custom behind it and the socioeconomic milieu in which it has functioned. Institutions may be analyzed in any of a number of ways, and as it happens Bohannan (1963, Chap. 21), modifying earlier constructs by Malinowski, has constructed a functional model for the study of institutions in their relation to cultural and social change. The model is comprised of four "systems"—material, social, idea, and event, the latter providing the necessary historical continuum. In discussing land, Bohannan stresses its relationship to economic institutions, suggesting that the *idea* system is based, in western culture, on property, but he notes that " 'property' is only one of the possible relationships of people to things" (p. 366). He suggests that in his model given sets of tasks in the working of land or the trading of products could comprise *events*; the land, technology, and products of the earth would represent *material*; and the organization of human labor would be an example of a *social* system.

Because Bohannan applies the model in a subsequent chapter to a relevant case study of the Omaha Indians, based on Mead's (1932) study of the "Antlers," it is germane to consider this model and example as pertinent literature. To my knowledge no other applicable institutional analysis has been developed. Mead's study of the Omaha Indians provides an excellent case example of a tribe that has undergone almost the full range of acculturative processes with commensurate loss of cultural norms and the like as their lands dwindled in the course of a century, through treaties, reservation, allotment, heirship, and alienation. It may be helpful to organize the data about the tribe around Bohannan's systems. Since material culture is normally primary in the analysis of land, we first consider, for example, the introduction of the plow, crops, and techniques of farming, so characteristic of numerous tribes in the reservation years (see Section BC). The events associated with treaties—establishment of the reservation, allotment, patenting in fee simple, and the process of attrition leading to alienation of landholdings—speak for themselves, as shown in Sections B and BC. Bohannan also identifies characteristic social phenomena, such as the role of village and family, and also the heirship group; ultimately he considers the relationship of the Indian as landlord to his white lessee (cf. Stern and Boggs 1971). Finally, he portrays the constellation of problems that revolves around the idea of private property and assimilation.

Of the "systems" of the model, that which deals with ideas—e.g., ideologies and lifestyles—has been least explored for most institutions according to Bohannan, and this is especially true of property. He observes, "Antlers applied their Western-derived notions of economic individualism to money derived from land sales; but in other respects the kinship hospitality rules of the traditional culture still held" (p. 389). One can observe similar situations for the majority of the tribes in one way or another, for seemingly ambivalent or contradictory behavior in response to Euro-American institutions is reported throughout the literature. Relevant data applicable to each system can readily be found; the range is boundless, as for example:

> *social*—division of labor, clan, kin, nuclear and extended family, tribal council, grazing association, Indian-white community or Indian-lessee relationship
>
> *material*—techniques, tools, crops, land, living standards
>
> *event*—treaty-writing, reservation, allotment, encroachment, termination, tribal reinstatement, the Pan-Indian movement, alienation
>
> *idea*—farming, holding private property, civilizing, assimilating, becoming landlords, regaining land or its equivalent in reimbursements, earning wages

Each of these elements has been reported again and again, and the following discussions, although not grouped in terms of the systems, do nonetheless reflect this model.

Tribes, Land and Culture Change

If a tribe is mainly an endogamous social group, an ethnic population, or a "nation" as the term was formerly used for American Indians, then it must at one time have occupied a discrete territory and possessed some attributes of a political body, recognizing and laying claim to this territory in the ways we ascribe to sovereign powers. Many scholars have explored the question of the political significance of the Indian tribe. Macleod, a keen observer of Indian land tenure changes, explored the notion of the state in terms of native Americans (1924); he came to stress the idea that primitives do set definite boundaries, as others had observed (see Section A). He suggested that all agricultural nations except the eastern Algonkians had national ownership of soil with freedom for all to hunt and subdivision by individual families only in the agricultural sector. In a later paper (1927) he suggested that conflicts among Indian nations or tribes over rights to trade with colonial powers provided further evidence for the existence of an explicit rivalry over territory. Such older interpretations were mostly speculative and came to no firm conclusions based upon ethnographic data.

As the discussion in Section AB implies, the debate over the pre-contact origins of the tribe and over the question of whether it flourished as a sociopolitical organization holding claims to territory received new impetus during the years of land-claims research. Berkhofer (1971) asserted in that debate that "tribal-wide, centralized systems of government arose in most cases only after, and often in response to, white contacts" (p. 371). Land-cession demands often triggered the need for the articulation of tribal-wide government, as was the case among the Cherokee and Navajo. But Wallace (1957) made a strong case for the Northeast, based on ethnographic and historical evidence, suggesting that eastern Algonkians did recognize exclusive territoriality. He noted too that such concepts of landownership perceived boundaries in terms of natural features or lines of sight, and that hunting grounds were as much a part of tribal territory as village areas. In reviewing these facts, Brasser (1971) concurred with earlier findings; yet he reminded readers that, for example, the Stockbridge settlement was an invention resulting from the amalgam of several groups (cf. Mochon 1968). This has a parallel in the later formation of the Warm Springs "tribe" (Hunt 1970) and several others in the Plains and in the Intermontane Region. On the other hand, Fenton (1971) noted that once the Iroquois were broken up and scattered, they lost much of their vitality and capacity for unified decisions; old lines of tribal distinction were broken down by mixed residence on small reserves.

This question of the antiquity of the tribe has produced parallel differences in opinion for much of the country and has opened up inquiries about the use, for example, of "time of taking" as the base on which to reconstruct culture change among various tribes. Bohannan, of course, borrowed data from Mead that did essentially commence its analysis at contact (with French trappers and early trade). But the most important institutional changes have arisen from the taking of land which necessitated the articulation of an aboriginal territoriality so that cession would have meaning to both parties. Such events form the foundation of almost all studies that examine changing Indian culture and society, and fortunately numerous studies have explored tribal conditions at time of taking in terms of the strength or weakness of native political organization. Manners, for example, in his review of Walapai territoriality (1957), rejected evidence of their pre-contact tribal status and favored Kroeber's (1955) position that the autonomous land unit comprised a smaller body of people. Wilson (1961) strengthened this view in a parallel observation that tribal authority arose only after the establishment of the Jicarilla Apache reservation, which legalized as a single people the bands that came to settle there. What followed was the diminution of the localized authority of the camp. At that level he found that boundary disputes arose over livestock movements, necessitating the augmentation of tribal regulatory powers that tended to ignore the traditional camp as a unit of Jicarilla society. Until the turn of the century the camp had been the effective social unit. M. E. Opler (1971) nonetheless concluded on the basis of both historical and ethnographic data that these people as of 1850—prior to taking—perceived a tribal territory.

Various interpretors have turned to similar themes in demonstrating the persistence of tribal customs in land matters. For the pre-removal period, for example, Cotterill (1963) briefly observed that

> In 1825 the Southern Indians were as strongly communistic as in 1775; the development of agriculture among them had not altered their conception of land as a tribal possession or inclined them to the acceptance of any private ownership thereof. (P. 230)

Yet of course within the following decade most of these Indians were forced either to accept allotments or relocate; after relocation they came to be allotted against their wishes (see Section BC). Aberle (1948) drew the inference that

> The struggles over land strengthened the Pueblo civil organization in its dealings with non-Indians and brought an internal cohesion to the group; while the success of the governing body throughout the years in keeping their resources added immeasurably to its prestige. Having land to distribute gave additional strength to their government. Throughout the centuries of the Indians' struggle

for land, there was probably a tacit recognition of the importance of land to the integrity of the governing body. (P. 63)

And whether it was an aboriginal or a post-contact phenomenon, Indians have recollections of their tribal capacity, as the historian Anson (1970) suggested of Miami self-identity:

> However, the dances, oral accounts of ancient religious practices and social customs, and genealogical labyrinths are of less interest to most Miami of today than recollections of the part played by their tribe in the long struggle to preserve Amerindian sovereignty south of the Great Lakes. (P. 299)

Without doubt, further articulation of the tribe resulted from the impact of U.S. law and Indian administration, which brought with it changes in both economic and political institutions. Kluckhohn and Hackenberg (in Kelly 1954) interpreted the IRA as having abetted the preservation of tribal views and the Indians' control of their own destinies. Changes in the sociopolitical organization of Indians and the emergence of "tribe" arose from both internal and external causes; the latter, more significant since contact times, included the flow of ideas, peoples, and material culture (including technology) from the surrounding environment or from various governments, businesses, or other institutionally organized bodies.

Changes in Indian culture since contact, and especially since the establishment of reservations, may be found in institutions other than political organization and land use. Perhaps one of the most dynamic changes that can be traced back to tribal problems in adapting to Euro-American institutions has been the evolution and articulation of the Sun Dance religion. Few books expand upon a theme as well as Jorgensen has (1972) in his search for explanations of the rise and spread of this religion among the Utes and Shoshones. He demonstrated that the misery and oppression resulting from the taking of land and the subsequent and almost uninterrupted exploitation of these lands by non-Indians set the stage for the appearance of the Sun Dance (cf. the discussion of his use of the metropolitan-satellite theory in Section C). The dance movement has had as its goal the total change or transformation of individual Indians through supernatural means and human effort, thus liberating Indians from surrounding problems, helping them to reject and castigate white society, and resolving conflicts between Protestant-ethic individualism and the collective ethic preached by Indians. Jorgensen's text includes a vast store of statistical and factual data about land, land use, and Indian numbers throughout the 90 years since the movement began. He notes clearly how demoralizing and depressing living conditions on the reserves have become over the decades, how the tribes have lost acreage to the railroads, and how land allotment has led to alienation and to heirship complexities. Urban migration has been one result; unearned income through lease contracts, which in any event tend to idle and disorient Indians, has been modest or meager. Unless readers are made aware that the book relates closely to land matters and goes to root causes to explain the rise of the Sun Dance movement, they may be misled by the title.

Another religious orientation—peyotism—seems to have been stimulated directly by changes in use-rights to resources on the Navajo Indian Reservation. Aberle (1966) reported that peyotism among the Navajo must be seen as a response to the deprivation experienced by the Indians during the livestock reduction program of the 1930s and later (cf. Fonaroff 1963 and 1964 and Boyce 1974; see Section C). Many Indians at this time chose non-compliance, others remained hostile although they accepted the edict of the government to thin their flocks. It was observed, for example, that those who lost most in flock size were the earliest to join the cult; peyotists apparently had been those who had held the larger flocks in pre-reduction days.

Several studies identify aspects of tribal attitudes toward the management of "corporate" resources and note the problems in maintaining the rights of tenants-in-common. Reynolds (1967) described the "resource controller" among Navajos, a person whom others consider most likely to be more competent than they to care for and maintain a given resource for the extended family. Within the Navajo normative framework, he is able to direct such aspects of resource allocation as the movement of sheep within a given grazing area, and since grazing territory is not owned by individuals, it must be controlled by a group of kinsmen according to a system of use-rights. The resource controller is the focal point of herd management and the most influential decision-maker.

The roles of resource controller and "outfit" (the latter is an occasionally cooperating kin group or "landholding" group) seem to stem from post-reservation introduction of animal husbandry. Fonaroff (1963, 1964) noted that reactions to economic or political changes, and especially reluctance to accept governmental economic advice, reflected Navajo efforts to continue to function as separate social units and yet move toward tribal unification. Tribal government has been characterized as having a "loose and elusive nature" (Fonaroff 1971); nevertheless, it has come to assert itself in spite of its post-contact origins and its exploitation as a pawn of government policy. Fonaroff stressed that most "recurrent problems were generated by different ideas of time, property and land-use concepts ..." and the fact that the Indians have had to reconcile differences within a single system (p. 443). (Cf. Witherspoon 1970 and

Kluckhohn and Leighton 1956 for relevant discussions of property rights, the extended family, and land use.)

While aboriginal patterns of land tenure can be identified easily, evidence suggests that most expressions of tenure by the tribe followed rather than preceded contact and probably the establishment of reservations, and therefore represent examples of culture change. The following sampling is eclectic and suggests how the corporate idea has emerged only with governmental efforts to encourage long-range resource development of the kind associated with the management of tribal timber stands and mineral or recreational resources. The tribe seems able to function better as a single entity, so reports indicate, where tenancy-in-common and not land allotment determines the use of multiple resources. Some tribes, for example, came to hold corporate resources by dint of the fact that when the reservation was allotted, surplus lands either were not opened to entry or were deemed ill-suited to farming (cf. Stern 1961-62; Sutton 1964). In other instances, tribes resisted allotment altogether, as happened among the Pueblos. Keesing (1939) noted that a strong corporate interest in the management of resources was the basis for Menominee rejection of land allotment. Rietz (1953) observed that the Sioux preferred tribal development, despite the fact that most of the Sioux country underwent land allotment. Sherman (1962) emphasized tribal cooperative enterprises and the fact that allotment did not work among the Red Lake Chippewa. In outlining evidence for a pre-contact "tribe-like" unit of social integration greater than an agglomeration of autonomous bands, Basehart (1967) considered the Mescalero as a resource-holding corporation, although ". . . it is not a group, it lacks authority posts, it has no decision making procedures" (p. 287). Yet it had continuity and was distinguished by the rights of its members to share its resource, and was therefore likened to a "jural entity."

Many examples cited in the literature reflect varying departures from aboriginal patterns and reveal both persistence and change in Indian sociopolitical organization as it relates to land tenure. The Hopis have often been depicted as highly traditional and resistant to external influences, yet changes in settlement patterns and behavior toward resources have been noted for several decades (Forde 1931b; Page 1940; Cox 1967; McIntire 1969). Cox reported, for example, disputes among these people where today girls at marriage want their own homes; because Indians can own their dwellings but not the land, which is held by the clan, there is a tendency toward individual ownership despite the absence of land allotment. For another Pueblo people, the Cochiti, Lange (1959) also noted the survival of traditional tenure patterns despite the gradual increase in emphasis on the family instead of the clan in landownership. Siegel (1967) interpreted Taos tradition as being reinforced by a greater awareness of the role of land tenure: "the most potent factor in keeping the old controls effective is the persistence of compact village life . . ." (p. 138). The need to perpetuate the Taos elite is exhibited in the maintenance of land as the locus of ceremonialism on which the Indian's identity depends. The tribe expressed fears that contact was affecting the continued integrity of their lifeways, and that increased numbers meant the need to expand into wage economy. Yet, despite individual ownership of land and houses (but communal ownership of pasturage), Taos cohesion is strong and they maintain a strong identification with all other Pueblos. The success of their bid for the return of Blue Lake in 1973 reflected the strength of their unified struggle to regain a sacred shrine.

Conflicts and confusion accompany many adaptations to Euro-American institutions, as the foregoing examples and others suggest. Getty (1961-62, 1963), in evaluating the relative success of San Carlos Apache grazing associations instituted by the tribe, noted that "these Indians incorporated the cattle industry into their slowly changing culture largely in terms of pre-reservation values . . . it represents, nevertheless, the one non-Apache activity in which they have achieved their greatest successes in terms of acculturation" (1961-62, p. 86). In contrast to the modest success of Apache animal husbandry, Simpson (1970) described the negative role of communal grazing and individually owned livestock among the Papago, for whom traditional values and fear of the loss of status have tended to interfere with the success of range conservation. Lack of success, it is suggested, seems to be due to an unwillingness to modernize communal grazing rules and to the fact that property rights remain largely unwritten, allowing for absentee ownership. And, too, the constraints placed upon the individual check his capacity to make decisions, even though cattle are held individually. Similarly, Garbarino (1972) found that Seminole Indians, on adopting cattle and tribal range management, had difficulty understanding the problems of the deteriorating natural range vs. the advantages of the artificially improved range, the use of which incurred some regulation of individual rights and the imposition of grazing fees. She reports much discontent, although stockraising constitutes the only economically viable way for many Indian families to stay on the reservation in familiar surroundings. She demonstrated a strong correlation between succcess in stockraising and political activity within the tribe.

In reassessing the success of the Arapahoe Ranch experiment, Fowler (1973) has shown that technological change and economic reorganization have benefitted the tribe. Although characterized as a model of scientific ranch management, the Araphoe Ranch is also regarded as "an extension and reaffirmation of Arapahoe conceptualizations about the relationship between economic organization and social process (p. 462). In terms of tenure, the ranch entity can lease grazing land more readily and cheaply, and as Fowler noted, it gives evidence of a consistent and unique style of Arapahoe adaptation that provides for continuity in community development. Despite problems and conflicts, Fowler felt, the ranch lends credence to the view that economic development in Indian communities can occur in ways consonant with Indian preferences and cultural identity (cf. Wilson 1972).

Finally, it should come as no surprise that such an eclectic literature as that which deals with the subject of the tribe has generated symposia disscussing the theme, in part set in motion by Fried's provocative paper (1966). Fried discussed the post-contact origins of tribalism and the legal status of the tribe in Indian-white relations. He noted that in the past linguistic discreteness had served as the criterion of tribal existence because other data were confusing; but common descent and autonomous political integration, he recognized, contributed to a sense of tribalism. His example was the Iroquois. In his overall review he stressed the importance of the role of residence, suggesting that a people termed a tribe may be stable synchronically, but it is likely to have shifted diachronically. Thus, he asserted that boundaries between tribes were no clearer than those separating bands.

The symposium stimulated by his study (Helm 1968) offered many cogent observations that reflect the opposing positions already summarized in this section. In this symposium Hymes, for example, argued that the tribe represented a secondary phenomenon reacting to Europeanization, and Colson asserted that tribes in North America and even in Africa have arisen in response to colonial influences and comprise products of administrative convenience or self-conscious nationalistic movements. Dole outlined how the term "tribe" has come to identify a people possessing, among other traits, a territory, language, name, awareness of unity, genealogy, and systems of economic and political organization. Gearing (1968) regarded the tribe as a "bounded political group or community," a jural community in which some form of law prevails; he referred, for example, to "little" sovereignties and larger ones. But all in all, no single explanation or definition suffices to answer the unresolved question, Just what in native American experience is a tribe, and did it originate in pre- or post-contact times?

Nonetheless, much of the preceding discussion does underscore several facts: (1) "tribe" as a term in use is surcharged with legal meaning and identifies a historical body of people, whether or not they hold land today; (2) varying bodies of people called Indians occupied and utilized territory, but many of these people came to articulate a territorial claim only when pressured by white demands for land cessions; and (3) the surviving native population in situ or as relocated continues to identify itself as a people historically involved in that land transaction. If the land issue is sufficient stimulus to cause even mixed native populations to identify a common cause and basis for unity, then the term "tribe" may come to mean less ethnographically but more legally. The literature on the American Indian tribe suggestively reflects bipolar positions: the ethnologist seeks cross-cultural generalization in which the Indian tribe can become part of a larger methodological context—i.e., can be interpreted in the light of universal human organizations. The legalist does not share this quest; he seeks a narrower definition that may be applied to specific situations in which the tribe constitutes a legal entity, comparable to the corporation or municipality. These antithetical positions may be explored better by reference to other aspects of the interaction between law and anthropology.[1]

Family Hunting Territories

One of the more interesting questions relating culture change to land tenure concerns the genesis of the family hunting territory in the Northeast and in eastern Canada. Its earliest student, Speck, established (1914-15, 1915) the original criteria by which to demonstrate its aboriginal origins, a thesis held by him and his colleague Eiseley (Speck and Eiseley 1939), and by Macleod (1922, 1927), J. M. Cooper (1938, 1939), A. E. Cooper (1942), and Hallowell (1949). The rise of family hunting territories as a form of private land tenure, whether it occurred during aboriginal or contact (fur trade) times, has stimulated a good deal of debate. The crucial point in this debate is the demonstration that dependence on small nonmigratory fauna such as the beaver and the hare could be best developed by family groups in well-defined land units, and that conservation practices could be best developed where family rights inhered in given land tracts. Hallowell's later elaborations took the opposing viewpoint that these territories were disparate in size and therefore not based on the work of family units. His stress was on ecological considerations: a normal territory would yield the yearly catch of the trapper, however large or small its bounds; the size was seen as a function of game abundance.

Criticism of the pro-aboriginal position was first enunciated by Leacock (1954) and has been restated with varying emphasis and occasional new data over the years by Hickerson (1967a/b, 1971); Bishop (1970); Knight (1965); and others. Leacock argued that family holdings came into existence in subarctic cultures only as a result of the emphasis on trapping for the European fur trade. This led the raising of beaver and other sedentary game on an individual basis to replace communal hunting of large game. Such views do not deny the aboriginal origins of the family hunting band itself. Hickerson's supportive evidence argues that with the increase of mobility of Indian families owing to encroaching white settlement in the late nineteenth century, the family hunting territory system became a permanent feature of Indian life in that region.

Bishop further noted that at least with respect to the Ojibwa, the decline of large game led to a commensurate dependence on smaller game such as hare and on fish. Larger groups that had hunted large game could no longer remain together continuously throughout the winter; thus splintering-off took place, leading to the rise of family hunting territories. Hickerson and Bishop assert separately that the influence of traders, who preferred dealing with individuals rather than entire groups, should not be overlooked in tracing the development of family hunting territories. Also the economic activity of snaring small game did not require group cooperation, but rather intense work by a few persons. These studies stress that the family hunting pattern became predominant only after the 1820s or 1830s. Overkill of large game and forced dependence upon smaller game, then, are suggested as factors contributing to the pattern.

Knight's fresh look at this question supported the view that private rather than tribal control was necessary for the development and maintenance of beaver conservation. In support of the fur-trade argument he suggests that a shift from cooperative caribou hunting to individualized fur trapping and dependence on trading for food led to competition for fur resources, thus encouraging the family territory. Unlike Leacock, he does not support the view that integration in and dependence on fur-trade economy per se could lead to or allow for maintenance of private control and restricted use of strategic resources. Knight emphasized that reliable physical security was requisite for family territoriality. He found that fluctuations in local fauna necessitated frequent and smooth readjustments of personnel over the band area and made private control and restricted use of resources unfeasible and unadaptive.

Comparing band organization in the Plateau and Basin areas of the West, Steward (1955a) cautioned against equating family-level organization in livelihood there with that in the Northeast; for the latter he did argue that such organization was a response to fur trade, but he found ecological arguments to explain why family territories were not really workable in the Basin, for "territorial interpenetration of families living in different localities was necessary to the survival of all. . . . The absence of property claims of local groups to delimitable areas of natural resources upon which work had not been expended was the corollary of the fragmented nature of Shoshonean society" (p. 108). Steward's earlier

(1936) paper on bands prompted a response by Speck and Eiseley (1939). Davidson (1928) had supported the claim of aboriginal origins in discussing hunting territories in the Northwest, since he could not show historical connections or diffusion for this complex of economic organization. He tended to feel that because this pattern of land tenure could arise independently, owing to its simplicity, there was no need to prove its aboriginal origin. He suggested, for example, that it might have been a system more ancient than the clan landownership so prevalent in northwestern North America. However, Lewis (1942), in discussing the fur trade in part of the Northwest, did not refer to hunting territories either in aboriginal or post-contact situations.

An economist has recently offered a new theoretical argument to the fur-trade controversy. Demsetz (1967), in constructing a broader theory of property rights, argued that private property arose among the Northeastern tribes when it became economical to deal effectively with external costs and benefits by a shift from tribal tenure. Property rights of this kind began to evolve under the impetus of the fur trade, which economically encouraged the husbandry of fur-bearing animals. Until some such advantage could be seen by the Indians, there was no urge to incorporate those costs and benefits of fur trapping and trading by means of a private property concept—i.e., a hunting territory. If the arguments for post-contact genesis are accepted, institutional changes in land tenure seem to have been triggered by changes in related economic institutions, based upon a set of events involving a given material culture—i.e., fur-bearing animals—exploited by a social group who had the idea to sequester privately a resource of limited availability and commensurately high value.

Hickerson (1967b) should be examined because of the inclusiveness of his review of the pertinent literature and because his study received the careful critical review especially identified with *Current Anthropology*, where it was published. The study goes beyond the immediate questions posed here, for he raises new questions about the particularization of property among hunting and gathering peoples and relates this question to the theories of Morgan, Engels, and such later anthropologists as Lowie. Hickerson sees this approach as relevant to land claims research—here applied to the Chippewa—and stresses that it is impossible to reassess adequately the property patterns of aboriginal times by examining contemporary reservation culture, in which persistence is paramount. Rather, one must conduct a more intensive historical analysis and assess changes subsequent to contact. Despite differences in interpretation of data, most of the literature of the past twenty years at least sustains the post-contact theory of the origin of the family hunting territory.

The Individual Indian and the Land

It seems only a short step now to the issues of individual Indian land holdings—not so much a question of aboriginal practice as one of the acceptance and incorporation of private property into modern Indian land use practice. One might ask: Does the holding of land as private property break up members of society in terms of the collective or group good? Overwhelming evidence in the Indian case certainly suggests that this is the case, especially where land allotment occurred too rapidly and without reinforcement of its long-term intent. In fact, Lurie's interpretation (1971) of the failure of the allotment system reads like an indictment; she argued that "the nature of the landholding group was not questioned . . ." and further noted that "allotment demonstrated that the government denied the right of Indians to persist as communities" (p. 433). Moreover,

> . . . allotment did not permit Indian people to take their place as individuals making free choices among the segments of the larger American society or to create their own segments as others had done; it picked out the rural agricultural segment for them. (P. 434)

The attitudes of various tribes toward land-allotment policies have indicated mixed feelings over whether individualizing land among the membership of a tribe was a blessing or a curse. There are tribes that accepted, even if reluctantly, allotment of land and that today exhibit strong tribal or corporate sentiments toward communal land; conversely we find that several tribes that once rejected allotment are now particularizing rights to land and resources. Both reflect significant institutional changes.

For example, the Hopis and the Navajos have been in conflict over an interzonal area claimed by both tribes (see Aberle 1974a/b and the discussion of Stephens 1961 in Section BC). The Hopis were advised to take allotments and homestead lands outside their mesa villages as a means to check the intrusion of Navajos into traditional Hopi territory, but the latter made only a poor and reluctant gesture toward accepting this land policy, and encroachment has continued to the present. On the other hand, with the attainment of grazing carrying capacity and the increase in the numbers of Indians dependent on forageable resources, there has been an increase in claims to family grazing areas and a parallel assertion of family proprietorship among the Black Rock Navajos, despite the tribal regulation of grazing-district lands (Downs 1964). Martin (1968) found among the Havasupais, whose reservation was not allotted, patterns of family land-holding akin in practice to private property. Here, land is held patrilocally and family heads resist dividing their holdings among their married sons. Such sons must cooperate with the extended family under these circumstances, and this leads to conflict when younger family members enter their thirties and wish to be heads of their own households. Burgeoning tourism based on packing-in on horseback has stimulated an effective economy that could provide income for younger families, were the need for additional pasturage satisfied by fathers giving up land to sons. The prestige accorded to the landholder, suggests Martin, is an important factor in denying land to sons and causing their exodus from the reservation. In some ways, this situation resembles the mixed communal/private rights in soil found among many peasant populations.

The avowed purpose of land allotment—to make farmers of the Indians, who were to reside on homesteads analogous to the family farm—has caused additional conflict as an idea and value, as the literature reports. The Teton Sioux, for example, encountered problems in trying to become farmers, for farming had little meaning for them, so they chose ultimately to lease land and raise cattle (Mekeel 1936). Macgregor (1970) noted efforts to consolidate land on the Fort Berthold reserve, where stockraising was preferred to farming, and Wilson (1972) observed that land not affected by allotment and subsequent heirship complexities encouraged Indians to switch from farming to ranching on the Wind River Reservation. In fact, most of the irrigable land has long been alienated. French (1961) found that despite the rise of individual property among the Wasco-Wishram, these Indians did not take up farming and their internal conflicts were mostly over fishing rights. Elkin (1940) reported that the Northern Arapaho did not take up farming either, and that much of their land lay idle owing to problems of heirship. Yet Macgregor (1946) noted that among modern Dakota Indians since the sale and rental of allotments began, the emphasis on property as an intrinsic value has been a chief problem for the second generation in the cattle industry.

Rejection of land allotments set in motion various economic and social problems among some tribes. Hoffmeister (1945) and M. K. Opler (1940, 1971) have drawn attention to the attitude of the Indians of the Ute Mountain group, who chose isolation which led to economic stagnation; as Opler (1940) put it, "The shrinkage of the reservation by treaty and land sales played a greater role in alienating the Weminutc from 'White ways' and farming than any alleged cultural conservatism" (p. 182). The loss of livelihood and consequent privation of the Shoshoni-Bannock grew out of persistence of traditional views toward communal land and inheritance. These views ran counter to Idaho state inheritance law, which rejects communal tenure (Sorensen 1971). According to Sorensen and to Hawley's review (1948) of Indian problems in New Mexico, native institutions function for the group, and Indians generally have not been acquainted with Euro-American land laws, the aims of individual landownership, or the white man's system of competition and progress. Yet even as communal rights in land survive as corporate rights in village communities, as seems to be the case among the Tlingits (cf. Averkieva 1971), American laws have tended to break down social controls and the authority of Indian leadership. In speaking of the Chippewas, Hickerson (1971) notes a major social reorientation from intensively discrete communal kinship to loosely aggregated small-family clusters, and he cites particularization of property as a contributing factor.

We also can find a few examples in which new institutions have been embraced, as Joffe's study of the Fox (1940) suggests:

> Whenever they received large sums of money . . . these were invested in more tribal land. . . . Whether by accident or perspicacity the Fox arrived at the method which permitted them to continue their old culture after the arrival of the Whites. Attachment to land was something which the White man not only understood, but was valued by him. The Fox hit at the crux of the situation when they acquired land through a channel acceptable to the Whites (by purchase). (PP. 260-61)

Leasing, of course, has represented another institutional change which has led to other events and social circumstances. For example, Stewart (1967) reported a decline in farming where leasing had become more advantageous, and Lang too observed (1953) a rejection of landowning and farming and a preference for leasing. Yet others have noted some modest successes through leasing, such as the symbiotic relationship that has developed between Umatilla Indians and white lessees (Stern and Boggs 1971). Market-oriented and wise enough to realize that they could better themselves by leasing and not by farming, the Umatillas entered into an arrangement that provides far more in special services and favors than merely income from the rental of land. Although reports of leasing income reveal that Indians make only a modest living at best, many studies have demonstrated how readily Indians have adopted the practice and become landlords (cf. Hoffmeister 1945; Longwell 1961; Sutton 1967; and others; see Section C).

Various kinds of changes in social organization and in the orientation of individual to group have come about as a result of allotment, land alienation, or inheritance patterns. It has been found that the breakup of long-standing social groups may result when land subdivision occurs. For example, Reynolds (1967) showed that among the Rimrock Navajos who acquired allotments, fragmentation of outfits and scattering of their members resulted as families took to moving onto their parcels. Macgregor (1970) reported that land allotment to the nuclear family among the Teton Sioux lessened the dependence on the extended family. Martin

(1969-70) reviewed the relocation of the Modoc from Oregon to Oklahoma, where they settled among the Quapaw. He suggested that the move was stimulated by the opportunity to gain a land allotment and secure rental income; with money secured in this manner, many of these Indians returned home—only to be ostracized by their own tribe on the Klamath Reservation. Many of these Modocs ultimately returned to Oklahoma.

A few studies reveal the internal conflicts that resulted from concentration of hunting and gathering bands on the reservations. Harris's study (1940) of the White Knife Shoshoni in Nevada underscored a basic conflict that has been a divisive force elsewhere: settling as communities rather than as families and taking up farming, these Indians at first made considerable adjustments to sedentary agrarian life, while they continued aboriginal patterns of communal work and sharing. But the discipline of traditional individual contributions of labor in exchange for equitable sharing of food began to break down for some members of the communities (or camps). The working members began to resent sharing in the traditional way and clamored for allotments. The government granted them allotments, although it did not take them out of tribal tenure; nevertheless, as a result of this process, the Indians came to perceive both land and livestock as individually owned. As Harris noted, this led to "a reversion to the economic independence of the immediate kin group" (p. 92).

Studies of land heirship reveal social changes also. Munsell's review of Papago kinship networks (1967) showed how traditional tenure practices, in responding to institutional change in the determination of heirs, have come to forfeit the rights of those who "drift out" (see Section BC). Shimkin (1970) evaluated Paiute efforts to trade landholdings as a means to consolidate larger single ownerships, and thereby strengthen the role of the extended family. Such efforts were undertaken especially as a means to allow co-heirs to work the land jointly. These extended families seem to have channeled ownership of land to elderly men who now "own" most of the family land; their adult married sons, mostly landless, work the land. Such consolidation has been accomplished through the emergence of strong bilateral extended family ties that also function in raising money for capital investments and land improvements. Such changes in social organization resulting from heirship have contributed significantly to strengthening extended family ties.

Sasaki's Fruitland Navajo study (1960) and Goldfrank's review of a Blackfoot tribe (1945) reported on more favorable aspects of the adoption of the allotment policy, yet they also reveal much about the inevitable outcome of this land scheme. Sasaki recounted the Indians' desire to secure a cash income from farming as a way to pay their debts. They had come to reject subsistence livelihood in favor of commercial ventures, however small. When the government sought to double the number of families on the land by dividing all units in half (from 20 to 10 acres each), resident Indians resented it and protested strenuously. Such maneuvers by the government made Indians fearful that their tenure in the land was temporal. Sasaki, like other observers, noted also that a breakdown in the customary pattern of aiding relatives had occurred following land allotment. Income from crops, for example, was no longer regarded as part of a traditional obligation toward relatives.

Goldfrank revealed that the younger men of the reservation supported farming as an enterprise and sought to cultivate as much land as possible, and that ultimately land tended to concentrate in the hands of the few. This led to the practice of ultimogeniture, although it later gave way.

All in all, land allotment has been severely criticized because of its disruptive effect on the continuity of tribal lifestyles (cf. Debo 1970). Yet even after review of its impact, Priest, a historian, came to write:

> If individual ownership of land could be made compatible with racial preservation by careful government administration the excesses of both past and present might be avoided. If not, the return to a policy of isolation will mean the defeat of fifty years of effort to solve the Indian problem. (Priest 1942, 1969 ed., p. 252)

The advent of the IRA in 1934 did not in actual fact begin an era of isolation for the tribes. Quite the contrary, more and more tribes have become involved with the "outside world," demonstrating increasingly that the reservation, whether seen as a corporate entity or as one held by tenants-in-common, is only a microcosm within the larger society.

The Reservation and the Larger Society

Seen as an isolate functioning under special laws and protections, the reservation is a unique political institution within the states (see Section AC). Its political autonomy may in some ways persist whether the land is held by the tribe or held in allotments, although when allotment opened up reservations and mixed Indian country resulted, tribal autonomy was challenged. But in its economic activity, the opened reservation has reflected the interaction that makes it part of the society that surrounds it. Whether we consider the situation of land leasing or the intermingling of landownership and residence by Indians and non-Indians on reservations (cf. Stern and Boggs 1971; Sutton 1967; Jorgensen 1971; Longwell 1961), these institutional shifts have come to involve Indians in ways that make for greater diffusion of new traits. Despite the values that are stressed in studies that consider the protective role of isolation and segregation (Colson 1953, 1967; Eggan 1943; Hudson 1970; Barnouw 1950; McKee 1971), the interaction of Indians and non-Indians in the utilization of reservation resources is seen as vital. For example, through leasing and the mobility exhibited by Indians who move freely from the reservation as a home base to work and social involvement outside the reservation, Indians come to understand the way the dominant society functions and how Indian land rights may play a role in furthering both tribal and individual aspirations (cf. Nielson 1967; Nagata 1971; Weightman 1972; Hackenberg 1969).

The increasing mix on the reservation has, of course, diminished the integrity of the tribal home and has contributed to dispersal onto homesteads and migration to agency towns or distant cities (Schusky 1970; Longwell 1961; Sutton 1964; Bruner 1961; Martin 1969-70; Hoffmeister 1945; Hewes 1942a/b). Out-migration (Vogt's "drifting out") has had a varying impact on Indian leadership and on those who could influence change from within, and it has perhaps made diffident numerous Indians who were born too late to come to hold an allotment and who are thus left landless. But the landed often do not fare much better; heirs to allotments might as well be landless in the numerous instances where so many share the title to land that it becomes nearly impossible to utilize. Even with out-migration, identity with place seems to remain strong and gives credence to the view that the existence of the reservation continues to hold meaning, even if Indians do not reside on the land or derive economic gain from the use of its resources.

Advocates and opponents of individualization of Indian land feel deeply that the Indian ultimately must become part of the society at large (cf. Manners 1962 and Collier's reply, both reprinted in Walker 1971). The question often asked is, Just what means should be employed to make this possible? The absence of a trust land base seems not always to hinder the survival of tribalism: the persistence of many Indian communities was reported by Brasser (1971) for the East, by Boissevain (1956, 1959) for the Narragansett, by Jacobson (1960) for the Koasati of Louisiana, and by Houser (1970) for those members of the Isleta Pueblo who fled during the Spanish reconquest of 1680 and whose lands in west Texas have only recently been placed under a state trusteeship. (For a newer, general study of eastern Indians, see Tamarin 1974).

Studies such as those edited by Nurge (1970) and Walker (1971) point to the existence of "reservation culture," a phenomenon that can be examined in ethnographic terms. Again and again students have discovered among the resident populations of reservations elements of cultural and social change that indicate modifications of aboriginal practices or adoptions of Euro-American practices of land tenure. Although further study should take the researcher to the cities to ask questions of urban Indians about the role of land in their socioeconomic circumstances, the reservation is likely to remain the focus of inquiry. The political changes wrought by new interactions and confrontations with state and local governments will lead many tribes to take new institutional directions in their functioning as jural communities with their states.

It has been my position throughout most of this volume that political and legal factors have contributed most to the demise or persistence of native American culture vis-à-vis the land. Indians and non-Indians writing about the problems of Indian land tenure continue to stress the importance of the land base—the locus of tribalism—and the psychological relaxation of anxieties that Indians experience when they at last come to feel that their land base is not going to be sacrificed to the interests of non-Indians. But many thinkers assert that a real issue, the crux of continued Indian-white confrontations, is the abridgement of tribal autonomy on reservations. Castile (1974) attributes the rise of these situations to the current administrative community; instead, he recommends a "sustained enclave" concept, which would turn over the bulk of decision-making to the tribes. He argues that to date too much decision-making has been outside the reservation by non-Indians, and this has all too often led to anomie and apathy among the Indians. The sustained enclave would eliminate the fear of termination and perhaps encourage "assisted culture change." Like other scholars today, Castile sustains the view that cultural enclaves are worthwhile and should be preserved within our society. But Castile apparently would not go as far as Deloria (1974; see Section AC) in urging a return to tribal sovereignty. All in all, strengthening tribal autonomy on reservations and preserving the land base itself are seen as essential to the continued existence of native American culture.

Notes

1. See, for example, the symposium in *Law and Society Review*, 1974, vol. 7, no. 4, and an earlier symposium on the "Ethnography of Law," L. Nader (ed.), *American Anthropologist* 67, no. 6, pt. 2 (1965).

Works Cited in Section ABC

Aberle, D., 1966, 1974a/b
Aberle, S., 1948
Anson, 1970

Averkieva, *1971
Barnett, 1956
Barnouw, 1950

Basehart, 1967
Beals, 1953
Berkhofer, 1971
Bishop, 1970
Bohannan, 1963
Boissevain, 1956, 1959
Boyce, 1974
Brasser, 1971
Bruner, 1961
Castile, 1974
Colson, 1953, 1967, *1968
Cooper, A. E., 1942
Cooper, J. M., 1938, 1939
Cotterill, 1963
Cox, 1967
Davidson, 1928
Debo, 1970
Deloria, 1974
Demsetz, 1967
Dole, *1968
Downs, 1964
Dozier, 1957
Driver, 1969
Eggan, D., 1943
Eggan, F., 1955, 1966
Elkin, 1940
Fenton, 1940, 1971
Fonaroff, 1963, 1964, 1971
Forde, 1931b
Fowler, 1973
French, 1961
Fried, 1966
Garbarino, 1972
Gearing, 1968
Getty, 1961-62, 1963
Goldfrank, *1945
Hackenberg, 1969
Hagan, 1961
Hallowell, 1949, 1957
Harris, 1940
Hawley, 1948
Helm, 1968
Hewes, 1942a/b
Hickerson, 1967a/b, 1971
Hoffmeister, 1945
Houser, 1970
Hudson, 1970
Hunt, 1970
Hymes, *1968
Jacobson, 1960

Joffe, *1940
Jorgensen, 1971, 1972
Keesing, 1939, 1953
Kelly, 1954
Kluckhohn & Leighton, 1956
Knight, 1965
Kroeber, 1955
Lang, *1953
Lange, 1959
Leacock, 1954
Leacock & Lurie, 1971 .
Lewis, 1942
Linton, 1940
Longwell, 1961
Lurie, *1971
Macgregor, 1946, 1970
Macleod, 1922, 1924, 1927
Manners, 1957, 1962
Martin, J. F., 1968
Martin, L. J., 1969-70
McIntire, 1969
McKee, 1971
McNickle, *1973
Mead, 1932
Mekeel, 1936
Mochon, 1968
Munsell, *1967
Murdock, 1949
Nagata, 1971
Nielson, 1967
Nurge, 1970
Opler, M. E., 1971
Opler, M. K., 1940, 1971
Ortiz, *1972
Page, 1940
Peterson, J. H., *1970
Price, 1973
Priest, 1942
Reynolds, 1967
Rietz, 1953
Sasaki, *1960
Schusky, 1970
Sherman, 1962
Shimkin, *1970
Siegel, 1967
Simpson, 1970
Sorensen, 1971
Speck, 1914-15, 1915, *1928b
Speck & Eiseley, 1939
Spicer, 1961, 1962, 1969b

Stafford, 1971
Stern, *1952, 1961-62
Stern & Boggs, 1971
Steward, 1936, 1955a/b
Stewart, *1966, *1967
Sutton, 1964, 1967
Tamarin, 1974
Thompson, *1950
Tuck, *1971b
Vogt, *1961

Waddell, *1969
Walker, 1971
Wallace, 1957
Washburn, 1971b
Weightman, 1972
Wilson, H. C., 1961
Wilson, P. B., 1972
Wissler, 1940
Witherspoon, 1970
Witthoft, 1961

---

*Denotes works not actually cited, but relevant to this section.

EPILOGUE

Notes Toward a Comparative Approach

Certain distinctions become apparent when we differentiate the ways an ethnically homogeneous population allocates land *among* its members and *between* majority and minority elements within its society. In those countries of the world where today one finds minority populations identifiable as indigenous peoples,[1] inequitable land division is commonplace; it has persisted under varying institutional arrangements since the explorations and discoveries that opened up new continents to Europeans, and for similar or even longer time periods in non-European realms. It seems axiomatic, though not logically necessary, that confrontations between Europeans on the one hand and such peoples as Australian aborigines, New Zealand Maoris, or the Buryats of Siberia on the other have invariably resulted in conflicts over territory. Whether by physical dispossession or by treaty negotiation and land cession, displacement of indigenous populations from their own ground has been a fairly constant accompaniment to the *leitmotif* of conquest and colonization. To a lesser degree, similar circumstances apply to the Japanese (Ainu), the Chinese (central Asian minorities), and the Hindus (hill tribes of India and Nepal), and to many other peoples of the Old World.

Few studies explicitly attempt to compare the outcome of contact between American Indians and whites to the outcome of other confrontations between indigenous peoples and more sophisticated societies. Scholars nevertheless continue to infer that similar events, ideologies, and social conflicts have existed in all such contact situations. The inferences suggest a large and fruitful field of research that has been inadequately developed to date. There is much evidence for the need for comparative research that would place the experience of the Indian in the perspective of the destinies of all indigenous peoples for whatever time period and geographic distribution one may have in mind. For example, studies of colonialism and colonial history suggest the importance, and in numerous cases demonstrate the vitality, of the comparative frame of reference. Similarly, "frontier" or contact histories have sought to fashion more cogent typologies in hopes of revealing nomothetic principles in human confrontations. Many of these studies examine situations of contact between sophisticated societies, with their markedly more elaborate human organization, institutions, and technology (including weaponry), and indigenous populations. Contemporary interpretations of native administration also show how much can be learned from a comparative approach to institutional and legal setting of economic development, resource use, and the allocation of land. And finally, in the interpretation of the acculturation of indigenous peoples, one finds several kinds of studies employing comparative data.

To date certain colonial histories have sought common themes, and—as the Peckham and Gibson symposium (1969) indicates—Indian and colonial policy, including specifically land acquisition and dispossession policy, are a fruitful area for research. Such works as Jennings's account of the origins of native land rights and review of colonial attitudes (1971b) clarify, for example, the idea that the European colonial experiences with native peoples everywhere are comparable simply for the reason that their institutional framework stems from common heritage. Applied to Anglo-America, we find that Narvey's legal-historical analysis (1974) of the Royal Proclamation of 1763 demonstrates that much of the land cession and reserve establishment in Canada and the United States arose out of common origins (see Section B). Although the two countries have forged somewhat different native land policies (for example, Canada has never succumbed to the allotment practice), common legal history dating back to British practices suggests that more is similar than is different in Indian administration (cf. Cardinal 1969). As for Hispanic America, the encomienda and the mission as colonial institutions also suggest the common bases for land practices involving Indians in nearly all regions, including the Mexican Cession area prior to 1848. Zavala (1965), in a heuristic paper that only touches upon land themes, inferred how comparative study of the differences in managing more densely settled agrarian Indians and migratory tribes could also constitute a common approach.

Studies examining common or divergent institutions in the conquest and occupancy of areas occupied by native populations are not lacking (Cook 1943; Snow 1921; Ribeiro 1971; Service 1955; Barnes 1960; Price

1973). Snow and Price especially examine the role of law; Price asked whether "principles of international law, common at least to European countries and characterizing colonial relationships, suggest any limit" to the treatment of native peoples. He extracted observations from writings dealing with other peoples and other countries or colonies as a means to broaden the context within which to interpret the experience of the American Indian in our legal system. An older survey of native policy around the world was prepared for the *Encyclopedia of Social Sciences* (1931-38).

Some frontier historians have sought to refine a working methodology based upon the precept that peoples of a common cultural heritage can be compared in their divergent frontier experiences, despite differences in time, distance, and cultures encountered. Sharp (1955), for example, suggested a set of controls for comparisons of the frontiers of English-speaking peoples in Australia, Canada, and the United States. He noted that (1) comparisons should be between settlements occurring during the same historical period; (2) the pioneers must possess a similar cultural heritage and a corresponding technology; and (3) the physical environments compared must be generally similar. He drew the inference that Canadian native policy proved more successful than that of Australia or the United States because it was orderly, well-planned, and honorably executed (cf. Raby 1973, for a more limited comparison of the United States and Canada). Sharp suggested that law extended west in Canada ahead of settlers, in contrast to what occurred in the other two countries, and that native peoples had a chance to adjust to sedentary life before whites engulfed them (see Sections B and BC; also note Cardinal, whose 1969 analysis of Canadian Indian policy suggests that it has not been so successful in the long run).

Several other comparative frontier studies provide useful factual support and theoretical frameworks for the study of land tenure in the confrontation of cultures. Patterson (1971, 1972) compared Indians in North America to Bantu and other African peoples in Ghana, Kenya, and South Africa. Allen (1959) commented on displacement and conquest, noting how the Australian aborigines were unable to unite and form alliances in order to stem white aggression, as many Indian groups had done in the United States. He observed that the U.S. Government was less able to resist popular pressures against Indians on the frontier; he found that the giving and taking of reserves in the United States had no parallel in Australia. It was his conclusion that "humanitarian sentiments were simply unable to prevail until the frontier was virtually closed, that is to say until it was plainly too late for them [native peoples] to be of any use" (p. 26). Other studies have made comparisons in the Americas

(Trimble 1912-13; Macleod 1928; Spicer 1962), between the Old and New Worlds (Strieby 1895; Macleod 1928; Fried 1952), in the Pacific realm (Price 1963), or between the Pacific realm and North America (Jacobs 1971, 1972). Several specific studies, while dealing only with a single frontier, suggest the range of writings on parallel themes (Elkin 1951; Leach 1960; Rayner 1962; Biskup 1968; Wards 1968; Solberg 1969).

Jacobs's studies (1954, 1971, 1972) not only pointed up the utility of comparing attitudes on several frontiers toward the land rights of wandering tribes, but also offered a word of caution on the application of the frontier theory to indigenous populations. He claimed, with reference to New Guinea and British land policy, that the taking of native land rights was never a concerted goal—perhaps because of the high-density settlement of well-entrenched native communities that held on to their villages and lands, ferociously resisting conquest. This contrasts with the experiences of native peoples in Australia and North America. With reference to the frontier thesis, he suggested that historians have focused too often on the development of white civilization and exploitation of the land, in which the native has played a minor role. Turner (1921), Jacobs thought, treated Indians as a "kind of geographical obstacle" to the westward movement (1971, p. 307) (cf. the comments on environmental determinism by geographers in Section A). In comparing North America to Australia, as based on the writings of other historians, he stressed the role indigenous peoples have played in influencing the character of the white societies that occupied their lands. But since European colonization played no significant role in New Guinea, he believed that such an approach to frontier history was inapplicable. As Jacobs put it:

> The frontier theory, an interpretation of the development of white characteristics in a new land, cannot be applied to a country where the natives still control the mass of their own land and outnumber the Europeans. (1971, p. 308)

If one focuses on problems of land administration and resource development, one can see additional parallels in corresponding institutions and objectives, and in the exploitation and economic status of various native peoples. This is most notable on land set aside for native occupancy by European majority populations (reserves, reservations, resguardos, etc.). These lands, in most cases, are remnants of aboriginal territory, but the living arrangement has undergone drastic alteration. Increased population densities and new livelihood and settlement patterns have led to the modification of ecological relations linking man and land. Price (1950) was among the first to observe comparatively the administration of natives in English-speaking countries (i.e., Australia, Canada, New Zealand, and the

United States); in these countries he referred to "invasions" as being of "similarities rather than contrasts," especially with reference to the "adoption of well meaning but ineffective palliatives—the herding of the unfortunate natives in meagre reservations . . ." (p. 190). A new interpretation of current resource expansion into indigenous areas, especially in English-speaking countries, has been made by Sanders (1974); this author is especially critical of legal maneuvers in the taking of land for reservoirs (cf. the discussion of dams in Section AC). However, when we come to contrast South African reserves with U.S. reservations (Horrell 1965), we find that the factors that led Price and Sanders to find similarities no longer apply (cf. Hill 1964; Niewenhuysen 1966; Carter et al. 1967).

Few other studies focus on comparisons, but together, a great many studies reveal how similar land policies in different countries and colonies have led to parallel situations in land reservation, economic stagnation, and problems of improving both the economic and sociopolitical well-being of indigenous populations. A pair of studies on Rhodesian land allocation (Floyd 1962; Roder 1964) demonstrates similarities there with the ideologies and events leading to ethnic segregation in South Africa; another pair of studies (Morgan 1963; Jones 1965) contrasts the circumstances of white land dominance in Kenya and the eventual white withdrawal upon independence in that colony. All in all, the situation in Africa is not readily comparable to that in most of the Americas, because in Africa the natives comprise the overwhelming majority. (For a survey of native administration in British Africa, see Hailey 1951.)

Individual studies of reserved lands focus on the sociocultural and institutional setting of the inhabitants of such places as the Blackfoot Reserve of Alberta (Hanks and Hanks 1950), the general reserve system in Canada (Inglis 1971), the Namagurla Reserve in South Africa (Carstens 1967), and the hundred small reservations occupied by the Mapuche Indians of southern Chile (Faron 1961). The introduction of land tenure changes in various societies can also be compared by referring to such works as Carter's study (1955) of Aymara Indians and agrarian reform in Bolivia, Thiesenhusen and Brown's study (1964) of the introduction of private property among Chilean Indians, Manners's analysis (1964) of the impact of private ownership on an African people, and even Spitz's account (1967) of the transplanting of the homestead practice from the mainland to native Hawaiians. For comparison with rural-urban patterns bearing on Indian socioeconomic mobility, other studies amply provide comparative data: Dunstan's analysis (1966) of aboriginal land rights and the Australian economy, Metge's discussion (1964) of the Maoris' participation in New Zealand society relative to their inhabitation of trust lands, studies by Bennett (1969) and Denton (1970) focusing on the urbanizing Indian in Canada and his involvement in some urban functions, and Sabbagh's assessment (1968) of the rural-urban interaction of native peoples under apartheid in South Africa. These studies suggest, among other possibilities, the kinds of processes and events that researchers could consider in cross-cultural comparisons of the status of indigenous peoples around the world.

With respect to factors contributing to native culture change, comparisons may be made of the role of introduced land institutions in several selected contexts. Maori acculturation, for example, reveals many parallels to that of Indian tribes, in that reservation-like areas have tended to abet the withdrawal of native peoples from involvement in their surroundings. Ausubel (1961) suggested that the Maori have made a greater entry into the national life of New Zealand than Indians have in the U.S., although one must note, too, how utterly different these two countries are in terms of institutional complexities, size of the dominant population, and land area. Spicer (1969a), in comparing Mexican native policy with that of the United States, showed how Mexico sought to institutionalize the goals of cultural homogeneity by denying the existence of separate Indian ethnicities, in marked contrast to U.S. policy, which was from the outset preoccupied with delimiting rather than destroying the territorial basis of native ethnicity. He suggested that proletarization of Indians in Mexico, which led to their mixing into the economy, was abetted by the loss of territorial limits.

We should note, of course, that many Indian communities in both Americas participate selectively in the economies of these countries from within reservations or without. Unlike examples in Canada and the United States (the contrast with Mexico and Chile is less pronounced), most of the Indian communities in the Andes function outside the protection that land trusteeship has provided most Indians in the United States. Aguirre Beltrán (1967) has provided a useful analysis of the territorial situation of Andean peoples who continue to occupy their homelands because, as he suggested, these are marginal lands not coveted by the dominant society. He regarded these areas as refuges, for they normally lie outside the general economic sphere of the countries in which they are found. However, in some instances, they are drawn into regional economy by virtue of the influence of non-Indian settlers, tradespeople, and officials domiciled in the area. They best compare, perhaps, with the Pueblos, whose persistence as distinct communities partaking of Euro-American social and economic life on their own terms is somewhat similar.

Readers will no doubt realize that the foregoing discussions have been limited to events and circumstances of European confrontation with native peoples. In part, this emphasis stems from the fact that so much has been written and is available to us about European-native contacts. But any effort to uncover parallels among the colonial confrontations of different countries will reveal that when one attempts to include the experiences of non-European colonizers (and, for certain purposes, even the practices of the Soviet Union), the results are not reconcilable into a single scheme. For one thing, land reserves and semiautonomous political units are not equivalent. It is true that in historical perspective we find that the Russian take-over of native lands on its frontiers (cf. Bacon 1966) and the Chinese expansion into its southwestern provinces duplicate many of the contact situations that occurred in the United States (Fried 1952). Nevertheless, the reservations in the U.S. lack representation in the body politic, while for the territorial enclaves in Russia and China, such representation has always been intended; the comparison therefore suggests at least one major distinction. Also several such autonomous enclaves are inhabited not by truly indigenous peoples, but rather, by ethnic populations that constitute minorities relative to the body politic (cf. the situation of the Magyars in Rumania—see Helin 1967; for a general discussion of ethnic boundaries, see Barth 1969).

Confrontations in the subarctic realm offer some marginally comparable situations (Armstrong 1966; Lantis 1966). Here both the Soviet Union and Canada include scattered native populations that have not quite entered the national life of their countries. While the Canadian subarctic is a kind of national trust for its native inhabitants, the land institutions affecting its administration cannot be said to compare to the structure of territoriality in the Russian Soviet Federated Socialist Republic (RSFSR), in which are found most of the native peoples of the entire Soviet Union. Unlike Canada, which is organized politically into provinces and dominion territories all based on political rather than ethnic factors, the Soviet Union is organized into a series of nested political units based on ethnicity. In their governmental system many indigenous populations are represented in distinct national republics such as the Kirghiz SSR or Georgian SSR; lesser autonomous units (the Autonomous Soviet Socialist Republics or ASSRs) lie within these larger republics; most of the 19 ASSRs are found within the RSFSR. Ethnicities within republics (SSRs) and autonomous republics (ASSRs) all participate in the Council of Nationalities. Much lesser status is accorded those indigenous peoples who have not yet achieved cultural maturity (e.g., political); these groups reside in autonomous *oblasts* and national *okrugs*. While the governmental systems of North American countries differ markedly from that of the USSR, one could suggest that reservations in the West compare most with the national *okrugs*, most of which are located in the RSFSR.

Lantis has noted that neither Canada nor the Soviet Union has had to compete with other powers for control of these vast northlands, in marked contrast to the international conflicts over minority peoples and their territories between the Soviet Union and the Chinese Peoples Republic farther south (Moseley 1967; Freeberne 1968). In little or none of the subarctic is land administration tied up with significant pioneer settlement; thus until recently the native inhabitants have been numerically dominant within the subarctic areas of Canada and the Soviet Union (whereas they long ago became a numerical minority in Alaska).

Armstrong's review of Soviet native policy (1966) showed it to stand in marked contrast to those of the western countries. He noted that the Soviet government abandoned an earlier plan to establish native reservations in the north, preferring a socialist approach as a means to elevate and move people forward in communist ideological terms. The government has sought to sustain nationality and foster unity among these peoples, and at the same time to convey the principles of the Soviet system of democracy. They first set up "native soviets" as the equivalent of "village" soviets elsewhere, but shifted to a policy of establishing national districts (*okrugs*) in which, for example, the native tongue would continue to be spoken. Under this plan different ethnic groups could proceed to advance in the Soviet democracy and perhaps ultimately achieve ASSR status. Yet in the meantime Russification, by means of planned immigration, has proceeded to reduce some indigenous peoples to a minority in their homelands. Thus their territorial units are no more sacred trusts than reservations are in the United States, and of course they cannot be compared in their political roles. If ever the Navajos attained commonwealth status (cf. the discussion of Stucki 1971 in Section AC), something comparable to the ASSR will have come about.

In other political arenas one may see parallels to the Soviet approach or to the situations that have flourished in the West. Buchanan (1970) briefly examined the geographic pattern of Chinese minority distribution, which reveals in its organization close affinities to the Soviet scheme of recognizing the independent rights of various nationalities in homogenous and mixed situations. (For a comparative discussion in the context of political geography, see Pounds 1963; 1970, Chap. 2.)

One historian noted that Ainu territory on the island of Hokkaido was perceived as an area in which to exploit the natives and settle Japanese farm families (Takakura 1960). Despite protective laws and eventual creation of native reservations, occupation by the Japanese reduced the Ainu to a dependent minority. Somewhat different has been the experience of hill tribes in the subcontinent of India. Hindu occupancy of Limbus territory in Nepal, for example, led to the reduction of native land status and the establishment of the colonists as landlords over their indigenous tenants (Caplan 1970). The author observed that because native life-ways have been so bound up with the preservation of territory, they disintegrated as the Hindus gained control and sought to terminate communal (*kipat*) tenure. The natives, in turn, resisted acculturation in an attempt to maintain their defense of traditional tenure concepts. One can see some similarity in the resistance to acculturation among Pueblos and Maoris, but the reduction of a native people to a tenant class has few parallels. (One may perhaps regard the tenant-like or feudal nature of encomiendas and haciendas in Latin America as near equivalents.)

Despite the availability of cross-cultural studies and a vast literature on land tenure that includes accounts of numerous native systems, only a few studies to date have sought to structure the subject matter so as to be useful to the further study of land institutions under contact conditions. Fried's very instructive analysis (1952) of American and Chinese advances on their own frontiers and the ensuing destruction, transformation, or incorporation of indigenous peoples provides a good working methodology that, to my knowledge, has not been imitated, perhaps because the researchers must be equally well versed in the literature of all the peoples under investigation, a seemingly insuperable demand. My own unpublished study (Sutton 1965) explored in a more limited way the generic characteristics of the reserve as a land medium for native administration within English-speaking societies. It attempted to demonstrate how utterly different non-European (as well as contemporary Soviet) experience with native peoples has been. No global scheme has been devised, notwithstanding the availability of a somewhat outdated world survey of indigenous peoples and their lands, prepared by the International Labor Office (1953) and a classificatory system of minorities by the United Nations Commission on Human Rights (United Nations 1950).

The only approximation to a cross-cultural typology of culture contacts from which land questions involving indigenous peoples can be extrapolated is an excellent heuristic paper by Forbes (1968). An ethnohistorian of the American Indian, Forbes has branched out to examine comparable situations and to define better the arena of ethnohistory. Many of his paired "contacts" consider indigenous situations. Other studies too have proposed gross headings under which to subsume relevant land data; for example, Schermerhorn (1970) spoke of a threefold scheme of colonization and applied it to the British experience. For Nigeria and Kenya he spoke of "limited settlement." For South Africa and Rhodesia he referred to "substantial settlement," since here the colonists, although outnumbered, had come to hold vast acreage. Finally, he referred to "massive settlement" for areas outside Africa, where the newcomers soon constituted the majority.

Others have also expressed the view that size and density of population and related demographic factors have contributed to the rise of colonial land policies that favor or disfavor the persistence of native inhabitation. In a very direct way it is expressed by Price (1963) in his analysis of European expansion in the Pacific realm and its continental margins. For this area he delineated two contrasting kinds of colonizers: sojourners and settlers. He applied the former label to countries and regions in which administrators, missionaries, traders, and soldiers have played the major role in institutional diffusion, as in India, parts of Southeast Asia, and Africa; the latter applies to the more permanent residents who colonized eastern and southern Africa, the Americas, and Australia (cf. the map of "Europeanization of the World" by Zelinsky 1966). Jacobs (1971) indirectly alluded to a similar contrast between European involvement in New Guinea and that in Australia and North America.

If similarities exist in the occupation, acquisition, or administration of native lands by several cultures, and if parallels can be found in the institutions, processes, and practices of those who instituted changes in indigenous land tenure, at least one scholar has urged some caution in coming to conclusions too quickly. Speaking of "recurrent sequences of change in contacts between non-literates and Europeans" (1961, p. 541), Spicer concluded a comparative analysis of six case studies of American Indian acculturation by referring to the work of Elkin (1951). The latter identified a set of events and processes in the occupation of Australia and suggested that they might be generic and thus applicable to other situations. But Spicer suggested that it was "meaningless to posit such invariant sequences without explicit statement of conditions of contacts as well as of the nature of the cultures in contact" (ibid.). Recognizing that some such sequences–e.g., native population decline and disruption of local group structure–have occurred, Spicer still felt that "nowhere is there evidence that Elkin's sequence is inherent in the contact of European and native cultures and must develop regardless of conditions once contact has been established" (ibid.).

Nonetheless, Fried (1952) made cogent comparisons of American and Chinese practices, fully attentive to the fact that emphasis on a comparative approach tended to obscure very real differences. He inferred from his limited comparison that acculturative types and determinants have both had universal application and that parallel processes can be educed by resort to a comparative methodology. Whether one subscribes to the more restrictive position taken by Spicer or to positions held by Elkin, or Fried, or others, there does seem to exist a basis for further comparative treatment of the themes that have been outlined in this book. This final section has had only one objective: to introduce the comparative view, keeping in mind that the answers to questions in social science research most often depend on a capacity to represent situations in terms of their similarities rather than their differences. At the comparative level a scholar must reject the impulse to elaborate on the plentiful distinctions between individual contact situations; instead one must search for universals. In this regard several scholars have already pointed the way toward a better understanding of how human confrontations change the customs and lifestyles of pre-literate or relatively unsophisticated populations, many of whom are fast becoming numerical minorities, either by dint of disastrous alterations in birth/death rates or by assimilation into the larger society. society.

Notes

1. Best defined as those comprising "descendents of the aboriginal population living in a given country at the time of settlement or conquest ... by some of the ancestors of the nonindigenous groups in whose hands political and economic power at present lies" (International Labor Office, 1953, p. 26).

Works Cited in the Epilogue

Aguirre Beltrán, 1967
Allen, 1959
Armstrong, 1966
Ausubel, 1961
Bacon, 1966
Barnes, 1960
Barth, 1969
Beeman, *1971
Bennett, 1969
Biskup, 1968
Buchanan, 1970
Caplan, 1970
Cardinal, 1969
Carstens, 1967
Carter, 1965
Carter, Karis, & Stoltz, 1967
Cook, 1943
Denton, 1970
Dunstan, 1966
Elkin, 1951
Encyclopedia of Social Sciences,
   1931-38

Faron, 1961
Floyd, 1962
Forbes, 1968
Freeberne, 1968
Fried, 1952
Hailey, 1951
Hanks & Hanks, 1950
Harper, *1947
Helin, 1967
Hill, 1964
Horrell, 1965
International Labor Office, 1953
Inglis, 1971
Jacobs, 1954, 1971, 1972
Jennings, 1971b
Jones, 1965
Lantis, 1966
Leach, 1960
Macleod, 1928
Manners, 1964
Metge, 1964
Mikesell, *1960

Morgan, 1963
Moseley, 1967
Narvey, 1974
Niewenhuysen, 1966
Patterson, 1971, 1972
Peckham & Gibson, 1969
Pounds, 1963, 1970
Price, A. G., 1950, 1963
Price, M. E., 1973
Raby, 1973
Rayner, 1962
Ribeiro, *1962, 1971
Roder, 1964
Sabbagh, 1968
Sanders, 1974
Schermerhorn, 1970
Schwarz, *1963
Service, 1955

Sharp, 1955
Snow, 1921
Solberg, 1969
Speck, *1926
Spicer, 1961, 1962, 1969a
Spitz, 1967
Strieby, 1895
Stucki, 1971
Sutton, 1965
Takakura, 1960
Tax, *1967
Thiesenhusen & Brown, 1964
Trimble, 1912-13
Turner, 1921
United Nations, 1950
Wards, 1968
Zavala, 1965
Zelinsky, 1966

---

*Denotes works not actually cited, but relevant to this section.

Bibliographical and Cartographic Sources

Bibliographical Sources

Despite the amount of literature generated by scholars, lawyers, public officials, and others, few valuable bibliographical sources exist. *Dissertation Abstracts* was of limited utility, as was Dockstader's (1957) compilation: of 3700 entries in the latter, hardly four dozen deserved citation or discussion. Ballas (1966) and Carlson (1972) listed manuscripts in geography. Freeman and Smith prepared a useful guide (1966) to the manuscripts of the American Philosophical Society. Snodgrass (1968) has incorporated all of the relevant government documents from 1930 to 1967 and has included, under the heading "natural resource administration," some important references to non-governmental publications on Indian land tenure. *House Report 2503* (U.S. Congress 1953) contains a comprehensive compilation of laws, treaties, statistics, and bibliographical sources on all tribes (pp. 221-670). Although they do not contain bibliographies, the discussions of sources by Litton (1955) and Gibson (1960) evaluate the National Archives and public and private libraries. Allen and Moristo (1971) provide a useful introduction to the California Indian archival materials housed at Federal Records Centers in the state. Jones (1955) has compiled a useful guide to the annual reports of the Bureau of Indian Affairs.

For ethnographic sources Murdock (1953) remains the definitive work (cf. Owen 1967). Keesing (1953), another anthropological source, examines the theme and methodology of acculturation studies and contains many citations, but it lacks any useful analysis of the land tenure literature written by anthropologists. Edwards (1942), now much out of date, retains its utility for older source materials on agriculture. Winther (1964) and Winther and Van Orman (1967) prepared exhaustive bibliographies of historical source materials and included citations from all of the state and regional historical quarterlies, which have comprised a constant outlet for writings on Indian land policy, cessions, treaties, and other matters germane to this study. Hagan (1963) offers the only (albeit brief) historiographic interpretation of Indian affairs, but does not develop a discussion of land tenure. Only more recently have compilations of legal sources come into print (*American Indian Law Newsletter* 1968, 1971; Sabatini 1973; Price 1973). The Native American Rights Fund has published an index to Indian legal materials and resources (1973b); Smith (1974) is a more general recent bibliography.

The range of bibliographies, of course, extends from the footnotes of any one study to detailed digests of sources on a single tribe. Older sources of some small value include Field (1873) and DePuy's compilation and brief discussion (1917) of English colonial treaties with the Indians. There are always useful references in tribal bibliographies such as those for the Five Civilized Tribes (Jones 1967), the Iroquois (Weinman 1969), the Utes (Stewart 1971), the Navajo (Kluckhohn 1940); and in state and regional bibliographies such as those for the Indians of California (Riddell 1962), California and Nevada (Forbes 1969), the Great Basin (Fowler 1970), Louisiana (Neuman and Simmons 1969), and Wisconsin (Fay 1965). General bibliographical sources rarely cite more than a few relevant texts. Readers may wish to examine Marken (1973), Klein and Icolari's sourcebook (1967), or the annotated bibliography prepared by Torrans (1960), who offers excellent assessments of the content and usefulness of several books discussed in this volume. The *Indian Historian Press* publishes annual lists of titles (1971, 1972, 1973), but only a few pages under the headings of land or law directly relate to themes under review here. One cannot afford to overlook anthologies, for they reprint useful samples of laws, treaties, judicial decisions, speeches, articles, and scholarly interpretation, and they include some studies that have been prepared by Indians (Armstrong 1971; Deloria 1971; Ellis 1972; Forbes 1964, 1967, 1969; Josephy 1971; Moquin and Van Doren 1973; Prucha 1973; Vanderwerth 1971; Vogel 1972; Walker 1971; Washburn 1964, 1973).

Cartographic Sources

The cartographic representation of Indian distributions, patterns of territoriality and land tenure, and forms of settlement constitutes an important vehicle by which to record past and present tribal claims to land. Perhaps as many as a quarter of the studies under review contain maps of some kind. Certainly, studies such as those by Swanton (1922), Beauchamp (1900), and Stewart (1966a) discuss in elaborate detail original compilations of mappable data or reproduce historic maps of considerable utility to later researchers. The literature is filled with original maps of tribal distributions, often defined in terms of lingual patterns, clans, settlement types, or boundaries; as is suggested in Section AB, the cartographic renditions related to land claims litigation are perhaps among the best reconstructions to date. General map sources include Kelsay's (1954) archival compilation, which cites maps of cessions, reservations, and allotments, state by state; Sturtevant's briefer compilation of maps (1958); and Royce's (1899, 1971) classic presentation of land cession maps together with detailed listings of executive and congressional actions affecting cession and reservation of lands. A wall-map rendition of land cessions, utilizing Royce data, appeared as a supplemental publication to a geographical periodical (Hilliard 1972). [For a compilation of data on federal and state reservations, including statistical, economic, and related historical information (but unfortunately lacking maps), consult Economic Development Administration (1971).]

Several state atlases should be consulted. Morris and McReynolds (1965) have prepared the best of the handful of historical atlases that include useful Indian land data. More than two dozen plates portray cessions, reservations, land openings, and leases and allotments among the Five Civilized Tribes and the smaller emigrant groups as well as among the indigenous Plains tribes residing within Indian Territory and the State of Oklahoma. Their plate 13, for example, delineates removal areas (cf. Figure 3 in this volume). Each plate includes a summary bibliography. A Kansas atlas by Socolofsky and Self (1972) contains only a few plates covering tribal distributions, emigrant Indian homelands, reservations, missions, and treaty sites; but it does not actually show cession areas. Lonsdale's (1967) North Carolina atlas displays, on two maps, aboriginal distributions relative to colonization and Indian boundaries in colonial times, as prepared by De Vorsey (see his 1966 book and the discussion in Section B). Other, somewhat less useful, atlases include Beck and Haase's for New Mexico (1969), and California (1974). Both atlases include plates showing Indian lands; the latter also shows the relationship between the unratified California Indian treaties and later reservations (plate 57).

Works Cited in This Section

Allen & Moristo, 1971   Armstrong, 1971
American Indian Law Newsletter,   Ballas, 1966
    1968, 1971   Beauchamp, 1900

220

Beck & Haase, 1969, 1974
Carlson, 1972
Deloria, 1971
DePuy, 1917
De Vorsey, 1966
Dockstader, 1957
Economic Development Administration, 1971
Edwards, 1942
Ellis, 1972
Fay, 1965
Field, 1973
Forbes, 1964, 1967, 1969
Fowler, 1970
Freeman & Smith, 1966
Gibson, 1960
Hagan, 1963
Hilliard, 1972
Jones, J. A., 1955
Jones, W. K., 1967
Josephy, 1971
Keesing, 1953
Kelsay, 1954
Klein & Icolari, 1967
Kluckhohn, 1940
Litton, 1955
Lonsdale, 1967
Marken, 1973

Moquin & Van Doren, 1973
Morris & McReynolds, 1965
Murdock, 1960
Native American Rights Fund, 1973-74
Neuman & Simmons, 1969
Owens, 1967
Price, 1973
Prucha, 1973
Riddell, 1962
Royce, 1899, 1971
Sabatini, 1973
Smith, 1974
Snodgrass, 1968
Socolofsky & Self, 1972
Stewart, 1966a, 1971
Sturtevant, 1958
Swanton, 1922
Torrans, 1960
U.S. Congress, House, 1953
Vanderwerth, 1971
Vogel, 1972
Walker, 1971
Washburn, 1964, 1973
Weinman, 1969
Winther, 1964
Winther & Van Orman, 1967

Bibliography

A Bibliographical Note

If literature denotes, as one definition suggests, a body of writings on a particular subject, then the bounds of this study may be set anywhere. It is not likely to be inclusive, since, frankly, manuscript materials cannot always be located and the vast store of government documents defies exhaustion. A realistic working method has required some selectivity, whether with reference to manuscripts, documents, periodical literature, monographs, or books; not every relevant title has been cited, nor have all of those cited undergone review in the bibliographical essays. The typology speaks for itself, and its literature suggests, if this endeavor has been successful, the full range of writings on the subject of Indian land tenure, through the review of a comprehensive sample. Thus government documents, which make up a field in themselves, have received careful examination, and those titles have been included in the bibliography and discussion which comprise the only source that amply treats a given topic, or which represent the best compilation of cartographic, bibliographical, or statistical information. One should keep in mind that government publications and processed materials are the sum and substance of a considerable literature in Indian affairs; where applicable, the discussion has drawn attention to the utility of such sources. Similarly, curtailment of the citation and discussion of case law reflects the fact that the more important litigation has been interpreted in other publications which should suffice as source material for the avid researcher. And in general, it has been necessary to limit citations in the fields of history and ethnography, where my concern has been to suggest the scope and orientation of the work of a vast number of scholars. Consequently, certain studies that may seem to have been overlooked were actually omitted because additional references might have proved redundant. Finally, some references cited in the bibliography do not receive any mention in the text; these are supplemental and useful studies, which may be located through the indexes or the citations at the end of each chapter.

Since the essays revolve around the typology (Figure 1), each section has its own self-contained, alphabetized reference list including author and date only; it did not seem necessary to provide full citations within each section, since the present comprehensive bibliography is provided. These brief bibliographies do make it possible to locate easily all literature relevant to each section. On the other hand, users will find the tribal, geographical, and subject indexes helpful in searching for information on specific tribes or topics. We have included these indexes so that the reader does not have to rely exclusively on the typology as a means of getting at the important sources on any topic. The combination of the detailed table of contents, threefold indexing, and the brief bibliographies which follow the sections should provide ample access to the literature for the researcher.

Finally, I should note areas of omission in this bibliographical study. Without doubt, certain works of journalism, oral history, and even fiction should be considered relevant land tenure literature. However, as categories of published materials, none of the three offers any significant quantity of source material or interpretation at this date. One can cite, for example, an excellent series of articles on Indian land problems in the *Christian Science Monitor* (ca. summer-fall, 1970) or the Pulitzer Prize-winning series on the controversial guardianship issues of the Palm Springs (Agua Caliente) Indians in California, written by George Ringwald in the *Riverside Press-Enterprise* in 1967-68. Two Indian newspapers provide varying coverage of land-related matters nationally, regionally, or by tribes—*Wassaja* (published by the American Indian Historical Society, San Francisco) and *Akwesasne Notes* (published by the Mohawk Nation in upstate New York). One may expect that ultimately oral history will include important recordings of the thoughts of Indians who still recall past situations bearing on land rights, homelands, and the like. Similarly, one can refer to numerous published Indian speeches (several anthologies cited in the preceding section include relevant examples on land matters). To date, neither oral history nor Indian oratory has been interpreted from the specific orientation of land tenure. In passing, one might also note the contribution of film by way of a single example recently released by the University of California Extension: The Pit River Indian Nation's dispute over a land settlement has been sensitively interpreted in an Emmy Award-winning 16mm production entitled "Forty-Seven Cents" (see *Lifelong Learning*, 43, no. 3, July 9, 1973; see also Section AB).

Abbreviations used in the Bibliography

AA	American Anthropologist	FBJ	Federal Bar Journal
AAA	Memoir, American Anthropological Association	GPJ	Great Plains Journal
		GPO	Government Printing Office
AAAG	Annals, Association of American Geographers	GR	Geographical Review
AAAS	American Association for the Advancement of Science	HO	Human Organization (note: former name, Applied Anthropology is written out in full)
AAAPSS	Annals, American Academy of Political and Social Science	IH	Indian Historian
		IMH	Indiana Magazine of History
AES	American Ethnological Society	INM	Indian Notes and Monographs (Heye Foundation, New York)
AH	Agricultural History	JAH	Journal of American History (formerly Mississippi Valley Historical Review)
AHR	American Historical Review		
AI	Annals of Iowa		
AILN	American Indian Law Newsletter (Albuquerque)	JEH	Journal of Economic History
AILR	American Indian Law Review (Norman)	JFE	Journal of Farm Economics
AmI	América Indígena	JG	Journal of Geography
AMNH	American Museum of Natural History (New York)	JW	Journal of the West
		L.R.	Law Review (various)
APCG	Association of Pacific Coast Geographers	LSO	Law and Social Order (Arizona State Law Journal)
APS	American Philosophical Society	NMHR	New Mexico Historical Review
ArW	Arizona and the West	MRBIP	Missouri River Basin Indian Project
AR	Anthropological Record (University of California)	MVHR	Mississippi Valley Historical Review
AW	Annals of Wyoming	NRJ	Natural Resources Journal
BAE	Bureau of American Ethnology	NRL	Natural Resources Lawyer
CHSQ	California Historical Society Quarterly	OHQ	Oregon Historical Quarterly
CO	Chronicles of Oklahoma	PHR	Pacific Historical Review
CSSH	Comparative Studies in Society and History	PMAAE	Peabody Museum of American Archeology and Ethnology
EG	Economic Geography		
EH	Ethnohistory	PNWQ	Pacific Northwest Quarterly
ET	Ethnology		

224

RMMLI	Rocky Mountain Mineral Law Institute	SWJA	Southwestern Journal of Anthropology
SCQ	Southern California Quarterly (Historical Society of Southern California)	UCPAAE	University of California Publications in American Archaeology and Ethnology
SWHQ	Southwest Historical Quarterly	UHQ	Utah Historical Quarterly

A dagger (†) is used to mark those works that have not been seen by the author, but are known by title only or through an abstract (as in *Dissertation Abstracts*) or a review. Because many university libraries refuse to lend manuscripts, it has been necessary to infer the contents of some of the more promising titles. An asterisk (*) signifies that the reference and discussion are based mainly on correspondence with an author, librarian, colleague, or other person, especially in connection with doctoral dissertations in progress or books in press at the time of the inquiry.

Numbers enclosed in brackets following entries refer to pages *in this volume* where the work is discussed.

Abbott, George W., 1960. "The American Indian, Federal Citizen and State Citizen." *FBJ* 20: 248-54.

Abel, Annie H., 1904. "Indian Reservations in Kansas and the Extinguishment of Their Title." *Transactions, Kansas State Historical Society* [Collection] *1903-04,* 8: 72-109. [116, 117]

————, 1908a. "History of Events Resulting in Indian Consolidation West of the Mississippi." *Annual Report,* American History Association *1906,* 1: 233-450. [46]

————, 1908b. "Proposals for an Indian State, 1778-1878." *Annual Report,* American History Association *1907,* 1: 89-104. [46]

Aberle, David F., 1966. *The Peyote Religion Among the Navaho.* (Chicago: Aldine). [187, 189]

————, 1974a. "Navajo Rights in Land; Use Rights; Grazing Rights; Rights in Livestock; Rights in Habitation Sites, Habitations, and Improvements; and Miscellaneous Rights: Germane to Legislation Concerning the Disputed Territory and the Moencopi Area." [Statement prepared for the Navajo Tribal attorney, Sept., 1974, processed.] 17pp. [26, 124, 196]

————, 1974b. "Statement of David F. Aberle for Submission to the Senate Committee on Indian and Insular Affairs. [Statement presented at the hearings, July 24, 1974, processed.], 64pp. [124, 196]

Aberle, Sophie D., 1948. *The Pueblo Indians of New Mexico: Their Land, Economy and Civil Organization. AAA Memoir* 70 [*AA* 50, no. 4, pt. 2]. [88, 122, 187-88]

Abernethy, Alonzo, 1913-15. "Early Iowa Indian Treaties and Boundaries." *AI* 11: 241-259; 358-380. [53]

Abourezk, James G., 1966. "South Dakota Indian Jurisdiction." *South Dakota L.R.*, 11: 101-118. [155]

Aguirre Beltrán, Gonzalo, 1967. *Regiones de Refugio: el Desarrollo de la Comunidad y el Proceso Dominical en Mestizo America.* (Mex., D.F., Ediciones Especiales 46, Instituto Indigenista Interamericano). [Reviewed by R. C. Hunt, *AA* 71 (1969): 545-52]. [210]

Ainsworth, Ed., 1965. *Golden Checkerboard.* (Palm Desert: Desert-Southwest Publishing Co.). [121, 134]

†Akright, Ora F., 1924. "Indian Land Cessions to the United States." Unpublished masters thesis, Univ. of Kansas. [53]

Alden, John R., 1944. *John Stuart and the Southern Colonial Frontier: A Study of Indian Relations, War, Trade, and Land Problems in the Southern Wilderness, 1754-1775.* (Ann Arbor: Univ. of Michigan Press). [43]

Allen, H. C., 1959. *Bush and Backwoods: A Comparison of the Frontier in Australia and the United States.* (East Lansing: Michigan State Univ. Press). [207]

Allen, Jack and Moristo, Dennis, 1971. "An Introduction to the Bureau of Indian Affairs–Agency Records and Bureau of Indian Affairs–Archival Records Housed in the San Francisco and Bell Federal Records Centers." *Native American Series*, pamphlet no. 1. (Los Angeles: American Indian Culture Center, Univ. of California). [217]

Alvord, Clarence W., 1917. *The Mississippi Valley in British Politics: A Study of the Trade, Land Speculation, and Experiments in Imperialism Culminating in the American Revolution.* (Cleveland: Arthur Clark). [40]

American Friends Service Committee, 1970. *Uncommon Controversy: Fishing Rights of the Muckleshoot, Puyallup, and Nisqually Indians.* (Seattle and London: Univ. of Washington Press). [147, 161]

American Indian Law Newsletter 1968, vol. 1, no. 25; 1971, vol. 4, no. 7. [218]

Ames, David W. and Fisher, Burton R., 1959. "The Menominee Termination Crisis: Barriers in the Way of a Rapid Cultural Transition." *HO* 18, no. 3: 101-11. [139-40]

*Anderson, George E., 1956. "The Hoopa Valley Indian Reservation in Northwestern California: A Study of Its Origins." Unpublished masters thesis, Univ. of California, Berkeley. [70, 81, 117]

Angle, J., 1959. *Federal, State, and Tribal Jurisdiction on Indian Reservations in Arizona. American Indian Series* 2, Bureau of Ethnic Research, Univ. of Arizona (Tucson). [155]

Anonymous, 1955. "Minnesota's Chippewas: Treaties and Trends." *Minnesota L.R.* 39 (June): 853-72. [158, 160]

—————, 1960. "Tribal Property Interests in Executive Order Reservations: A Compensable Indian Right." *Yale L.R.* 69 (May): 627-42. [116, 123]

—————, 1966. "The American Indian–Tribal Sovereignty and Civil Rights." *Iowa L.R.* 51: 654-69. [150]

—————, 1968a. "Indians: Better Dead than Red?" *Southern California L.R.* 42, no. 1 (Feb.): 101-25. [151]

—————. 1968b. "Regulation of Treaty Indian Fishing." *Washington L.R.* 43: 670-83. [161]

—————, 1969. "The Indian Bill of Rights and the Constitutional Status of Tribal Governments." *Harvard L.R.* 82: 1343-73. [150]

—————, 1972. "Toward a New System for the Resolution of Indian Resource Claims." *New York Univ. L.R.* 47, no. 6: 1107-49. [148]

—————, 1973. "Res Judicata–Judgment in Suit between Navajo and Hopi Tribes Held to Estop Individual Navajo Indians Not Parties to the Prior Suit from Asserting Aboriginal Title Claims to Ancestral Lands." *Rutgers L.R.* 26 (Summer): 909-28. [124]

Anson, Bert, 1964. "Variations of the Indian Conflict: The Effects of the Emigrant Indian Removal Policy, 1830-54." *Missouri Historical Review* 59, no. 1 (Oct.): 64-89. [49, 108, 188]

—————, 1970. *The Miami Indians.* (Norman: Univ. of Oklahoma Press). [50, 92, 188]

Armstrong, Terence, 1966. "The Administration of Northern Peoples: the USSR." In Macdonald, R. St. J. (ed.): 57-88. [211, 212]

Armstrong, Virginis I. (comp.), 1971. *I Have Spoken: American History through the Voices of the Indian.* (Chicago: Swallow Press). [98, 218]

†Arnold, Winston C., 1967. *Native Claims in Alaska.* (Anchorage). [109]

Aschenbrenner, P. J., 1971. "State Power and the Indian Treaty Right to Fish." *California L.R.* 59, no. 2 (March: 485-524). [160, 161]

Aschmann, Homer H., 1963. "Environment and Ecology in the 'Northern Tonto' Claim Area." [Before the Indian Claims Commission, Docket no. 22-J.] (Riverside, Calif.: processed manuscript). [108]

—————, 1966. "The Head of the Colorado Delta." In Eyre, S. R. and Jones, G. R. J. (eds.). *Geography as Human Ecology* (London: Arnold): 231-263. [87, 108]

—————, 1970. "Athapaskan Expansion in the Southwest." *Yearbook, APCG* 32: 79-97. [29-30]

Aumann, F. R., 1906. "The Acquisition of Iowa Lands from the Indians." *AI* 7 [3rd ser.] (Jan.): 283-90. [50]

Ausubel, D. P., 1961. "Maori: A Study in Resistive Acculturation." *Social Forces* 39 (March): 218-27. [210]

Averkieva, Julia, 1971. "The Tlingit Indians." In Leacock and Lurie (eds.): 317-342.

Babbitt, Hattie, 1971. "State Taxation of Indian Income." *LSO* 1971, no. 2: 355-369. [157-58]

†Bach, Arthur L., 1937. "The United States Government Indian Land Policy." Unpublished masters thesis in history, Univ. of North Dakota. [70]

Bacon, Elizabeth E., 1966. *Central Asians under Russian Rule: A Study in Culture Change.* (Ithaca: Cornell Univ. Press). [211]

†Baenen, J. A., 1965. "Hunting and Fishing Rights of the Nez Perce Indians: A Chapter in Recent Ethnohistory." Unpublished masters thesis in anthropology, Washington State Univ. [160]

†Bailey, M. T., 1972. *Reconstruction in Indian Territory: A Study of Avarice, Discrimination and Opportunism.* (New York: Kennikat Press). [See review in *AILN* 5, no. 9 (Nov.1972).] [117]

Ballas, Donald J., 1960. "Notes on the Population, Settlement, and Ecology of the Eastern Cherokee Indians." *JG* 59 (Sept.): 258-67. [50, 132]

—————, 1962. "The Livelihood of the Eastern Cherokees." *JG* 61 (Nov.): 342-49. [50, 81, 132]

—————, 1966. "Geography and the American Indian." *JG* 65 (April.): 156-68). [217]

†—————, 1970. "A Cultural Geography of Todd County, South Dakota, and the Rosebud Indian Reservation." Unpublished doctoral dissertation in geography, Univ. of Nebraska. [73, 81, 86]

Barker, Robert W., 1960. "The Indian Claims Commission–the Conscience of the Nation in Its Dealings with the Original American." *FBJ* 20: 240-47. [94]

Barlowe, Raleigh, 1970. *Land Resource Economics*. (Englewood Cliffs, N.J.: Prentice-Hall). [10]

Barnes, J. A., 1960. "Indigenous Politics and Colonial Administration, with Special Reference to Australia." *CSSH* 2, no. 2: 133-49. [206]

Barnett, Homer G., 1956. *Anthropology in Administration*. (Evanston: Row, Peterson). [12, 179-80]

Barney, Ralph A., 1955. "Legal Problems Peculiar to Indian Claims Litigation." *EH* 2 (Fall): 315-325. [94, 99]

– – – – –, 1960. "Some Legal Problems under the Indian Claims Commission Act." *FBJ* 20: 235-39. [94, 99]

– – – – –, 1963. "Indian Claims." *Appraisal Journal* 31 (April): 169-77. [94, 104-6]

Barnouw, Victor, 1950. *Acculturation and Personality Among the Wisconsin Chippewa. AAA Memoir* 72 [*AA* 52, no. 4, pt. 2]. [201]

Barrett, L. A., 1926. "Land and Economic Conditions of the California Indians." *Transactions of the Commonwealth Club of California* 21, no. 3 (June): 118-125. [132]

Barrett, Samuel K., 1908. *The Ethno-Geography of the Pomo and Neighboring Indians. UCPAAE* 6: 1-332. [29]

Barth, Frederick, (ed.), 1969. *Ethnic Groups and Boundaries: the Social Organization of Culture Differences*. (Bergen and Oslo: Universitetsforlaget). [211]

Bartlett, Katherine, 1945. "The Distributions of the Indians of Arizona in 1848." *Plateau* 17, no. 3: 41-45.

Basehart, Harry W., 1967. "Resource-holding Corporation among the Mescalero Apache." *SWJA* 23 (Autumn): 277-91. [190]

Bauman, Robert, 1960. "Iroquois Empire." *Northwest Ohio Quarterly* 32, no. 4: 138-172. [47]

Baumhoff, Martin A., 1958. "California Athabascan Groups." *AR* 16, no. 5: 157-237. [32]

†Bayard, Charles J., 1956. "The Development of the Public Land Policy, 1783-1820, with Special Reference to Indians." Unpublished doctoral dissertation in history, Indiana Univ.

Beaglehole, Ernest, 1936. "Ownership and Inheritance in An American Indian Tribe." *Iowa L.R.* 20 (Jan.): 304-16. [25]

Beals, Ralph A., 1953. "Acculturation." In Kroeber, A. L. (ed.), *Anthropology Today*. (Chicago: Univ. of Chicago Press): 621-41. [180]

– – – – – and Hester, James A., Jr., 1956. "A New Ecological Typology of the California Indians." *Selected Papers of the 5th International Congress of Anthropological and Ethnological Sciences* (Sept. 1-9, Philadelphia, Univ. of Pennsylvania): 411-19. [21]

Beauchamp, W. M., 1900. *Aboriginal Occupation of New York. Bulletin*. New York State Museum (Albany) 7, no. 32. [30, 219]

Bechham, S. D., 1971. *Requiem for a People: The Rogue Indians and the Frontiersmen*. (Norman: University of Oklahoma Press).

Beck, Warren A. and Haase, Ynez D., 1969. *Historical Atlas of New Mexico*. (Norman: Univ. of Oklahoma Press). [219]

– – – – –, 1974. *Historical Atlas of California*. (Norman: Univ. of Oklahoma Press). [219]

Beeman, R. R., 1971. "Labor Forces and Race Relations: A Comparison of the Colonization of Brazil and Virginia." *Political Science Quarterly* 86 (Dec.): 609-36.

Bender, Averam B., 1952. *The March of Empire: Frontier Defense in the Southwest, 1848-60.* (Lawrence: Univ. of Kansas Press). [53]

Benge, William B., 1960. "Law and Order on Indian Reservations." *FBJ* 20: 223-229.

Bennett, Elmer F., 1960. "Federal Responsibility for Indian Resources." *FBJ* 20: 255-62. [71]

Bennett, J. W., 1969. *Northern Plainsmen: Adaptive Strategy and Agrarian Life.* (Chicago: Aldine Publishing Co.). [210]

Bennett, Robert, 1970. "Indian Land Development: Good or Bad Economics?" In *Indian Voices: The First Convocation of American Indian Scholars.* (San Francisco: American Indian Historical Society): 247-281. [78]

Berger, Edward B., 1968a. "Indian Land–Minerals–Related Problems." *RMMLI* 14: 89-122. [71, 72, 171]

––––––, 1968b. "Indian Mineral Interest–A Potential for Economic Advancement." *Arizona L.R.* 10, no. 3: 675-89. [71, 171]

–––––– and Mounce, William J., 1971. "Applicability of State Conservation and Other Laws to Indian and Public Lands." *RMMLI* 16: 347-97. [72, 171]

Berkhofer, Robert F., Jr., 1965. *Salvation and the Savage: An Analysis of Protestant Missions and American Indian Response, 1787-1862.* (Lexington: Univ. of Kentucky Press).

––––––, 1969. "Barrier to Settlement: British Indian Policy in the Old Northwest, 1783-1794." In *The Frontier in American Development: Essays in Honor of Paul W. Gates.* D. M. Ellis (ed.). (Ithaca: Cornell Univ. Press): pp. 249-276. [46]

––––––, 1971. "The Political Context of a New Indian History." *PHR* 40, no. 3: 357-82. [12, 38, 39, 186]

Berkman, R. L. and Viscusi, W. K., 1973. *Damming the West.* (New York: Grossman) Chap. 7, "Indians Sold Down the River," 151-96. [Ralph Nader's Study Group on the Bureau of Reclamation.] [163, 166]

Berreman, J. V., 1937. *Tribal Distributions in Oregon. AAA Memoir* 47 [*AA* 39, no. 3, pt. 2]. [31]

Berthrong, Donald J., 1956. "Federal Indian Policy and the Southern Cheyennes and Arapahoes, 1887-1907." *EH* 3: 138-48. [117]

––––––, 1971. "Cattlemen on the Cheyenne-Arapaho Reservation, 1883-1885." *ArW* 13, no. 1: 5-32. [119]

Bertrand, A. L. and Corty, F. L. (eds.), 1962. *Rural Land Tenure in the United States.* (Baton Rouge: Louisiana State Univ. Press). [10, 11]

Billington, Ray A., 1974. *Westward Expansion: A History of the American Frontier.* (New York: Macmillan, 4th ed.). [10, 43, 44, 120]

Bishop, Charles A., 1970. "Emergence of Hunting Territories among the Northern Ojibwa." *ET* 9 (Jan.): 1-15. [193-4]

Biskup, P., 1968. "White-Aboriginal Relations in Western Australia: An Overview." *CSSH* 10 (July): 447-56. [208]

Blackmar, F. W., 1891. *Spanish Institutions in the Southwest.* Johns Hopkins Univ. Studies in History and Political Science, Extra vol. 10 (Baltimore: Johns Hopkins Univ. Press).

Bledsoe, S. T., 1909. *Indian Land Laws; being a treatise on the laws of acquiring title to, and the alienation of, allotted Indian lands.* (Kansas City). [51]

Block, W. E., Jr., 1971. "Alaska Native Claims." *NRL* 4, no. 2 (April): 223-50. [109]

Blumenthal, W. H., 1955. *American Indians Dispossessed; Fraud in Land Cessions Forced upon the Tribes.* (Philadelphia: G. S. MacManus).

Blunt, Joseph, 1825. *Historical Sketch of the Formation of the Confederacy, particularly with reference to the provincial limits and the jurisdiction of the general government over Indian tribes and the public territories.* (New York: Geo. & Chas. Carvill). [40]

Bodine, J. J., 1973. "Blue Lake: A Struggle for Indian Rights." *AILR* 1, no. 1 (Winter): 13-22. [110]

Bogue, Allan G., Phillips, Thomas D., and Wright, James E., 1970. *The West of the American People.* (Itasca, Illinois: Peacock). [44]

Bohannan, Paul, 1963. *Social Anthropology.* (New York: Holt, Rinehart and Winston). [11, 131, 184-5, 187]

––––––, 1965. "The Differing Realms of the Law." *AA* 67, no. 6, pt. 2: 33-42. [4]

Boissevain, Ethel, 1956. "The Detribalization of the Narragansett Indians: A Case Study." *EH* 3, no. 3: 225-45. [140-41, 156, 180, 201]

––––––, 1959. "Narragansett Survival: A Study of Group Persistence through Adopted Traits." *EH* 6, no. 4: 347-62. [140-1, 156, 180, 201]

Bolton, R. P., 1920. *New York City in Indian Possession. INM* 2, no. 7: 225-395. [30]

Bonnin, G., Fabens, C. H. and Sniffen, M. K., 1924. *Oklahoma's Poor Rich Indians, an Orgy of Graft and Exploitation of the Five Civilized Tribes–Legalized Robbery.* Publication 127, 2nd series (Philadelphia: Indian Rights Association). [125]

Bounds, John H., 1971. "The Alabama-Coushatta Indians of Texas." *JG* 70, no. 3 (March): 175-82. [70, 87]

Bourke, John G., 1894. "The Laws of Spain in Their Application to the American Indians." *AA* 7, no. 2 [old ser.]: 193-201. [96]

Bourne, Arthur R., 1953. "Some Major Aspects of the Historical Development of Palm Springs between 1880 and 1938, and in Addition a Continuation of the Historical Changes in the Indian Land Problems and Four Cultural Institutions until 1948." Unpublished masters thesis in history, Occidental College, California. [70, 81]

Boyce, George A., 1974. *When Navajos Had Too Many Sheep: The 1940's.* (San Francisco: The Indian Historian Press). [83, 189]

Branam, J. T., 1974. "Property Rights: Intertribal Mineral Rights in the Arkansas Riverbed." *AILR* 2, no. 1 *(Sum*mer): 125-36. [171]

Brant, Charles S. (ed.), 1969. *Jim Whitewolf: The Life of a Kiowa Apache Indian.* (New York: Dover). [132]

Brasser, T. J. C., 1971. "The Coastal Algonkians: People of the First Frontiers." In Leacock and Lurie (eds.) 64-91. [186, 201]

Brayer, H. O., 1938. *Pueblo Indian Land Grants of the "Rio Abajoo," New Mexico.* Univ. of New Mexico *Bulletin* 334, History Series 1, no. 1, [subsequently published as a book: (Albuquerque: Univ. of New Mexico Press, 1939)]. [122]

†Brohough, Gustav O., 1906. "Sioux and Chippewa Half-breed Scrip and Its Application to the Minnesota Pine Lands." Unpublished masters thesis in history, Univ. of Wisconsin.

Brookfield, H. C., 1964. "Questions on the Human Frontiers of Geography." *EG* 40, no. 4: 283-303. [10]

Brophy, William and Aberle, Sophie, 1966. *The Indian: America's Unfinished Business.* (Norman: Univ. of Oklahoma Press). [69, 79, 137, 138, 146, 172]

Brosius, S. M., 1904. *Needs of Protecting Indian Allotments.* Publication 67, 2nd ser. (Philadelphia: Indians Rights Association). [125]

Brown, Loren N., 1944. "The Appraisal of the Lands of the Choctaws and Chickasaws by the Dawes Commission." *CO* 22, no. 2: 177-191. [128]

†Brown, Lula L., 1930. "The Cherokee Neutral Lands Controversy." Masters thesis in history, Univ. of Colorado. [Pittsburg, Kansas, 1930]. [53]

Brown, Robert C., 1931. "Taxation of Indian Property." *Minnesota L.R.* 15 (Jan.): 182-209. [157]

Browne, J. Ross, 1861. "The Coast Rangers, a Chronicle of Events in California, pt. 2, Indian Reservations in California." *Harpers Magazine* 23, no. 135 (Aug.): 306-16. [54]

Brugge, D. M., 1965. "A Linguistic Approach to Demographic Problems: the Tonto-Yavapai Boundary." *EH* 12, no. 4: 355-372. [102]

Bruner, E. M., 1961. "Mandan." In Spicer, E. H. (ed.): 187-277. [169, 201]

Buchanan, Charles M., 1915. "Rights of the Puget Sound Indians to Game and Fish." *Washington Historical Quarterly* 6 (April): 109-18. [160]

Buchanan, Keith, 1970. *The Transformation of the Chinese Earth.* (London: Bell and Sons). [212]

Buffalohead, William R., 1964. "A Study of the Administration of the Indian Reservation System on the Sioux Reservation from 1879-1889." Unpublished masters thesis in history, Univ. of Wisconsin. [132]

Buffington, A. H., 1921. "The Policy of Albany and English Westward Expansion." *MVHR* 8: 327-66. [40]

Buntin, Martha, 1932. "Beginning of the Leasing of Surplus Grazing Lands of the Kiowa and Comanche Reservation." *CO* 10, no. 3: 369-82. [119]

Burke, J. C., 1969. "Cherokee Cases: a Study in Law, Politics, and Morality." *Stanford L.R.* 21 (Feb.): 500-31. [48, 146]

Burnett, Donald L., Jr., 1970. "Indian Hunting, Fishing and Trapping Rights: the Record and the Controversy." *Idaho L.R.* 7 (Spring): 49-75. [160, 161]

————, 1972. "An Historical Analysis of the 1968 Indian Civil Rights Act." *Harvard Journal on Legislation* 9, no. 4 (May): 557-626. [150, 154]

Burney, Dudley H., 1936. "The Indian Policy of the United States Government, 1870 to 1906, with particular reference to land tenure." Unpublished doctoral dissertation in history, Stanford Univ. [118, 126]

†Burns, Melton J., 1954. "Administration of Indian Affairs in the Allotment and Citizenship Period, 1887 to Date." Unpublished masters thesis in history, Univ. of Idaho. [126]

Burns, T., 1961. "Micropolitics: Mechanisms of Institutional Change." *Administrative Science Quarterly* 6, no. 3 (Dec.): 257-81. [75]

Burrill, Robert M., 1972. "The Establishment of Ranching on the Osage Indian Reservation." *GR* 62, no. 4 (Oct.): 524-43. [82, 119, 129]

Busselen, H. J., Jr., 1962. "A Study of the Federal Termination of a California Rancheria and Its Effects upon the Social and Economic Integration of the Indian Population Involved." Unpublished masters thesis in history, California State University, Sacramento. [21, 140]

Cady, D. I., 1926. "Indian Land Legislation from 1887 to 1895." Unpublished masters thesis in history, Univ. of South Dakota. [126]

Cahn, Edgar S. (ed.), 1969. *Our Brother's Keeper: the Indian in White America.* (Washington, D.C.: New Community Press). [69, 146]

Cain, Gordon, 1917-18. "Indian Land Titles in Minnesota." *Minnesota L.R.* 2: 177-191. [155]

Calef, Wesley C., 1948. "Land Associations and Occupance Problems in the Uinta Country." Doctoral dissertation in geography. (Chicago: Univ. of Chicago Press). [73]

Campbell, S. M., 1974. "A Proposal for the Quantification of Reserved Indian Water Rights." *Columbia L.R.* 74, no. 7 (Nov.): 1299-1321. [164-5]

Caplan, Lionel, 1970. *Land and Social Change in East Nepal–Study of Hindu-Tribal Relations.* (London: Routledge & Kegan Paul). [213]

Cappannari, S. C., 1960. "The Concept of Property Among Shoshoneans." In Dole, G. E. and Carneiro, R. (eds.), *Essays in the Science of Culture.* (New York: Crowell): 133-45. [25]

Cardinal, Harold, 1969. *The Unjust Society.* (Edmonton: M. G. Hurtig Ltd.). [206, 207]

* Carlson, Alvar W., 1971. "The Río Arriba: A Geographical Appraisal of the Spanish-American Homeland (Upper Rio Grande Valley, New Mexico)." Unpublished doctoral dissertation in geography, Univ. of Minnesota. [122, 217]

—————, 1972. "A Bibliography of the Geographical Literature on the American Indian, 1920-1971." *Professional Geographer* 24, no. 3 (Aug.): 258-63.

Carstens, P., 1967. *The Social Structure of a Cape Coloured Reserve.* (New York: Oxford Univ. Press). [209]

Carter, Gwendolyn M., Karis, Thomas, and Stultz, Newell M., 1967. *South Africa's Transkei: the Politics of Domestic Colonialism.* (Evanston: Northwestern Univ. Press). [209]

Carter, William E., 1965. *Aymara Communities and the Bolivian Agrarian Reform. Social Science Monographs* 24. (Gainesville: University of Florida).

Castetter, Edward F. and Bell, Willis H., 1942. *Pima and Papago Indian Agriculture.* (Albuquerque: Univ. of New Mexico Press).

—————, 1951. *Yuman Indian Agriculture: Primitive Subsistence on the Lower Colorado and Gila Rivers.* (Albuquerque: Univ. of New Mexico Press).

Castile, G. P., 1974. "Federal Indian Policy and the Sustained Enclave: An Anthropological Perspective." *HO* 33, no. 3 (Fall): 219-228. [4, 202]

Chambers, Reid P., 1971. "Discharge of the Federal Trust Responsibility to Enforce Claims of Indian Tribes: Case Studies of Bureaucratic Conflict of Interest." *AILN* 4, no. 16 (Sept.): 1-20. [145, 148, 163]

————— and Price, Monroe E., 1974. "Regulating Sovereignty: Secretarial Discretion and the Leasing of Indian Lands." *Stanford L.R.* 26 (May): 1061-1096. [147-8]

Chandler, Alfred N., 1945. *Land Title Origins: A Tale of Force and Fraud.* (New York: Robert Schalkenbach Foundation). [45, 48]

Chapman, Berlin B., 1933. "Establishment of the Wichita Reservation." *CO* 11, no. 4: 1044-55. [49, 53, 54]

—————, 1936. "Dissolution of the Iowa Reservation." *CO* 14, no. 4: 467-77. [92]

—————, 1942-43. "Dissolution of the Osage Reservation." *CO* 20, no. 3: 244-54; no. 4: 375-87; 21, no. 1: 78-88; no. 2: 171-82. [119, 129]

—————, 1943. "Establishment of the Iowa Reservation." *CO* 21, no. 4: 366-77. [53]

—————, 1944. "Dissolution of the Wichita Reservation." *CO* 22, no. 2: 192-209; no. 3: 300-14. [92]

—————, 1946. "The Pottawatomie and Absentee Shawnee Reservation." *CO* 24, no. 3: 293-305. [53]

—————, 1948. "The Otoe and Missouria Reservation." *CO* 26, no. 2: 132-58. [130]

—————, 1957. "The Nemaha Half-Breed Reservation." *Nebraska History Magazine* 38, no. 1: 1-23. [109]

—————, 1962. "The Day in Court for the Kiowa, Comanche and Apache Tribes." *GPJ* 2: 1-21. [109]

—————, 1965. *The Otoe and Missourias: a Study of Indian Removal and the Legal Aftermath.* (Oklahoma City: Times Journal Publishing Co.). [92, 102]

†Chowen, R. H., 1941. "The History of Treaty Making with the Potawatomi Nation of Indians." Unpublished masters thesis in history, Northwestern Univ.

Clark, I. G., 1947. "The Railroads and the Tribal Lands: Indian Territory, 1838-1890." Unpublished doctoral dissertation in history, Univ. of California, Berkeley. [120]

Clark, Robert E., 1971. "Water Rights Problems in the Upper Rio Grande Watershed and Adjoining Areas." *NRJ* 11, no. 1: 48-68. [164]

Clawson, Marion, 1968. *The Land System of the United States.* (Lincoln: Univ. of Nebraska Press). [10]

Clemmer, Rochard O., 1974. "Northern and Eastern Nevada, 1858-1971: Land Use Patterns and Aboriginal Rights." *IH* 7, no. 1: 24-41, 47-49. [160]

Coan, C. F., 1914. "Federal Indian Policy in the Oregon Country, 1849-55." Unpublished masters thesis in history, Univ. of California, Berkeley.

—————, 1920. "The Federal Indian Policy in the Pacific Northwest, 1849-1870." Unpublished doctoral dissertation in history, Univ. of California, Berkeley. [55]

—————, 1922. "The Adoption of the Reservation Policy in the Pacific Northwest." *Oregon Historical Quarterly* 23, no. 1: 1-38.

Coffeen, William R., 1972. "The Effects of the Central Arizona Project on the Fort McDowell Indian Community." *EH* 19, no. 4: 345-77. [99, 170]

Cohen, Felix S., 1937. "Anthropology and Problems of Indian Administration." *Southwestern Social Science Quarterly* 18: 171-80. [65, 72, 137]

—————, 1941, 1971. *Handbook of Federal Indian Law.* (Washington, D.C.: GPO) [Reprinted by Univ. of New Mexico Press, Albuquerque, 1971. Also reprinted 1942, 1945.]. [50, 70-1, 74, 83, 96, 121-2, 126, 145, 146, 172]

—————, 1942. "The Spanish Origin of Indian Rights in the Law of the United States." *Georgetown Law Journal.* [Reprinted in Cohen, L. K. (ed.); 230-52]. [96, 101, 121-2, 149]

—————, 1945. "Indian Claims." *American Indian.* [Reprinted in Cohen, L. K. (ed.): 264-272.] [94]

—————, 1947. "Original Indian Title." *Minnesota L.R.* 32, (Dec.): 28-59. [Reprinted in Cohen, L. K. (ed.): 273-304.] [45, 91, 95-6]

—————, 1953. "The Erosion of Indian Rights—1950-53; a case study in bureaucracy." *Yale Law Journal* 62 (Feb.): 348-90. [69, 150]

Cohen, L. K. (ed.), 1960. *The Legal Conscience: Selected Papers of Felix S. Cohen.* (New Haven: Yale Univ. Press). [70, 96, 122]

Cohen, Warren H. and Mause, Philip J., 1968. "The Indian: The Forgotten American." *Harvard L.R.* 81: 1818-58. [150]

Colgrove, K. C., 1911. "Pioneers and Indians." *Iowa Journal of History and Politics* 9: 196-302. [46]

Colley, Charles C., 1973. "The Struggle of Nevada Indians to Hold Their Lands, 1847-70." *IH* 6, no. 3: 5-17. [54]

Collier, John, 1932. "Needs in Administration of Indian Property." *National Conference of Social Work*, 1932: 627-39. [68]

––––––, 1949. *On the Gleaming Way.* (Denver: Sage). [Reprinted 1962.] [1, 68, 98]

Colson, Elizabeth, 1953. *The Makah Indians: A Study of an Indian Tribe in Modern American Society.* (Manchester: Univ. of Manchester Press). [201]

––––––, 1967. "Assimilation of an American Indian Group." In Bohannan, Paul and Plog, Fred (eds.), *Beyond the Frontier: Social Process and Cultural Change.* (New York: Natural History Press): 209-226. [201]

––––––, 1968. "Contemporary Tribes and the Development of Nationalism." In Helm, J. (ed.): 201-206. [192]

––––––, 1971. "Indian Reservations and the American Social System." In Walker, D. E., Jr. (ed.): 7-11. [74-5]

Condra, G. E., 1907. "Opening of the Indian Territory." *Bulletin of the American Geographical Society* 39: 321-40. [116]

† Congdon, Charles E., 1967. *Allegany Oxbow: A History of Allegany State Park and the Allegany Reserve of the Seneca Nation.* (Little Valley, N.Y.: Straight). [118]

Connelley, W. E. (ed.), 1925. "Indian Treaties and Councils Affecting Kansas: Dates and Places, Where Held, Names of Tribes, Commissioners and Indians Concluding Same." *Collections Kansas State Historical Society* 16. [51]

Cook, Sherburne F., 1943. *The Conflict between the California Indian and White Civilization. Ibero-Americana* 21, 22, 23, 24. [206]

† Cooper, A. E., 1942. "Ecological Aspects of the Family Hunting Territory System of the Northeastern Algonkians." Unpublished masters thesis in anthropology, Univ. of Chicago. [193]

Cooper, John M., 1938. "Land Tenure Among the Indians of Eastern and Northern North America." *Pennsylvania Archaeologist* 8: 55-59. [193]

––––––, 1939. "Is the Algonquian Family Hunting Ground System Pre-Columbian?" *AA* 41: 66-90; reply, 42: 179. [193]

Corkran, David H., 1967. *The Creek Frontier, 1540-1783.* (Norman: Univ. of Oklahoma Press). [43]

† Cornett, Lloyd H., Jr., 1954. "Leasing and Utilization of Land of the Cheyenne and Arapaho Indians, 1891-1907." Unpublished masters thesis in history, Univ. of Oklahoma. [119]

Cory, C. E., 1903-04. "The Osage Ceded Lands." *Collections Kansas State Historical Society* 8: 187-99. [53]

Cotroneo, R. R. and Dozier, J., 1974. "A Time of Disintegration: The Coeur d'Alene and the Dawes Act." *Western Historical Quarterly* 5, no. 4 (Oct.): 405-19. [129, 132, 136]

Cotterill, R. S., 1963. *The Southern Indians: The Story of the Civilized Tribes before Removal.* (Norman: Univ. of Oklahoma Press). [48, 187]

Covington, James W., 1951. "Federal Relations with the Colorado Utes, 1861-65." *Colorado Magazine* 28: 257-65.

Cox, Bruce A., 1967. "Hopi Trouble Cases: Cultivation Rights and Homesteads." *Plateau* 39, no. 4: 145-56. [190]

Cree, Linda, 1974. "Extension of County Jurisdiction over Indian Reservations in California: Public Law 280 and the Ninth Circuit." *Hastings Law Journal* 25 (May): 1451-1506. [21]

Crevelli, J. P., 1959. "Four Hundred Years of Indian Affairs in the North Bay Counties of California." Unpublished masters thesis in history, Univ. of California, Berkeley. [117]

Crouter, Richard E. and Rolle, Andrew F., 1960. "E. F. Beale and the Indian Peace Commissioners in California, 1851-54." *SCQ* 42, no. 2: 107-32. [20, 52, 54, 55]

Currie, Anne H., 1957. "Bidwell Rancheria." *CHSQ* 36, no. 4: 313-25.

Cuykendall, Clydia J., 1973. "State Taxation of Indians–Federal Preemption of Taxation against the Backdrop of Indian Sovereignty." *Washington L.R.* 49, no. 1: 191-212. [157]

Dale, Edward E., 1942. "The Cheyenne-Arapaho Country." *CO* 20, no. 4: 360-71. [21, 119]

––––––, 1949. *The Indians of the Southwest.* (Norman: Univ. of Oklahoma Press). [68, 117-18, 125]

Danforth, S. C., 1973. "Repaying Historical Debts: The Indian Claims Commission." *North Dakota L.R.* 49, no. 2 (Winter): 359-403. [94-95]

Danziger, E. J., Jr., 1973. "They Would Not Be Moved: The Chippewa Treaty of 1854." *Minnesota History* 43 no. 3 (Spring): 175-85. [53]

––––––, 1974. *Indians and Bureaucrats; Administering the Reservation Policy During the Civil War.* (Urbana: University of Illinois Press).

Dart, Henry P. (ed.), 1921. "Louisiana Land Titles Derived from Indian Tribes." *Louisiana Historical Quarterly* 4, no. 1: 134-44. [96]

Davidson, D. S., 1928. *Family Hunting Territories in Northwestern North America. INM* 46. [195]

Davies, Glen E., 1966. "State Taxation of Indian Reservations." *Utah L.R.* 1966 (July): 132-151. [157]

†Davis, Edward, 1919. "Tribal Land Titles in Oklahoma." Unpublished masters thesis in history, Univ. of Oklahoma. [116]

Davis, Lawrence, 1959. "Criminal Jurisdiction over Indian Country in Arizona." *Arizona L.R.* 1: 62-101. [155]

d'Azevedo, Warren L., 1964. "Comments on Tribal Distributions." In d'Azevedo, W. L., et al. (eds.): 315-334. [103]

––––––, Davis, Wilbur A., Fowler, Don D., and Suttles, Wayne (eds.), 1966. *The Current Status of Anthropological Research in the Great Basin: 1964.* Social Science and Humanities Publication No. 1. (Reno: Desert Research Institute).

Deardorff, Merle H., 1941. "The Cornplanter Grant in Warren County." *Western Pennsylvania Historical Magazine* 24, no. 1: 1-22 [117]

Debo, Angie, 1940. *And Still the Waters Run.* (Princeton: Princeton Univ. Press). [Reprinted 1966.] [126, 127-8, 156, 172, 178, 182, 200]

––––––, 1951. *The Five Civilized Tribes of Oklahoma; Report on Social and Economic Conditions.* (Philadelphia: Indian Rights Association). [88]

––––––, 1970. *A History of the Indians of the United States.* (Norman: Univ. of Oklahoma Press). [37, 68, 138]

DeForest, J. W., 1851. *History of the Indians of Connecticut: From the Earliest and Known Period to 1850.* (Hartford: J. W. Hamersely). [Reprinted with an introduction by W. E. Washburn, by Archan Books, Hamden, Conn., 1964.] [40]

de la Garza, Rudolph, Kruszewski, Z. A., and Arciniega, T. A., 1973. *Chicanos and Native Americans: the Territorial Minorities.* (Englewood Cliffs, N.J.: Prentice-Hall).

Delaney, Robert W., 1971. "The Southern Utes a Century Ago." *UHQ* 39 (Spring): 114-22. [54]

Dellwo, R. D., 1971. "Indian Water Rights–the Winters Doctrine Updated." *Gonzaga L.R.* 6 (Spring): 215-240. [164]

Deloria, Vine, Jr., 1970. "Implications of the 1968 Civil Rights Act in Tribal Autonomy." In *Indian Voices: The First Convocation of American Indian Scholars.* (San Francisco: American Indian Historical Society): 85-104. [77, 83, 151, 170]

–––––, (ed.), 1971. *Of Utmost Good Faith* (San Francisco: Straight Arrow Books). [44, 52, 99, 218]

–––––, 1974. *Behind the Trail of Broken Treaties.* (New York: Delta). [122, 169, 173, 202]

†Delorme, David P., 1955. "A Socio-economic Study of the Turtle Mountain Band of Chippewa Indians, and A Critical Evaluation of Proposals Designed to Terminate Their Federal Warship Status." Unpublished doctoral dissertation in sociology, Univ. of Texas. [140]

Demsetz, Harold, 1967. "Toward a Theory of Property Rights." *American Economic Review* 57, no. 2: 347-59. [62, 63, 195]

†Denton, T. D., 1970. "Strangers in Their Land: A Study of Migration from a Canadian Indian Reserve." Unpublihsed doctoral dissertation in anthropology, Univ. of Toronto. [210]

DePuy, H. R., 1917. *A Bibliography of the English Colonial Treaties with the American Indians, incl. a synopsis of each treaty.* (New York: printed for the Lennox Club). [51, 218]

DeRosier, A. H., Jr., 1966. *The Removal of the Choctaw Indians.* (Knoxville, Univ. of Tennessee Press). [49]

Deutsch, Herman J., 1956. "Indian and White in the Inland Empire: The Contest for the Land, 1880-1912." *PNWQ* 47: 44-51.

De Vorsey, Louis, Jr., 1966. *The Indian Boundary in the Southern Colonies, 1763-1775.* (Chapel Hill: Univ. of North Carolina Press). [43, 48, 219]

–––––, 1971. "Early Maps as a Source in the Reconstruction of Southern Indian Landscapes." In Hudson, C. M. (ed.) *Symposium on Indians in the Old South: Red, White, and Black.* (Athens: Southern Anthropological Society): 12-30. [43]

Diamond, S., Sturtevant, W. C., and Fenton, W. N., 1964. "Memorandum Submitted to Subcommittee on Indian Affairs of the Senate and House of Representatives." *AA* 66, no. 3: 631-3. [73, 170-1]

Dick, Everett, 1970. *The Lure of the Land.* (Lincoln, Univ. of Nebraska Press). [10, 45]

Dietrich, Margretta S., 1950-51. "The Navajo in No-Man's Land." *New Mexico Quarterly* 20 (Winter): 439-50. [156]

Dockstader, F. J. (comp.), 1957. *The American Indian in Graduate Studies: A Bibliography of Theses and Dissertations, Contributions from the Museum of the American Indian*, 15. (New York: The Heye Foundation). [217]

Dole, Gertrude E., 1968. "Tribe as the Autonomous Unit." In Helm, J. (ed.): 83-100.

Donaldson, Thomas, 1884. *The Public Domain: Its History, with statistics.* House Miscellaneous Document no. 45, pt. 4, 47th Congress, 2nd Session. (Washington, D.C., GPO). [118]

Dorner, Peter, 1961. "Needed: A New Policy for the American Indian." *Land Economics* 37, no. 2 (May): 162-73. [78]

Downes, Randolph C., 1945. "A Crusade for Indian Reform, 1922-1934." *MVHR* 32: 331-54. [68]

Downs, James F., 1964. *Animal Husbandry in Navajo Society and Culture. Univ. of California Publications in Anthropology* 1. [83, 196]

––––––, 1966. *The Two Worlds of the Washo: An Indian Tribe of California and Nevada.* (New York: Holt, Rinehart and Winston).

Dozier, Edward P., 1953. *The Hopi-Tewa of Arizona. UCPAAE* 44, no. 3: 259-376. [25]

––––––, Simpson, G. E., and Yinger, J. M., 1957. "The Integration of Americans of Indian Descent." *Annals, American Academy of Political and Social Science* 311 (May): 158-165. [In Simpson, G. E. and Yinger, L. M. (eds); 158-165]. [180]

Dozier, Jack, 1962. "Coeur D'Alene Country: The Creation of the Coeur D'Alene Reservation in Northern Idaho." *Idaho Yesterdays* 6, no. 3: 2-7.

Driver, Harold, 1969. *Indians of North America.* (Chicago: Univ. of Chicago Press). [Original edition 1961.] [26, 179]

–––––– and Massey, William C., 1957. *Comparative Studies of North American Indians, Transactions.* American Philosophical Society 47, pt. 2: 165-456. [26]

––––––, et al., 1953. *Indian Tribes of North America. Indiana Univ. Publications in Anthropology and Linguistics.* Memoir no. 9. [32, 104]

Drucker, Peter, 1937. *Culture Elements Distribution: V, Southern California. AR* 1, no. 1. [25]

Duin, V. N., 1971. "Problems of Indian Poverty: Shrinking Land Base and Ineffective Education." *Albany L.R.* 36 (Fall): 143-181.

Dukelow, Gayle L. and Zakheim, Rosalyn S., 1972. "Recovering Indian Lands: The Land Patent Annulment Suit." *Ecology Law Quarterly* 2 (Winter): 195-224. [1, 98, 111-12]

Dunbar, Gary, 1969. [Review of De Vorsey, 1966.] *Economic Geography* 45, no. 2: 181-82. [43]

Dunham, Harold H., 1937. "Some Crucial Years of the General Land Office, 1875-1890." *AH* 11: 117-41. [116]

––––––, 1941. *Government Handout: A Study in the Administration of Public Lands, 1875-1891.* (Ann Arbor: Edwards Bros.). [116]

Dunstan, D. A., 1966. "Aboriginal Land Title and Employment in South Australia." In Sharp, I. G. and Tatz, Colin M. (eds.), *Aborigines in the Economy.* (Melbourne: Jacaranda Press): 314-344. [209]

Dyer, R. C., 1945. "The Indians' Land Title in California: A Case of Federal Equity, 1851-1942." Unpublished masters thesis in history, Univ. of California, Berkeley. [21, 109]

Dykshorn, J., 1972. "Public Law 83-280 and the Reasons for Its Failure." Unpublished masters thesis in history, Univ. of South Dakota. [155]

Eastvold, D. and Broz, R. F., 1954. "A Report Compiled for the Department of Game and Fisheries of the State of Washington on Legal Problems Concerning Indians and Their Rights under Federal and State Law." Typescript. [161]

Eblen, J. E., 1968. *The First and Second United States Empires: Governors and Territorial Government, 1784-1912.* (Pittsburgh: Univ. of Pittsburgh Press). [53]

Economic Development Administration, 1971. *Federal and State Indian Reservations an EDA Handbook.* (Washington, D.C.: GPO). [219]

Edman, J., 1959. "The Appraisal Docket, Right to Condemn Indian Lands." *Appraisal Journal* 27 (April): 265-66. [168]

Edwards, E. E., 1942. *A Bibliography on the Agriculture of the American Indian.* U.S. Department of Agriculture Miscellaneous Publications 447. (Washington, D.C.: GPO). [217]

Eggan, Dorothy, 1943. "The General Problem of Hopi Adjustment." *AA* 45, no. 3, pt. 1: 356-73. [201]

Eggan, Fred, 1950. *Social Organization of the Western Pueblos.* (Chicago: Univ. of Chicago Press).

————, (ed.), 1955. *Social Anthropology of North American Tribes.* (Chicago: Univ. of Chicago Press). [178]

————, 1966. *The American Indian: Perspectives for the Study of Social Change.* (Chicago: Aldine). [178]

Eicher, Carl K., 1961-62. "An Approach to Income Improvement on the Rosebud Sioux Indian Reservation." *HO* 20, no. 4: 191-96.

Eiseley, Loren C., 1947. "Land Tenure in the Northeast: A Note on the History of a Concept." *AA* 49: 680-81.

Eisinger, Chester E., 1948. "The Puritans' Justification for Taking the Land." *Essex Institute Historical Collections* 84: 131-43. [97]

Elazar, D. J., 1968. "Land Space and Civil Society in America." In *Land Settlement Policy, Proceeedings,* Workshop on Land Settlement Policy, Agricultural Policy Institute Series 32, *Southern Land Research Publications* 7 (Raleigh: North Carolina State Univ.). [Reprinted in *Western Historical Quarterly* 5, no. 3 (July): 261-84.] [149]

Elkin, A. P., 1951. "Reaction and Interaction: A Food Gathering People and European Settlement." *AA* 53: 164-86. [208, 214]

Elkin, H., 1940. "Northern Arapaho of Wyoming." In Linton, R. (ed.): 207-255. [197]

Ellis, H. W., 1974. "Federal Taxation: Exclusion of Earnings on Allotted Indian Land from Federal Income Taxation." *AILR* 2, no. 1 (Summer): 119-124.

Ellis, Richard N. (ed.), 1972. *The Western American Indian: Case Studies in Tribal History.* (Lincoln: Univ. of Nebraska Press). [218]

Ellison, William H., 1922. "The Federal Indian Policy in California, 1846-1860." *MVHR* 9, no. 1: 37-67. [54]

————, 1925. "Rejection of California Indian Treaties, A Study of Local Influence on National Policy." *Grizzly Bear* 37 (May): 4-5, 86; (June): 4-5; (July): 6-7. [20, 55, 109]

Elmendorf, W. W., 1971. "Coast Salish Status Ranking and Intergroup Ties." *SWJA* 27: 353-380. [27]

Embry, Carlos B., 1956. *America's Concentration Camps: The Facts about Our Indian Reservations Today.* (New York: David McKay). [74]

Encyclopedia of Social Science, 1931-38. "Native Policy." 11-12: 252-282. [207]

Ericson, R. and Snow, D. R., 1970. "The Indian Battle for Self-Determination." *California L.R.* 58, no. 2: 445-490. [146, 152, 154]

Euler, Robert C. and Dobyns, Henry F., 1961-62. "Ethnic Group Land Rights in the Modern State: Three Case Studies." *HO* 20, no. 4: 203-07. [168]

Ewers, John C., 1958. *The Blackfeet: Raiders on the Northwestern Plains.* (Norman: Univ. of Oklahoma Press). [122]

Ezell, Paul, 1955. "Indians under the Law of Mexico, 1821-47." *AmI* 15, no. 3: 199-214. [96, 121]

Faron, Louis C., 1961. *Mapuche Social Structure.* Illinois Studies in Anthropology 1 (Urbana: Univ. of Illinois Press). [209]

Farrand, M., 1905. "The Indian Boundary Line." *AHR* 10 (July): 782-91. [43]

Faulhaber, Dwight L., 1970. "Power of a State to Impose an Income Tax on Reservation Indians." *Willamette Law Journal* 6: 515-24. [157-8]

Fay, George E. (comp.), 1965. *Bibliography of the Indians of Wisconsin.* Museum of Anthropology Miscellaneous Series 2. (Oshkosh: Wisconsin State University). [218]

───── (comp./ed.), 1967-72. *Charters, Constitutions, and By-Laws of the Indian Tribes of North America.* Occasional Publications in Anthropology, Ethnology Series. (Univ. of Northern Colorado, Museum of Anthropology). [79]
1967 Vol. 1 Part I: Sioux Tribes of South Dakota
1967 Vol. 2 Part II: Indian Tribes of Wisconsin (Great Lakes Agency)
1967 Vol. 3 Part IIa: Northern Plains
1967 Vol. 4 Part III: Southwest (Apache-Mohave)
1967 Vol. 5 Part IV: Southwest (Navajo-Zuni)
1968 Vol. 6 Part V: Indian Tribes of Oklahoma
1968 Vol. 7 Part VI: Indian Tribes of Oklahoma, cont.
1970 Vol. 8 Part VII: Indian Tribes of California
1970 Vol. 9 Part VIII: Indian Tribes of California, cont.
1970 Vol. 10 Part IX: Northwest and Alaska
1970 Vol. 11 Part X: Northwest and Alaska, cont.
1971 Vol. 12 Part XI: Basin-Plateau Tribes
1971 Vol. 13 Part XII: Basin-Plateau Tribes, cont.
1972 Vol. 14 Part XIII: Midwestern Tribes
1972 Vol. 15 Part XIV: Great Lakes Agency: Minn.-Mich.
1972 Vol. 16 Part XV: Northwest and Alaska, cont.
in press Vol. 17 Part XVI: Northwest and Alaska, cont.
in press Vol. 18 Part XVII: Tribes of the Eastern United States
in press Vol. 19 Part XVIII: Miscellaneous Indian Tribes

───── (comp.), 1970. "Land Cessions in Utah and Colorado by the Ute Indians, 1861-1899." Museum of Anthropology Miscellaneous Series, no. 13. (Univ. of Northern Colorado). [51]

───── (comp.), 1967. [Treaties] "Winnebago." Museum of Anthropology Miscellaneous Series, no. 1; 1970, "Menominee," no. 12. [51]

Federal Field Committee for Development Planning in Alaska, 1968. *Alaska Natives and the Land.* (Washington, D.C.: GPO): ch. 5, "The Land Issue," 427-516. [109]

Feit, Harvey A., 1973. "Twilight of the Cree Hunting Nation." *Natural History* 82, no. 7: 48-56.

Fenton, William N., 1940. *Problems Arising from the Historic Position of the Iroquois.* Smithsonian Institution, Miscellanous Collection 100. (Washington, D.C.: GPO): 159-251. [28, 181]

─────, 1948. "The Present Status of Anthropology in Northeastern North America: A Review Article." *AA* 50: 494-515.

————et al., 1957. *American Indian and White Relations to 1839: Needs and Opportunities for Study.* (Chapel Hill: Univ. of North Carolina Press). [38-39]

—————, 1971. "The Iroquois in History." In Leacock and Lurie (eds.): 129-168. [186]

Fey, Harold E. and McNickle, D'Arcy, 1959; 1970. *Indians and Other Americans.* (New York: Harper and Row). [37, 97, 126, 135, 138, 139, 140]

Field, T. W., 1873. *An Essay Towards an Indian Bibliography.* (New York: Scribner, Armstrong). [Reprinted by Long's College Book Co., Columbus, 1951.] [218]

Fielding, R. Kent, 1952. "Establishing the Value of Indian Lands in the West, 1850-1900." Unpublished masters thesis in history, Brigham Young Univ. [116]

FIL, 1958. *Federal Indian Law see* U.S. Department of the Interior, 1958.

Firey, Walter, 1960. *Man, Mind and Land.* (Glencoe: Free Press).

†Flekke, Marie, 1935. "The Opening of the Black Hills in 1876." Unpublished masters thesis in history, Univ. of New Mexico. [53]

Fletcher, Alice, 1885. "Lands in Severalty among the Indians: Illustrated by Experiences with the Omaha Tribe." *Proceedings 1884,* AAAS 33, pt. 2: 654-65. [128]

Floyd, Barry N., 1962. "Land Apportionment in Southern Rhodesia." *GR* 52 (Oct.): 566-82. [209]

Fonaroff, Leonard S., 1963. "Conservation and Stock Reduction on the Navajo Tribal Range." *GR* 53 (April): 200-223. [81, 83, 189]

—————, 1964. "Aid and the Indian: A Case Study in Faulty Communication." *The California Geographer* 5: 57-68. [81, 83, 189]

—————, 1971. "Political Process and Culture Change Among the Navajo." *GR* 61 (July): 442-44. [75, 189]

Fontana, Bernard L., 1963. "The Hopi-Navajo Colony on the Lower Colorado River—A Problem in Ethnohistorical Interpretation." *EH* 10, no. 2: 162-82. [124]

Forbes, Gerald, 1936. "The International Conflict for the Lands of the Creek Confederacy." *CO* 14, no. 4: 478-98. [41, 48]

—————, 1941. "Oklahoma Oil and Indian Land Tenure." *AH* 15 (Oct.): 189-94. [135-6]

Forbes, Jack D. (ed.), 1964. *The Indian in America's Past.* (Englewood Cliffs, New Jersey: Prentice-Hall). [52, 98, 218]

—————, 1965a. "A Comprehensive Program for Tribal Development in the United States." *HO* 24, no. 2: 159-61. [77-8]

—————, 1965b. "The 'Public Domain' of Nevada and Its Relationship to Indian Property Rights." *Nevada State Bar Journal* 30, no. 3: 16-47.

————— (ed.), 1967. *Nevada Indians Speak.* (Reno: Univ. of Nevada Press). [129, 218]

————— 1968. "Frontiers in American History and the Role of the Frontier Historian." *EH* 15, no. 2: 203-235. [213]

—————, 1969. *Native Americans of California and Nevada: A Handbook.* (Healdsburg, California: Naturegraph). [218]

Forde, C. Daryll, 1931a. *Ethnography of the Yuma Indians.* UCPAAE 28, no. 4: 83-278. [25, 29]

—————, 1931b. "Hopi Agriculture and Land Ownership." *Journal, Royal Anthropological Institute* 61: 357-405. [25, 83, 84, 190]

—————, 1934. *Habitat, Economy, and Society: A Geographical Introduction to Ethnology.* (London: Methuen). [Reprinted 1957.] [26]

Foreman, Grant, 1932. *Indian Removal.* (Norman: Univ. of Oklahoma Press). [46]

–––––, 1933. *Advancing the Frontier, 1830-1860.* (Norman: Univ. of Oklahoma Press). [44, 46, 49]

–––––, 1936. *Indians and Pioneers: The Story of the American Southwest before 1830.* (Norman: Univ. of Oklahoma Press). [44]

–––––, 1941. "Historical Background of the Kiowa-Comanche Reservation." *CO* 19, no. 2: 129-40. [53]

–––––, 1948. "Texas Comanche Treaty of 1846." *SWHQ* 51 (April): 313-32. [54]

Fowler, C. S., 1970. *Great Basin Anthropology . . . A Bibliography.* Social Sciences and Humanities Publication 5. (Reno: Desert Reserach Institute). [218]

Fowler, Loretta, 1973. "The Arapahoe Ranch: An Experiment in Cultural Change and Economic Development." *Economic Development and Cultural Change* 21, no. 3: 446-64. [191-2]

†Frederick, Aurora L., 1923. "Indian Land Cessions in Missouri, 1804-1816." Unpublished masters thesis in history, Washington Univ. (St. Louis).

Freeberne, M., 1968. "Minority Unrest and Sino-Soviet Rivalry in Sinkiang, China's Northwestern Frontier Bastion, 1949-1965." In Fisher, C. A. (ed.), *Essays in Political Geography* (London: XYZ Publ Co.). [212]

Freeman, John F. and Smith, Murphy D., 1966. *A Guide to Manuscripts Relating to the American Indian in the Library of the American Philosophical Society.* APS Memoir 65. [217]

French, D., 1961. "Wasco-Wishram." In Spicer, E. H. (ed.): 337-430. [197]

Fretz, Burton D., 1966. "The Bill of Rights and American Indian Tribal Government." *NRJ* 6 (Oct.): 581-616. [151]

Fried, Morton H., 1952. "Land Tenure, Geography, and Ecology in the Contact of Cultures." *American Journal of Economics and Sociology* 11: 391-412. [45, 95, 208, 211, 213, 214]

–––––, 1966. "On the Concept of 'Tribe' and 'Tribal Society.'" *Transactions,* New York Academy of Science, Ser. II) 28, no. 4: 527-40. [Reprinted in Helm, J. (ed.), 1968.] [27, 192]

–––––, 1967. *The Evolution of Political Society: An Essay in Political Anthropology.* (New York: Random House).

Frison, T. H., 1965. "Acquisition of Access Rights and Rights of Way on Fee, Public Domain and Indian Lands." *RMMLI* 10: 217-259. [174]

Fritz, Henry E., 1963. *The Movement for Indian Assimilation, 1860-90.* (Philadelphia: Univ. of Pennsylvania Press). [125, 127]

Fryer, S. R., 1942. "Navajo Social Organization and Land Use Adjustment." *Scientific Monthly* 55, no. 5: 408-22. [81]

Fynn, A. J., 1907. *The American Indian as a Product of Environment.* (Boston: Little, Brown). [24]

Garbarino, Merwyn S., 1972. *Big Cypress: A Changing Seminole Community.* (New York: Holt, Rinehart and Winston). [191]

Garrow, P. H., 1974. "An Ethnohistorical Study of the Powhatan Tribes." *The Chesopiean* 12, nos. 1-2 (Feb.-April): 1-79. [41]

Gates, Merrill E., 1886. "Land and Law as Agents in Educating Indians." *17th Annual Report,* 1885, Board of Indian Commissioners. (Washington, D.C.: GPO): 13-35. [Reprinted in Prucha, F. P. (ed.), 1973.] [125]

Gates, Paul W., 1936. "The Homestead Law in an Incongruous Land System." *AHR* 41, no. 4: 652-81. [125]

–––––, 1937. "A Fragment of Kansas Land History: The Disposal of the Christian Indian Tract." *Kansas Historical Quarterly* 6, no. 3: 227-40. [53, 117]

–––––, 1942. "Introduction" to Robertson, N. A. and Riker, D. (eds.), *The John Tipton Papers.* (3 vols., Indianapolis): vol. 1: 3-58.

–––––, 1954. *Fifty Million Acres: Conflicts over Kansas Land Policy, 1854-1890.* (Ithaca: Cornell Univ. Press). [45, 54, 172]

–––––, 1968. *History of Public Land Law Development.* (Washington, D.C.: GPO). [10, 45, 120]

–––––, 1971. "Indian Allotments Preceding the Dawes Act." In Clark, J. G. (ed.), *The Frontier Challenge: Responses to the Trans-Mississippi West.* (Lawrence: Univ. of Kansas Press): 141-170. [126]

Gearing, Fred, 1968. "Sovereignties and Jural Communities in Political Evolution." In Helm, J. (ed.): 111-119. [192]

Getty, Harry T., 1961-62. "San Carlos Apache Cattle Industry." *HO* 20, no. 4: 181-86. [81-2, 191]

–––––, 1963. *The San Carlos Indian Cattle Industry, Anthropological Papers.* (Univ. of Arizona), 7. [81-2, 191]

Gibbons, Francis M., 1965. "Examination of Indian Mineral Titles." *RMMLI* 10: 73-105. [71]

Gibson, Arrell M., 1960. "Sources for Research on the American Indian." *EH* 7, no. 2: 121-36. [217]

–––––, 1963. *The Kickapoos: Lords of the Middle Border.* (Norman: Univ. of Oklahoma Press). [117]

Gifford, Edward W., 1918. *Clans and Moieties in Southern California. UCPAAE* 14: 155-219. [20, 25]

–––––, 1923. *Pomo Lands on Clear Lake. UCPAAE* 20: 77-94.

–––––, 1926. "Miwok Lineages and the Political Unit in Aboriginal California." *AA* 28, no. 2: 389-401. [25, 27]

Gilbert, William H. and Taylor, John L., 1966. "Indian Land Questions." *Arizona L.R.* 8: 102-133. [78, 88, 110, 136, 150]

Gilbreath, Kent, 1973. *Red Capitalism: an Analysis of the Navajo Economy.* (Norman: Univ. of Oklahoma Press). [83, 158]

Gilmore, Melvin R., 1928. *"Some Indian Ideas of Property."* INM 5: 137-144.

Gittinger, Roy, 1917. "The Separation of Nebraska and Kansas from the Indian Territory." *MVHR* 3, no. 4: 442-61. [117]

Gladen, Frank H., 1970. "Public School Lands in Arizona: History and Management." *JW* 9, no. 1: 110-24. [121]

Glasscock, C. B., 1938. *Then Came Oil: The Story of the Last Frontier.* (Indianapolis: Bobbs-Merrill). [72]

Glassner, Martin I., 1974. "The New Mandan Migrations: From Hunting Expeditions to Relocation." *JW* 13, no. 2: 59-74. [169]

Goding, M. Wilfred, 1958. "The Management of Tribal Land." *Land,* the Yearbook of Agriculture. (Washington, D.C.: GPO): 96-102. [78]

Goldfrank, Esther, 1945; 1966. *Changing Configurations in the Social Organization of a Blackfoot Tribe during the Reserve Period. AES Monograph* 8 (Seattle: Univ. of Washington Press).

Goldschmidt, Walter R. and Haas, Theodore H., 1946. *Possessory Rights of Natives of Southeastern Alaska.* A Report to the Commissioner of Indian Affairs. [109]

Goodrich, Chauncey S., 1926. "Legal Status of California Indians." *California L.R.* 14, no. 2: 83-100; no. 3: 157-187. [21, 157]

Gordon, Leon M., 1950. "The Red Man's Retreat from Northern Indiana." *Indiana Magazine of History* 46, no. 1: 39-60. [50]

†Gordon, Suzanne, 1973. *Black Mesa: The Angel of Death.* (New York: John Day). [171]

Goshute Tribe, [1971]. *Petitioner's Proposed Findings of Fact and Brief in Support Thereof.* [Before the Indian Claims Commission, docket no. 326-J, prepared by R. W. Barker, Atty. (3 vols. Washington, D.C.: Wilkinson, Cragun, and Barker).] [107]

Graebner, Norman A., 1945. "The Public Land Policy of the Five Civilized Tribes." *CO* 23, no. 2: 107-118. [129]

Green, Charles L., 1928. "The Indian Reservation System of the Dakotas to 1889." *South Dakota Historical Collections* 14: 307-416.

––––––, 1939. "The Administration of the Public Domain in South Dakota." Unpublished doctoral dissertation in history, Univ. of Iowa. [118]

†Green, E., 1923. *The Indians of Southern California and Land Allotment.* (Long Beach). [128]

Greever, William St. C., 1954. *Arid Domain: The Santa Fe Railway and Its Western Land Grant.* (Stanford: Stanford Univ. Press). [120-1]

Grinnell, George B., 1907. "Tenure of Land Among the Indians." *AA* 9: 1-11. [24]

Gulick, John, 1960. *Cherokees at the Crossroads.* (Chapel Hill: Univ. of North Carolina Press). [50]

Gunther, Gerald, 1958-59. "Governmental Power and New York Indian Lands—a Reassessment of a Persistent Problem of Federal-State Relations." *Buffalo L.R.* 8: 1-26. [155, 168]

†Gutkoski, Joseph L., 1938. "Wyoming Valley Lands Controversy." Unpublished masters thesis in history, Columbia Univ.

†Guttman, A., 1965. *States' Rights and Indian Removal: The Cherokee Nation vs. the State of Georgia.* (Boston: Heath). [48]

Haas, Theodore H., 1957. "The Legal Aspects of Indian Affairs from 1887 to 1957." In Simpson, G. E. and Yinger, J. M. (eds.), 12-22. [64, 70, 126]

Haas, William H., 1925. "The American Indian and Geographic Studies." *AAAG* 15: 86-91. [12]

Hackenberg, Robert A., 1972. "Restricted Interdependence: The Adaptive Pattern of Papago Indian Society." *HO* 31, no. 2: 112-125. [76-201]

Hacker, P. E., Meier, D. C., and Pauli, D. J. 1974. "State Jurisdiction over Indian Land Use; an Interpretation of the 'Encumbrance' Savings Clause of Public Law 280." *Land and Water L.R.* 9, no. 2: 421-56. [154]

Haddon, Sam E., 1965. "Access and Wharfage Rights and the Territorial Extent of Indian Reservations Bordering on Navigable Water—Who Owns the Bed of Flathead Lake?" *Montana L.R.* 27: 55-77. [165]

Hafen, L. R., Hollon, W. E. & Rister, C. C., 1970. *Western America.* (Englewood Cliffs, New Jersey: Prentice-Hall, rev. ed.). [44]

Hagan, William T., 1956. "Private Property, the Indian's Door to Civilization." *EH* 3: 126-37. [126, 127]

––––––, 1961. *American Indians.* (Chicago: Univ. of Chicago Press). [37, 128, 178, 182]

––––––, 1963. *The Indian in American History.* Publication no. 50 of the Service Center for Teachers of History, of the American Historical Association. (New York: Macmillan). [12, 218]

—————, 1971a. "Squaw Man on the Kiowa, Comanche, and Apache Reservation: Advance Agents of Civilization or Disturbers of the Peace?" In Clark, J. G. (ed.), *The Frontier Challenge: Reponses to the Trans-Mississippi West.* (Lawrence: Univ. of Kansas Press): 171-202. [53, 128]

—————, 1971b. "Kiowas, Comanches and Cattlemen, 1867-1900: A Case Study of the Failure of United States Reservation Policy." *PHR* 40 (April): 333-55. [115, 119]

Haile, Berard, 1954. *Property Concepts of the Navajo Indians.* Anthropological Series 17. (Washington, D.C.: Catholic Univ. of America Press). [25]

Hailey, William M., 1951. *Native Administration in the British African Territories, 1950-53.* (London: Her Majesty's Stationery). [209]

Halbert, Henry S., 1923. "Indian Land Cessions in Alabama." *Arrow Points* 7, no. 1: 6-10. [48]

†Haley, J. C., 1940. "The Opening of the Kiowa and Comanche Country." Unpublished masters thesis in history, Univ. of Oklahoma. [116]

Hallowell, A. Irving, 1943. "Nature and Function of Property as a Social Institution." *Journal of Legal and Political Sociology* 1: 115-38. [5]

—————, 1949. "The Size of Algonkian Hunting Territories: A Function of Ecological Adjustments." *AA* 51: 35-45. [193]

—————, 1957. "The Backwash of the Frontier: The Impact of the Indian on American Culture." In Wyman, W. D. and Kroeber, C. B. (eds.), *Frontiers in Perspective.* (Madison: Univ. of Wisconsin Press): 229-58. [5, 11, 181]

Halsey, F. W., 1901. *The Old New York Frontier; Its Wars with Indians and Tories; Its Missionary Schools, Pioneers and Land Titles, 1614-1800.* (New York: Charles Scribner's Sons). [40]

Hanks, Lucian M., Jr. and Hanks, Jane R., 1950. *Tribe under Trust: A Study of the Blackfoot Reserve of Alberta.* (Toronto: Univ. of Toronto Press). [209]

Harmon, George D., 1930-31. "The United States Indian Policy in Texas, 1845-1860." *MVHR* 17: 377-403. [54]

—————, 1941. *Sixty Years of Indian Affairs: Political, Economic, and Diplomatic, 1789-1850.* (Chapel Hill: Univ. of North Carolina Press). [46]

†Harner, N. S., 1965. "History of the Pyramid Lake Indians, 1842-1959." Unpublished masters thesis in history, Univ. of Nevada. [81]

Harper, Allan G., 1943. "Salvaging the Wreckage of Indian Land Allotment." In LaFarge, O. (ed.): 84-102. [126-7]

—————, 1947. "Canada's Indian Administration: The Treaty System." *AmI* 7: 129-48.

Harris, J. S., 1940. "White Knife Shoshoni of Nevada." In Linton, Ralph (ed.): 39-116. [199]

Harris, Marshall, 1953. *Origins of the Land Tenure Systems in the United States.* (Ames: Iowa State Univ. Press). [56, 126]

Harrison, Jonathan B., 1887. *Latest Studies on Indian Reservation.* (Philadelphia: Indian Rights Association). [125]

Hart, Paxton, 1959. "The Making of Menominee County." *Wisconsin Magazine of History* 43 (Sept.): 20-29. [138]

Harvey, Herbert R., 1961. *Report on Land Use and Occupancy of the Yuma Indian Reservation.* [Docket 320, before the Indian Claims Commission]. (Washington, D.C.: GPO). [21, 108]

— — — — —, n.d. *Ethnohistory and the Cahuilla Indians.* [Docket 80, before the Indian Claims Commission]. (Cambridge, Mass., processed manuscript.) [108]

Hastings, J. R., 1971. "California Ethnohistory: Anglo-World View and the Indian Laws, 1850-63, A.D." Masters thesis in anthropology, California State Univ., Sacramento. [54]

Hawley, F. M., 1948. *Some Factors in the Indian Problem in New Mexico.* Division of Research, 15. (Albuquerque: Univ. of New Mexico Press). [197-8]

Heaston, M. D., 1971. "Whiskey Regulation and Indian Land Titles in New Mexico Territory, 1851-1861." *JW* 10, no. 3: 474-83.

Heizer, Robert F., 1941. "Alexander S. Taylor's Map of California Indian Tribes, 1864." *CHSQ* 20: 171-80. [32]

— — — — —, 1966. *Languages, Territories and Names of California Indian Tribes.* (Berkeley and Los Angeles: Univ. of California Press). [32, 104]

— — — — and Hester, Thomas R., 1970. "Shasta Village and Territory." In "Papers on California Ethnography," *Contributions of the Univ. of California Archeological Research Faculty* 9: 119-58. [29]

— — — — and Almquist, Alan F., 1971. *The Other Californians: Prejudice and Discrimination under Spain, Mexico, and the United States to 1920.* (Berkeley and Los Angeles: Univ. of California Press), Chap. 3, "The Indian and the Lands of His Fathers."

Helin, Ronald A., 1967. "The Volatile Administrative Map of Rumania." *AAAG* 57, no. 3: 481-502. [211]

Helm, June (ed.), 1968. *Essays on the Problem of Tribe, Proceedings, 1967. AES.* (Seattle: Univ. of Washington Press). [27, 192]

Herbert, C. W., 1962. "Land of the White Mountain Apache." *Arizona Highways* 37, no. 7: 4-39. [81]

Herman, M. W., 1956. "Social Aspects of Huron Property." *AA* 58 (Dec.): 1044-58. [221 (footnote)]

Herskovits, Melville J., 1952. *Economic Anthropology: The Economic Life of Primitive Peoples.* (New York: Knopf). [Reprinted by Norton, New York 1965.] [4-5, 10, 26]

Hertzberg, Hazel W., 1971. *The Search for an American Indian Identity: Modern Pan-Indian Movements.* (Syracuse: Syracuse Univ. Press). [74]

Hewes, Leslie, 1942a. "The Oklahoma Ozarks as the Land of the Cherokees." *GR* 32: 267-81. [82, 128, 132, 202]

— — — — —, 1942b. "Indian Land in the Cherokee Country of Oklahoma." *EG* 18, no. 4: 401-12. [50, 82, 128, 132, 202]

— — — — —, 1944. "Cherokee Occupance in the Oklahoma Ozarks and Prairie Plains." *CO* 22, no. 3: 324-37. [82, 132]

†Hey, George A., 1939. "The Policies of Senator Henry L. Dawes in Solving the Indian Problem." Unpublished masters thesis in history, Trinity College. [126]

Hibbard, Benjamin H., 1924. *A History of the Public Land Policies.* (New York: Macmillan). [Reprinted by Univ. of Wisconsin Press, Madison, 1965]. [10]

Hickerson, Harold, 1965. "The Virginia Deer and Intertribal Buffer Zones in the Upper Mississippi Valley." In Leeds, A. and Vayda, A. P. (eds.), *Man, Culture and Animals: the Role of Animals in Human Ecological Adjustments,* American Association for the Advancement of Science, Publication 78. (Washington, D.C.): 43-65. [103]

––––––, 1967a. *Land Tenure and the Rainy Lake Chippewa at the Beginning of the 19th Century. Smithsonian Contribution to Anthropology* 2, no. 4: 41-63. [193]

––––––, 1967b. "Some Implications of the Theory of the Particularity, or 'Atomism,' of Northern Algonkians." *Current Anthropology* 8, no. 4: 313-343. [193, 195]

––––––, 1971. "The Chippewa of the Upper Great Lakes: A Study in Socio-political Change." In Leacock and Lurie (eds.): 169-199. [193, 198]

Hill, Christopher R., 1964. *Bantustans: The Fragmentation of South Africa.* (New York: Oxford Univ. Press). [209]

Hill, Edward E., 1974. *The Office of Indian Affairs, 1824-1880: Historical Sketches.* (New York: Clearwater Publishing Co.). [130]

Hill, Esther V., 1930. "The Iroquois Indians and Their Land since 1783." *New York History* 11: 335-53. [41, 81]

Hill, Joseph, 1927. *History of Warner's Ranch and Its Environs.* (Los Angeles: privately published). [117]

Hill, William W., 1936. "Notes on Pima Land Law and Tenure." *AA* 38: 586-89. [25]

Hilliard, Sam B., 1971. "Indian Land Cessions West of the Mississippi." *JW* 10, no. 3: 493-510. [52]

––––––, 1972. "Indian Land Cessions." [Map Supplement to *AAAG* 62, no. 2]. [See review in *PHR* 42, (1973) no. 1: 108.] [52, 219]

Hinsdale, W. B., 1932. *Distribution of the Aboriginal Population of Michigan.* Museum of Anthropology, *Occasional Contributions* 2. (Ann Arbor: Univ. of Michigan Press).

†Historical Society of Pennsylvania, 1938. *Indian Treaties Printed by Benjamin Franklin.* Introduction by Carl van Doren, notes by Julian P. Boyd. (Philadelphia: Historical Society of Pennsylvania). [51]

Hobbs, Charles A., 1964. "Indian Hunting and Fishing Rights." *George Washington L.R.* 32: 504-32. [160]

––––––, 1969. "Indian Hunting and Fishing Rights." *George Washington L.R.* 37: 1251-1273. [160, 169]

Hodge, R. A., 1973. "Getting Back the Land: How Native Americans Can Acquire Excess and Surplus Federal Property." *North Dakota L.R.* 49, no. 2 (Winter): 333-42. [110]

Hoebel, E. Adamson, 1940. *The Political Organization and Law-Ways of the Comanche Indians. AAA Memoir.* 54 [*AA*, 42, no. 3, pt. 2]. [25, 28]

Hoffman, Bernard G., 1964. *Observations on Certain Ancient Tribes of the Northern Appalachian Province. Bulletin 191, Anthropological Papers* 70, *BAE.* (Washington, D.C.: GPO): 191-246. [28, 30]

Hoffmeister, Harold, 1945. "The Consolidated Ute Indian Reservation." *GR* 35, no. 4: 601-23. [73, 84, 86, 197]

Hogan, Thomas E., 1974. "City in a Quandary: Salamanca and the Allegany Leases." *New York History* 55, no. 1: 79-101. [134]

†Holmes, J. D. L., 1969. "Spanish Treaties with West Florida Indians, 1784-1802." *Florida Historical Quarterly* 48. [51]

Hood, S., 1972. "Termination of the Klamath Indian Tribe of Oregon." *EH* 19, no. 4: 379-392. [139]

Hooker, Barbara, 1972. "Surplus Lands for Indians: One Road to Self-Determination." *Vital Issues* 22, no. 1. |78, 111|

Hoopes, Alban W., 1932. *Indian Affairs and Their Administration; with Special Reference to the Far West, 1849-60.* (Philadelphia: Univ. of Pennsylvania Press).

Hoover, J. W., 1930. "Tusayan: The Hopi Indian Country of Arizona." *GR* 20, no. 3: 425-44. [87]

———, 1931a. "Geographic and Ethnic Grouping of Arizona Indians." *JG* 30, no. 6: 235-46.

———, 1931b. "Navajo Nomadism." *GR* 21, no. 4: 429-445. [121]

———, 1935. "Generic Descent of the Papago Villages." *AA* 37, no. 2: 257-64. [28]

———, 1936. "The Jicarilla Indian Country of New Mexico." *Bulletin, Geographical Society of Philadelphia*, 34, no. 1: 1-12. [87]

———, 1941. "Cerros de Trincherias of the Arizona Papagueria." *GR* 31, no. 2: 228-39.

Horrell, Muriel, 1965. *Reserves and Reservations; a Comparison of Plans for the Advancement of Underdeveloped Areas in South Africa and the United States, incl. information about development of the African reserves in South Africa as of June 1965.* (Johannesburg: South African Institute of Race Relations). |209|

Horsman, Reginold, 1967. *Expansion and American Indian Policy, 1783-1812.* (East Lansing: Michigan State Univ. Press). [45, 91]

Hough, Henry W., 1967. *Development of Indian Resources.* (Denver: World Press). [64, 78]

Houghton, Frederick, 1920. *History of the Buffalo Creek Reservation. Publication of the Buffalo Historical Society* 24: 3-181.

Houghton, N. D., 1945. " 'Wards of the U.S.'–Arizona Applications: A Study of the Legal Status of the Indians." *Univ. of Arizona, Social Science Bulletin* 16, no. 3. [155]

Houser, N. P., 1970. "The Tigua Settlement of Ysleta del Sur." *Kiva* 36, no. 2: 23-40. [201]

Howard, James H., 1972. "Notes on the Ethnogeography of the Yankton Dakota." *Plains Anthropologist* 17, no. 58, pt. 1: 281-307.

Howard, R. P., 1969. "A Historiography of the Five Civilized Tribes: A Chronological Approach." *CO* 47, no. 3: 312-331. [12]

†Huber, G. H., 1933. "Indian Policy of Pennsylvania." Unpublished masters thesis in history, Univ. of Buffalo. [172]

Hudson, Charles M., 1970. *The Catawba Nation. Monograph* 18. (Athens: Univ. of Georgia Press). [201]

Hudson, John, 1973. "Two Dakota Homestead Frontiers." *AAAG* 63, no. 4: 442-462. [119]

Humphrey, Seth K., 1905. *The Indian Dispossessed.* (Boston: Little, Brown). |65, 118|

Humphreys, A. G., 1971. "The Crow Indian Treaties of 1868: An Example of Power Struggle and Confusion in United States Indian Policy." *AW* 43 (Spring): 73-89. |53|

Hunt, Jack, 1970. "Land Tenure and Economic Development of the Warm Springs Indian Reservation." *JW* 9, no. 1: 93-109. |77, 81, 82, 169, 186|

Huntington, Ellsworth, 1919. *The Red Man's Continent: A Chronicle of Aboriginal America.* |Part 1 of *The New Continent.*| (New Haven: Yale Univ. Press). |24|

Hutchinson, C. Alan, 1964-65. "The Mexican Government and the Mission Indians of Upper California, 1821-35." *Americas* 21: 335-362. |121, 126|
—————, 1969. *Frontier Settlement in Mexican California.* (New Haven: Yale Univ. Press). |126|
Hyde, W., 1971. "Residual Trusteeship: the Possibility of a Tribe Retaining Some of Its Trust Relationship after Termination." Typescript. (Albuquerque: Univ. of New Mexico, School of Law). |138|
Hymes, Dell, 1968. "Linguistic Problems in Defining the Concept of 'Tribe.' " In Helm, J. (ed.): 23-48. |192|
†Iden, Thomas L., 1929. "A History of the Ute Indian Cessions of Colorado." Unpublished masters thesis in history, Western Colorado College (Gunnison).
ILIDS, 1972. *Indian Legal Information Development Service.* 1, no. 9: 34-38. |124|
Indian Claims Commission, 1968. *Annual Report.* |102|
Indian Historian Press, 1970, 1971, 1972. *Index to Literature on the American Indian.* (Indian Historian Press: San Francisco). |218|
† Inglis, Gordon B., 1971. "The Canadian Indian Reserve: Community, Population, and Social System." Unpublished doctoral dissertation in anthropology, Univ. of British Columbia. |209|
International Labor Office, 1953. *Indigenous People.* (Geneva). |213|
Israel, D. H. and Smithson, T. L., 1973. "Indian Taxation, Tribal Sovereignty, and Economic Development." *North Dakota L.R.* 49, no. 2 (Winter): 267-302.
Jackson, Helen H., 1881, 1965. *A Century of Dishonor: A Sketch of the United States Government's Dealings with Some of the Indian Tribes.* [Reprinted by Harpers, New York, 1965, A. F. Rolle (ed.).] |65, 118|
†Jackson, J., 1938. "State Jurisdiction of Indian Affairs in South Dakota." Unpublished masters thesis in political science, State Univ. of Iowa. |155|
†Jackson, Leroy F., 1909. "The Extinguishment of the Land Title of the Eastern Tribes of the Dakota Nation Previous to the Outbreak of 1862." Unpublished masters thesis in history, Univ. of Chicago. |53|
Jackson, W. Turrentine, 1945. "Indian Affairs and Politics in Idaho Territory, 1863-1870." *PHR* 14, no. 3: 311-25.
Jacobs, Wilbur R. (ed.), 1954; 1967. *The Appalachian Indian Frontier: The Edmond Atkin Report and Plan of 1755.* (Lincoln: Univ. of Nebraska Press). |39, 43, 49, 208|
—————, 1971. "The Fatal Confrontation: Early Native-White Relations on the Frontiers of Australia, New Guinea, and America–A Comparative Study." *PHR* 40, no. 3: 283-309. |208, 214|
—————, 1972. *Dispossessing the American Indian: Indians and Whites on the Colonial Frontier.* (New York: Charles Scribner's Sons). |39, 43, 49, 208|
Jacobson, Daniel, 1960. "The Origin of the Koasati Community of Louisiana." *EH* 7, no. 2: 97-120. |201|
James, A. L., 1894. *English Institutions and the American Indian, Johns Hopins Univ. Studies in History and Political Science.* 12 ser. no. 10. (Baltimore: Johns Hopkins Univ. Press). |56|
Janke, Ronald A., 1967. "The Development and Persistence of Land Tenure Problems on Indian Reservations in the United States." Unpublished masters thesis in geography, Univ. of Wisconsin, Milwaukee. |87|

Jefferson, James, Delaney, Robert W., and Thompson, Gregory C., 1972. *The Southern Utes: A Tribal History.* (Ignacio, Colo., Southern Ute Tribe).

Jennings, Francis, 1965a. "The Delaware Interregnum." *Pennsylvania Magazine of History and Biography* 89: 174-198. [39, 41-2]

————, 1965b. "Miquon's Passing: Indian-European Relations in Colonial Pennsylvania, 1674-1755." Doctoral dissertation in history, Univ. of Pennsylvania. [39, 41-2]

————, 1966. "The Indian Trade of the Susquehanna Valley." *Proceedings, APS* 110, 6: 406-424. [39, 41-2]

————, 1968a. "Glory, Death and Transfiguration: The Susquehannock Indians in the Seventeenth Century." *Proceedings APS* 112, 1: 15-53. [39, 41-2]

————, 1968b. "Incident at Tulpehocken." *Pennsylvania History* 35, 4 (Oct.): 335-355. [39, 41-2]

————, 1970. "The Scandalous Indian Policy of William Penn's Sons: Deeds and Documents of the Walking Purchase." *Pennsylvania History* 37, 1 (Jan.): 19-39. [39, 41-2]

————, 1971a. "The Constitutional Evolution of the Covenant Chain." *Proceedings APS* 115, 2: 88-96. [39, 41-2]

————, 1971b. "Virgin Land and Savage People" *American Quarterly* 23, 4 (Oct.): 519-41. [39-42, 95, 206]

*————, in press [1975]. *The Invasion of America: Indians, Colonialism, and the Cant of Conquest.* (Chapel Hill: Univ. of North Carolina Press). [42]

Jensen, Kenneth D., 1964. "A Land Utilization Survey of the Turtle Mountain Indian Reservation, Belcourt, North Dakota." Unpublished masters thesis in geography, Univ. of North Dakota. [87]

Joffe, N., 1940. "Fox of Iowa." In Linton, Ralph (ed.): 259-332. [198]

Johnson, D. C., 1974. "State Taxation of Indians: Impact of the 1973 Supreme Court Decisions." *AILR* 2, no. 1 (Summer): 1-28. [157]

Johnson, Kenneth, 1966. *K-344, or the Indians of California vs. the United States.* (Los Angeles: Dawson's Book Shop). [109]

†Johnson, K. W., 1973. "Sovereignty, Citizenship and the Indian. *Arizona L.R.* 15, no. 4 (November):

Johnson, Ralph W. (ed.), 1970. *Studies in American Indian Law.* Typescript. (Seattle: Univ. of Washington, School of Law).

Johnston, Sr. Mary A., 1948. *Federal Relations with the Great Sioux Indians of South Dakota, 1887-1933, with particular reference to the land policy under the Dawes Act.* Doctoral dissertation published by Catholic Univ. of America (Washington, D.C.). [132]

Jones, D. C., 1966. *The Treaty of Medicine Lodge.* (Norman: Univ. of Oklahoma Press). [49]

Jones, G. T., 1974. "Enforcement Strategies for Indian Landlords." *AILR* 2, no. 1 (Summer): 41-60. [135]

Jones, J. A., 1955. "Key to the Annual Reports of the U.S. Commissioner of Indian Affairs." *EH* 2 no. 1: 58-62. [217]

Jones, N. S. Carey, 1965. "The Decolonization of the White Highlands of Kenya." *Geographical Journal* 131, no. 2: 186-201. [209]

Jones, R. S., 1973. "A History of the Alaska Native Claims Settlement of 1971, together with a history of the determination and disposition of the property rights of native Hawaiians, being a comparison of those two situations in the light of proposing a settlement of Hawaiian Native land claims." Typescript, Legislative Reference Service. (Washington, D.C.: Library of Congress).

Jones, Volney H., 1950. "The Establishment of the Hopi Reservation and Some Later Developments Concerning Hopi Lands." *Plateau* 23, no. 2: 17-25. [123]

Jones, W. K., 1967. "General Guide to Documents on the Five Civilized Tribes in the University of Oklahoma Library Division of Manuscripts." *EH* 14, no. 1-2: 47-76. [218]

Jorgensen, Joseph G., 1971. "Indians and the Metropolis." In Waddell, J. O. and Watson, O. M. (eds.). *The American Indian in Urban Society* (Boston: Little, Brown): 67-113. [74, 75]

−−−−−, 1972. *Sun Dance Religion.* (Chicago: Univ. of Chicago Press). [74, 188]

Josephy, Alvin M., Jr. (ed.), 1961. *The American Heritage Book of Indians.* (New York). [46]

−−−−−, 1971. *Red Power: The American Indian's Fight for Freedom.* (New York: American Heritage Press). [218]

Juergensmeyer, J. C. and Wadley, J. B., 1974. "The Common Lands Concept: A 'Commons' Solution to a Common Environmental Problem." *NRJ* 14, no. 3 (July): 361-381. [98]

Kane, Albert E., 1965. "Jurisdiction over Indians and Indian Reservations." *Arizona L.R.* 6: 238-255. [152, 154]

Kappler, Charles J., 1903-38. *Indian Affairs, Law and Treaties.* (Washington, D.C.: GPO), 5 vols. [Reprinted as *Indian Treaties* by Interland Publishing Co., New York, 1972. Also reprinted by AMS Press, New York, 1972.] [51, 96, 122]

Kasch, C., 1947. "The Yokayo Rancheria." *CHSQ* 26, no. 3: 209-15. [21, 117]

Kawashima, Yasu, 1969a. "Jurisdiction of the Colonial Courts over the Indians in Massachusetts, 1689-1763." *New England Quarterly* 42 (Dec.): 532-50. [156]

−−−−−, 1969b. "Legal Origins of the Indian Reservation in Colonial Massachusetts." *American Journal of Legal History* 13, no. 1: 42-56. [56, 156]

−−−−−, 1974. "Indians and Southern Colonial Statutes." *IH* 7, no. 1: 10-16. [56-7]

Keesing, Felix M., 1939. *The Menomini Indians of Wisconsin; a Study of Three Centuries of Cultural Contact and Change. APS Memoir* 10. [190]

−−−−−, 1953. *Culture Change: An Analysis and Bibliography of Anthropological Sources to 1952.* (Stanford: Stanford Univ. Press). [11, 178, 217]

Keith, Shirley, 1974. "A Rebuttal to 'the Pre-emption Doctrine and Colonias de Santa Fe.'" *NRJ* 14 (April): 283-292. [159]

Keller, R. H., Jr., 1972. "On Teaching Indian History: Legal Jurisdiction in Chippewa Treaties." *EH* 19, no. 3: 209-18. [58n.]

Kelly, Isabel T., 1932. *Ethnography of Surprise Valley Paiute. UCPAAE* 31, no. 3. [29]

−−−−−, 1938. "Southern Paiute Bands." *AA* 36, no. 4: 548-560. [29]

Kelly, J. M., 1971. "Indians–the Extent of the 'Fair and Honorable Dealings' Section of the Indian Claims Commission Act." *Saint Louis Univ. Law Journal* 15, no. 3: 491-507. [94]

Kelly, Lawrence C., 1963. "The Navaho Indians: Land and Oil." *NMHR* 38, no. 1: 1-28. [72, 122, 150, 171]

—————, 1968. *The Navajo Indians and Federal Indian Policy, 1900-35.* (Tucson: Univ. of Arizona Press). [81]

Kelly, William H., 1953. *Indians of the Southwest: A Survey of Indian Tribes and Indian Administration in Arizona.* Bureau of Ethnic Research, *Annual Report* 1. (Tucson: Univ. of Arizona Press). 70, 155, 172]

—————, 1954. *Indian Affairs and the IRA: the Twenty Year Record.* (Tucson: Univ. of Arizona Press). [188]

Kelsay, Laura E. (comp.), 1954. *List of Cartographic Records of the Bureau of Indian Affairs.* Special Lists no. 13. (Washington, D.C.: National Archives). [219]

Kelsey, Harry, 1973. "The California Indian Treaty Myth." *SCQ* 15, no. 3: 225-35. [55]

Kennard, E. A. and Macgregor, Gordon, 1953. "Applied Anthropology in Government: U.S." In Kroeber, A. L. (ed.) *Anthropology Today: An Encyclopedic Inventory.* (Chicago: Univ. fo Chicago Press): 832ff. [11]

Kerr, J. R., 1969. "Constitutional Rights, Tribal Justice and the American Indian." *Journal of Public Law* 18: 311-38. [150]

Kickingbird, Kirke and Ducheneaux, Karen, 1973. *One Hundred Million Acres.* (New York: Macmillan). [1-2, 64, 65, 77, 88, 109, 110-11, 173]

Kimmey, Fred M., 1960. "Christianity and Indian Lands." *EH* 7, no. 1: 44-60. [43, 97]

Kinney, Jay P., 1937. *A Continent Lost—A Civilization Won: Indian Land Tenure in America.* (Baltimore: Johns Hopkins Univ. Press). [Reprinted by Octagon Books, New York, 1975.] [7, 44, 46, 49, 51, 68, 71, 77, 96, 126, 127, 133]

—————, 1950. *Indian Forest and Range; A History of the Administration and Conservation of the Redman's Heritage.* (Washington, D.C.: Forestry Enterprises). [62,78]

Klein, B. and Icolari, D. (eds.), 1967. *Reference Encyclopedia of the American Indian.* (New York: B. Klein). [218]

Kluckhohn, Clyde, 1940. *Bibliography of Navajo Indians.* (New York: J.J. Augustin). [218]

————— and Leighton, Dorothy, 1956. *The Navaho.* (Cambridge: Harvard Univ. Press). [190]

Knight, Rolf, 1965. "A Re-examination of Hunting, Trapping, and Territoriality among the Northeastern Algonkian Indians." In Leeds, A. and Vayda, A. P. (eds.), *Man, Culture, and Animals: The Role of Animals in Human Ecological Adjustments.* Publication 18 (Washington, D.C.: American Association for the Advancement of Science): 27-42. [193-4]

Knoepfler, Karl J., 1922. "Legal Status of American Indian and His Property." *Iowa Law Bulletin* 7, no. 1: 232-49. [126, 158]

Knoop, A., 1941. "The Federal Indian Policy in the Sacramento Valley, 1846-1860." Unpublished masters thesis in history, Univ. of California, Berkeley. [54-5]

Koch, Lena C., 1924-25, 1925-26. "The Federal Indian Policy in Texas, 1845-1860." *SWHQ* [Texas State Historical Association] 28, no. 3: 223-234; no. 4: 259-286; 29, no. 1: 19-35; no. 2: 98-127. [54, 117]

Koons, M. E., Jr. and Walker, H. C., Jr., 1960. "Jurisdiction over Indian Country in North Dakota." *North Dakota L.R.* 36, no. 1: 51-62. [155]

Kowalke, O., 1956. "The Settlement of the Stockbridge Indians and the Survey of Land in Outagamie County, Wisc." *Wisconsin Magazine of History* 40 (March): 31-35. [50]

Kroeber, Alfred L., 1925; 1953. *Handbook of the Indians of California. BAE Bulletin* 78. (Washington, D.C.: Smithsonian Institution). [Reprinted by California Book Co., Berkeley.] [20, 27, 29, 32]

—————, (ed.), 1935. *Walapai Ethnography. AAA Memoir*, 42. [25]

—————, 1939. *Cultural and Natural Areas of Native North America. UCPAAE* 38. [Reprinted by Univ. of California Press, Los Angeles and Berkeley, 1963.] [31]

—————, 1951. *A Mohave Historical Epic. AR* 11, no. 2: 71-176. [25, 101]

—————, 1955. "Nature of the Land-Holding Group." *EH* 2, no. 2: 303-14. [27, 34, 101, 187]

—————, 1962. "The Nature of Land-Holding Groups in Aboriginal California." *Reports of the University of California Archeological Survey*, no. 56: 83-120. [Also in Heizer, R. F. (ed.), *Aboriginal California: Three Studies in Culture History* (Los Angeles and Berkeley: Univ. of California Press, 1963): 81-120.] [20, 27, 34, 101]

Kunkel, Peter H., 1974. "The Pomo Kin Group and the Political Unit in Aboriginal California." *Journal of California Anthropology* 1, no. 1: 7-18. [27]

LaFarge, Oliver (ed.), 1943. *The Changing Indian.* (Norman: Univ. of Oklahoma Press). [68]

—————, 1957. "Termination of Federal Supervision: Disintegration and the American Indian." *AAAPSS* 311 (May): 41-46. [138]

LaFontaine, Frank S., 1973. "Indian Property and State Judgment Executions." *Oregon L.R.* 52, no. 3: 313-24.

Laidlaw, Sally J., 1960. *Federal Indian Land Policy and the Fort Hall Indians. Occasional Papers* 3, Idaho State College (Univ.) Museum (Pocatello). [70, 81]

†LaManna, Virginia C., 1934. "A Study of Land Frauds on the Western Lands of the United States, 1875-1900." Unpublished masters thesis in history, New York Univ. [118]

Lambert, Paul F., 1973. "The Cherokee Reconstruction Treaty of 1866." *JW* 12, no. 3: 471-89.

Lang, Gottfried O., 1953. *A Study in Culture Contact and Culture Change: The Whiterock Utes in Transition. Anthropological Papers* 15, Univ. of Utah. [130, 198]

Lange, Charles H., 1959; 1968. *Cochiti: A New Mexico Pueblo: Past and Present.* (Austin: Univ. of Texas Press). [Reprinted by Southern Illinois Univ. Press, Carbondale.] [190]

Langone, Stephen A., 1969. "The Heirship Land Problem and Its Effect on the Indian, the Tribe, and Effective Utilization." In *Toward Economic Development for Native American Communities* 91st Congress, 1st Session, Joint Economic Committee. (Washington, D.C.: GPO): v. 2: 519-548. [136]

Lankes, Frank, 1962. *An Outline of West Seneca History.* (West Seneca, N.Y.: West Seneca Historical Society). [41]

—————, 1964. *The Senecas on Buffalo Creek Reservation.* (West Seneca, N.Y.: West Seneca Historical Society). [41]

Lantis, Margaret, 1966. "The Administration of Northern Peoples: Canada and Alaska" In Macdonald, R. St. J. (ed.): 89-119. [211, 212]

Large, Donald W., 1973. "This Land is Whose Land? Changing Concepts of Land as Property." *Wisconsin L.R.* 1973, no. 4: 1039-1083. [98]

Lass, W. E., 1963. "The Removal from Minnesota of the Sioux and Winnebago Indians." *Minnesota History* 38 (Dec.): 353-64. [50]

Lazarus, Arthur A., Jr., 1960. "Indian Rights under the Federal Power Act." *FBJ* 20: 217-222. [169-170]

Lazewski, Tony, 1973. "Geographic Research and Native Americans." [Introductory commentary to special interest session on Native Americans in Contemporary Society: Problems and Issues, annual meeting, AAG, Atlanta, Ga.] [13]

Leach, Douglas E., 1966. *The Northern Colonial Frontier, 1607-1763.* (New York: Holt, Rinehart and Winston). [40, 41]

Leach, E., 1960. "The Frontiers of 'Burma.' " *CSSH* 3: 49-73. [208]

Leacock, Eleanor, [1954]. *The Montagnais Hunting Territory and the Fur Trade. AAA Memoir,* 78. [24, 193-4]

————— and Lurie, Nancy O. (eds.), 1971. *North American Indians in Historical Perspective.* (New York: Random House). [21, 25, 179]

LeDuc, Thomas, 1957. "The Work of the Indian Claims Commission under the Act of 1946." *PHR* 26, no. 1: 1-16. [94]

Lee, S. W., 1967. *A Survey of Acculturation in the Intermontane Area of the United States. Occasional Papers* 19, Idaho State Univ. Museum (Pocatello).

†Leidy, Edgar E., 1929. "The Extinction of the Indian Title in Ohio beyond the Greenville Treaty Line." Unpublished masters thesis in history, Ohio State Univ. [50]

Leonard, Charles B., 1928. "Federal Indian Policy in the San Joaquin Valley: Its Applications and Results." Unpublished doctoral dissertation in history, Univ. of California, Berkeley. [54-5]

Leupp, Francis E., 1909. "Indian Lands: Their Administration with Reference to Present and Future Use." *AAAPSS* 33 (May): 620-30. [65, 77, 125]

—————, 1910. *The Indian and His Problem.* (New York: Charles Scribner's Sons). [51, 65]

Levitan, Sar A. and Hetrick, Barbara, 1971. *Big Brother's Indian Programs—with Reservations.* (New York: McGraw-Hill Book Co.) [79]

Levy, Jerrold E. and Kunitz, Stephen J., 1971. "Indian Reservations, Anomie, and Social Pathologies." *SWJA* 27, no. 2: 97-128. [74]

Lewis, Oscar, 1942. *The Effects of White Contact upon Blackfoot Culture with Special Reference to the Role of the Fur Trade. AES Monographs* 6. [Reprinted 1966 by Univ. of Washington Press, Seattle.] [195]

Liljeblad, Sven, 1958. "Epilogue: Indian Policy and the Fort Hall Reservation." *Idaho Yesterdays* 2, no. 2: 14-19. [81]

Lindquist, Gustavas E., 1948-49. "Indian Treaty Making." *CO* 26, no. 4: 416-48. [52]

Linton, Ralph (ed.), 1940. *Acculturation in Seven American Indian Tribes* (New York: D. Appleton-Century; reprint by Peter Smith, Gloucester, 1963). [178]

—————, 1943. "Land Tenure in Aboriginal America." In LaFarge, O. (ed.): 42-54. [26]

Lipps, O. H., 1932. *The Case of the California Indians.* (Chemawa, Oregon). [20, 109]

Litton, G., 1955. "The Resources of the National Archives for the Study of the American Indian." *EH* 2, no. 3: 191-208. [217]

Lockmiller, David A., 1928. "Land Grants of the Cherokee Nation." Unpublished masters thesis in history, Emory Univ.

†Long, Anton V., 1949. "Senator Bursum and the Pueblo Indian Lands Act of 1924." Unpublished masters thesis in history, Univ. of New Mexico.

Longwell, Alden R., 1961. "Lands of the Omaha Indians." Unpublished masters thesis in geography, Univ. of Nebraska, Lincoln. [72, 86, 198, 200, 201]

Lonsdale, Richard E. (ed.), 1967. *Atlas of North Carolina.* (Chapel Hill: Univ. of North Carolina Press). [219]

Loomer, C. W., 1955. *Land Tenure Problems in the Bad River Indian Reservation of Wisconsin.* University of Wisconsin, Agricultural Experimental Station, *Research Bulletin* 188: 1-48. [70, 73, 84-5, 156]

Loper, Ethel V., 1955. "The Alienation and Utilization of the Pawnee Lands, 1874-1921." Unpublished masters thesis in history, Univ. of Oklahoma. [136]

Loram, C. T. and McIlwraith, T. F. (eds.), 1943. *The North American Indian Today.* (Toronto: Univ. of Toronto Press). [69]

Loud, Llewellyn L., 1918. *Ethnography and Archeology of the Wiyot Territory. UCPAAE* 14, no. 2: 221-436. [29]

Lower Pend D'Oreille, [1957]. *Petitioner's Proposed Findings of Fact and Brief.* [Docket 94, before the Indian Claims Commission, prepared by J. W. Cragun: Wilkinson, Cragun and Barker, Attorneys, Washington, D.C.] [107]

Lurie, Nancy O., 1955. "Problems, Opportunities, and Recommendations." *EH* 2 (Fall): 357-75. [95, 100]

————, 1956. "A Reply to Land Claims Cases." *EH* 3 (Summer): 256-76. [95, 100]

————, 1957. "The Indian Claims Commission Act." *AAAPSS* 311 (May): 56-70. [95, 100, 102]

————, 1966. "Women in Early American Anthropology." In Helm, J. (ed.), *Pioneers of American Anthropology: The Uses of Biography.* (Seattle: Univ. of Washington Press): 43-54. [130-1]

————, 1969. "Wisconsin Indians: Lives and Lands." *Wisconsin Magazine of History* 53 (Autumn): 2-20. [81]

————, 1971. "Menominee Termination." *IH* 4, no. 4: 31-43. [140, 179, 180, 196]

————, 1972. "Menominee Termination: from Reservation to Colony." *HO* 31, no. 3: 257-269. [140, 149]

Lysyk, K., 1973. "Approaches to Settlement of Indian Title Claims: the Alaskan Model." *Univ. of British Columbia L.R.* 8: 321-42. [109]

Macdonald, R. St. J. (ed.), 1966. *The Arctic Frontier.* (Toronto: Univ. of Toronto Press).

†Macfarlane, Ronald O., 1933. "Indian Relations in New England, 1620-1760: A Study of a Regulated Frontier." Unpublished doctoral dissertation in history, Harvard Univ. [56]

Macgregor, Gordon, 1946. *Warriors without Weapons.* (Chicago: Univ. of Chicago Press). [12, 197]

————, 1949. "Attitudes of the Fort Berthold Indians Regarding Removal from the Garrison Reservoir Site and Future Administration of Their Reservation." *North Dakota History* 16, no. 1: 31-60. [99, 168-9]

————, 1970. "Changing Society: The Teton Dakotas." In Nurge, E. (ed.): 92-106. [74, 197, 198]

Macleod, William C., 1922. "The Family Hunting Territory and Lenape Political Organization." *AA* 24, no. 4: 1448-63. [193]

————, 1924. *The Origin of the State, Reconsidered in Light of the Data of Aboriginal North America.* (Philadelphia). [186]

————, 1927. "Trade Restrictions in Early Society [in Relation to Land Tenure]." *AA* 29, no. 2: 271-278. [186, 193]

————, 1928. *The American Indian Frontier.* (New York: Alfred A. Knopf). [37, 56, 208]

————, 1939. "Contacts of Europe with the American Aborigines." In *The Relations of Europe with Non-European Peoples*, vol. 7 of Eyre, Edward (ed.), *European Civilization: Its Origins and Development.* (Oxford: Oxford Univ. Press): 813-1062.

Madsen, Brigham D., 1958. *The Bannock of Idaho.* (Caldwell: Caxton), Chap. 11, "Land Cessions and Allotments." [132, 169]

Malin, James C., 1921. *Indian Policy and Westward Expansion. Bulletin, Univ. of Kansas Humanistic Studies* 2, no. 3. [44-5]

Malone, Henry T., 1956. *Cherokees of the Old South: A People in Transition.* (Athens; Univ. of Georgia Press). [50]

†Manley, Henry S., 1947. "Buying Buffalo from the Indians." *New York History* 28 (July). [41]

————, 1960. "Indian Reservation Ownership in New York." *New York State Bar Bulletin.* [Journal] 32, no. 2: 134-38. [70]

Manners, Robert A., 1956. "The Land Claims Cases: Anthropologists in Conflict." *EH* 3, no. 1: 72-81. [99]

————, 1957. "Tribe and Tribal Boundaries: the Walapai." *EH* 4, no. 1: 1-26. [101, 187]

————, 1962. "Pluralism and the American Indian." *AI* 22, no. 1: 23-38. [Reprinted in Walker, D. (ed.): 124-1453]. [201]

————, 1964. "Colonialism and Native Land Tenure: A Case Study in Ordained Accommodation." In Manners, R. A. (ed.), *Process and Pattern in Culture: Essays in Honor of Julian H. Steward.* (Chicago: Aldine): 266-80. [209]

————, 1974. *Southern Paiute and Chemehuevi: An Ethnohistorical Report.* (New York and London: Garland Publishing Co.).

Mannypenny, George W., 1880. *Our Indian Wards.* (Cincinnati: Robert Clarke and Co.). [51, 65]

Mardock, R. W., 1971. *The Reformers and the American Indian.* (Columbia: Univ. of Missouri Press). [125, 127]

Marken, J. W. (ed.), 1973. *Indians and Eskimos of North America. A Bibliography of Books in Print through 1972.* (Vermillion: Dakota Press). [218]

Martin, John F., 1968. "A Reconstruction of Havasupai Land Tenure." *ET* 7, no. 4: 450-60. [84, 196-7]

————, 1973. "The Organization of Land and Labor in a Marginal Economy." *HO* 32, no. 2: 155-60. [84]

Martin, L. J., 1969-70. "A History of the Modoc Indians: An Acculturation Study." *CO* 47 (Winter): 398-446. [198-9, 201]

Martone, R., 1974. "The United States and the Betrayal of Indian Water Rights." *The Indian Historian* 7, no. 3 (Summer): 3-11. [163]

Matthews, M. A., 1973. "Indian Law: the Pre-Emption Doctrine and Colonias de Santa Fe." *NRJ* 13 (July): 535-45. [159]

Mattison, Roy H., 1955. "The Indian Reservation System in the Upper Missouri, 1865-90." *Nebraska History Magazine* 36, no. 3: 141-72. [53]

McArthur, C. L., 1949. "Oklahoma Indian Land Laws." *Oklahoma Bar Association Journal* 20 (July): 1165-81. [70]

McCluggage, Robert W., 1970. "The Senate and Indian Land Titles, 1800-1825." *Western Historical Quarterly* 1 (Oct.): 415-25. [48-9]

McCullar, Marion R., 1973. "The Choctaw-Chickasaw Reconstruction Treaty of 1866." *JW* 12, no. 3: 462-70.

McFeeley, Mark B., 1972. "Need for a Federal Policy in Indian Economic Development." *New Mexico L.R.* 2 (Jan.): 71-80. [158-9]

McIntire, Elliot G., 1969. "Hopi Colonization on the Colorado River." *California Geographer* 10: 7-14. [124, 190]

⸻, 1971. "Changing Patterns of Hopi Indian Settlement." *AAAG* 61, no. 3: 510-21.

McKee, Jesse O., 1971. "The Choctaw Indians: A Geographical Study in Cultural Change." *Southern Quarterly* 9, no. 2: 107-140. [201]

McLane, A. E., 1955. *Oil and Gas Leasing on Indian Lands.* (Denver: F. H. Gower). [72]

McLoone, J. J., 1968. "Indian Hunting and Fishing Rights." *Arizona L.R.* 10, no. 3: 725-739. [160]

†McNeely, John H., Jr., 1939. "History of Tribal Claims of the Dakota Sioux Indians against the United States." Unpublished masters thesis in history, George Washington Univ. [92]

†McNickle, D'Arcy, 1946. "Rescuing Sisseton." *The American Indian* 3, no. 2. [See Fey, H. and McNickle, D. (1970), Chap. 9, for discussion.] [132]

⸻, 1949. *They Came Here First: The Epic of the American Indian.* (Philadelphia & New York: Lippincott). [37]

⸻, 1962; 1973. *Indian Tribes of the United States: Ethnic and Cultural Survival.* (London: Oxford Univ. Press). [Rev. ed. entitled *Native American Tribalism: Indian Survivals and Renewals*; see review, *JW* 13, no. 1: 143 (1974).] [37]

Mead, Margaret, 1932. *The Changing Culture of an Indian Tribe. Columbia Univ. Contributions to Anthropology* 15. (New York: New York Univ. Press). [Reprinted 1969.] [131, 184-5]

⸻ and Bunzel, Ruth (eds.), 1960. *The Golden Age of American Anthropology.* (New York: G. Braziller). [11]

Mekeel, Scudder, 1936. *The Economy of a Modern Teton Dakota Community. Publications in Anthropology* 6. (New Haven: Yale Univ. Press). [197]

Meriam, Lewis, et al., (1928). *The Problem of Indian Administration. Studies in Administration* 17. (Baltimore: Brookings Institution for Government Research). [62, 68, 126]

Meserve, Charles F., 1896. *The Dawes Commission and the Five Civilized Tribes of Indian Territory, A Report.* (Philadelphia: Indian Rights Association). [125]

⸻, 1933. "The First Allotment of Lands in Severalty among the Oklahoma Cheyenne and Arapahoe Indians." *CO* 11, no. 4: 1040-1043. [132]

Metge, Joan, 1964. *A New Maori Migration.* (London: Athlone Press). [209]

Meyer, Roy W., 1964. "The Establishment of the Santee Reservation, 1866-69." *Nebraska History* 45, no. 1: 59-97. [53]

⸻, 1967. *History of the Santee Sioux: United States Indian Policy on Trial.* (Lincoln: Univ. of Nebraska Press). [128]

†⸻, 1968. "The Fort Berthold Reservation and the Garrison Dam." *North Dakota History* 35, no. 3-4: [169]

Mikesell, Marvin W., 1960. "Comparative Studies in Frontier History." *AAAG* 50, no. 1: 62-74.

Miller, Gerald R., 1957. "Indians, Water, and the Arid Western States—Prelude to the Pelton Decision." *Utah L.R.* 5 (Fall): 495-510. [164, 170]

†Mills, Lawrence, 1919. *The Lands of the Five Civilized Tribes: A Treatise upon the Law Applicable to the Lands of the Five Civilized Tribes in Oklahoma.* (St. Louis: F. H. Thomas Law Book Co.). [70]

Mitchell, Robert D., 1972. "The Shenandoah Valley Frontier." *AAAG* 62, no. 3: 461-86. [42-3, 44]

M.K.M.B., 1942. "Indian Law—Occupancy Rights of Indians in Mexican Cession Area—What Constitutes Extinguishment of Occupancy Rights." *George Washington L.R.* 10 (April): 753-55. [121]

†Mobley, Keith, 1970. "The Klamath Indians: Federal Trusteeship, 1864-1954." Unpublished masters thesis in law, Univ. of Oregon. [81]

† Mochon, M. J., 1968. "Stockbridge-Munsee Cultural Adaptions: 'Assimilated Indians.' " *Proceedings*, APS 112: 182-219. [186]

Mohr, Wallace H., 1933. *Federal Indian Relations, 1744-1788.* (Philadelphia: Univ. of Pennsylvania Press). [46]

Monahan, Forrest D., Jr., 1967-68. "The Kiowa-Comanche Reservation in the 1890s." *CO* 45, no. 3: 451-463. [119]

Moore, C. A., 1973. "The Preservation of Unallotted Tribal Lands: Concurrent Federal and Tribal Jurisdictions." *Columbia Journal of Law and Social Problems* 9 (Winter): 279-307. [148]

†Moore, Clydene H., 1952. "The Opening of Oklahoma Indian Lands." Unpublished masters thesis in history, East Texas State College. [116]

Moorehead, Warren K., 1914. *The American Indian in the United States—Period 1850-1914.* (Andover, Mass.: The Andover Press). [Reprinted by Books for Libraries Press, Freeport, N.Y., 1969). [65]

Moquin, Wayne and Van Doren, Charles, 1973. *Great Documents in American Indian History.* (New York: Praeger). [98, 99, 218]

Morgan, Arthur E., 1971. *Dams and Other Disasters: A Century of the Army Corps of Engineers in Civil Works.* (Boston: Porter Sargent). [166-8, 170]

Morgan, Dale L., 1948. "The Administration of Indian Affairs in Utah, 1851-1858." *PHR* 17, no. 4: 383-409.

Morgan, W. T. W., 1963. "The White Highlands of Kenya." *Geographical Journal* 129, no. 2: 140-55. [209]

Moriarty, James R., 1973. "Federal Indian Reservations in San Diego County." *American Indian Culture Center Journal* 4, no. 2: 13-25.

Morris, John W. and McReynolds, E. C., 1965. *Historical Atlas of Oklahoma.* (Norman: Univ. of Oklahoma Press). [117, 219]

Morse, Jedidiah, 1822. *A Report to the Secretary of War of the United States on Indian Affairs, Comprising a Narrative of a Tour Performed in the Summer of 1820 . . . for the Purposes of Ascertaining, for the Use of the Government, the Actual State of the Indian Tribes of Our Country.* (New Haven: Converse). [51]

Moseley, G., 1967. *A Sino-Soviet Cultural Frontier: The Ili Kazakh Autonomous Chou. Harvard East Asian Monographs* 22. (Cambridge: Harvard Univ. Press). [212]

Mosk, Sanford A., 1944. *Land Tenure Problems in the Santa Fe Railroad Grant Area.* (Berkeley and Los Angeles: Univ. of California Press). [120-1, 150]

†Mosley, J. P., 1935. "Land Legislation in the Forty-first Congress, 1869-1871." Unpublished masters thesis in history, Univ. of Kansas. [Refers to Indian policy.]

MRBIP, 1952. *Appraisal of Indian Property on the Oahe Reservoir Site within the Cheyenne River Indian Reservation, S.D.* Missouri River Basin Indian Project, Report 132. (Billings, Mont.). [169]

—————, 1963. *Seneca Indians Who Will be Affected by the Kinzua Dam Reservoir.* Missouri River Basin Indian Project, Report 175. (Billings, Mont.). [163]

Muckelroy, Anna, 1922-23. "Indian Policy of the Republic of Texas." *SWHQ* 25, no. 4: 229-60; 26, no. 1: 1-29; no. 2: 128-48; no. 3: 184-206. [54]

Mundt, K. E., 1967. "Indian Autonomy and Indian Legal Problems." *Kansas L.R.* 15: 505-11.

*Munsell, Marvin R., 1967. "Land and Labor at Salt River: Household Organization in a Changing Economy." Unpublished doctoral dissertation in anthropology, Univ. of Oregon. [137, 199]

Murdock, George P., 1949. *Social Structure.* (New York: Macmillan). [179]

—————, 1953. *Ethnographic Bibliography of North America.* (New Haven: Human Relations Area Files; 3rd ed. 1960). [217]

Murray, Raymond H., 1945. "A Survey of Indian Policy in 1934 with Special Reference to the Dawes Act of 1887." Unpublished masters thesis in history, Univ. of South Dakota. [126]

†Murray, S. N., 1953. "A Study of Indian Land Relations as Illustrated through the History of the Lake Traverse Reservation." Unpublished masters thesis in history, Univ. of Wisconsin. [81]

Nagata, Shuichi, 1971. "The Reservation Community and the Urban Community: Hopi Indians of Moenkopi." In Waddell, J. O. and Watson, O. M. (eds.), *The American Indian in Urban Society.* (Boston: Little, Brown): 114-59. [76, 201]

Nammack, Georgiana C., 1969. *Fraud, Politics, and the Dispossession of the Indians: the Iroquois Land Frontier in the Colonial Period.* (Norman: Univ. of Oklahoma Press). [40-1]

Narvey, Kenneth M., 1974. "The Royal Proclamation of 7 October 1763, the Common Law and Native Rights to Land within the Territory Granted to the Hudson's Bay Company." *Saskatchewan L.R.* 38: 123-249. [43-4, 206]

Nash, Douglas, 1970. "Tribal Control of Extradition from Reservations." *NRJ* 10, no. 3: 626-34. [146, 152, 155]

—————, 1971. "Remedy for a Breach of the Government-Indian Trust Duties." *New Mexico L.R.* 1 (Jan.): 321-34. [71]

Nash, Gary, 1967. "The Quest for the Susquehanna Valley: New York, Pennsylvania, and the Seventeenth Century Fur Trade." *New York History* 48, no. 1: 3-27. [41]

Nathan, Harriet (ed.), 1972. *America's Public Lands: Politics, Economics and Administration.* (Berkeley: Univ. of California, Institute of Government Studies). [109]

†Native American Rights Fund, 1973a. *Index to Indian Claims Commission Decisions.* (Boulder, Colo: Native American Rights Fund). [107]

†—————, 1973b. *Catalogue: An Index to Indian Legal Materials and Resources.* Vol. 1, 1973-74. (Boulder, Colo: Native American Rights Fund). [218]

Neil, William M., 1956. "Territorial Governor as Indian Superintendent in the Trans-Mississippi West." *MVHR* 43 (Sept.): 213-37. [53]

Neils, Elaine M., 1971. *Reservation to City: Indian Migration and Federal Relocation. Research Paper* 131, Department of Geography. (Chicago: Univ. of Chicago Printing Dept.). [3]

Nelson, Bruce, 1946. *Land of the Dacotahs.* (Minneapolis: Univ. of Minnesota Press). [53, 76]

†Neuhoff, Dorothy A., 1922. "The Platte Purchase." Unpublished masters thesis in history, Washington Univ. (St. Louis). [53, 54]

Neuman, Robert W. and Simmons, Lanier A. (comps.), 1969. *A Bibliography Relative to Indians of the State of Louisiana. Anthropological Study* 4 (Baton Rouge: Department of Conservation, Louisiana Geological Survey). [218]

Neumann, H. R., 1953. "Implications of Federal Withdrawal from Indian Affairs in California." Unpublished masters thesis in political science. Univ. of California, Berkeley. [140]

†Newkirk, Alfred F., 1928. "Some Phases of the Descent Law Applicable to Indian Allotments in Oklahoma." Published doctoral dissertation in law. [Univ. of Illinois, Collection of Law Theses.] [137]

Newman, Nicholas C., 1970. "Jurisdiction over Indians and Indian Lands in Washington." In Johnson, R. W. (ed.): 232-84. [155]

Nichols, Rosalie, 1970. "Right-wing Rationale of Non-recognition of Indian Rights." *IH* 3, no. 2: 25-36, 65. [97]

Nielsen, Richard A., 1973. "American Indian Land Claims: Land Versus Money as a Remedy." *Univ. of Florida L.R.* 25, no. 2: 308-326. [112]

Nielson, John D., 1967. "The Geography of Selected Aspects of Cultural Change among the Navajos of the Aneth Area, Southeastern Utah." Unpublished masters thesis in geography, Univ. of Utah. [201]

Niewenhuysen, John, 1966. "Economic Development in the African Reserves of South Africa." *Land Economics* 42, no. 2: 195-202.

Nurge, Ethel (ed.), 1970. *The Modern Sioux: Social Systems and Reservation Culture.* (Lincoln: Univ. of Nebraska Press). [74, 201]

Oblasser, Bonaventure, 1936. "Papagueria, the Domain of the Papagos." *Arizona Historical Review* 7, no. 2: 3-9. [28]

O'Callaghan, Jerry A., 1951. "Extinguishing Indian Titles on the Oregon Coast." *OHQ* 52 (June): 139-44.

––––––, 1952. "Klamath Indians and the Oregon Wagon Road Grant, 1864-1938." *OHQ* 53 (March): 23-28. [120]

†O'Connor, Mary H., 1942. "Potawatomie Land Cessions in the Old Northwest." Unpublished masters thesis in history, Cornell Univ. [50]

Oliphant, Orin J., 1950. "Encroachment of Cattlemen on Indian Reservations in the Pacific Northwest, 1870-1890." *AH* 24, no. 1: 42-57. [119]

Oliver, Robert W., 1959. "Legal Status of the American Indian Tribes." *Oregon L.R.* 38: 193-245. [93, 146, 150, 151]

Oliver, S. C., 1962. *Ecology and Cultural Continuity as Contributing Factors in the Social Organization of the Plains Indians. UCPAAE* 48, no. 1. [28]

Olson, J. C., 1965. *Red Cloud and the Sioux Problem.* (Lincoln: Univ. of Nebraska Press). [52]

Olson, T. W., 1972. "Indian-State Jurisdiction over Real Estate Development on Tribal Lands." *New Mexico L.R.* 2, no. 1: 81-90. [158, 159]

O'Neil, Floyd A., 1971. "The Reluctant Suzerainty: the Uintah and Ouray." *UHQ* 39 (Spring): 129-44.

Opler, Marvin K., 1940. "The Southern Ute of Colorado." In Linton, Ralph (ed.): 119-203. [197]
————, 1971. "The Ute and Paiute Indians of the Great Basin Southern Rim." In Leacock and Lurie (eds.): 257-88. [197]
Opler, Morris E., 1971. "Jicarilla Apache Territory, Economy, and Society in 1850." *SWJA* 27, no. 4: 309-29. [30, 102, 187]
O'Reilly, M., 1970. "The Bureau of Indian Affairs and Its Discretionary Powers over Land." Typescript. (Albuquerque: Univ. of New Mexico, School of Law Library). [71]
Orfield, Gary, 1966. "A Study of the Termination Policy." (Denver: National Congress of American Indians [1966]. [Reprinted in U.S. Senate, 91st Congress, 1st session, Subcommittee on Indian Education, *The Education of American Indians: The Organization Question*, vol. 4 (Washington, D.C.: GPO): 673-816. [139-40]
————, 1973. "Menominee Restoration." In [Symposium on Indian Affairs]: 35-40. [140]
Ortiz, Alfonso (ed.), 1972. *New Perspectives on the Pueblos.* (Albuquerque: Univ. of New Mexico Press).
Osgood, Cornelius, 1936. *The Distribution of the Northern Athapaskan Indians. Publications in Anthropology* 7. (New Haven: Yale Univ. Press). [28]
Osgood, W. S., 1973. "Indian Land Retention in Colonial Metztitlán." *Hispanic American Historical Review* 53 (May): 217-38.
Oswalt, Wendell H., 1966. *This Land Was Theirs: A Study of the North American Indian.* (New York: Wiley). [2nd ed., 1973.] [26]
Otis, D. S., 1934; 1973. "History of the Allotment Policy." In *Readjustments of Indian Affairs*, Hearings before the Committee on Indian Affairs, House of Representatives, 73rd Congress, 2nd Session. (Washington, D.C.: GPO). [Reprint edited by Prucha, F. P., *The Dawes Act and the Allotment of Indian Lands.* (Norman: Univ. of Oklahoma Press).] [126-7]
†Otis, H., 1947. "History of Klamath Indian Reservation, 1864-1900." Unpublished masters thesis in history, Univ. of Oregon. [117]
O'Toole, Francis J. and Tureen, Thomas M., 1971. "State Power and the Passamaquoddy Tribe: 'A Gross National Hypocrisy.'" *Maine L.R.* 23, no. 1: 1-39. [155]
Owen, Robert (ed.), 1967. *The North American Indians: A Source Book.* (New York: Macmillan). [217]
†Padelford, Philip S., 1936. "The Ordinances of 1784 and 1787." Unpublished masters thesis in history, Univ. of Washington. [45]
Page, Gordon, 1940. "Hopi Land Pattern." *Plateau* 13, no. 2: 29-36. [83, 123, 190]
Painter, Cornelius C., 1883. *The Proposed Removal of Indians to Oklahoma.* (Philadelphia: Indian Rights Association). [125]
————, 1887. *The Dawes Land in Severalty Act and Indian Emancipation.* (Philadelphia: Indian Rights Association). [125]
————, 1888. *The Condition of Affairs in Indian Territory and California, A Report.* (Philadelphia: Indian Rights Association). [125]
Painter, L. K., 1970. "The Seneca Nation and the Kinzua Dam." *Niagara Frontier* 17 (Summer): 30-35. [168]
Park, W. Z., et al., 1938. "Tribal Distribution in the Great Basin." *AA* 40: 622-38. [24-5, 31]

Parker, Arthur C., 1924. "The Status of New York Indians." *New York State Museum Bulletin* 253: 67-82. [155]

†——————, 1925. "The White Man Takes Possession." In Doty, L. (ed.), *History of the Genessee.* (Chicago: S. J. Clarke Publ. Co.). 4 vols. V. 1: 261-284. [41]

†Parker, T. V., 1907. *The Cherokee Indians, with special reference to their relations with the United States Government.* (New York: Grafton Press).

Parman, D. L., 1971. "The Indian and the Civilian Conservation Corps." *PHR* 40, no. 1: 39-56.

Patterson, E. Palmer II, 1971. "The Colonial Parallel: A View of Indian History." *EH* 18, no. 1: 1-18. [207]

——————, 1972. *The Canadian Indian: A History since 1500.* (Don Mills, Ont.: Collier-Macmillan Ltd.). [207]

Paulson, Howard W., 1971. "The Allotment of Land in Severalty to the Dakota Indians before the Dawes Act." *South Dakota History* 1, no. 2: 132-44. [126]

Pearce, Roy H., 1953. *The Savages of America.* (Baltimore: Johns Hopkins Press). [2nd ed., *Savagism & Civilization*, 1967.] [97]

Pease, Gregory, 1969. "Constitutional Revision—Indians in the New Mexico Constitution." *NRJ* 9, no. 3: 466-70. [155]

Peckham, H. and Gibson, C. (eds.), 1969. *Attitudes of Colonial Powers Toward the American Indians.* (Salt Lake City: Univ. of Utah Press).

Pennington, Kenneth J., 1970. "Bartolomé de las Casas and the Tradition of Medieval Law." *Church History* 39 (June): 149-61. [96, 122]

Peterson, E. M., 1934. "Oregon Indians and Indian Policy, 1849-1871." Published masters thesis in history, *Univ. of Oregon thesis series*, no. 3 [1939]. [138]

†Peterson, John H., 1970. "The Mississippi Band of Choctaw Indians: Their Recent History and Current Social Relations" Unpublished doctoral dissertation in anthropology, Univ. of Georgia. [Abstract appeared in *Dissertation Abstracts*, 1971.]

Peterson, Rod, 1970. "The History, Meaning, and Effect of Termination of Federal Supervision over Indian Reservations." In Johnson, Ralph W. (ed.): 1-47.

Phillips, George H., 1973. "Indian Resistance and Cooperation in Southern California: The Garra Uprising and Its Aftermath." Doctoral dissertation in history, U.C.L.A. [In press, as *Chiefs and Challengers: Indian Resistance and Cooperation in California.*] (Berkeley and Los Angeles: Univ. of California Press). [55]

Phillips, R. G., Jr., 1972. "Indian Fishing Rights." *Willamette Law Journal* 8 (June): 248-60. [160]

Philp, K. R., 1968. "John Collier and the American Indian, 1920-1945." Doctoral dissertation in history (Lansing: Michigan State Univ.). [68]

Platt, Robert S., 1959. "Summary Memorandum on the Bad River Indian Reservation, Based on Reports of Field Study." In Platt, R. S., *Field Study in American Geography, Research Paper* 61, Dept. of Geography. (Chicago: Univ. of Chicago Printing Department): 242-51. [86]

Pomeroy, K. B. and Yoho, J. G., 1964. *North Carolina Lands: Ownership, Use and Management of Forest and Related Lands.* (Washington, D.C.: American Forestry Association). [56]

†Popoff, N., 1970. "A Study of Management Policies and Practices of the Bureau of Indian Affairs . . . on Lands Held in Federal Trust on the Quinault Indian Reservation." Unpublished masters thesis (?), Univ. of Washington.

Pounds, C. W., 1922. "Nationals without a Nation: the New York State Tribal Indians." *Columbia L.R.* 22, no. 2: 97-102. [155]

Pounds, N. W. J., 1963, 1970. *Political Geography.* (New York: McGraw-Hill), Chap. 2. [212]

Prather, G., 1943. "The Struggle for the Michigan Road." *IMH* 39, no. 1: 1-25. [120]

—————, 1944. "The Construction of the Michigan Road." *IMH* 40, no. 3: 243-279. [120]

Price, A. Grenfell, 1950. *White Settlers and Native Peoples.* (Melbourne: Georgian House; Cambridge: Cambridge Univ. Press). [208-9]

—————, 1963. *The Western Invasions of the Pacific and Its Continents: A Study of Moving Frontiers and Changing Landscapes, 1513-1958.* (London: Oxford Univ. Press). [208, 214]

Price, Monroe E., 1969. "Lawyers on the Reservation: Some Implications for the Legal Profession." *LSO* 1969, no. 2: 161-206. [21, 71, 72-3, 160]

—————, 1973. *Law and the American Indian: Readings, Notes, and Cases.* (Indianapolis: Bobbs-Merrill). [7, 51, 55, 71, 79, 96, 122, 139, 145, 154, 160, 172, 206-7, 218]

Priest, Loring B., 1942. *Uncle Sam's Stepchildren: The Reformation of United States Indian Policy, 1865-1887.* (New Brunswick: Rutgers Univ. Press). [Reprinted by Octagon, New York, 1969.] [125, 127, 200]

Pritchett, L. Bow, Jr., 1963. "Problems of State Jurisdiction over Indian Reservations." *De Paul L.R.* 13 (Autumn-Winter): 74-98. [152, 154]

Province, John, 1956. "Tenure Problems of the American Indian." In Parsons, K. H., Penn, R. J., and Raup, P. M. (eds.), *Land Tenure.* (Madison: Univ. of Wisconsin Press): 420-28. [78]

Prucha, Francis P., 1962. *American Indian Policy in the Formative Years: The Trade and Intercourse Acts, 1790-1834.* (Cambridge: Harvard Univ. Press). [46, 49]

—————, 1963. "Indian Removal and the Great American Desert." *IMH* 59 (Dec.): 299-322. [49]

—————, 1967. *Lewis Cass and American Indian Policy.* (Detroit: Wayne State Univ. Published for the Detroit Historical Society). [49, 53]

—————, 1969. "Andrew Jackson's Indian Policy: A Reassessment." *JAH* 56 (Dec.): 527-39. [39, 45]

—————, 1971. "New Approaches to the Study of the Administration of Indian Policy." *Prologue* 3 (Spring): 15-19. [12, 73, 128]

—————, 1973. *Americanizing the American Indians: Writings by the "Friends of the Indians" 1880-1900.* (Cambridge: Harvard Univ. Press). [125-6, 218]

Quail, Keith F., 1937. "Tragic Story of Pueblo Indian Land Titles." *Journal, Bar Association of Kansas* 6 (Nov.): 158-63. [122]

Raby, Stewart, 1973. "Indian Land Surrenders in Southern Saskatchewan." *Canadian Geographer* 17, no. 1: 36-52. [207]

Radloff, F. E., 1966. "Survey after Lease Issues—Federal and Indian Lands." *RMMLI* 11: 473-501. [71-2]

Rae, J. B., 1952. "The Great Northern's Land Grant." *JEH* 12 (Spring): 140-45. [120]

Rainey, George, 1933. *The Cherokee Strip.* (Guthrie, Oklahoma: Co-operative Publishing Co.). [117]

Rand, James H., 1913. *The Indians of North Carolina and Their Relations with the Settlers. James Sprunt Historical Publications* 12, no. 2. (Chapel Hill: North Carolina Historical Society). [43]

Ranquist, Harold A., 1971. "Effects of Changes in Place and Nature of Use of Indian Rights to Water Reserved under the 'Winters Doctrine.'" *NRL* 5, no. 1: 34-41. [164]

Ransom, R. E. and Gilstrap, W. G., 1971. "Indians–Civil Jurisdiction in New Mexico–State, Federal and Tribal Courts." *New Mexico L.R.* 1 (Jan.): 196-214. [155]

Ratcliff, James L., 1973. "What Happened to the Kalapuya? A Study of the Depletion of Their Economic Base." *IH* 6, no. 3: 27-33. [55]

Ray, Dorothy J., 1967. "Land Tenure and Polity of the Bering Strait Eskimos." *JW* 6, no. 3: 371-94.

Ray, Verne F., 1936. "Native Villages and Groupings of the Columbia Basin." *PNWQ* 27, no. 2: 99-152. [29]

-----, 1955a. "Anthropology and Indian Claims Litigation: Papers presented at a Symposium Held at Detroit in December, 1954." *EH* 2, no. 4: 287-291. [100]

-----, 1955b. [Review of] *Indian Tribes of North America* by H. E. Driver, et al. (1953). *AA* 57: 145-46. [104]

-----, et al., 1938. "Tribal Distributions in Eastern Oregon and Adjacent Regions." *AA* 40, no. 3: 384-415. [24, 31]

Raymer, Patricia, 1974. "Wisconsin's Menominees: Indians on a Seesaw." *National Geographic Magazine* 146, no. 2: 228-251.

Rayner, W. M., 1962. *The Tribe and Its Successors: An Account of African Traditional Life and European Settlement in Southern Rhodesia.* (New York: Faber and Praeger). [208]

Reeve, Frank D., 1937-38. "Federal Indian Policy in New Mexico, 1858-1880." *NMHR* 12, no. 3: 218-69; 13, no. 1: 14-62; no. 2: 146-91; no. 3: 261-313. [54]

-----, 1946. "A Navajo Struggle for Land." *NMHR* 21, no. 1: 1-21. [54]

-----, 1946-47. "The Apache Indians in Texas." *Texas State Historical Association Quarterly* 50: 189-219. [54]

-----, 1956. "Early Navajo Geography." *NMHR* 31: 290-309. [28]

Reifel, Ben, 1950. "Problem of Relocating Families on the Fort Berthold Indian Reservation." *JFE* 32 (Nov.): 644-46. [168]

†-----, 1952. "Relocation on the Fort Berthold Indian Reservation: Problems and Programs. Doctoral dissertation (?), Harvard Univ. [168]

Relander, Click, 1962. *Strangers on the Land: A Historiette of a Longer Story of the Yakima Indian Nation's Effort to Survive Against Great Odds.* (Yakima: Franklin Press).

Reynolds, O. M., Jr., 1974. "Zoning the Reservation–Village of Euclid Meets Agua Caliente." *American Indian L.R.* II, 2 (Winter): 1-16. [158]

Reynolds, Terry R., Lamphere, L., and Cook, C. E., Jr., 1967. "Time, Resources and Authority in a Navajo Community." *AA* 69, no. 2: 188-99. [189, 198]

Rhodes, Benjamin F., 1920. "The Opening of the Cherokee Outlet." Unpublished masters thesis in history, Univ. of Oklahoma. [116]

Ribeiro, Darcy, 1962. "The Social Integration of Indigenous Populations in Brazil." *International Labor Review* 85 (April): 325-46.

-----, 1971. *The Americans and Civilization.* Tr. from Portuguese by L. L. Barrett and M. McD. Barrett. (New York: E. P. Dutton).

†Richards, Arthur L., 1922. "The Distribution of the Lands of the Five Civilized Tribes." Unpublished masters thesis in history, Univ. of Chicago. [53]

Richardson, Rupert N., 1933. *The Comanche Barrier to Southern Plains Settlement: A Century and a Half of Savage Resistance to the Advancing White Frontier.* (Glendale: A. H. Clark). [54]

Riddell, Francis A. (comp.), 1962. "General Bibliography of the Indians of California." *Ethnographic Report* 1. (Sacramento: Resources Agency, Department of Parks and Recreation). [218]

Rietz, Robert W., 1953. "Leadership, Initiative, and Economic Progress of an American Indian Reservation." *Economic Development and Cultural Change* 2, no. 1: 60-70. [81, 82, 190]

Riley, C. L., 1968. "The Makah Indians: A Study of Political and Economic Organization." *EH* 15, no. 1: 57-95. [25]

Riley, F. L., 1904. "Choctaw Land Claims." *Publications Mississippi Historical Society* 8, no. 21: 345-95.

Ringwald, George, n.d., "The Agua Caliente Indians and Their Guardians." [Reprint of selections from Pulitzer Prize-Winning Entry for Meritorious Service (Riverside: Press-Enterprise, n.d.).] [134]

Rister, Carl C., 1936. "A Federal Experiment in Southern Plains Indian Relations, 1835-1845." *CO* 14: 434-55. [49, 54]

Robbins, Roy M., 1942. *Our Landed Heritage: The Public Domain, 1776-1936.* (Princeton: Princeton Univ. Press). [Reprinted, Lincoln: Univ. of Nebraska Press, 1962). [10, 45]

Robbins, William G., 1974. "Extinguishing Indian Land Title in Western Oregon." *IH* 7, no. 2: 10-14. [55]

Roberts, William O., 1943. "Successful Agriculture within the Reservation Framework." *Applied Anthropology* 2, no. 3: 37-44. [81-2]

Rockwell, Wilson, 1956. *The Utes: A Forgotten People.* (Denver: Sage Books). [108]

Roder, Wolf, 1964. "The Division of Land Resources in Southern Rhodesia." *AAAG* 54, no. 1: 41-58. [209]

Rohrbough, M. J., 1968. *The Land Office Business: The Settlement and Administration of American Public Lands, 1789-1837.* (New York: Oxford Univ. Press). [45]

Rosenfelt, Daniel M., 1973. "Indian Schools and Community Control." *Stanford L.R.* 25, no. 4: 492-550. [158]

Ross, Norman A. (ed.), 1973a. *Index to the Decisions of the Indian Claims Commission.* (New York: Clearwater Publishing Co.). [107]

───── (ed.), 1973b. *Index to the Expert Testimony Before the Indian Claims Commission: The Written Reports.* (New York: Clearwater Publishing Co.). [107]

Rountree, H. C., 1972. "Powhatan's Descendants in the Modern World: Community Studies of Two Virginia Reservations, with notes on five non-reservation enclaves." *The Chesopieans*, 10, no. 3 (June): 62-97. [41]

─────, 1973. "Indian Land Loss in Virginia: A Prototype of United States Federal Indian Policy." Doctoral dissertation in anthropology, Univ. of Wisconsin, Milwaukee. [41]

Royce, Charles C. (comp.), 1899. *Indian Land Cessions in the United States. 18th Annual Report, 1896-97. pt. 2, BAE* (Washington, D.C.:GPO): 521-997. [Reprinted by AMS Press, New York, 1971.] [44, 45, 52, 219]

Ruby, R. H. and Brown, J. A., 1970. *The Spokane Indians: Children of the Sun.* (Norman: Univ. of Oklahoma Press). [103, 108, 129]

Rushmore, Elsie M., 1914. *The Indian Policy During Grant's Administration.* Published doctoral dissertation in political science. (Jamaica, N.Y.: Marion Press). [118]

Ruttenber, E. M., 1971. *History of the Indian Tribes at Hudson's River.* [Reprint of the original 1872 ed., as Empire State Historical Publications Series 95 (New York: Kennikat Press).]

Sabatini, Joseph D. (comp.), 1973. *American Indian Law: A Bibliography of Books, Law Review Articles and Indian Periodicals.* (Albuquerque: American Indian Law Center, School of Law, Univ. of New Mexico). [145, 218]

Sabbagh, Michael E., 1968. "Some Geographical Characteristics of a Plural Society: Apartheid in South Africa." *GR* 58, no. 1: 1-28. [210]

Sady, Rachel R., 1947. "The Menominee: Transition from Trusteeship." *Applied Anthropology* 6, no. 2: 1-14. [139]

Sanchez, Jamie, 1972. "The Nisqually Indian Reservation." *IH* 5, no. 1: 31-36. [161]

Sanders, D. E., 1974. "Native People in Areas of Internal National Expansion." *Saskatchewan L.R.* 38: 63-87. [209]

Sasaki, Tom T., 1960. *Fruitland, New Mexico: A Navaho Community in Transition.* (Ithaca: Cornell Univ. Press). [130, 199-200].

†Satz, R. W., 1974. *American Indian Policy in the Jacksonian Era.* (Lincoln: Univ. of Nebraska Press).

†Savage, W. W., Jr., 1972. "The Cherokee Strip Livestock Assn: The Impact of Federal Regulation on the Caatleman's Last Frontier." Unpublished doctoral dissertation in history, Univ. of Oklahoma. [119]

Scaife, H. L., 1896. *History and Conditions of the Catawba Indians of South Carolina.* (Philadelphia: Indian Rights Association). [118, 125]

Schaab, William C., 1968. "Indian Industrial Development and the Courts." *NRJ* 8 (April): 303-330. [148, 159]

Schenck, W. E., 1926. *Historical Aboriginal Groups of the California Delta Region. UCPAAE* 23, no. 2: 123-146. [29]

Schermerhorn, R. A., 1970. *Comparative Ethnic Relations: A Framework for Theory and Research.* (New York: Random House).

Schifter, R., 1954. "Indian Title to Land." *American Indian* 7, no. 1: 37-47. [97]

–––––, 1970. "Trends in Federal Indian Administration." *South Dakota L.R.* 15 (Winter): 1-21. [71]

Schlesinger, R. A., 1967. *The California Indian Lease.* California Practice Book 35. (Berkeley and Los Angeles: Univ. of California Press). [72]

Schmeckebier, Lawrence F., 1927. *Office of Indian Affairs; History, Activities and Organization. Service Monograph* 48. (Baltimore: Brookings Institution for Government Research). [Reprinted by AMS Press, New York, 1972.] [51, 68, 72]

Schoolcraft, Henry R., 1853. *Information Respecting the History, Condition, and Prospects of the Indian Tribes of the United States.* (Philadelphia: Lippincott), 6 vols. [Reprinted by AMS Press, New York, 1969. See also, Nichols, F. S. (comp.), *Index to Schoolcraft's "Indian Tribes of the United States." BAE Bulletin* 152. (Washington, D.C.: GPO, 1954).] [51]

Schusky, Ernest, 1959. *Politics and Planning in a Dakota Indian Community.* (Vermillion: Institute of Indian Studies, Univ. of South Dakota). [70, 140, 169, 201]

–––––, 1970. "Culture Change and Continuity in the Lower Brule Community." In Nurge, E. (ed.): 107-122.

†Schwarz, Henry G., 1963. "Policies and Administration of Minority Areas in Northwest China and Inner Mongolia, 1949-59." Unpublished doctoral dissertation in political science, Univ. of Wisconsin.

Selander, K. J., 1947. "Section 2 of the Indian Claims Commission Act." *George Washington L.R.* 15 (June): 388-425. [93-4]

Sells, C., 1917. "Land Tenure and the Organization of Agriculture on Indian Reservations in the United States." *International Review of Agricultural Economics* 77, no. 1: 63-76. [77]

Semple, W. F., 1952. *Oklahoma Indian Land Titles, Annotated.* (St. Louis, Thomas Law Book Co.). [70]

Service, Elman R., 1947. "Recent Observations on Havasupai Land Tenure." *SWJA* 3, no. 4: 360-66. [84]

————, 1955. "Indian-European Relations in Colonial Latin America." *AA* 57 (June): 411-25. [206]

Seymour, C. F., 1906. "Relations between the United States Government and the Mission Indians of Southern California." Unpublished masters thesis in history, Univ. of California, Berkeley. [117]

Seymour, F. W., 1924. "Land Titles in the Pueblo Indian Country." *American Bar Association Journal* 10 (Jan.): 36-41. [122]

Shames, D. (ed.), 1972. *Freedom with Reservation: The Menominee Struggle to Save Their Land and People.* (Madison, Wisconsin Indian Legal Services for National Committee to Save the Menominee People and Forests).

Shane, Ralph M., 1959. "A Short History of the Fort Berthold Reservation." *North Dakota History* 26, no. 4: 181-214. [81, 169]

Sharp, P. F., 1955. "Three Frontiers: Some Comparative Studies of Canadian, American and Australian Settlement." *PHR* 24 (Nov.): 369-77. [207]

Sharum, A. E., 1947. "Ad-Valorem Taxation of Land Affecting the Five Civilized Tribes." *Journal of the Oklahoma Bar Association* 18: 94-111. [157]

Sheehan, Bernard, 1969. "Indian-White Relations in Early America: A Review Essay." *William and Mary Quarterly* 26: 267-286. [40, 97]

Sheldon, Addison E., 1936. *Land Systems and Land Policies in Nebraska: A History of Nebraska Land, Public Domain and Private Property. Publications of the Nebraska State Historical Society* 22 (Lincoln). [45]

Shepard, Ward, 1935. "Land and Self Government for Indians: The Wheeler-Howard Bill." *National Conference of Social Work* 1935: 539-47. [128]

————, 1943. "Land Problems in an Expanding Indian Population." In LaFarge, O. (ed.): 72-83. [128]

Shepardson, Mary, 1963. *Navajo Ways in Government. AAA Memoir*, 96 [*AA* 65, no. 3, pt. 2]. [155]

———— and Hammond, B., 1966. "Navajo Inheritance Patterns: Random or Regular?" *ET* 5, no. 1: 87-96. [137]

Sherman, Merle, 1962. "A Geographic Study of the Red Lake Chippewa Indian Band of Minnesota." *Proceedings Minnesota Academy of Sciences*, 30: 60-66. [81, 82, 190]

†Sherman, Paschal, 1920. "Our Indian Land Law." Unpublished doctoral dissertation (?), Catholic University of America.

Shimkin, Dimitri B., 1940. "Shoshone-Comanche Origins and Migrations." *Proceedings, 6th Pacific Scientific Congress*, vol. 4. (Berkeley and Los Angeles: Univ. of California Press): 17-26.

———, 1970. "Socio-Cultural Persistence among Shoshoneans of the Carson River Basin (Nevada)." In Swanson, E. H., Jr., (ed.), *Languages and Cultures of Western North America: Essays in Honor of Sven S. Liljeblad.* (Pocatello: Idaho State University Press): 172-200. [199]

Siegel, Bernard J., 1967. "Suggested Factors of Culture Change at Taos Pueblo." In Tax, S. (ed.), *Acculturation in the Americas, Proceedings & Selected Papers, 29th International Congress of Americanists.* (New York: Cooper Square Publ.): 133-40. [190-1]

Silver, J. W., 1944. "Land Speculation Profits in the Chickasaw Cession." *Journal of Southern History*, 10 (Feb.): 84-92. [48]

Simoons, Frederick J., 1953. "Changes in Indian Life in the Clear Lake Area Along the Northern Fringe of Mexican Influence in Early California." *AmI* 13: 103-06.

Simpson, George E. and Yinger, J. Milton (eds.), 1957. "American Indians and American Life." *AAAPSS* 311 (May): 1-204. [69]

Simpson, J. R., 1970. "Uses of Cultural Anthropology in Economic Analysis: a Papago Indian Case." *HO* 29 (Fall): 162-8. [191]

Singh, Ram Raj Prasad, 1966. *Aboriginal Economic System of the Olympic Peninsula Indians, Western Washington. Sacramento Anthropological Society Paper,* 4. [25]

†Smead, W. H., 1905. *Land of the Flatheads, A Sketch of the Flathead Reservation, Montana: Its Past and Present, Its Hopes and Possibilities for the Future.* (St. Paul, Minn: Pioneer Press).

†Smith, Dwight L., 1949. "Indian Land Cessions in the Old Northwest, 1795-1809. Unpublished doctoral dissertation in history, Indian Univ.

———, 1956-57. "Indian Land Cessions in Northern Ohio and Southeastern Michigan." *Northwest Ohio Quarterly* 29: 27-55. [50]

——— (ed.), 1974. *Indians of the United States and Canada: A Bibliography.* Introduction by J. C. Ewers (Santa Barbara: ABC-Clio). [218]

Smith, Michael T., 1970. "The History of Indian Citizenship." *Great Plains Journal* 10, no. 1: 25-35.

———, 1973. "The Constitutional Status of American Indians. In [Symposium on Indian Affairs]: 10-15. [150]

Smith, W. and Roberts, J. M., 1954. *Zuni Law: A Field of Values. Reports of the Rimrock Project Values Series 4, Papers, PMAAE* (Harvard) 43, no. 1. [24, 25]

Snodgrass, Marjorie P. (comp.), 1968. *Economic Development of American Indians and Eskimos, 1930 through 1967, a Bibliography.* Bibliographical Serial 10. (Washington, D.C.: Bureau of Indian Affairs.) [69, 87, 135, 217]

Snow, Alpheus H., 1921. *The Question of Aborigines in the Law and Practice of Nations.* (New York: Putnam's Sons). [96-7, 206-7]

Snyderman, G. S., 1951. "Concepts of Land Ownership Among the Iroquois and Their Neighbors." In Fenton, William (ed.), *Symposium on Local Diversity in Iroquois Culture, BAE Bulletin* 149. (Washington, D.C.: Smithsonian Institution): 15-34. [25]

Socolofsky, Homer and Self, Huber, 1972. *Historical Atlas of Kansas.* (Norman: Univ. of Oklahoma Press). [219]

Solberg, C. E., 1969. "A Discriminatory Frontier Land Policy: Chile, 1870-1914." *Americas* 26, no. 2: 115-33. [208]

Sondheim, Harry B. and Alexander, John R., 1960. "Federal Indian Water Rights: A Retrogression to Quasi-Riparianism." *Southern California L.R.* 34, no. 1: 1-61. [21, 163, 164]

Sonosky, Marvin J., 1960. "Oil, Gas, and Other Minerals on Indian Reservations."
    FBJ 20: 230-34. [71]
Sorenson, Randolph J., 1971. "Indian-American Land Tenure Conflict: A Case Study
    of the Shoshone-Bannock Fort Hall Indian Reservation, Fort Hall, Idaho."
    Unpublished masters thesis in geography, Univ. of Washington. [81, 197-8]
Sorkin, Alan L., 1971. *American Indians and Federal Aid.* (Washington, D.C.:
    Brookings Institution). [79]
—————, 1973. "Business and Industrial Development on American Indian Reser-
    vations." *Annals of Regional Science* 7, no. 2: 115-129. [62, 77]
Sparks, J. P., 1968. "The Indian Stronghold and the Spread of Urban America."
    Arizona L.R. 10, no. 3 (Winter): 706-24. [158]
Speck, Frank G., 1914-15. "Basis of American Indian Ownership of the Land." Univ.
    of Pennsylvania, *University Lectures* 2: 181-96. [193]
—————, 1915. *Family Hunting Territories and Social Life of Various Algonkian
    Bands of the Ottawa Valley. Memoir* 70. (Ottawa, Can., Geological Sur-
    vey). [193]
—————, 1926. "Land Ownership Among Hunting Peoples in Primitive America and
    the World's Marginal Areas." *22nd International Congress of Americanists*, vol. 2:
    323-332.
—————, 1928a. "Chapters on the Ethnology of the Powhatan Tribes of Virginia."
    INM 1, no. 5.
—————, 1928b. *Territorial Subdivisions and Boundaries of the Wampanoag, Massa-
    chusetts, and Nauset Indians. INM* misc. no. 44.
—————, 1940. *Penobscot Man: The Life History of a Forest Tribe in Maine.*
    (Philadelphia: Univ. of Pennsylvania). [Reprinted by Octagon Books, New York,
    1970.]
————— and Eiseley, Loren C., 1939. "Significance of Hunting Territory Systems of
    the Algonkian in Social Theory." *AA* 41: 269-80. [24, 27, 193, 195]
Spicer, Edward H., 1959. "European Expansion and the Enclavement of South-
    western Indians." *ArW* 1: 132-45. [54]
————— (ed.), 1961. *Perspectives on Indian Culture Change.* (Chicago: Univ. of
    Chicago Press). [178, 180, 181, 214]
—————, 1962. *Cycles of Conquest: The Impact of Spain, Mexico and the United
    States on the Indians of the Southwest, 1533-1960.* (Tucson: Univ. of Arizona
    Press). [54, 180, 208]
—————, 1969a. "Política Gubernamental e Integración Indigenista en México y
    Estatos Unidos." *Anuario Indigenista* 29 (Dic.): 29-48. [210]
—————, 1969b. *A Short History of the Indians of the United States.* (New York: D.
    Van Nostrand). [178, 182]
Spier, Leslie, 1923. *Southern Diegueno Customs. UCPAAE* 20: 297-358. [25]
—————, 1928. *Havasupai Ethnography. Anthropological Papers, AMNH* 29:
    81-392. [24, 25, 29]
—————, 1930. *Klamath Ethnography. UCPAAE* 25: 1-338. [24, 29]
—————, 1936. *Tribal Distribution in Washington. General Series in Anthropology* 3.
    (Menasha, Wisc.: G. Banta). [29]
Spitz, Allan, 1967. "Transplantation of American Democratic Institutions: The Case
    of Hawaii." *Political Science Quarterly* 82 (Sept.): 386-98. [209]
*Stafford, John W., 1971. "Crow Cultural Change: A Geographical Analysis." Unpub-
    lished doctoral dissertation in geography, Michigan State Univ. [182]

†Stanley, George, 1950. "The First Indian 'Reserves' in Canada." *Revue d'Histoire del'Amerique Francaise* 4, no. 2: 178-210.

Stanley, Ray, 1954. "Political Geography of the Yuma Border District." Unpublished doctoral dissertation in geography, U.C.L.A.; ch. 2, "Aboriginal Occupance and Tribal Patterns of the Upper Delta Region." [108]

Steiner, Rodney, 1966. "Reserved Land and the Supply of Space for the Southern California Metropolis." *GR* 56, no. 3: 344-62. [77, 134, 158]

Stephens, C. H., 1961. "The Origin and History of the Hopi-Navajo Boundary Dispute in Northern Arizona." Unpublished masters thesis in history, Brigham Young Univ. [123]

Stern, Theodore, 1952. "Chickahominy: The Changing Culture of a Virginia Indian Community." *Proceedings APS* 96, no. 2: 219-23.

————, 1956. "The Klamath Indians and the Treaty of 1864." *OHQ* 57, no. 3: 229-273. [55]

————, 1961-62. "Livelihood and Tribal Government on the Klamath Indian Reservation." *HO* 20, no. 4: 172-80. [81, 82, 190]

————, 1965. *The Klamath Tribe: A People and Their Reservation. AES Monograph* 41 (Seattle). [55, 73, 129, 139]

———— and Boggs, James P., 1971. "White and Indian Farmers of the Umatilla Indian Reservation." In Walker, D. E., Jr. (ed.): 37-76. [87, 131, 185, 198, 200]

Steward, Julian H., 1933. *Ethnography of Owens Valley Paiute. UCPAAE* 33, no. 3. [29]

————, 1936. "The Economic and Social Basis of Primitive Bands." In Lowie, R. H. (ed.), *Essays in Anthropology presented to A. L. Kroeber.* (Berkeley and Los Angeles: Univ. of California Press): 331-350. [195]

————, 1937. "Linguistic Distributions and Political Groups of the Great Basin Shoshoneans." *AA* 39: 625-34. [31]

————, 1938. *Basin-Plateau Aboriginal Socio-Political Groups, BAE Bulletin* 120. (Washington, D.C.: Smithsonian Institution). [31]

————, 1939. "Some Observations of Shoshonean Distributions." *AA* 41: 261-65. [29]

————, 1955a. *Theory of Culture Change: The Methodology of Multilinear Evolution.* (Urbana: Univ. of Illinois). [31, 178, 194]

————, 1955b. "Theory and Application in a Social Science." *EH* 2 (Fall): 292-302. [99-100, 181]

————, 1970. "The Foundations of Basin-Plateau Shoshonean Society." In Swanson, E. H., Jr. (ed.), *Languages and Cultures of Western North America: Essays in Honor of Sven S. Liljeblad.* (Pocatello: Idaho State Univ.): 113-51.

————, 1974. *Aboriginal and Historical Groups of the Ute Indians of Utah: An Analysis with Supplement.* (New York and London: Garland Publishing Co.).

Stewart, D. A., 1933. "The Government and the Development of Oklahoma Territory." Unpublished doctoral dissertation in history. Univ. of Oklahoma. [116-17]

Stewart, F. H., 1932, 1972. *Indians of Southern New Jersey.* (Port Washington, N.Y.). [Reprinted by Kennikat Press, N.Y. as *Middle Atlantic States Historical Publication* 8.] [40]

Stewart, Kenneth M., 1969. "The Aboriginal Territory of the Mohave Indians." *EH* 16, no. 3: 257-75. [28, 101]

Stewart, Omer C., 1943. *Notes on Pomo Ethnography. UCPAAE* 40, no. 2: 29-62. [28, 29, 94]

–––––, 1958. "The First American and His Land." *The Delphian Quarterly* 41: 23-28, 38. [106]

–––––, 1959. "Chippewa Indian Claims." *The Delphian Quarterly* 42, no. 4: 35-40.

–––––, 1961. "Kroeber and the Indian Claims Commission Cases." *Kroeber Anthropological Society Papers* 25: 181-90. [21, 100, 101, 106, 108, 109]

–––––, 1966a. "Tribal Distributions and Boundaries in the Great Basin." In d'Azevedo, W. L., et al. (eds.), *The Current Status of Anthropological Research in the Great Basin: 1964.* (Reno: Desert Research Institute): 167-237. [101, 103, 219]

–––––, 1966b. "Ute Indians: Before and After White Contact." *UHQ* 34: 38-61.

–––––, 1967. "Southern Ute Adjustment to Modern Living." In Tax, S. (ed.), *Acculturation in the Americas, Proceedings & Selected Papers, 29th International Congress of Americanists.* (New York: Cooper Square Publ.): 80-87. [198]

–––––, 1970. "The Question of Bannock Territory." In Swanson, E. H., Jr. (ed.), *Languages and Cultures of Western North America: Essays in Honor of Sven S. Liljeblad.* (Pocatello: Idaho State Univ. Press): 201-231. [101-103]

–––––, 1971. *Ethnohistorical Bibliography of the Ute Indians of Colorado. Univ. of Colorado Series in Anthropology* 18). [218]

–––––, in press. "Recent Litigation and Its Effects." [California Indian Land Claims] in Heizer, R. F. (ed.), *California,* vol. 3, *Handbook of North American Indians.* (Washington, D.C.: Smithsonian Institution). [109]

Stewart, William J., 1964. "Settler, Politician, and Speculator in the Sale of the Sioux Reserve." *Minnesota History* 39, no. 3: 85-92. [50]

†Stormfels, Mabel C., 1934. "Land Policy in Congress, 1867-1869." Unpublished masters thesis in history, Univ. of Kansas.

Strieby, M. E., 1895. "Scotch-Highlanders and American Indians: the Process of Civilizing Them Compared." *27th Annual Report,* Board of Indian Commissioners, 58-63.

Strong, William D., 1929. *Aboriginal Society in Southern California. UCPAAE* 26, no. 1. [Reprinted by Malki Museum Press, Banning, California, 1972.] [25, 27, 29]

Stucki, Larry R., 1971. "The Case against Population Control: the Probable Creation of the First American Indian State." *HO* 30, no. 4: 393-398. [152, 154]

Sturtevant, William C. (comp.), 1958. *Selected Bibliography of Maps Relating to the American Indian. BAE.* (Washington, D.C.: Smithsonian Institution). [219]

–––––, 1966. "Anthropology, History, and Ethnohistory." *EH* 13, no. 1-2: 1-51. [12]

–––––, 1967. "Early Indian Tribes, Culture Areas, and Linguistic Stocks." [Map], in *The National Atlas of the United States of America.* (Washington, D.C.: Geological Survey, 1970). [32]

Summers, George A., 1937. "The Leased District Claims of the Choctaw-Chickasaw Nation." Unpublished masters thesis in history, Oklahoma A. & M. (State Univ.). [92, 117]

Suttles, W., 1960. "Affinal Ties, Subsistence, and Prestige Among the Coast Salish." *AA* 62: 296-305. [27]

–––––, 1963. "The Persistance of Intervillage Ties Among the Coast Salish." *ET* 2: 512-25. [Reprinted in Walker, D. E., Jr. (ed.): 665-77.] [27, 76]

—————, 1968. "Coping with Abundance: Subsistence on the Northwest Coast." In Lee, R. B. and DeVore, I. (eds.), *Man the Hunter*: 55-68. (Chicago: Aldine). [27]

Sutton, Imre, 1964. "Land Tenure and Changing Occupance on Indian Reservations in Southern California." Unpublished doctoral dissertation in geography, U.C.L.A. [21, 29, 55, 73, 76-7, 84, 86, 109, 117, 121, 130, 149, 170, 190, 201]

—————, 1965. "The Administration of Indigenous Peoples: The Experience with the Reserve in English-Speaking Countries." Social Science Colloquium Paper, California State University, Fullerton. [213]

—————, 1967. "Private Property in Land Among Reservation Indians in Southern California." *Yearbook, APCG* 29: 69-89. [21, 73, 77, 84, 132, 134, 158, 198, 200]

—————, 1968. "Geographical Aspects of Construction Planning: Hoover Dam Revisited." *JW* 7, no. 3: 301-344. [168]

—————, 1970a. "Dams and the Environment." *GR* 60, no. 1: 128-29.

—————, 1970b. "Land Tenure in the West: Continuity and Change." *JW* 9, no. 1: 1-23. [10, 64, 131]

Swanton, John R., 1922. *Early History of the Creek Indians and Their Neighbors. BAE Bulletin* 73. (Washington, D.C.: Smithsonian Institution). [28, 30, 219]

—————, 1946. "Indians of the Southeastern United States." *BAE Bulletin* 137. (Washington: Smithsonian Institution).

—————, 1952 [1953]. *The Indian Tribes of North America. BAE Bulletin* 145. (Washington, D.C.: Smithsonian Institution). [32]

Sweeney, Marian H., 1924. "Indian Land Policy since 1887 with Special Reference to South Dakota." Unpublished masters thesis in history, Univ. of South Dakota. [132]

Swierenga, Robert P., 1966. "Land Speculator 'Profits' Reconsidered: Central Iowa as a Test Case." *JEH* 26, (March): 1-28. [45, 52, 106]

—————, 1968. *Pioneers and Profits: Land Speculation on the Iowa Frontier.* (Ames: Iowa State Univ. Press). [10, 45]

"Symposium on the Concept of Ethnohistory," 1961. *EH* 8, no. 1: 12-92. [12]

[Symposium on Indian Affairs], 1973. *Civil Rights Digest* 6, no. 1: 3-56.

Takakura Shinichiro, 1960. *The Ainu of Northern Japan: A Study in Conquest and Acculturation.* Tr. by J. A. Harrison, *Transactions, APS* n.s. 50, pt. 4. [212]

†Tamarin, A., 1974. *We Have Not Vanished; Eastern Indians of the United States.* (Chicago: Follett Publishing Co.). [174, 201]

Tax, Sol (ed.), 1967. *Acculturation in the Americas, Proceedings and Selected Papers, 29th International Congress of Americanists.* (New York: Cooper Square Publ).

Taylor, B. J., 1970. "The Reservation Indian and Mainstream Economic Life." *Arizona Business Bulletin* 17, no. 10 (Dec.): 12-22. [78]

Taylor, Theodore W., 1972. *The States and Their Indian Citizens.* (Washington, D.C.: GPO). [172]

Teit, James A., 1928. *The Middle Columbia Salish. Publ. in Anthropology* 2, no. 4, Univ. of Washington. [31]

Thayer, J. B., 1888. "The Dawes Bill and the Indian." *Atlantic Monthly* 61 (March): 315-22. [126]

Thiesenhusen, W. C. and Brown, M. R., 1964. "Chile Distributes Land to its Southern Indians." *Land Tenure Center Newsletter* 17 (May-June): 15-21. [209]

Thomas, David H., 1973. "Empirical Test for Steward's Model of Great Basin Settlement Patterns." *American Antiquity* 38 (April): 155-76. [34(footnote)]

Thomas, Robert K., 1966a. "Colonialism: Classic and Internal." *New University Thought* 4, no. 4: 37-44. [4, 75]

—————, 1966b. "Powerless Politics." *New University Thought* 4, no. 4: 44-53. [4, 75]

Thompson, Gregory C., 1972. *Southern Ute Lands, 1848-1899; the Creation of a Reservation. Occasional Papers of the Center of Southwest Studies* 1. (Durango: Fort Lewis College).

Thompson, Laura, 1950. *Culture in Crisis: A Study of the Hopi Indians.* (New York: Harper and Bros.).

Thwaites, R. G., 1900. *Some Wisconsin Indian Conveyances, 1793-1836. Collections,* Wisconsin State Historical Society 15. [51]

Tibbles, Thomas H., 1958. *Buckskin and Blanket Days: Memoirs of a Friend of the Indians.* (London: Oldbourne). [Written in 1905.] [131]

Torrans, Thomas, 1960. "General Works on the American Indian, a Descriptive Bibliography." *ArW* 2: 79-103. [218]

†Townsend, Charles V., 1939. "The Opening of the Cheyenne and Arapahoe Country." Unpublished masters thesis in history, Oklahoma A. & M. (State University). [53]

Travis, Joan D., 1968. "Agrarian Problems and Prospects of the Colorado River Indian Reservation." Unpublished masters thesis in geography, U.C.L.A. [21, 88, 125]

Treat, Payson J., 1910. *The National Land System, 1785-1820.* (New Hampshire: E. B. Treat and Co.). [Reprinted by Russell and Russell, New York, 1967.] [45]

Trelease, Allen W., 1960. *Indian Affairs in Colonial New York: the Seventeenth Century.* (Ithaca: Cornell Univ. Press). [40, 172]

Trenholm, Virginia C. and Carley, Maurine, 1964. *The Shoshonis: Sentinels of the Rockies.* (Norman: Univ. of Oklahoma Press). [128]

*Trennert, Robert A., 1969. "The Far Western Indian Frontier and the Beginnings of the Reservation System, 1846-1851." Unpublished doctoral dissertation in history, Univ. of California, Santa Barbara. [54, 57]

Trimble, W. J., 1912-13. "The Indian Policy of the Colony of British Columbia in Comparison with That of the Adjacent American Territories." *Proceedings Mississippi Valley Historical Association* 1: 276-86. [208]

Troiel, Marie Y., 1924. "Certain Phases of the Land Problem in New Mexico and Arizona." Unpublished masters thesis in history, Univ. of California, Berkeley. [122]

Tuck, James A., 1971a. "The Iroquois Confederacy." *Scientific American* 224, no. 2: 32-42.

—————, 1971b. *Onondaga Iroquois Prehistory: A Study in Settlement Archeology.* (Syracuse: Syracuse Univ. Press). [30]

Turner, Frederick Jackson, 1921. *The Frontier in American History.* (New York) [208]

Turner, Orsamus, 1852. *History of the Pioneer Settlement of the Phelps and Gorham's Purchase.* (Rochester, N.Y.: W. Alling). [41]

Tuttle, R. L., 1971. "Economic Development of Indian Lands." *Univ. of Richmond L.R.* 5 (Spring): 319-29. [79]

Tyler, S. Lyman, 1964a. *Indian Affairs, A Study of the Changes in Policy of the United States toward Indians.* Publication of the Institute of American Indian Studies. (Provo: Brigham Young Univ.). [69]

—————, 1964b. *A Work Paper on Termination: with an Attempt to Show Its Antecedents. Indian Affairs,* [2], Institute of American Indian Studies. (Provo: Brigham Young Univ.). [138]

—————, 1973. *A History of Indian Policy.* (Washington, D.C.: Bureau of Indian Affairs). [79, 80, 126, 138]

†Uhler, S. P., 1950. "Pennsylvania's Indian Relations to 1754." Doctoral dissertation in history, Temple Univ. [Published doctoral dissertation, Allentown, Pa., 1951.] [43]

Underhill, Ruth M., 1953. *Red Man's America: A History of Indians in the United States.* (Chicago: Univ. of Chicago Press)., [26]

United Nations, 1950. *Definition and Classification of Minorities.* (New York: Commission on Human Rights). [213]

U.S. Congress, House, 1953. *Report with Respect to the House Resolution . . . to Conduct an Investigation of the Bureau of Indian Affairs. H.R. 2503.* (Washington, D.C.: GPO). [21, 32, 217]

—————, 1960. *Indian Heirship Land Study.* 86th Congress, 2nd Session, House Committee Print 27. (Washington, D.C.: GPO). [135]

—————, 1966. *Indian Fractionated Land Problems Hearings.* 89th Congress, 2nd Session. (Washington, D.C.: GPO). [135]

U.S. Congress, Senate, 1958. *Indian Land Transactions; an Analysis of the Problems and Effects of Our Diminishing Indian Land Base, 1948-57.* 85th Congress, 2nd Session. (Washington, D.C.: GPO). [69]

—————, 1961. *[Report . . . Relating to the] Indian Heirship Land Problem. Hearings.* 87th Congress, 1st Session. 2 pts. (Washington, D.C.: GPO).

U.S. Department of the Interior, 1958. Office of the Solicitor, *Federal Indian Law.* (Washington: GPO). [Reprinted by the Association of American Indian Affairs, 1966.] [70-1, 72, 74, 146, 172]

U.S. Department of Justice, 1964. *Defendant's Requested Findings of Fact, Objections to Petitioner's Proposed Findings of Fact, and Brief.* [Docket 320 before the Indian Claims Commission, prepared by Ramsey Clark, Assistant Attorney General, in the Quechan Tribe case. (Washington, D.C.: GPO). [108]

U.S. National Resources Board, 1935. *Indian Land Tenure, Economic Status, and Population Trends. Report,* pt. 10, Land Planning Committee. (Washington, D.C.: GPO). [126, 136]

U.S. President, 1912. *Executive Orders Relating to Indian Reservations, 1855-1912.* 2 vols., House Committee on Indian Affairs. (Washington, D.C.: GPO). [116]

†Unrau, William E., 1964. "The Role of the Indian Agent in the Settlement of the South-Central Plains, 1861-1868." Unpublished doctoral dissertation in history, Univ. of Colorado. [53]

—————, 1971. *The Kansa Indians: A History of the Wind People, 1673-1873.* (Norman: Univ. of Oklahoma Press). [50, 53]

Utley, Robert M., 1963. *The Last Days of the Sioux Nation.* (New Haven: Yale Univ. Press). [53]

Vance, John T., 1969. "The Congressional Mandate and the Indian Claims Commission." *North Dakota L.R.* 45 (Spring): 325-336. [94]

Van De Mark, D., 1956. "The Raid on the Reservations." *Harper's Magazine* 212 (March): 48-53; (May): 4; and (July): 8. [69]

Vanderwerth, W. C., 1971. *Indian Oratory: Famous Speeches by Noted Indian Chieftains.* (Norman: Univ. of Oklahoma Press). [98, 218]

Van Every, D., 1966. *Disinherited: The Lost Birthright of the American Indian.* (New York: W. Morrow). [48]

Vaughan, Alden T., 1965. *The New England Frontier: Puritans and Indians, 1620-1675.* (Boston: Little, Brown). [40]

Veeder, William H., 1965. "Winters Doctrine Rights–Keystone of National Programs for Western Land and Water Conservation and Utilization." *Montana L.R.* 26: 149-72. [163]

–––––, 1969. "Federal Encroachment on Indian Water Rights and the Impairment of Reservation Development." In U.S. Congress, Joint Economic Committee, *Toward Economic Development for Native American Communities,* 91st Congress, 1st Session. (Washington, D.C.: GPO): 2 vols; vol. 1: 460-518. [163]

–––––, 1971. "Indian Private and Paramount Rights to Use of Waters." *RMMLI* 16: 631-68. [163]

–––––, 1972. "Water Rights: Life or Death for the American Indian." *IH* 5, no. 2: 4-21. [163]

–––––, 1973. "Indian Water Rights and the National Water Commission." In [Symposium on Indian Affairs]: 28-33. [163]

Voegelin, Charles F. and Voegelin, Erminie W., 1944. *Map of North American Indian Languages. Publ.* 20, AES (Menasha, Wisc.: G. Banta). [32]

Voegelin, Erminie W., 1955. "The Northern Paiute of Central Oregon: A Chapter in Treaty-making." *EH* 2: 95-132, 241-72. See also Wheeler-Voegelin.

Vogel, Virgil J., 1972. *This Country Was Ours; A Documentary History of the American Indian.* (New York: Harper and Row). [99, 218]

Voget, Fred (ed.), 1961-62. "American Indians and Their Economic Development." *HO* 20, no. 4: 157-248. [62, 78]

Vogt, Evon Z., 1961. "Navaho." In Spicer, Edward (ed.): 278-336.

Waddell, Jack O., 1969. *Papago Indians at Work. Anthropological Papers* 12, Univ. of Arizona. [76]

Wait, William, 1912. "The Hudson, Its Aboriginal Occupation, Discovery and Settlement." *Proceedings,* New York State Historical Association 11: 152-65. [41]

Walker, Deward E., Jr. (ed.), 1971. "An Exploration of the Reservation System in North America." *NW Anthropological Research Notes* 5, no. 1: 1-140. [73, 201, 218]

––––– (ed.), 1972. *The Emergent Native American: A Reader in Culture Contact.* (Boston: Little, Brown).

Walker, Francis A., 1874. *The Indian Question.* (Boston: J. R. Osgood). [46, 65]

Wallace, Anthony F. C., 1947. "Woman, Land, and Society: Three Aspects of Aboriginal Delaware Life." *Pennsylvania Archaeologist* 17: 1-35.

–––––, 1957. "Political Organization and Land Tenure Among the Northeast Indians." *SWJA* 13: 301-21. [27, 28, 101, 108, 186]

–––––, 1970. *The Death and Rebirth of the Seneca.* (New York: A. A. Knopf). [12]

Wallace, E. and Hoebel, E. Adamson, 1952. *The Comanches: Lords of the South Plains.* (Norman: Univ. of Oklahoma Press). [119]

Wallace, Paul A. W., 1961. *Indians in Pennsylvania*. (Harrisburg: Pennsylvania Historical and Museum Commission). [43, 172]

Wallen, Woodrow, 1970. "Indian Hunting and Fishing Rights: Northwest Developments." In Johnson, Ralph (ed.): 375-422. [160]

Ward, Ralph E., et al., 1956. *Indians in Agriculture: I—Cattle Ranching on the Crow
Reservation*. Bulletin 522, Missouri River Basin Investigations Project, B.I.A., in
cooperation with Montana State College (Univ.), Agricultural Experiment Station
(Bozeman). [87]

Wards, Ian, 1968. *The Shadow of the Land: A Study of British Policy and Racial
Conflict in New Zealand, 1832-1852.* (Wellington: Historical Publications Branch,
Dept. of Internal Affairs). [208]

Warner, Sr. Mildred, 1970. "Indians Challenge the Nebraska Territorial Government:
I"; "The Attitude of the Nebraska Territorial Government Toward the Indians:
II." *GPJ* 9 (Spring): 53-58; 59-66. [117]

Washburn, Wilcomb E., 1957. "A Moral History of Indian-White Relations." *EH* 4,
no. 1: 47-61. [97]

—————, 1959. "The Moral and Legal Justification for Dispossessing the Indians." In
Smith, James M. (ed.), *Seventeenth-Century America: Essays in Colonial History*.
(Chapel Hill: Univ. of North Carolina Press): 16-25. [97]

————— (ed.), 1964. *The Indian and the White Man*. (New York: Doubleday). [52, 218]

—————, 1965. "Indian Removal Policy: Administrative, Historical, and Moral
Criteria for Judging Its Success or Failure." *EH* 12, no. 3: 274-78. [39, 49]

—————, 1971a. "The Writing of American Indian History." *PHR* 40, no. 3:
261-81. [12, 39]

—————, 1971b. *Red Man's Land/White Man's Law: A Study of the Past and Present
Status of the American Indian*. (New York: Charles Scribner's Sons). [7, 44, 45,
49, 51, 68, 91, 95, 96-7, 100, 126, 138, 145, 181-2]

————— (ed.), 1973. *The American Indian and the United States: A Documentary
History*. (New York: Random House). [52, 218]

—————, in press. *The Assault on Indian Tribalism: The General Allotment Law
(Dawes Act) of 1887*. (Philadelphia: Lippincott). [126]

Waterman, T. T., 1920. *Yurok Geography*. UCPAAE 18, no. 5. [29]

Watkins, Arthur V., 1957. "Termination of Federal Supervision: Removal of Restrictions over Indian Property and Person." In Simpson, G. and Yinger, J. (eds.):
47-55. [138]

Watkins, T. H., 1974. "Ancient Wrongs and Public Rights." *Sierra Club Bulletin* 59,
no. 8: 15-16, 37-39. [110, 111]

Wax, Murray L., 1971. *Indian Americans: Unity and Diversity*. (Englewood Cliffs,
N.J.: Prentice-Hall). [156]

Weatherford, G. D., 1974. "Indian Water Rights: Legal Variables in Regional Water
Management." [Papers of the] *AAAS*, 140th meeting, section on Environmental
Sciences, "Lake Powell and Lake Tahoe in Environmental Transition," San
Francisco, February 25-March 1. 12pp.

Weightman, Barbara A., 1972. "The Musqueam Reserve: A Case Study of the Indian
Social Milieu in an Urban Environment." Unpublished doctoral dissertation in
geography, Univ. of Washington. [76, 201]

Weinberg, Albert K., 1963. *Manifest Destiny*. (Chicago: Univ. of Chicago Press).
[46]

Weinman, Paul L., 1969. *A Bibliography of the Iroquois Literature (Partially Annotated)*. New York State Museum and Science Service *Bulletin* 411. [218]

Weslager, C. A., 1972. *The Delaware Indians: A History*. (New Brunswick, N.J.: Rutgers Univ. Press). [41, 50]

Westphall, Victor, 1965. *The Public Domain in New Mexico, 1854-1891*. (Albuquerque: Univ. of New Mexico Press). [118]

W. F. C., Jr., 1965. "The Constitutional Rights of the American Tribal Indian." *Virginia L.R.* 51: 121-42. [154]

Whalen, Sue, 1971. "The Nez Perces' Relationship to Their Land." *IH* 4, no. 3: 30-33. [1, 25]

Whatley, J. T., 1969. "The Sage of Taos Pueblo: The Blue Lake Controversy." *IH* 2, no. 3: 22-28. [110]

Wheeler-Voegelin, Erminie, 1956. "History and Ethnohistory, and a Case in Point." In Wallace, A. F. C. (ed.), *Men and Cultures. Selected Papers, 5th International Congress of Anthropological and Ethnographical Sciences*. (Philadelphia: Univ. of Pennsylvania Press): 364-67. [104]

See also Voegelin.

†White, J. V. 1972. *Taxing Those They Found Here*. (Albuquerque: Univ. of New Mexico, Institute for the Development of Indian Law). [157]

White, Raymond C., 1963. *A Reconstruction of Luiseno Social Organization*. *UCPAAE* 48, no. 2. [25, 29]

†Whitten, Frederick E., 1950. "The Platte Purchase and Its Significance in Frontier History." Unpublished masters thesis in history, Kansas City (?). [53, 54]

Wilkinson, Glen A., 1966. "Indian Tribal Claims before the Court of Claims." *Georgetown Law Journal* 55: 511-28. [91]

Willey, Elizabeth S., 1969. "The Lands and History of the Hopi Indians." Unpublished masters thesis in geography, Univ. of Utah. [83]

Williams, Ethel J., 1970. "The Indian Heirship Land Problems." In Johnson, Ralph W. (ed.): 150-231. [136-7]

—————, 1971. "Too Little Land, Too Many Heirs—the Indian Heirship Land Problem." *Washington L.R.* 46, no. 4: 709-44. [136-7]

†Williams, Mary C., 1922. "The Opening of the Oklahoma Territory." Unpublished masters thesis in history, Columbia Univ. [116]

*Wilms, Douglas C., 1973. "Cherokee Indian Land Use in Georgia, 1830-1838." Unpublished doctoral dissertation in geography, Univ. of Georgia. [50]

—————, 1974a. "Cherokee Settlement Patterns in Nineteenth Century Georgia." *Southeastern Geographer* 14, no. 1 (May): 46-53. [50]

*—————, 1974b. "Georgia's Land Lottery of 1832," *CO* 52 (Spring). [50]

Wilson, Benjamin D., [1852], 1952. *Indians of Southern California in 1952*, (ed.) John W. Caughey. (San Marino: Huntington Library). [54]

Wilson, Edmund, 1959. *Apologies to the Iroquois*. (New York: Farrar, Straus and Cudahy). [99, 166-8]

Wilson, H. Clyde, 1961. *Changes in the Jicarilla Apache Political and Economic Structures: 1880-1960*. *UCPAAE* 48, no. 4: 297-360. [75, 187]

*Wilson, Paul B., 1972. "Farming and Ranching on the Wind River Indian Reservation, Wyoming." Unpublished doctoral dissertation in geography, Univ. of Nebraska, Lincoln. [Abstract as "Relationships of the Indian Reservation Land Tenure System to Land Use on the Wind River Indian Reservation." *AAAG* 57 (1967): 809.] [86-7, 136, 197]

Winther, O. O. (ed.), 1964. *A Classified Bibliography of the Periodic Literature of the Trans-Mississippi West (1811-1957).* (Bloomington: Indiana Univ. Press). [217-18]

————— and Van Orman, R. A. (eds.), 1967. *A Classified Bibliography . . . A Supplement (1957-67).* Bloomington: Indian Univ. Press). [218]

Wise, Jennings C., 1971. *The Red Man in the New World Drama: A Politico-Legal Study with a Pageantry of American Indian History.* Ed. and rev., with introduction by Vine Deloria, Jr. (New York: Macmillan). [Originally published 1931.] [3]

Wissler, Clark, 1926. *Relation of Nature to Man in Aborginal America.* (New York: Oxford Univ. Press). [31]

—————, 1938a. *The American Indian.* (New York: Oxford Univ. Press; 3rd ed.). [5, 27]

—————, 1938b. *Red Man Reservations.* (New York: Sheridan House).

—————, 1940. *Indians of the United States: Four Centuries of Their History and Culture.* (New York: Doubleday, Doran). [178]

Witherspoon, Gary, 1970. "New Look at Navaho Social Organization." *AA* 72, no. 1: 55-65. [189-90]

Witthoft, John, 1961. *Eastern Woodland Community Typology and Acculturation.* In "Symposium on Cherokee and Iroquois Culture," no. 9, *BAE Bulletin* 180. (Washington, D.C.: Smithsonian Institution): 67-76. [With comments by J. M. Goggin, 77-81.] [183-4]

Wolff, A., 1973. *Unreal Estate.* (San Francisco: Sierra Club), Chap. 8, "Giving it to the Indians." [174]

Wroth, L. C., 1928. "The Indian Treaty as Literature." *The Yale Review* n.s. 17, no. 4: 749-66. [51]

Wylie, Helen, 1905-07. "The Acquisition of Iowa Lands from the Indians." *AI* 7, no. 4: 283-290.

Young, Mary, 1955. "The Creek Frauds: A Study in Conscience and Corruption." *MVHR* 52, no. 3: 411-37. [48]

—————, 1958. "Indian Removal and Land Allotment: The Civilized Tribes and Jacksonian Justice." *AHR* 64, no. 1: 31-45. [48]

—————, 1961. *Redskins, Ruffleshirts and Rednecks: Indian Allotments in Alabama and Mississippi, 1830-1860.* (Norman: Univ. of Oklahoma Press). [48, 126]

Zavala, Silvio, 1965. "The Frontiers of Hispanic America." In Wyman, W. D. and Kroeber, C. B. (eds.), *The Frontier in Perspective.* (Madison: Univ. of Wisconsin Press). [Originally published in 1957]: 35-58. [206]

Zelinsky, Wilbur, 1966. *A Prologue to Population Geography.* (Englewood Cliffs, N.J.: Prentice-Hall). [214]

Zigmond, M. L., 1938. "Kawaiisu Territory." *AA* 40, no. 4: 634-38. [29]

†Zimmerman, W., 1955. "Some Problems Relating to Indian Treaties; Problem of Tax Exemption." In *Proceedings of the Conference on Indian Tribes and Treaties.* (Minnesota: Center for Continuation Study). [157]

Subject Index

This book contains three indexes: (1) a *Subject Index*, which provides a broad range of subject headings and cross-references; (2) a *Tribal Index to Authors*, which indexes tribes and bands, and also reservations where the name of the reservation differs from that of the Indians inhabiting it; and (3) a *Geographical Index to Authors*, which cites states, territories, regions, locales or other identifiable places (i.e., those that bear toponyms associated with Indian affairs, such as the Black Hills, Hudson Bay, etc.).

The Subject Index includes most of the headings found in the Tribal and Geographical Indexes and leads directly to the pages in this book where each subject is discussed. It also includes a great many headings not found in either of the other indexes. The Tribal and Geographical Indexes do not refer to pages in the text; rather they lead directly to significant works by author and date. They are intended primarily as quick-reference guides to the literature, and they will probably prove most useful as indexes to the Bibliography. (The Bibliography includes page citations for all studies that have been discussed in this book; it thus doubles as an author index.)

The Tribal and Geographical Indexes are, to a degree, mutually exclusive. For example, studies that deal specifically with the Indians of a particular state generally will not be indexed under the various tribal names, while studies that deal with individual tribes will be cited in the Tribal Index but not in the Geographical Index.

Tribal Index to Authors

This index will lead readers to works included in the Bibliography which discuss significantly specific tribes or bands, or reservations whose names do not coincide with tribal names. Bracketed page numbers in the Bibliography indicate pages in this book where these works are discussed. The *Subject Index* includes most of the headings in this index and leads directly to the relevant pages in this volume, but does not provide the names of authors cited.

Geographical Index
to Authors

This index will lead readers to works included in the Bibliography which discuss significantly the Indians of geographical areas, such as states, territories, regions, locales or other identifiable places associated with Indian affairs. Bracketed page numbers in the Bibliography indicate pages in this book where these works are discussed. The *Subject Index* includes most of the headings in this index and leads directly to the relevant pages in this volume, but does not provide the names of authors cited.